The Mysterious Death of
Mary Rogers

STUDIES IN THE HISTORY OF SEXUALITY

Judith Brown and Guido Ruggiero, *General Editors*

IMMODEST ACTS
The Life of a Lesbian Nun in Renaissance Italy
Judith Brown

THE EVOLUTION OF WOMEN'S ASYLUMS SINCE 1500
From Refugees for Ex-Prostitutes
to Shelters for Battered Women
Sherrill Cohen

SEXUALITY IN THE CONFESSIONAL
A Sacrament Profaned
Stephen Haliczer

COMMON WOMEN
Prostitution and Sexuality in Medieval
England
Ruth Mazo Karras

MASCULINITY AND MALE CODES OF HONOR
IN MODERN FRANCE
Robert A. Nye

THE BOUNDARIES OF EROS
Sex Crime and Sexuality in Renaissance Venice
Guido Ruggiero

THE MYSTERIOUS DEATH OF MARY ROGERS
Sex and Culture in Nineteenth-Century New York
Amy Gilman Srebnick

Further volumes are in preparation

The
Mysterious Death
of Mary Rogers

SEX AND CULTURE IN
NINETEENTH-CENTURY
NEW YORK

Amy Gilman Srebnick

OXFORD UNIVERSITY PRESS
New York   Oxford

Oxford University Press

Oxford   New York
Athens   Auckland   Bangkok   Bogotá   Bombay   Buenos Aires
Calcutta   Cape Town   Dar es Salaam   Delhi
Florence   Hong Kong   Istanbul   Karachi
Kuala Lampur   Madras   Madrid   Melbourne
Mexico City   Nairobi   Paris   Singapore
Taipei   Tokyo   Toronto

and associated companies in
Berlin   Ibadan

Library of Congress Cataloging-in-Publication Data
Srebnick, Amy Gilman.
The mysterious death of Mary Rogers :
sex and culture in nineteenth-century New York /
Amy Gilman Srebnick.
p.   cm.—(Studies in the history of sexuality)
Includes bibliographical references (p.   ) and index.

ISBN-13 978-0-19-511392-1 (Pbk.)

1. Rogers, Mary, 1820–1841
2. Murder—New York (N.Y.)—History—19th century.
3. Sex crimes—New York (N.Y.)—History—19th century.
4. Sex role—New York (N.Y.)—History—19th century.
5. City and town life—New York (N.Y.)—History—19th century.
6. New York (N.Y.)—Social life and customs—19th century.
I. Title.   II. Series.   HV6534.N5S69   1995   364.1'523'092—dc20   94-38995

Printed in the United States of America

FOR WALTER
CON BRIO ED AMORE

ACKNOWLEDGMENTS

This project developed out of a short paper I presented at a conference many years ago. It grew slowly into a book, taking me into a wide range of academic subjects—the history of crime and criminal justice, the literary genres of mid-nineteenth century American culture, the politics of urban life, the history of sexuality and the study of cultural representation. Because these areas of study were often new to me, friends and colleagues have been especially important and helpful: the former encouraging me to take some intellectual leaps of faith, the latter catching me when those leaps became too precarious. It is with great pleasure that I am, at last, able to thank them in print.

Let me begin by acknowledging those institutions and libraries which quite literally made this study possible. The resources of The New York Public Library and The New-York Historical Society remain invaluable collections for anyone studying the history of New York City. In addition, special thanks go to Columbia University, The American Antiquarian Society, The Connecticut State Library, The New London Historical Society and The New York Genealogical Society. I am especially grateful to Michael Joseph, formerly of the New York Historical Society and now at Rutgers University Library, for his help with sources and prints over the years, and Georgia Barnhill of the American Antiquarian Society.

Teaching at a state college means heavy teaching loads, many students, and infinite institutional responsibilities. I would never have been able to complete this book without the help offered in a variety of ways, but especially in the form of reduced teaching schedules, by Montclair State University. An uninterrupted semester under the auspices of the Distinguished Scholar Program, as well as a sabbatical leave, allowed me to complete the writing and prepare the work for publication. Since these rewards are granted by a continuous process of peer review, I wish to thank all those colleagues on various committees who saw the value of this project and helped to issue that institutional support. And special thanks go to Philip Cohen, formerly Dean of Social Sciences and Humanities, who helped make possible an early trip to Paris where this work received its first significant attention.

This French connection has proved especially important—not only in determining some of the book's content and flavor, but in introducing me to a whole set of new colleagues through the International Association for the Study of Crime and Criminal Justice. Thanks especially go to Wilbur Miller who extended the invitation to that IACCJ conference in Paris in the fall 1988, and to Robert Muchembled for publishing an early essay in *Mentalités*. It was at that same conference in Paris that I met Guido Ruggiero whose initial enthusiasm led to my contract with Oxford and the book's inclusion in the History of Sexuality series. Guido's faith in the project, his patience in waiting for it to happen, his helpful critical suggestions and, most of all, his cheerful and timely letters and calls have guided me through this project. At Oxford, my editor, Nancy Lane, ran with this project at a very early stage. I thank her for her confidence and for her continued help. Thomas Le Bien patiently took care of many of the endless details of publication, and Rosemary Wellner did a careful job of editing my mistakes and omissions.

When I began this work I knew little about the history of crime and criminal justice, nineteenth-century abortion law, and less about the work of Edgar Allan Poe. Learning something about these new areas as well as others has helped to make this project a continuing act of discovery. It has also brought me into contact with scholars in many different fields. Their careful readings and critical comments and suggestions have been invaluable. Stephen Jaffe openly shared his own work with me, and Pat Cline Cohen, Daniel Cohen, and the late Ray Paul offered helpful suggestions. I am especially grateful to Carrol Smith-Rosenberg, Eric Monkkonen, and David Papke who read earlier versions of this work at conferences and to Eric Sundquist and James Mohr who very kindly read final chapters on Poe and abortion respectively.

Many friends—all of whom listened endlessly to the tale of Mary Rogers—deserve special thanks. Merry and Mort Young provided a beach house at a key moment in the final writing and Mort saved me with his infinite patience and floppy discs from a computer disaster late in the game. Jay Livingston, the WordPerfect mavin, answered endless dumb questions and also read an early version of the chapter on crime. Peter Freund, George Martin, Pleun Bouricius, the late Stephen Friedman, and Ann Weissman did the same for other chapters. Janet Cutler not only encouraged and read pieces, she kept me entertained with her stories during the sometimes eternal commute to New Jersey. David Greenstein found the engraving which now graces the cover and forms the central image of Chapter 4. Ann Prival dragged me out to lunch during an especially reclusive period and understood the mother/daughter connections which lurked, almost silently and very personally, within this study. Carole Turbin encouraged me to wander off with this project from the start. Lee Lowenfish, as always, has provided warmth, laughter, and music. Ann Alter, Ellen Schrecker, and Marvin Gettleman read various sections along the way and prepared some very good meals as well. And very special gratitude goes to Tom Benediktsson, both friend and colleague, who saw this project hatch when we first started team teaching interdisciplinary courses in American literature and history over ten years ago. Much of the content of this book was worked out in preparing and teaching these courses, and Tom's knowledge and understanding of American literature infuses many different aspects of this book. Over the years he has also read and edited, offering help, both editorial and otherwise, at critical points all along the way.

For my family more than thanks are necessary. My father, Beryl Gilman, has always made nineteenth-century American intellectual life a place of familiarity and comfort and he and Bluma Gilman were the first to introduce me to the artifacts of early American culture. My mother, Jean Gilman Zion, whose memory is a continuous spirit in my work, understood the true meaning of city culture—especially for women. And it is hard to convey in words how Walter, Joshua, and Daniel Srebnick have individually and collectively created a household where work is intimately bound with everyday existence and daily life. When I began this project my sons, Joshua and Daniel, were boys who wondered, I am sure, about their mother's strange obsesssion with the death of Mary Rogers. Now grown from boys to men, with interests not so far afield (as well as unique talents of their own), and with a shared love of the city they were raised in, they continue to keep me laughing and my perspective and priorities about the world more or less in balance. My husband, Walter, has been with this project every minute of its existence. He listened, read, traveled, edited time and again, and was always my best and most caring critic. It may be trite to say that this book would not have happened without him, but it is true nonetheless. Most important, his faith in me over these many years has provided me with the energy, confidence, and happiness so necessary to do any work at all.

An early version of the ideas set forth in this book appeared in *Mentalités*. Earlier versions of Chapters 4 and 6 appeared in *Legal Studies Forum* and *The Mythmaking Frame of Mind: Social Imagination and American Culture*, respectively. I am grateful for permission to reprint.

CONTENTS

INTRODUCTION

My first encounter with Mary Rogers was quite accidental. As part of an extended project on the history of gender, work, and early New York industrialization, I was reading popular novels of the 1840s in search of representations of poor and working women in popular urban culture. What I later understood to be a fictionalization of the Rogers saga formed the basis of one such sentimental novel, *Lilla Hart*, written by Charles Burdett, a New York–based writer who was also a journalist— one of the new breed of reporters covering the city beat. Burdett's novel, written in 1846, told a sentimental tale of loss and redemption figured around a young woman of the city who persevered against enormous odds: unrelenting poverty, the loss of both her parents, forced abduction, and ultimately even the threat of violent and willful death. In the end the heroine prevailed; she was returned unharmed by her captor and rewarded for her noble heart and Christian charity with a reconstructed family, wealth, and a happy marriage. This transformation of the impoverished working girl into a wealthy young bride was, I soon discovered, merely one version of one of the period's most compelling popular news events: the disappearance and brutal death in the summer of 1841 of Mary Cecilia Rogers, known widely as the "Beautiful Cigar Girl." Through a series of equally serendipitous literary encounters, I continued to find elements of the so-called "Mary Rogers Mystery" in the literature of antebellum New York City. Eventually, fascinated by this story, I abandoned (or so I thought) my earlier project to pursue the history of this enigmatic young woman whose tragic death so entertained her nineteenth-century contemporaries. My own fascination with the Rogers story, I soon discovered, was not altogether surprising, given the role she had played in the nineteenth century.[1]

The saga of Mary Rogers, the chronicles of her violent death, the pursuit of her would-be murderer, the descriptions of her battered naked body, were the subjects of many narratives subsumed within the larger history of New York City during its critical period of growth in the two decades before the Civil War. Narratives about the disappearance of attractive young women, or their forced abduction and eventual magical transformation, formed other recurring motifs in the antebellum literature. Mary Rogers herself, or some imagined version of her, appeared in various forms: the disappeared victim in an unusually violent and sexually motivated death, the virtuous working girl of popular fiction, and, most notably, as Marie, the mysterious subject of Edgar Allan Poe's early work in detective fiction, "The Mystery of Marie Roget." Eventually Rogers figured prominently as a force in other, less likely, forms of contemporary discourse: the literature advocating police and criminal justice reform as well as the crusades to criminalize abortion. Indeed, what Lydia Child had called "The Mary Rogers Tragedy" was more than just a famous crime—it was an event of unusual and perplexing importance in the culture of 1840s New York.

My interest in the Rogers story was by no means unique: an extensive Rogers literature already existed. As a historian however, my concerns were different from the detective buffs, Poe scholars, and journalists (all male) who had preceded me. I was less interested in solving the "mystery" of Mary's death, or ascertaining whether or not Poe had solved the crime, and more concerned with why the Rogers story was so compelling (in its own time and subsequently), and with what it told about the connections between the genesis of American urban culture, violent crime—especially violent sexual crimes against women—and the sensational popular text. Perhaps not surprisingly, I found myself still contending with one of the central questions in my earlier project: the historical place of women in the economic and social transformations during this period of rapid change and modernization. Rogers's life and death presented a way of refocusing those interests in the history of the relationship of women, social class, and urban culture, while simultaneously offering me a way of contending with a series of cultural and historical themes with which I was increasingly engaged: the history of sexuality, the crisis of modernity, the relationship between gender and culture (especially between women and cities), the varieties of cultural representation. In time, my work took me into still other areas I had never seriously considered: the history of criminal justice, the growth of detective and mystery fiction. In short, Rogers became not only a vehicle though which I could continue my exploration of antebellum urban society and culture, she became the connecting link between the more traditional approaches to social, women's, and urban history, and the new discourses of critical studies and cultural theory.

As a college student in the late 1960s, I chose a concentration (and eventually graduate studies as well) in history because I understood historical studies to be fundamentally an interdisciplinary inquiry about culture and its transmission over time. My youthful conviction that the subject matter of historical analysis was open-ended, and that in order to grasp the complexities of the past the limiting categories of academe had to be challenged, has not fundamentally changed. With time, however, it has become both a more acceptable approach and a far more complicated one, as the parameters of the discipline itself, as well as the methods of historical and intellectual inquiry generally, have developed and expanded.

Not the least of these changes has been the legitimation of unusual or even fanciful topics as viable subjects for the historian. Cat massacres, penopticism, the carnevalesque, the stories of social outcasts and criminals have proven to be not only engaging topics for study, but, more important, useful pathways into our understanding of what the French have identified as *mentalités*. The work of several students of French history and culture has been particularly important here: Natalie Davis, Robert Darnton, Alain Corbin, and Robert Muchembled. Their work, infused by the pioneering cultural theory of Antonio Gramsci, the complex analysis of discourse, knowledge, and the technologies of power, explored by Michel Foucault, and the emphasis on literary texts and language itself, offered by Foucault, and Roland Barthes as well as others, has opened the doors of historiography. Recent studies in women's history and gender studies, including Judith Walkowitz's important new work, *City of Dreadful Delight: Narratives of Sexual Danger in Late-Victorian London*, and the theoretical and critical studies of Joan Scott, Laura Mulvey, and Jane Tompkins, have transformed the analytic categories within which we work. But while cultural history has yielded a broad range of innovative studies in European, English, and especially French history, the application of culture studies to topics in American history has been somewhat slower to take hold. Recently, however, new work in African-American history, women's studies, and that elusive blend known as American studies, have made interdisciplinary studies more fashionable, if not more respectable. The work of historians like Lawrence Levine, Carrol Smith-Rosenberg, and Karen Halttunen and the cultural frameworks of anthropologists—most notably Clifford Geertz—have blended with feminist theory and the techniques of literary analysis to define new historical subjects as well as new modes of investigation. I hope that *The Mysterious Death of Mary Rogers* will serve as an offering in this new direction.[2]

Clearly, in choosing the death of a rather ordinary young woman, Mary Rogers, as the subject for an historical study, I have drawn upon these new intellectual frameworks. This book is about Mary Rogers, her mysterious life, and the phenomenon that her sad and puzzling death became. But, in a larger way, this book is a chronicle, through the narrativizations of this one particular event, of the modernization of urban antebellum culture. A study in American cultural history, it uses the mystery of Rogers's death to explore themes in the history of sexuality and of urban mass culture and cultural representation. My intent is not to solve the crime (many others have tried with more or less success) but to understand how and why the death of this young woman became a source of mystery and romance and what it can tell us about the genesis of modern urban culture. In the sense that Foucault defined, Rogers thus becomes a sexual subject, just as her death marks the "point

where discourse emerged" about sexuality, about women in urban culture, about the relationship between public policy and private life, and
about the spectacle of violent female death as a source of narrative.[3]
   Fredric Jameson implores us at the beginning of *The Political Unconscious* to "Always Historicize." I understand this imperative to foreground the overriding importance of context for understanding both
cultural expressions and the politically unconscious meanings inscribed
within such expressions. His argument starts with the notion that we
apprehend texts, and presumably cultural events as well, through what
he calls "sedimented layers of previous interpretations." In this spirit,
this study explores a cultural event, its fictive and journalistic representations, as well as the social and political narratives it inspired, by con-
textualizing them within the time and space of the nineteenth-century
city, and locating them in the elaborate system of gender and class relations of that cultural moment.[4]
   Mary Rogers's New York was a city undergoing rapid change. Already the foremost metropolis of the new nation, its experience of accelerated growth and cultural diversity signaled the complexities of
urban life and culture for years to come. In particular, the period around
Mary's death, the late 1830s and 1840s, witnessed enormous changes in
all areas of social and cultural life as modern American culture began
to take on its contemporary forms and dimensions. Partly this was
caused by the relative openness of the cultural landscape that was made
possible by the newness of the nation and its significant breaks with
Europe and European culture. Partly this was the result of modernization—the expansion of capitalism and the new conceptions of the marketplace that accompanied it—the development of new technologies,
and vastly changed character of work, culture, and daily life that
heralded the modern city. Just as mechanization revolutionized the
character of work, so new printing techniques transformed and commercialized the dissemination of knowledge. Simultaneously, a new
reading public came of age—much of it working class and female—
which seemed to have an insatiable appetite for narratives that featured
events from "real life."
   Without the new concepts of public news and information and without this reading public, the story and the mystery of Mary Rogers would
probably have gone almost unnoticed. But Rogers's life and death occurred at the very moment that a new urban and commercial written
culture was taking shape. The newspaper, the dime novel, the sensational pamphlet, and the magazine with its serialized stories were the
places where the Rogers story was both created and popularized. Mary
Rogers became a "mystery" of the mysterious city, configured in an
endless variety of narratives which, like the narratives of the city itself,
filtered her story through what Jameson referred to as an endless sedi-
ment of meaning and interpretation. As the subject of the new popular
and commercial culture, Rogers symbolized the different and often con-

tending visions of gender, sexuality, and female identity. Her story enables us to understand how issues of gender and sexuality figured in the cultural production of the antebellum period and how definitions of female sexuality and behavior fit into an emerging discourse about social and sexual order in the new republic.

In spite of my new interest in the development of the sensational narrative and the vagaries of cultural representation, the domain of the real is still a troubling place for a historian. As I proceeded with my work, one issue above all continued to plague me: Who was Mary Rogers? For while Mary Rogers has been the subject of narratives and detective work for over one hundred and fifty years, her identity had remained elusive. Figured in everybody's image but her own, Rogers remained a woman without a family, without a past—without an identity and definable genealogy. None of her earlier chroniclers gave any information about her origins, her family, or the circumstances of her life. From the moment of her disappearance, attention had been focused on her gruesome death and the men most likely responsible for it. As this project took shape, however, I found myself increasingly uncomfortable with the degree to which Mary had become so completely a cultural construction, defined by her sexuality and her apparently violent death. If I developed a personal obsession with this case, it was to "find" Mary, to restore her as a person, to reconstruct her heritage, and to give her voice in my own account. My search for her yielded surprising results, but it also made clear to me the persistent invisibility of women in history and the importance of restoring them to the historical record.

From the start I had been able to locate Mary's putative mother, Phebe Rogers, in the 1840 manuscript census records for New York City and in city directories. Here she was listed as the head of household at 126 Nassau Street and as the widow of Daniel Rogers, respectively. The census included the other household residents, and validated what earlier writers had known—namely that she ran a boardinghouse at that address. But the historical record seemed frozen at that point; there were no records of Phebe Rogers after 1841 or before 1840, and no records of a Daniel Rogers appeared prior to that time. (I did find a Phebe Rogers in Castile, New York, as the head of household in an 1830 census, but further excavation of that information, including a trip to Castile and its environs, yielded not even a tombstone.) Without knowing Phebe's maiden name, I had no way to trace her family roots and none of the Daniel Rogers I found in the extant records squared with what information I already had. On a final hunch, well after I had "completed" the research and was into the writing, I began to check the genealogies for New England. In a search of privately published family histories I discovered that a Daniel Rogers of New London had married a widow named Phebe Wait Mather. Phebe's first husband, it turned out, was a man named Ezra Mather, a prosperous Connecticut merchant and direct descendant of the Connecticut wing of the famous New England Mathers. I now had my clue. By working back through the census records for Connecticut I was able to locate Phebe Mather and what turned out to be her rather extensive family. The discovery that Phebe was married to a Mather was like finding a historian's gold (testified to by my indelicate shriek in the rather weighty, leather-bound premises of the New York Genealogical Society). The rest was relatively easy. Mathers and Rogers were the stuff of eighteenth-century society and culture and information seemed to tumble out at every point, except for one nagging piece of evidence—I was (and still am) unable to find a birth record for Mary Rogers herself, a fact that I explain in Chapter 2.

The discovery of Mary's identity was the final piece of the puzzle, and its importance was underscored by the way it fit so cleanly into what my other evidence had already determined. Most important, however, it restored Mary and located her in a family as well as within a geographic and social context. In a larger way it provided a kind of historical reality or validity to what had been essentially a study in cultural representation: Mary and her mother were in fact part of the massive rural to urban migration of the early national period. Their experiences as women in the new city told a familiar tale of family disintegration and downward mobility. Widowhood and economic loss were not unusual and their move to the city provided them with a new and very different life from the one they had known. Here the experiences of work of these women fit a familiar pattern of early nineteenth-century female labor, just as their changed circumstances led them to carve out new urban identities characteristic of the changing social world of nineteenth-century American life. At this point their lives also veered sadly in another direction, with Mary's death and its place in nineteenth-century culture distinguishing them from the thousands of mothers and daughters who lived out their lives in the streets, neighborhoods, and workshops of the new metropolis. Yet even in death Mary was in some way a representative, if exaggerated, version of the urban experience of the nineteenth-century female. She was, after all, a young woman who experienced both the freedom and the perils of the city and it was because of this that she served as such a useful symbol for nineteenth-century commentators and writers struggling to depict and understand the urban scene.

The prologue to *The Mysterious Death of Mary Rogers* sets the stage for the Rogers story, indicating the significance of the event in 1840s New York, and suggesting how Rogers's life and death became myth. Chapter 2 tells the sequence of events as it was reconstructed at the time: the known events preceding her disappearance and the chronicle of the discovery of her body. It also introduces the principal characters in Mary's life and provides possible solutions to her death. Chapter 3 focuses on identity, suggesting how female identity became its own problematic in

the context of antebellum New York. Here I recount the legacy of
Mary's past and the urban world into which she and her putative
mother, Phebe Rogers, fled. These issues are closely connected to the
relationship between women and public space and questions about the
construction of gender in modern urban culture. Chapter 4 introduces
the subject of representation, particularly the way the death of Rogers
moved into the public imagination through the agency of the newspaper.
The voice of James Gordon Bennett, the enfant terrible of the new urban journalism, was critical here: he was the man who more than any
other set the frames within which the Rogers story came to be known
and understood. In constructing different and conflicting versions of
Mary, Bennett's narrative pushed Mary into the center of a debate about
criminal justice already underway. Chapter 5 considers this debate about
criminal justice and argues that both police reform and the criminali-
zation of abortion were rooted in concerns about sexual order, and that
both were also interrelated aspects of a larger debate about the relationship between the private and public in modern urban life. Chapter 6
moves back to the issue of representation, focusing specifically on Poe's
rendering of the Mary Rogers story, "The Mystery of Marie Roget."
Poe's tale of Mary ultimately superseded all other fictional versions of
the event; his fictive Marie replaced Mary and became the basis for all
later tellings. Here I focus on Poe's interpretation of the story and on
how it fits within a larger conversation about women and things urban.
Chapter 7 moves from Poe's reading to the ways the Rogers tale was
spun into other nineteenth-century urban narratives—"fictional"
stories—that were not only significant as popular reading, but helped
urbanites of various classes locate themselves within the new metropolis.
In these narratives, Mary became not the source of disorder and sexual
disarray she had been as a one-time symbol of desire, but a tamed,
domesticated, or reduced version of her former self. These novels thus
offered symbolic strategies of containment for the period's most viable
source of transgression and rebellion—the sexual urban woman who is
the at once alluring and threatening figure at the heart of this whole
study.

The Mysterious Death of
Mary Rogers

I

PROLOGUE:
THE MARY ROGERS
TRAGEDY

*And to illustrate both our pressing need to ask the question why and the
proposition that history begins with our sense of wrong, I used to ask you
to liken the study of history to an inquest. Suppose we have on our hands
a corpse—viz., the past. A corpse not always readily identifiable but now
and then taking a specific and quite personal form. . . . Do we say of this
corpse, Well a corpse is a corpse and corpses don't revive? No, we do not.
We ask: Why did this corpse come to be a corpse? Answer: by accident. . . . At which you would laugh, and prove your inquisitive minds,
your detective spirit—your historical consciousness.*

Graham Swift, *Waterland* (1983)[1]

*I*N September 1841, Lydia Maria Child, the celebrated writer and
abolitionist, visited the scene of what she and others described as
the "Mary Rogers Tragedy." The event she referred to was the mysterious death of Mary Cecilia Rogers, a young woman of New York
City who had mysteriously disappeared on a hot Sunday in late July
from the boardinghouse she ran with her elderly mother on Nassau
Street, in the heart of the city. More commonly known as the "Beautiful Cigar Girl" when she had tended the counter at John Anderson's
popular cigar store, her body, badly bruised and waterlogged, had been
found three days later, floating in the shallow waters of the Hudson
River just a few feet from the shore, near Hoboken, New Jersey. Standing at this site, "the beautiful promontory near Sybil's cave where her
body was found half in and half out of the water," just a few weeks
after the death, Child was struck by the beauty of the setting and overwhelmed by a complex mixture of thoughts, feelings, and associations.[2]

Before descending the embankment down to the river, Child had
walked the scenic three-mile stretch on the cliffs between Hoboken
("beautiful beyond imagining") and Weehawken, which had figured
prominently in the newspaper reports of Mary's death. Stopping at the
open glade known as the Elysian Fields, a popular recreation spot,
"where a poet's disembodied spirit might well be content to wander,"

she then walked north to Weehawken—as lovely as "a nook of Paradise, before Satan entered its gardens." Here "the steep, well wooded bank descended to the broad bright Hudson," and she could see where "the sparkling water peeps between the twining boughs, like light through the rich tracery of gothic windows; and the cheerful twittering of birds alone mingles with the measured cadence of the plashing waves." Arriving in the moonlight at the water's edge, the "presumed scene" of the tragedy, Child was struck by the stillness of the place. "All else was still—still—so fearfully still," she said, "that one might almost count the beatings of the heart." But what caused her consternation, what literally "caused her heart to beat," was not the thought of the "murdered girl—the recollection of *her* gave me no uneasiness," she wrote, but rather the proximity of danger from the city just across the water. "I could not forget," she continued, "that the quiet lovely path we were treading was near to the city, with its thousand hells, and frightfull easy of access."[3]

Child's eerie description of this site caught the dissonance between the sylvan scene and the city just beyond. Here was an edenic setting— "Paradise before Satan"—so easily violated by forces of the city that intruded "with her vices into this beautiful sanctuary of nature." Departing on a boat that would return her to the city, Child was struck, however, not by fear or even sadness (although she did note that the moon shone with a "saddened glory"), but rather by a "delightful sensation of elasticity and vigour which one feels when riding a fiery steed." In the distance the "rockets rose from Castle Garden and dropped their blazing jewels on the billow bosom of the bay."[4]

In this juxtaposition of nature and civilization, innocence and violation, fear and erotic energy, and especially in her reckoning with the demons of the city, Child's musings indicate the range of associations provoked by the Mary Rogers tragedy. The death of Rogers was a public event, defined by the city and the uniqueness of a historical moment. And just as Mary faded from the foreground of Lydia Child's consciousness, replaced by the images of the city, so too did Mary's own identity fade into a public persona melded with that of the extraordinary metropolis in which she lived.

It was not unusual for bodies to be found floating in the waters around New York, the new nation's largest and most busy city. These were almost ordinary occurrences, attesting to the frequency of suicides, accidental drownings, or even foul play.[5] But from her position at Anderson's, a popular haunt for the journalists and politicians who would turn this death into a cause célèbre, Mary was a well-known figure and her disappearance and presumed murder immediately became an issue of concern, curiosity, and eventually outrage. It was for its time an emblematic crime, one of those events that occurs at a critical historical moment and enters the public imagination in surprisingly complex ways that far transcend the actual importance of the events or its principal players. Moreover, the death seemed unusually brutal for its time; the coroner's report said (with the following explications) that "from marks and bruises, there were evident signs of the body having been violated . . . and that the bruises about the head and face, as well as . . . was sufficient to cause death . . . by persons or persons unknown." It was immediately assumed that she had been raped and murdered; clearly, the death of Mary Rogers was not an ordinary event.[6]

Public reaction was swift. The New York *Herald* asserted that "a young and beautiful girl has been seduced and murdered within hail of this populous place." The next day it followed with the information that "The city was full of rumors [about the murder] yesterday, got up for the basest and most mercenary matters." "The horrible murder of Miss Rogers excites daily a deeper and wider interest in our city," wrote the New York *Tribune*. Crowds were "daily hurrying to the Sybil's Cave to look at the scene of the deed and the shore where her body was first discovered." "It was," concluded the *Herald*, an "awful atrocity . . . agitated among all classes." Hoboken's Chief Magistrate (and the presiding official when the body was found) noted the "great but just excitement prevailing in the community, relative to the mysterious and desperate murder of Mary C. Rogers." Deluged by requests for information he could or would not provide, he made a public plea for any knowledge of Mary's whereabouts prior to her death.[7]

The police made little headway in solving the crime. In response to what they considered a dragging official investigation, and asserting that the public demanded action, a "Committee of Safety" was formed under the auspices of James Gordon Bennett, editor of the New York *Herald*. In a statement the committee deplored the slow response of the police, offered a reward for "information leading to the apprehension and conviction of any one of the murderers," and urged city residents to form vigilante groups to search out the killers.[8] Almost one month after the event, the Governor of New York, William Seward, under considerable public pressure, offered a proclamation boldly stating that "Mary C. Rogers . . . was lately ravished and murdered" and offered a reward for information leading to the conviction of "any person guilty of said crimes."[9]

Looking back, George Walling, who later became the city's Chief of Police, recounted the Rogers death in his *Recollections*, listing it among the "great crimes that startled the country." He too spoke of the "excitement following the murder of Mary Rogers [which] was conspicuously felt by the prominent New Yorkers of the day."[10] One such prominent New Yorker was Philip Hone, former Mayor, successful merchant, and noted diarist, who was otherwise preoccupied with awaiting the final decision on Clay's Bank Bill, but who took time to chronicle the "shocking murder" in his dairy. Apparently well informed of the events, Hone wrote: "the body of a young female named Mary Cecilia

Rogers was found on Thursday last in the river near Hoboken, with
horrid marks of violation and violence on her person. She was," he
added, "a beautiful girl."[11]

There were several theories as to how and at whose hand Mary Rogers died: that she had been brutally violated and killed by an urban gang;
that she had been murdered by a lone assassin either known to her or
not; that her death was a suicide; or even that she had not died but
merely disappeared and that the body found belonged to some other
unfortunate young woman. All these speculations had an explicit subtext
rife with fear and fantasy about the city, its complex mix of residents,
it growing identification with unrestrained sexuality, and its reputation
for danger and violent death. The case was never "solved"; there were
no indictments, no trial, and no formal resolution. With time, however,
it was generally acknowledged that Rogers had died during an abortion
gone awry, her body dragged to the river in an attempt to cover up the
crime.[12]

Mary Rogers and her mother, Phebe Wait Mather Rogers, were refugees
to New York, part of the large migration that so overwhelmed early
nineteenth-century cities in the twenty years before the Civil War. At
time of their arrival in the late 1830s, New York was a city on the brink
of transformation. Defined by its excellent port and its traditional commercial role, it had already displaced its economic rivals, Boston and
Philadelphia, as the new nation's foremost entrepôt and commercial
center. By the 1840s it would assume its place as the country's largest
industrial center as well. Culture followed commerce and the city soon
emerged as what Edward Spann has called an "American Metropolis,"
a city to rival London and Paris in the sheer amount of its activity,
cultural diversity, and cosmopolitan flavor.[13]

With economic growth came population growth, new demographic
diversity, and geographic expansion. What was a relatively compact, if
crowded, city in 1820 with 156,056 people almost all living and working
at the city's southern edge, grew in just twenty years to contain a population more than twice as large. By 1840, just one year before Mary's
death, the city had 391,114 people and its residential and commercial
areas extended north as far as 35th Street. That same year the New
York *Mirror* lamented that the Common Council had "destroyed nearly
all the good shaded nooks" that had been intended as public squares.
Twenty years later, on the eve of the Civil War, the city contained over
one million inhabitants, its settled areas extended to the high 80s, and
the area designated as Central Park was well under construction.[14] In
just forty years the city had become a sprawling metropolis filled with
widely different groups of people and a complex economic and social
life that anticipated in almost every way our modern definitions of city
life.[15] By the early 1840s writes the modern historian Neil Harris in his
biography of Phineas Barnum, "The city was not only America's largest

but also its most heterogeneous and, by reputation, its wickedest, filled, according to the exposes that found their way into print, with gamblers and seducers, criminals and confidence men, who took advantage of foreign immigrants and country bumpkins."[16]

The transformation of New York into a city unlike any other in the new republic inspired responses and commentary from those who, like Lydia Child, experienced its energy, intensity, and complexity. Child had arrived in New York the spring before Mary's death and, in comparison to her native Boston, she found it one large cacophony of contrasting sounds and sights. Calling the city a "great Babylon," "a vast emporium of poverty and crime where wealth dozes on French couches, thrice piled, and canopied with damask, while Poverty camps in the dirty pavement," a place of "bloated disease, and black gutters, and pigs uglier than their ugly kind," she remarked upon the "noisy discord of the street-cries [that gave] the ear no rest."[17]

Yet another visitor to the city, George Lippard, the popular novelist and reformer, writing out of a different style and tradition than Child, also saw the city as a place of opposites, a veritable dazzle of activity and constant change. He noted the transformation of Manhattan from a "green Island, where once the swelling hills arose and the quiet brooklets sparkled" to an urban "wilderness of stone and brick and mortar" with a "million of lives swarming beneath its countless roofs, and along its tortuous streets." Asking his reader to "image the Empire city," he answers himself that it is a "a voluptuous Queen sitting in her gorgeous palace, drunk with wine and blinded by the glare of the festival of lights." And the empire over which this Queen reigns is both "an empire of wealth that blinds you with its glare, and misery, that strikes you dumb with its anguish, an empire of palaces and hovels, garlands and chains, churches and jails."[18]

New York continually inspired such expansive images and metaphors. Always overwhelming, this city of the 1840s was a formidable space to be reckoned with, one unlike any other—a site of glittering lights and dark hard stone, of vast wealth and desperate poverty. Into its narrow streets collected men and women from everywhere and from every walk of life. "It throbbed," said Lippard, with a "million lives and held in her streets the people of every tongue." Here in one small space was the heterogenous mix of the new nation; it was, proclaimed the journalist and urban flaneur George Foster, nothing less than a "Republican Metropolis."[19]

Mary and Phebe Rogers were part of this new "Republican Metropolis." Migrating to New York from Connecticut during the depression year of 1837, they joined the large initial wave of immigration that transformed urban centers in the quarter century before the Civil War. The descendants of two illustrious Connecticut families, these two women came with few financial resources and were in flight from a complicated family legacy. One of the allures of the city was that it offered personal sanctuary from old ways, from the narrow controls of family life and provincial village culture. It was the "new," the site of a bustling commerce, lively public culture, and abundant opportunity; in this it was also a place of presumed freedom where life could start anew and individual identity could be recast. For Mary and Phebe Rogers the city was a such a haven from their previous lives and they sought its promised anonymity and freedom. Once in New York their lives changed dramatically. At least for Mary, the city allowed her a life unimaginable in the world of her New England ancestors. In her roles as cigar seller and later boardinghouse keeper she entered a public culture unlike any other she had known. However, in offering relative freedom from past restraints, the city, at least in the mind's eye, put youths, both male and female, at risk.

As the quintessential urban space, New York was inscribed in the extensive literature of the period as both dangerous and sexual. By the time of Mary's death this "Republican Metropolis" had become an American anti-type, the presumed site of social danger where traditional notions of order and restraint had broken down. Urban violence, the legacy of the uprisings and popular rebellions of the 1830s and increased crime, had already become a familiar aspect of urban existence and a source of public concern. Gangs were a common feature of city culture, and rowdies and miscreants of all sorts were said to plague the city streets, constantly endangering the citizenry. Poverty and disease were endemic, not only in well-known slum areas such as the Five Points, but throughout the town, a consequence of a dramatically increasing population, crowded conditions, and insufficient municipal facilities. This urban space, the organic microcosm of the new republic, had become not only the dreaded sore of Jefferson's body politic, but also the epitome of a promiscuous public realm.[20]

In regarding cities as dark, dangerous, and inherently sexual, nineteenth-century Americans drew on a complex legacy with roots in both the Judeo-Christian and classical traditions. Both the city of the New Jerusalem and the City of Babylon as well as those of Athens and Rome were available as metaphoric and literary representations. In choosing the nineteenth-century construction of Babylon, the city of vice, as their predominant literary construction of the urban, Americans were not only refusing a more optimistic version of their present and their future, they were rejecting their own historical utopic version of the City Upon the Hill as well. This choice of the dark and dangerous city over that of one of light and hope says a great deal about nineteenth-century concerns and fears while simultaneously suggesting the depth of the suspicion of urban culture characteristic of both our past and present.[21]

Cities, and New York particularly, existed in sharp distinction to the bourgeois home. As many critics have suggested, antebellum culture was delineated into two exclusive and antithetical domains, forming an essential cultural dialectic of public and private space. On the one hand there was the city—the untamed male province of commerce and public life; on the other, the refined female and largely private place of the home—the site of household and family. The city and the public culture associated with it existed, it seemed, definitively outside the parameters prescribed by the simultaneously emerging bourgeois codes of antebellum America.

But the essence of this urban danger was not only that associated with urban gangs, panel thieves, or even Five Points' disease—although of course it included these as well. Rather, it was the sexual danger ascribed to city culture that filled the endless tracts and advice books published during this antebellum period. The expansion of the commercial sex industry in the 1830s contributed to the city's reputation as a place of promiscuity and sexual danger. The array of brothels and bawdy houses was a familiar feature of city life. Prostitutes of all types were said to have taken over city streets, luring men to sin and becoming an endless source of popular comment and political debate. Moreover, prostitution thrived not in any given district, but on the city's major thoroughfares, near the homes of the city's wealthy, in crowded clusters in the Five Points or along the East River, and in every area of the city.[22] But the association of the city with sexuality, and perhaps more important with sexual danger, transcended the preoccupation with prostitution common to evangelical reformers and anti-vice crusaders. In a broader context, the city was the locus of a large and expanding public culture of pleasure and entertainment. Dance halls, theaters, promiscuous crowds on public promenades—these were the stuff of urban culture, and they identified the city as a place of secular and sensual pleasure.

If the city was dazzling and glittery, forbidding and dangerous, mysterious and seductive, it was also defined by a specifically female identity. Images of the city were laden with female-gendered associations and references—at once full-bosomed and maternal "upon whose bay held the ships of every sea, and whose streets held the people of every tongue." This female self of New York was at once benevolent, like the Temperance societies who "threw a silken cord to the fallen and the perishing"; and a Babylon ridden with commerce which with "her loaded drays and haded skeletons is busy as ever fulfilling the World's contract with the Devil." She is explicitly personified as a sexual and seductive harlot—the "wonderfully beautifully featured girl; scarlet cheeked, glaringly arrayed and of a figure all natural grace but unnatural vivacity" who tempts the protagonist of Herman Melville's novel *Pierre*, causing him to shudder and proclaim, "My God . . . the town's first welcome to youth." A vast, mysterious space, this womanly city was to be entered into, conquered, carved into manageable pieces, and ultimately possessed and understood. But whichever female visage she inspired, the city in the minds of writers as vastly different as Melville, Lippard, or Child was a distinctly gendered female force—overpowering and deeply mysterious.[23]

In its rise, this city gave birth to an explosion of new forms of culture. Among them was the appearance of all types of print culture: the popular penny newspaper, the cheap commercial novel, the serialized detective story. All these developed in the ten years around Mary's death, serving the arrival of a newly expanded reading public; all were specifically urban in their content and sensibility. Mary Rogers' life and death became a text, or many texts really, of this new urban print culture. Through her story urban journalists and fiction writers invented complex tales of urban life figured around the violent death of a beautiful young woman. As one of the earliest sensational narratives of urban commercial culture, the Rogers story invited, just as Rogers herself did, an exploration of city culture, with its romance, its sex, and its violence. Matters hitherto considered outside the purview of public discourse— Mary's beaux, her sexual history, and even her mutilated body—became legitimate information, even "newsworthy."

The new penny press, only six years old, found in this tale of violent death an instant "city story" and a means to sell papers to the new readership that increasingly included women and men of the working classes. Following every possible lead in the case, and often inventing them, papers such as the *Herald*, the Evening *Post*, and even the more understated and reform-minded *Tribune* engaged in a competitive race with one another to cover the story that they had in large measure created. Thus emerged a serialized "real life mystery story," enacted on the city streets and featuring an unending cast of city characters. In the name of public information, and in the cause of pursuing justice, the press published detailed and medically specific coroner's reports, printed the depositions of private citizens, and in the case of James Gordon Bennett, appropriated the death as a vehicle for political agitation.[24]

Subsequent to the newspaper coverage, Mary Rogers became the subject of popular fiction and, in an anticipation of postmodern literary inventions, the first "real" subject of that peculiarly modern urban form, the detective story. Using the new penny papers, which he ironically referred to as the "public prints," Edgar Allan Poe wove the second story of his pioneering detective trilogy around the crime in "The Mystery of Marie Roget," first published in Snowden's *Ladies' Magazine*, in the fall and winter of 1842–43. Poe muddled his attempt to solve the crime, but in focusing his attention on the enigma of Mary herself and the distinctly urban quality of the event—the importance of the city setting, the collection of male characters who figured prominently in the investigation—he foregrounded the important issues in the case and simultaneously established several important ingredients of the detective genre.[25]

Using Poe as their inspiration, writers of cheap popular fiction, many of whom were themselves close to the city's press and publishing industry, and several who surely knew Poe, quickly followed his model. Mary's story, or some imagined variation of it, became one of the featured sagas of the urban mystery novels gaining popularity in the 1840s. Borrowing the literary form pioneered by the French writer, Eugene Sue, these would-be authors followed Poe's attempt to use Mary Rogers as the subject of their novels, while simultaneously exploring the contrasting dimensions of urban life, focusing especially on its lurid and sensational aspects. The Rogers story also inspired other ephemeral forms—crime narratives, a gallows confession, sentimental verse.[26]

Mary Rogers, however, served not only as a source of cultural representation; the representations of her served a variety of other purposes as well. In her name political agendas were fought and social and legislative policy enacted. Unable to solve the crime, the city's police and system of policing came under fire, fueling an already ongoing crisis about rising crime rates, criminal justice, and social order in the growing city. At issue was not only the inefficiency of the police, but the nature of policing itself, which many critics contended was designed for post facto detection instead of the prevention of crime. With the death of Mary Rogers serving as a constant source of rhetorical power, police reform was enacted in the Police Reform Act of 1845 that effectively modernized the system and established a more organized form of social and political surveillance. And the sexual implications of Rogers' death added to an already ongoing attempt to regulate social and sexual behavior. Most significant in this regard was an 1845 law criminalizing abortion; the passage of this law was explicitly related in several ways to the Rogers tragedy.[27]

As the subject of all forms of social discourse—the newspaper, the mystery novel, and even that of legislators and reformers—Rogers was the embodiment of all that antebellum middle-class culture named as unspeakable, but actually, according to the modern critic of the history of sexuality, Foucault, integrated into a "regulated and polymorphous" variety of discourses. Mary Rogers was the new urban woman who used her sexuality to obtain an as yet unlikely freedom; her sexuality gave her access to the public and male spaces of the city, while it distanced her from the beau ideal of woman as wife and mother. Thus removed from the interiority of the home, Rogers became the public woman who inspired a constant discussion about nonprocreative sex, the female body, abortion, and some notion of the dangers of sexuality. As the subject of these extended conversations, Rogers was simultaneously a symbol of social transgression, the source of social danger to be contained, controlled, and even legislated against.[28]

In all of the discourse about Rogers—in the penny press, in popular fiction and tracts, even in legislative debates—references and images of Mary were intertwined with those of the city; the mystery of Mary Rogers fused with the mystery of the city itself. Like the city, she was a source of wonder, mystery, and fear, provoking desire and inspiring narrative. Mary was a woman of the city, its intimate inhabiter who knew Lippard's "tortuous streets" and pleasure haunts. Like the city she became an object of desire, the "feminine enigma" that, in the words of Teresa de Lauretis, is an "inspiration for narrative."²⁹ Mary was not only the subject of urban mysteries, she *was* the mystery. She was the essence of the mysterious woman whose body held the secrets of her sexual life, of her sexually violent death, and even of endless crimes perpetrated against her. These unknowns inspired a prolific and emotionally charged discussion about her life and how she died, just as they engendered endless commentary about social and sexual danger, and legislation and social policy intended to police life within the city itself. And, in a Foucauldian sense, she provoked an endless discourse about sex and an exploration of things hidden and unknown.

The following description of events tells the story of the "Tragedy of Mary Rogers" as it emerged from these city texts. Thus recapitulated as a narrative, it depicts a story of a death, but more important it also tells the story of a life—that of Mary Rogers—and of the complex urban social world of which she was a part. As the title of Poe's story suggests, however, the *tragedy* of Mary Rogers quickly became the *mystery* of Mary Rogers, for reasons I hope the following pages will make clear.

2
A Body Floating
Between Two Tides

LINES ON THE DEATH OF MARY ROGERS
Death comes to all in wayward form,
In peaceful guise or vengeful storm,
    All must his presence share.
Around the dark and lurid bed
Of those whose tortured spirits shed,
    A terror on the air. . . .

Hark! heard ye not that note of fear
Burn wildly on the palsied ear,
    Far in the tangled wood?
Merciful God! what sound was there—
What deed of sin pollutes the air—
    What sickening taint of blood.

Oh! shield me from that fearful sight—
That crime of darkest, blackest night,
    Appalling even the brave.
Wild shriek on shriek, and pray'r on pray'r
And deepest curses mingle there—
    Oh God! in pity save.

Who heads they shrieks, poor helpless maid?
There is no arm with strength to aid—
    No heart that has the will.
One last wild cry that reaches heaven,
One bitter pray'r for mercy given—
    Tis past!—and all is still. . . .

Alas! the scene is passing fair,
Yet foul pollution revels there,
    And crime too black for name.
Far, far from all whose arm might save,
Welcome the cold, and bloody grave,
    That hides a wretch's shame.

Tho' tears above that grave be shed,
Not tears of blood may wake the dead,
    Yet weep we when she fell.

> But One *is just to all alike,*
> *And God's right arm is hard to strike*
> *The coward down to hell.*
>
> Anonymous (1841)[1]

*T*HE Rogers boardinghouse at 126 Nassau Street was a three-story red brick building with a flat roof, typical of the small buildings that flanked the downtown streets of lower Manhattan in the first half of the nineteenth century. Located on the east side of the street between Beekman and Ann streets, it formed part of a group of similar houses built in the late 1820s with the city's northward expansion. Nassau Street itself was a winding stretch that reached from Broad Street and continued to Park Row, ending just one block short of intersecting with City Hall Park. Along it was the usual jumble of stores, workshops, boardinghouses, and residences that defined the character of the early city, a bustling urban space where rich and very poor often lived next to each other, where work and recreation took place in the same city blocks, and where the social segregation of neighborhoods by class, race, and ethnicity had not yet fully taken hold.[2]

In the ten short years since the house had been built, Nassau Street had attained a particular identity, one that set it off from the usual maze of narrow intersecting streets. As the seat of the city's burgeoning printing and publishing industry, it was, said the astute observer George Foster, "the city's brain."[3] The choice of Nassau Street as the home of the city's newspapers and print culture was a consequence of its strategic location. At the hub of the hectic city, it was practically adjacent to City Hall and equidistant from South Street to the east, the city's thriving port area with its attendant workshops and businesses, and Wall Street to the south, the center of commerce and trade. To the northwest, in back of City Hall, was the infamous Five Points, Manhattan's worst slum and the city's most powerful symbol of urban disorder and poverty. And almost surrounding the Rogers house itself were the city's most important landmarks—Trinity and St. Paul's Church, Theatre Alley, and just two short blocks away "shining like a track of fire" was Broadway, the city's most famous street for shopping, and strolling.[4]

With its central location, Nassau Street was also a good location for a boardinghouse, probably as good as any in the city. And it was here in 1840 that Phebe Rogers let the house at 126 from Peter Aymar, a man who owned many similar buildings in the neighborhood.[5] The widow Phebe was sixty when she set up house and already elderly and frail. But she still had charge of her youngest child, Mary Cecilia Rogers, and needed the small income that this meager property would provide. Mary was then twenty, unmarried, and by all accounts quite beautiful.

It was she who really managed the house, tended its small rooms, and took in the boarders—young single men come to town in search of work. Between 1840 and the summer of 1841 the house was filled with activity, home to Mary, Phebe, one servant girl, and a changing cast of men. Among these at one time or other were: Arthur Crommelin, probably a clerk; Daniel Payne, a corkcutter; William Kiekuck, a sailor; and Arthur Padley, whose occupation remains unknown.[6]

Bound by the created world of the boardinghouse, these people shared common quarters but probably shared more as well. Boardinghouses, especially those of the modest sort, were more than a collection of rooms peopled by strangers; in the absence of traditional town and family life they often became home, providing friendship and community in the new and strange setting of the impersonal city. Whatever the nature of this found household, it was shortlived. By the last week in July 1841, Mary was dead, Phebe had moved to her sister's house, and the boarders, all drawn into the drama over Mary's death, had moved on to other rented rooms.

The Discovery

At the Rogers boardinghouse, Sunday, July 25, began in an uneventful way. Mary, wearing a white dress, leghorn hat, and carrying a parasol, was dressed for a hot midsummer day. She interrupted Daniel Payne, a boarder at the house and her lover, in the midst of "making his toilet," to tell him that she was going to visit her aunt, Mrs. Downing, uptown on Jane Street, and that she would return later that evening. Payne bid Mary good-bye and announced his intention to wait for her at the omnibus stop on the dark corner of Broadway and Ann, as he usually did when she returned home late.[7]

Sunday in New York was different from all other days in the usually noisy and hectic metropolis. On Sunday the whole city changed character; work stopped, commerce ceased, and shops and taverns closed. At least until the late afternoon the streets were quiet, even empty, visited only by the occasional early stroller or men and women walking on their way to or from church. Edgar Poe noted that while the streets of the city were generally "thronged with people . . . on Sunday alone, the town had a peculiarly deserted air [which] no observing person can have failed to notice." The change on Nassau Street was especially palpable: "On Sunday," observed Foster, "even the beating of the presses was stilled by the Sabbath-day closing of the newspaper offices."[8] Mary, walking alone on Sunday morning, would have cut a lonely figure as she hurried to her destination. Writing of his imagined Mary Rogers, Marie Roget, Poe concluded that "It was not only possible, but as very far more than probable, that Marie might have proceeded, by any one of the many routes between her own residence and that of her aunt, without meeting a single individual whom she knew, or by whom she was known."[9]

We do not know who saw the *real* Mary that quiet Sunday morning, nor do we know where she might have gone. In fact, we know little with any certainty about the rest of Mary's day. What she did, with whom, and why, remain cast in mystery, the subject of much conjecture, the story behind the story that became the Mary Rogers tragedy. What we do know is that Mary never returned to Nassau Street that Sunday night. And within a few days her body was found near the Jersey shore— the victim of an unusually violent death.

Daniel Payne, the corkcutter, had come to board at the Rogers house in the fall of 1840. Shortly thereafter he became romantically involved with Mary and they were engaged to be married. Unlike Mary, Daniel Payne stayed home that hot Sunday morning, not venturing out until about eleven when, in his words, he "walked directly to his brother John Payne's on 33 Warren Street, staying in and around his brother's company until about 1:00." Payne said that they visited Scott's Bazaar on Dey Street, then walked up Broadway and parted company near St. Paul's Church. He went on alone, stopping at James Street at Mr. Bickford's for about an hour to "read the newspapers," and then heading downtown again, where he joined the dense crowd that filled Broadway on Sunday evenings.[10]

If Sunday morning in the city was an unusually quiet time, by evening it was again transformed, taking on a festive air. "Sunday evening," said George Foster, "the City undergoes a change as sudden and great as magic. Broadway . . . now swarms with a dense crowd of men and women who do not, through the week, find leisure for a promenade. The great bulk of them are servant-girls, with their beaux and brothers, lovers and friends, who wait eagerly through the whole week for the setting of the Sabbath sun, that they may rush into the streets, and for a few hours enjoy the luxury of being free to do as they please. Bookfolders, the seamstresses, the fly-girls, the type-rubbers, the strawbraiders—all the working girls from all parts of the City and every occupation—have also found their sweethearts, and are out for a promenade in Broadway."[11]

After his stroll in this urban crowd, Payne headed toward home, still expecting to wait for Mary at the street corner. But as he approached Ann Street he noticed a "heavy storm coming on." Concluding that on account of the rain, Mary would spend the night at her aunt's house, he decided not to wait for her and instead proceeded directly home.[12] By the next morning, however, Mary had still not returned and it was soon clear that she had never arrived at her aunt's.

Payne began what in retrospect seemed a frantic search for her, traversing what would have been, even in 1841 with public transportation, very large distances, "all the time enquiring of different persons . . . if they had seen any person of her description." He went first to Harlem at the northern end of Manhattan, then to Williamsburg in Brooklyn and then across the Hudson to Hoboken, and even to Staten Island.[13] Meeting with no success, he returned by boat to South Ferry in lower Manhattan and walked to the offices of the *Sun* where he placed a missing persons notice for Tuesday's edition of the paper:

> Left her home on Sunday Morning, July 25, a young lady, had on a white dress, black shawl, blue scarf, leghorn hat, light colored shoes and parasol light colored; it is supposed some accident has befallen her. Whoever will give information respecting her at 126 Nassau Street shall be rewarded for their trouble.[14]

Payne continued his fruitless search the following day, calling "upon a keeper of a public house on the corner of Duane and William Streets" where he heard that "a girl of Mary's description had been seen . . . for several hours on the previous Sunday." Then he again returned to Hoboken "where he asked for her at several places along the shore . . . at the ferry, and three times at sites between the ferry and a watering spot known as the Elysian Field's House." Finding no trace of her, Payne returned to the city by early afternoon, paid a visit to the shop where he worked as a corkcutter, and returned home again at seven.[15]

Word that Mary was missing traveled quickly. Arthur Crommelin knew by the next day, Monday, July 26. Crommelin, a former boarder and also Mary's former lover, had lived at the Rogers's for six months, beginning on December 7, 1840, and leaving the following June. But if Crommelin knew about Mary's disappearance on Monday, it was not until Wednesday, when he was shown Tuesday's newspaper notice, that he became alarmed and commenced his own fevered search for her. He began with a visit to Mary's Nassau Street house where he heard, he said, "first hand" about her disappearance "from the old lady," referring to Phebe Rogers. Believing that "Mary was forcibly detained in some assignation house or some other place, he went," he reported, "immediately to the police," for some undisclosed reason seeking a particular officer named Hayes, who was not to be found. Proceeding next to a tavern near the Shakespeare Hotel, he told his companions that he was going over to Hoboken to search for her. A friend, Archibald Padley, who currently shared boardinghouse quarters with him on John Street and had also once lived at the Rogers's Nassau Street house, accompanied him on this quest.[16]

The Jersey side of the Hudson was connected directly to New York City by three steamboats that continually crossed the river.[17] The boats landed near a hotel and tavern and a short walk brought visitors to the Elysian Fields, the glade described by Lydia Maria Child. It was "a truly lovely spot," wrote Child's fellow Bostonian, Samuel Dexter Ward: this "cleared place of about four or five acres, surrounded on three sides by trees and open on the other to the river . . . a truly lovely spot." "There were," he continued, "places of amusement and exercise, such as flying deer, swings &c" and a "well patronized refreshment house" known as Nick Moore's House.[18] The Elysian Fields provided a green, cool space where city dwellers could "enjoy the pleasures and health bearing breezes of the Country without purchasing them at the dear rate of sweating over dusty roads."[19] By the 1840s it was a popular resort for the "heated and tired inhabitants of the metropolis," a place to walk, play, or gather at any number of popular watering spots or hotels that served the day traffic along the cliffs high above the Hudson.

James Boulard and Henry Mallin were walking along this stretch of country bordering the Hudson on Wednesday, July 28, presumably enjoying a respite from the hot city, when they saw an unlikely sight, "a body floating between two tides, two or three hundred yards from shore." They ran as far as the Elysian Fields Dock, "procured a boat and rowed to the body that they had sighted and brought it ashore." They then secured the body with a rope and a stone until the coroner could examine it.[20]

When Arthur Crommelin arrived at this same spot shortly thereafter, the body was already on shore. He reported that he saw a group of people gathered around the body of a "drowned female," a body he recognized almost immediately as that of his friend, Mary Rogers. Crommelin cut open the sleeve of her dress and "rubbed her arm to identify her," and, he said, "made use of every proper means for the same purpose." He took a piece of her skirt, as well as a piece from the ripped sleeve, presumably to aid in further identification. He then "remained with the body all afternoon until the coroner had taken an inquest which was nearly 9 o'clock at night."[21]

Dr. Richard Cook, the Hoboken coroner Crommelin referred to, was notified of the discovery of the body. Arriving at the scene in the company of two jurors, they proceeded to examine the body. His initial report indicated that Mary had been raped and beaten and that she had been injured sufficiently to cause her death.[22] A more detailed report issued later described in graphic detail a violent and horrible death; Mary had been gagged, tied, raped by several men, and finally strangled. Her body was then discarded into the Hudson where it was subsequently found. Dr. Cook confirmed that Mary had not met her death by drowning: "frothy blood," he said, was "still issuing from the mouth," her face was "suffused with dark blood—bruised blood" and "was swollen, the veins . . . highly distended." These post-mortem symptoms as well as others—the presence of an echymose marks that led him to believe she had been throttled and partially choked by a man's hand, and a "piece of fine lace trimming" tied tightly and hidden in the flesh of her neck—indicated that she had died from strangulation.[23]

"Much of Cook's testimony," reported the *Herald*, was "of such a nature that it cannot be given in detail." It related, the paper continued, "to the appearance of the body, which enabled the doctor to state positively that the poor girl had been brutally violated." Cook also added that "previous to this shocking outrage, she had evidently been a person of chastity and correct habits; that her person was horribly violated *by more than two or three persons* . . . [and] . . . he stated distinctly . . . that there was not the slightest trace of pregnancy."[24]

By the time Crommelin was ready to leave for home, it was late and the ferries had stopped running until morning. He remained that night at the Jersey City Hotel, returning to the city the next morning, carrying the news of Mary's death and some pieces of her clothing. These included a "section of her dress which he had cut, flowers from inside and outside of Mary's hat, a garter, the bottom of her pantalette, a shoe and a curl of her hair, all given to him by the coroner." Phebe Rogers identified the clothing as that worn by her daughter, who "had the same on her person when she left her house on Sunday morning." Crommelin then went back to Hoboken to keep a scheduled meeting with the coroner, where, "in consequence to the great heat of the weather," it was decided "to temporarily inter the body, which was done at two feet from the surface of the earth, and in a double coffin."[25]

Mary's body remained in its shallow Hoboken grave until the middle of August when, at the request of New York's Acting Mayor Purdy, it was disinterred and brought to the Dead House in City Hall Park for further identification. Mary's death was officially registered by the city on August 11, 1841. Even though the Jersey coroner had determined that the cause of death was strangulation, the New York City coroner registered the cause of death as "drowned." Mary Rogers's body was finally buried (apparently without ceremony) at the cemetery of the West Presbyterian Church, located at the northern end of Varick Street.[26]

Of Boarders and Other Suspects

And within a short time, as I have already suggested, there were many different explanations for her violent death. Foremost among these was the theory that an individual had killed her—perhaps one of her known beaus. Another view proposed that she had been raped and killed by an urban gang. Still other interpretations would suggest that her death was a suicide, or that the body found was not that of the well-known cigar girl, but another anonymous female victim of unexplained violence. All of these suggestions alluded to the imagined fears and dangers of urban life, the association of the city with both sexual license and social danger.

The New York City police, presumably acting on the information that Mary had been accompanied by an unidentified man in the hours before her death, proceeded to try to locate him. As a result, several men were sought for questioning in the weeks following Mary's death and some (it is unclear who or how many) were arrested and detained. Included in this group were Arthur Crommelin and Daniel Payne; William Kiekuck, a sailor who had also once boarded with the Rogers; Joseph Morse, a wood engraver who worked down the block; and John Anderson, Mary's former employer. All provided statements to the police concerning their whereabouts on Sunday, July 25, and what they knew about Mary's habits and activities. With the notable exception of the cigar store owner, John Anderson, the newspapers were privy to these conversations with the police and printed them verbatim, often the very next day. These depositions have proven to be rich narrative sources, not only for the light they shed on Rogers and the events around her death, but for what they tell about the daily activities of a diverse group of (mostly) single urban men in 1841. Forced to prove their innocence, these men revealed much not only about their involvement with Mary, but about their lives, their associations, and their families. In publishing these narratives under provocative banners, the press generated a sense of mystery, urgency, and danger about the case, while simultaneously revealing in print information previously unexplored in public discourse. Consequently, while vicariously participating in the endless quest for her killer, readers became well acquainted with Mary and the young men of her circle.

Some fragmentary details about Mary and her mother, Phebe, also emerged from this early testimony and quickly became public, providing what little information we have about Mary, her friends, and her actual life. With time, of course, these fragments of information would form the basis of elaborate imaginary narratives about the life of a young and beautiful woman and her widowed mother in the antebellum city. The *Post*, for example, reported that a "colored servant" woman told the police that she had overheard a conversation between Phebe and Mary Rogers "relative to her intended marriage to Payne," and that Phebe Rogers had obtained Mary's "pledge that she would not marry him." The paper added the information that when Phebe heard that her daughter was missing, she uttered the "fear that she would never see Mary again."[27] Mrs. Rogers never went to Hoboken to see Mary's body, an issue that caused some commentary, and little was heard from her again, except a small notice in the *Herald* on August 25, indicating that the Nassau Street house was "untenanted" and that Phebe Rogers had removed to the residence of Mr. O'Hara on Jane Street.

At the inquest the day after the body was discovered, Arthur Crommelin was asked to tell what he knew of the deceased. He reported that "he knew her for a considerable time, having boarded in her mother's house about six months while [Mary] was the officiating manager of the family, and the main support of an infirm and aged mother, with the whole charge of conducting the boardinghouse." Crommelin consistently, and perhaps disingenuously, stressed Mary's gentility and propriety, stating that she was "seldom in the habit of going out on the Sabbath, except to church, and then not frequently with young men." He was "unable to account for her going to Hoboken on Sunday, the 25th of July" and supposed that she was "decoyed there by malice." "She was," he said, "formerly much attached to a young man in New York—but has some time since discarded him." He went on to add that he had "no knowledge of her going to Hoboken on the 25th of July, [she] was generally at home and domestic." He added that Mary was "for some time attached to Mr. . . . but for some time past rejected him, and is now attached to Mr. . . . to whom it was supposed she would have been married." He said that "during the whole time the witness has known her [she had] borne an irreproachable character for chastity and veracity. She was amiable and pleasing, and rather fascinating in her manners. [He] never heard her virtue questioned in the least."[28]

Later Crommelin offered more information about his own relationship with Mary. He left his room at Nassau Street in June 1841 when he was replaced in Mary's affections by Payne. At that time he reportedly told Mary that he disapproved of her involvement with the corkcutter, a man he regarded as "dissipated." Crommelin supposedly also admonished Mary that "he was sorry for the step she was taking" (presumably her marriage to Payne) and that "if she were ever in trouble to call him." Apparently, in the week before her death, Mary was in some form of trouble and even Phebe turned to him for help. According to Crommelin, either Mary or Phebe "called every day at Crommelin's asking him to call at their residence," a request Crommelin did not respond to because "he had been coldly received when last there." On Saturday, July 24, the day before she vanished, Mary left a final message on the slate attached to his door, adding a final poignant touch: a rose in the keyhole.[29]

Arthur Crommelin actually revealed relatively little about himself, and indeed he seems to have had an unusual role in the entire affair. Crommelin, whose occupation was never disclosed, was clearly of a different class than the other men connected with the case. Most likely a clerk, Crommelin appears to have functioned as a representative of the family and an aid to the police. When Mary disappeared, Crommelin knew exactly where to look for her; articulate and keen in contending with the authorities, he knew the family well and was familiar with Mary's habits and haunts.[30]

Archibald Padley, Crommelin's companion who accompanied him on his initial quest for Mary and was with him when he identified the body, also testified at the initial inquest. He stated that he knew Mary Rogers because he had also boarded at the Rogers' house and, to Mary's character, he said that "she was a worthy girl of irreproachable character, was attached, [and] had heard that she was at Hoboken on Sunday, the 25 of July but [had] no knowledge of her associates or companion on that occasion, and that [she] had been absent since some time on Sunday last, which had caused great anxiety and alarm in the family. [He] has no knowledge of hostile feeling or ill will on the part of any one toward [her]. . . . She was respected and much esteemed."[31]

Some additional and especially relevant information was obtained from Frederika Kallenbarack Loss, the innkeeper at Nick Moore's House, a popular tavern near the Elysian Fields. Loss, who would later figure prominently in the case, reported that Mary had visited the tavern on Sunday, July 25, "in company with several young men, and that she drank some lemonade offered by one of them."[32]. This added credibility to the press releases speculating that Mary had been seen that Sunday with any number of unidentified men.

Several weeks after Mary's death, on Friday, October 8, 1841, Payne, at first a prime suspect in the case, was dead. Found drunk, with a broken vial of laudanum beside him, near the spot where Mary's body had been discovered, he was initially presumed to have committed suicide. (The Hoboken coroner, however, found no trace of poison and was unable to identify a precise cause of death; he indicated that Payne was intoxicated and may have fallen.) The news of Payne's death traveled fast, reaching the city that evening and, as with all other events related to the Rogers case, it "occasioned great excitement." The New York City Mayor and Justice Taylor crossed the river in a small boat in the midst of a storm.[33] The following day the Mayor held an inquest on Payne's death; its contents were, per usual, reported in the papers. It was attended by various witnesses, the Hoboken coroner, Dr. Cook, Payne's brother, John Payne, the innkeeper, Mrs. Loss, Arthur Crommelin, and several of Payne's acquaintances. The testimony provided interesting information about Payne, but with the exception of Loss' statement that although she thought she recognized Payne, having seen him "once in New York and once out here gunning . . . he did not correspond at all with the person [she] saw with Mary Rogers in July," it shed little light on Mary's murder.[34]

Payne had apparently been in a very bad way since Mary's death. John Payne, his brother, identified the dead man's belongings and reported that he had worn a crepe band on his hat since the death of Miss Rogers. "He was a habitually a drinking man," he said, and had been "out of his mind since the affair of Mary Rogers." He added that when he saw his brother a few days earlier he was "very dejected and appeared to have been drinking." Payne had apparently left the city on Thursday, October 7 and traveled to Hoboken where he presented himself at the Phoenix Hotel at around ten in the evening. "He looked red and a little intoxicated and he seemed weak and could hardly stand up," said Samuel Whitney, a patron of the bar that evening. Payne reportedly spoke little except to ask, "Suppose you know me? . . . Well I'm the man who was to have been married to Mary Rogers—I'm a man of a good deal of trouble." The next day he wandered the area in a drunken state until he was found by two New Yorkers, Doctors Griswold and Clement, both New York physicians, out for a walk. Griswold reported that at about five o'clock they saw Payne, "lying on the bank, head on the bench—loosened his collar and roused him up, but he died in a few minutes." In his pocket a note was found which read: "To the World—Here I am on the spot: God forgive me for my misfortune in my misspent time."[35]

William Kiekuck, the sailor, was another suspect. Arrested "on suspicion" of involvement with the assumed murder, according to the *Herald* he was incarcerated at the Tombs at his own request, claiming that he wished to remain in custody "until the authorities are satisfied of his innocence."[36] Kiekuck had boarded with the Rogers for a short stay— two and one half weeks in the spring of 1840—when he was on leave from the *U. S. S. North Carolina* and again in early July 1841 when he "went again to Mrs. Rogers, where he saw Mary C. Rogers, having previously known her." As for his relationship with Mary, the *Courier* attributed the revealing comment to him that "far from being intimate with her [Mary], he had never walked out with her in his life."[37]

Kiekuck's story was interesting primarily because of what it revealed about working-men's culture, casual prostitution, and a sailor's stay in New York. Like Payne, Kiekuck had to account for his activities on the day of Mary's disappearance. He reported that he stayed at his sister's house on Saturday, July 24, the night of his arrival. He had breakfast with her on the morning of Sunday, July 25, and then went to visit another relative—his sister-in-law, Mrs. Anderson, who lived on 17th Street near Broadway. After that visit, he walked over to Ninth Avenue, where he met a friend, John Miller, and together they walked the city, stopping to take a bath and get a drink at a porter house on Thirteenth Street. He had supper at his sister's, then met his brother, and took a walk to "the hook on Walnut Street," an area known for prostitution. The next day he visited his shipmates at Robinson's, a sailors' boardinghouse, then "went uptown, or rather to the Five Points—went to bed with a girl," and, after getting some clothes at his sister's, went on board the *North Carolina* and shipped out.[38]

By the middle of August considerable suspicion was focused on the accomplished wood engraver, Joseph Morse, who worked at 120 Nassau Street, just a few doors south of the Rogers house. In a column headlined ARREST OF THE SUSPECTED MURDERER, the *Tribune* and the other penny papers closely followed the police investigations and initiated an ongoing and complicated narrative of the pursuit of Morse. The *Tribune* set the tone for the Morse story, describing him as "strongly built with handsome black whiskers . . . very neatly and fashionably dressed . . . exceedingly licentious in his conduct, the companion of gamblers and sometimes a gambler himself." Although Morse insisted that he had never met Rogers, the paper claimed that he had been a "frequent inmate of the store of Mr. Anderson when tended by Miss Rogers and evidently knew her well."[39] Rumors quickly circulated that

Morse was the unidentified man seen with Mary that fateful Sunday, both in New York and Hoboken. Acting on this assumption, the police pursued Morse in a dramatic chase to West Boylston, Massachusetts, a town seven miles from Worcester, where he was found "loitering about" under an assumed name. Arrested by Officer Hilliker of the New York Upper Police, he was returned to the city by steamboat and intensively interrogated by the Mayor and the District Attorney.[40]

Morse, a married man who lived on Greene Street, maintained that he had spent Sunday, July 25, not at Hoboken as initially reported, but on Staten Island, another recreation retreat within a ferry ride of lower Manhattan. Morse described his day to the police:

> [I] met a young lady about noon, in Bleecker Street. . . . She was dressed in black: I had met her before, and persuaded her to go with me to Staten Island. We went there; to the Pavilion; and had some refreshments and I kept her mind employed till after the last boat departed. I then persuaded her to agree to pass the night with me and to sleep in the same room. She did so; I tried to have connexion with her in the night but did not succeed. On Monday morning I came to the city with her, and left her in good friendship at the corner of Greenwich and Barclay Street.

Morse claimed that he did not know the girl's name but that it "might be Mary Rogers," adding that "if it is I had no hand in murdering her! as I left her in good feeling."[41]

Morse's story was corroborated by the young woman, Mary Haviland, who eventually came forward in his defense. Her own account of the day centered on their sexual encounter: "He persuaded me to stay in the hotel," she said, "and I did not know what was for the best and stayed." Responding to questions from the police she stated that "He kissed me and hugged me a good deal, and tried to persuade me to yield to his wishes; but I resisted all night." She said, "I can't say that he tried to use force. But he did lay down on the bed and . . . [I] . . . did undress 'partly' and did not get any sleep." "He tried," she continued, "to persuade me to consent to his wishes in every way; but I refused." She agreed, he "did not violate her in any way."[42]

Morse's connection with the Rogers death initially grew out of a marital squabble that followed his amorous outing. When he returned from Staten Island the following Monday he was greeted by an irate wife. What followed was a dispute between them that moved from the relative privacy of their boardinghouse onto the street and eventually ended in abusive language and violence. They were heard arguing on the corner of Broome and Greene streets; Morse, "screaming" at his wife, Martha, "tore part of his wife's earring out, struck her and then ran away." Morse really did run away, fleeing the city for Massachusetts. Two days later, on July 27, Martha Morse used the resources available to her and went to the Upper Police station on the Bowery to swear an assault and battery complaint against her husband to Officer Hilliker. In her deposition (preserved in the Police Court Records, but not recounted in the papers) Martha Morse claimed that on July 26, 1841, she was "violently assaulted and beaten by her husband, Joseph Morse, who struck . . . [her] in the face and abused her with much insulting and abusive language."[43]

Having taken the complaint of Martha Morse, Officer Hilliker made the understandable, but nevertheless mistaken, assumption that Morse's Sunday companion had been Mary Rogers. On a lead, he pursued him to Massachusetts where he promptly arrested him on suspicion of "having violated and murdered Mary Rogers." Indeed, Morse had fled the city because he thought he was suspected in the Rogers case. He too assumed that the young woman he picked up on Sunday July 25 was actually Mary herself. Ultimately, with Haviland's testimony (and additional testimony from her mother), Morse convinced the police of his innocence in the Rogers murder and was cleared of all charges. His difficulties with his wife, however, proved harder to surmount; although released on bail, it was not until Martha Morse dropped her assault and battery charges a month later (September 16, 1841) that Morse was a free man.[44] The papers, reluctant to give up a good story, continued the saga of Joseph Morse, his wife, his girlfriend, and her mother, by printing public testimonials to Morse's good character and his professional excellence as an accomplished engraver.[45]

In the story of Joseph Morse several important elements in the Mary Rogers case came together. The search for Morse, his dramatic seizure by the police, the public disclosure of the details of his romantic encounter, and the story of his altercation with his wife were all played out in the public press. Here was a tale of pursuit, discovery, and true-life romance as thrilling and as dramatically told as any to be found in city mystery tales. Falsely accused, Morse actually proved his innocence on charges of murdering Mary Rogers to the waiting public in the penny press. He succeeded, but only at the price of his reputation and public exposure of the details of his private life. In the public telling of his personal affairs, the boundaries between public and private had been daringly but safely crossed; the press had taken a significant and symbolic step in redefining the content of the news and claiming for the public the right to information once considered private; the principle of freedom of information was now yoked in public discourse to voyeurism and melodrama, and all these elements were to remain significant features of the Mary Rogers tragedy.

The information and accounts these men provided to the authorities and the newspapers constitute a unique set of narratives of social and community life. They recreate a world of largely single men and women who were connected by street culture, by neighborhood relationships, and by family ties. In reporting these accounts, the press, ostensibly

Figure 2–1 *The cover illustration of the* Tragic Almanack, *a pamphlet published in 1843, portrayed one imagined and highly dramatic version of Rogers's death. (Collection of The New-York Historical Society.)*

pursuing a murderer, inadvertently recreated a complex social world of ordinary men and women—the world of Mary Rogers. A distinctly urban world, as yet publicly unchronicled, it was given voice and public recognition as a consequence of Mary's death.

One man's testimony is absent from all the extant records. The newspapers, which routinely printed the depositions of men like Payne or Morse, were uncharacteristically silent on the subject of John Anderson, who does not show up in any archival records of the period. Anderson, however, had a significant role in Mary's life and information that came to light years later makes it clear that his testimony to the police was deliberately kept from the public to protect a man of considerable influence and power in the city. What information we do have about Anderson and his complicated relationship to Rogers was disclosed subsequent to these initial investigations and is taken up in the next chapter.

The Mary Rogers Mystery

In the years after her death, indeed into modern times, there have been several hypotheses about who killed Mary Rogers. Because of Poe's story, much attention in modern commentary has focused on exactly what Poe might have known. In "The Mystery of Marie Roget," he initially indicated that Mary had been actually killed by a lone assassin and in his first version of the tale he strongly implied that an unidentified "swarthy sailor" was responsible. One recent critic has even suggested that Poe wrote the story at the request of John Anderson in an effort to detract attention from himself. Another modern critic has argued that Poe believed the sailor to be a Captain William Spencer (1793–1854) who was awaiting orders from the Navy in New York during 1840–41. William Spencer was the brother of J. C. Spencer, Secretary of Navy (1841–43), and the son of Judge Ambrose Spencer (1765–1848), an important figure in New York politics. He was also the cousin of Philip Spencer, the young midshipman accused of the first attempted mutiny in the Navy and hung at sea by Captain Alexander Mackenzie. Mackenzie, in turn, was court-martialed for his action and eventually acquitted in a well-publicized trial held in the Brooklyn Navy Yard in 1842.[46]

A constant refrain in the weeks following Mary's death was that she had been murdered by one of the infamous gangs that plagued the city during this period. Composed of associational groups of young men organized around local firehouses and neighborhoods, groups like the Plug Uglies were often prone to violence and had become a common source of public consternation and complaint. Writing in 1839, Philip Hone noted in his diary that "The city is infested by gangs of hardened wretches . . . [who] patrol the streets making the night hideous and in-

sulting all who are not strong enough to defend themselves." Two years
later Mary's death led him to claim that she had "no doubt fallen victim to the brutal lust of some of the gang of banditti that walk unscathed and violate the laws with impunity in this moral and religious
city."[47]

Presenting the gang theory the *Post* boldly proclaimed that one James
Finnegan, "a rowdy of confirmed rascality," was arrested by the New
York police "under information amounting nearly to certainty, that he
is one of the wretches who committed the outrage and murder of Mary
C. Rogers." Creating one of many journalistic fictive narratives of violence, the *Post* said that Finnegan was part of a gang of "six or seven
persons, whose atrocities in various forms are familiar in the police annals; that two of them were known to Mary Rogers, and meeting her in
the street, on the morning of her murder, invited her to a sail to Hoboken, saying that they had hired a boat with oarsmen; that she accompanied them; was enticed, unsuspecting, to a retired part of the shore,
and there, after the accomplishment of their hellish purposes, brutally
murdered."[48]

James Gordon Bennett had insinuated the gang theory from the beginning of the case. The *Herald* argued both that Rogers's connection
to Anderson's store with its proximity to the "resort of gamblers, black-
legs, soaplocks and loafers, known as Headquarters," made that possibility all the more likely and, on another occasion, that she had been
murdered by a "gang of negroes."[49] In early September, over a month
after Mary's death, the gang theory was given greater credence. At that
time additional clothing was found in a thicket in Weehawken not far
from where Mary's body had first been discovered. The clothing at this
familiar place was "discovered" by the son of Frederika Kallenbarack
Loss, the innkeeper of Nick Moore's House. The area was overgrown
with boughs and briar bushes but there were "large stones, forming a
kind of seat, with back and footstool to it." Here, on these stones, a
boy found a shirt, woman's petticoat, silk scarf, parasol, and handkerchief marked with Mary's name. The *Herald* argued that a gang of "fire
rowdies, butcher boys, soap-locks, and all sorts of riotous miscreants . . . armed with sticks and clubs" came across the Hudson in two
boats ("one with six and the other with nine desperadoes in them").
After hanging about a small shanty next to Nick Moore's House, argued
the paper, they had killed Mary and taken off again rapidly in their
boats.[50] Later, describing the scene, the *Herald* created its own narrative
of imagined violation:

> A little farther off lay her gloves, turned inside out, as if they had been
> forcibly drawn from her hands in a hurry. And on one of the briar
> bushes, hung two pieces of her dress which had evidently been torn
> out, as she was dragged through this horrid place; one piece of the
> dress was so doubled as to have a thorn three times through it. The
> place was stamped about, and the branches were broken, and roots

bruised and mashed, all betokening that it had been the scene of a very violent struggle. The marks of a high heeled boot were very plain. And it appeared from the position of the articles, as if the unfortunate girl had been placed upon the middle broad scene, her head held forcibly back, and then and there horribly violated by several rowdies, and ultimately strangled.

The *Herald* went on to argue that the appearance of the clothing demonstrated that they could not have been placed there recently. "The things," they reported, "had all evidently been there at least three or four weeks."[51]

Over two weeks later, under the banner VIEW OF WEEHAWKEN—THE THICKET—THE SCENE OF THE MURDER—THE BAY, &c, the *Herald* published an annotated illustration of the thicket, detailing the scene of the crime. The wood engraving, one of several by Delsy Forbes the *Herald* published in conjunction with the death, accompanied a poem entitled "Weehawken" by Fitz-Greene Halleck. "Who that ever read the following beautiful lines on Weehawken," said the article, "would ever have supposed it could have been the scene of so horrible a tragedy." The engraving images the site in much the same way that Child described it: a wooded and bucolic site set against the built cityscape across the water.[52]

In time, however, it was acknowledged that the death of Mary Rogers was not the work of a single man or a rowdy gang; rather, it became an unspoken conclusion that her death was the result of an abortion gone awry. She had gone to Hoboken that fateful Sunday not to enjoy the pleasures of the Elysian Fields, but to end an unwanted pregnancy. This would account for her mother's fear, expressed after her disappearance, that she "would never see Mary again," and for the secrecy and mystery surrounding her disappearance in a community where people rarely just vanished without a trace. A botched abortion would explain why Mary's body showed undisclosed signs of sexual "violation," and why certain details could not be openly disclosed by the coroner; it would explain the otherwise disingenuous testimonials to Mary's "chastity," "virtue," and "domestic habits."[53]

Indeed, testimony that Mary Rogers died during an abortion was provided a year later by Frederika Loss, the innkeeper. In the fall of 1842 Loss was herself on the verge of death, the result of gunshot wounds apparently inflicted accidentally by her son. The *Tribune*, one of several papers that re-opened the Rogers case in the fall of 1842 in light of the Loss statement, printed the story that Loss, in a deathbed confession to Justice Merritt of Hoboken, had finally resolved the mystery of the death of Mary Rogers. Loss claimed that on Sunday, July 25, 1841, Rogers came to her house from the city in "company with a young physician who undertook to procure for her a premature delivery." Loss further maintained that Mary died "while in the hands of

VIEW OF

THE HOUSE WHERE MARY ROGERS WAS
LAST SEEN ALIVE.

Figure 2-2   *This headline in the New York* Herald *for September 17, 1841, depicted Nick Moore's House, a popular tavern near the Elysian fields. Over a year later, in a death-bed confession, the innkeeper, Frederika Loss, claimed that an abortion was performed on Mary at the inn, causing her death. (Courtesy, American Antiquarian Society.)*

her physician . . . and a consultation was then held as to the disposal of her body." The body was finally taken at night by the son of Mrs. Loss and "sunk in the river where it would be found." Mary's clothes were "first tied up in a bundle and sunk in a pond on the land of James G. King in that neighborhood; but it was afterwards thought that they were not safe there, and they were accordingly taken and scattered through the woods as they were found."[54]

From here on in the accounts become unclear. On the basis of Loss's information, Justice Merritt accused Loss and her sons of involvement in the Rogers death. He provided a deposition expressing his belief that "the murder of the said Mary C. Rogers was perpetrated in a house at Weehawken, called 'The Nick Moore House' then kept by one Frederika Loss . . . and her three sons . . . all three of whom [he] has reason to believe are worthless and profligate characters; and . . . that he has just reason to believe that the said sons and their mother, kept one of the most depraved and debauched houses in New Jersey, and that all of them had a knowledge of and were accessory to, and became participators in the murder of said Mary C. Rogers, and the concealment of her body."[55]

Loss's sons, the family doctor, and several others were questioned by the Hackensack police. The two oldest sons were arrested and held for a judicial hearing that took place on November 19th in Jersey City. However, no further action was apparently taken, probably for lack of conclusive evidence. Even Mrs. Loss's alleged deathbed confession proved legally irrelevant. This may have been because the dying Loss was delirious and lapsing in and out of consciousness; or perhaps because it was considered a final and therefore unreliable attempt at publicity. Ultimately, Justice Merritt, without explanation, denied the contents of the article providing Loss's confession.[56] Thus, like most of the leads surrounding Mary's disappearance and death, this one would remain inconclusive.

Despite the official disregard of Loss's revelations, the abortion theory put to rest all other speculation. The *Tribune* summed up the issues well: "Thus has this fearful mystery, which has struck fear and terror to so many hearts, been at last explained by circumstances in which no one can fail to perceive a Providential agency. . . . We rejoice most deeply at this revelation, and that the scene of the unhappy victim's death is relieved of some of the horrors with which conjecture, apparently well founded, has surrounded it."[57]

In a final acknowledgment of this probable resolution to the "fearful mystery," and as a fitting denouement to the affair, Edgar Allan Poe revised his story in 1845 to account for the likelihood that Mary had died during an abortion. By changing several key words in his text, he was able to insinuate this possibility without having to be explicit. In the public mind, however, the abortion theory was more than mere suggestion as Mary's death eventually dissolved into the already extensive debate about the proliferation and commercialization of abortion within the city. Indeed, the entire subject of abortion had become another sensational text of popular literature, figuring prominently in popular guidebooks and cheap fiction and in the accounts and transcripts of several key trials that occurred between 1839 and 1848. The history of Madame Restell, the most infamous abortionist of the period, played a significant role in many of these narratives. Whether Mary had in fact undergone an abortion performed by Madame Restell herself (or even by any of her alleged New Jersey associates) will probably never be resolved. But in a short time Mary Rogers and the abortion issue were inextricably linked. Curiously, in an odd and ironic twist, Mary would emerge ultimately not as a seductive femme fatale, but as the victim of this widely condemned but extensive practice. In fact, her death would contribute to the complicated set of events that culminated in the 1845 New York State law criminalizing the procedure itself.

Despite the public disclosure that Rogers died as the result of an abortion, the death of Mary Rogers has historically remained an unsolved mystery: a curious denial of this most plausible explanation. Without formal indictments and in the absence of a trial, there could never be any formal resolution. Perhaps this helps to explain why the narrative possibilities of this death have continued to endure in different forms. Containing all the dramatic components of modern city culture—sex, violence, and mystery in an urban setting—her death became a story, or really many stories. Retold from different points of view, and for diverging purposes, these stories offered radically disparate constructions of Mary, of the imagined crime, the criminals, and even of the city itself.

As a woman whose life and whose death were associated with the sexual freedom offered by the city, Rogers raised the crisis over gender and sexuality that came with new family and work arrangements and the more open culture of the modern city. Mary, single, relatively independent, and enjoying new and freer relationships with men, was the "new" woman, and as such she became a source of curiosity, desire, vulnerability, and fear. Blending with the larger mysteries of modern urban culture, the death of Mary Rogers had in short time become a mystery of the already mysterious city. Indeed, Mary's disappearance and death were mysteries in the two meanings of the word: a puzzle that required detection or solution, and a mystery in the older sense of the term—something hidden and unknown. By "detecting" and "solving" the puzzle, Mary's nineteenth-century contemporaries found a language to map the diverse and often troubling world that was the nineteenth-century city. It was a language allowing them to probe the unknown while at the same time giving them a way to talk to and about themselves—a language that provided shape for Philip Hone's assertion that New York was no longer a "moral and religious city."[58]

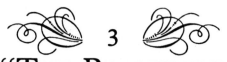

3

"THE BEAUTIFUL SEGAR GIRL": MARY IN THE CITY OF THE NEW WORLD

Nothing is more vague than impressions of individual identity.
Edgar Allan Poe, "The Mystery of Marie Roget" (1842–43)[1]

God hath in these latter ages raised up such lights in the world at several times as hath discovered much of the great mystery of iniquity; but they have always been accounted (at their first appearing) as deceivers and seducers and the like, by the dark world in general, and met with great opposition from the powers of this world, even from the powers of darkness.
John Rogers, Sr., *Epistles* (1705)[2]

City of Orgies, walks and joys,
City whom that I have lived and sung in your midst will one
day make you illustrious,
Not the pageants of you, not your shifting tableaus, your
spectacles, repay me,
Not the interminable rows of your houses, nor the ships at
the wharves,
Nor the processions in the streets, nor the bright windows
with goods in them,
Nor to converse with learn'd persons, or bear my share in
the soiree or feast;
Not those, but as I pass O Manhattan, your frequent and
swift flash of eyes offering me love,
Offering response to my own—these repay me,
Lovers, continual lovers, only repay me.
Walt Whitman, "Calamus,"
"City of Orgies" (1860)[3]

O NE of the important transitional passages in Melville's *Pierre; or, the Ambiguities*, published just over a decade after Mary's death, depicts the entry of Pierre and his half-sister Isabel into New York. They have left their rural family seat and the oppressive patriarchal past it represents for the presumed anonymity and imagined freedom offered by the town. In a foreshadowing of later events, the entry of these youthful characters is full of fearful expectation. As they approach the city limits, Pierre and his companion are quite literally jolted by the "great change in the character of the road" as it narrows from a wide and gentle country path to a hard city street: "The coach seems rolling over cannonballs of all calibers." Frightened, Isabel grabs Pierre's arm and "eagerly and forbodeingly demands what is the cause of this most strange and unpleasant transition?" In response, Pierre tells her that it is the pavement that marks the beginning of the town, hard stones that he likens to "the buried hearts of some dead citizens . . . come to the surface."[4]

If transition, peril, and even hard-hearted cruelty were aspects of urban culture that awaited newcomers to the city, another was the phenomenon of the crowd, Lippard's "million of lives swarming beneath the countless roofs and along its tortuous streets," that vast and often daunting collection of strangers associated with modern city life. For Poe this urban swarm was alienating but also curiously invigorating. In "The Man of the Crowd" the narrator gathers energy from "the tumultuous sea of human heads," which filled him with a "delicious novelty of emotion." For Walt Whitman this unique feature of urban life was a source of individual freedom and erotic possibility:

> I too walk'd the streets of Manhattan island, and bathed in the
>   waters around it,
> I too felt the curious abrupt questionings stir within me,
> In the day among crowds of people sometimes they came
> In my walks home late at night or as I lay in my bed they came
>   upon me. . . .[5]

The flight from rural to urban life, the encounter with the urban crowd, and the freedom and perils these provided were recurring motifs of early nineteenth-century America, motifs that were defining elements of the Mary Rogers saga. Like Whitman, Mary's New York and her own persona were erotically charged; like Pierre, Mary Rogers sought the freedom, anonymity, and opportunity offered by the city and its crowds and encountered an untimely death. Moreover, like Pierre, Mary was in flight from a complicated and disintegrating family legacy. Mary Rogers was the descendant of two of New England's most famous, even mythic, families: the Mathers, heirs of New England's ministerial elite and descendants of Richard Mather, one of Connecticut's first settlers; and the Rogerses, descendants of James Rogers, also an early Connecticut settler and associate of Winthrop's son and Connecticut founder, John Winthrop, Jr. In this aspect of her history Mary Rogers's progenitors left her and Connecticut a significant legacy. For the Mathers and the Rogerses, who were linked through the first and second marriage of Phebe Rogers, represented two distinct and opposite poles in the social and ecclesiastical history of New England. One tradition heralded back to Cotton Mather, the stern preacher of New England orthodoxy, and the other to John Rogers, the founder of Connecticut's most disruptive and troublesome sect—the Rogerenes.

In the transition to the context of the city and the world of the urban crowd, this historic familial identity faded away and was replaced in time, at least for Mary, by one both new and uniquely urban. The city, wrote Georg Simmel years later (and confronting another burst of urban expansion), "grants to the individual a kind and amount of personal freedom which has no analogy whatsoever under other conditions." More recently, Lynn Lofland and Richard Sennett have each described the city as a community composed of otherwise disassociated people brought together almost randomly: a collection of strangers. In this new environment, writes Sennett, where traditional codes of recognition had broken down and where social mobility, both upward and downward, overcame the inheritability of position, "it became difficult to place 'who' a stranger was simply by his family background." Nevertheless, "the anonymity offered by the city, the loss of familiar associations and traditions, the collection of strangers itself, all served to make the new city into what it was." [6]

Indeed, in New York Mary's past became invisible, even indiscernible from that of scores of other young women and men who sought the city as a refuge from some other place. In all the information about Mary Rogers, not one of her friends, nor any of the journalists or storytellers who recounted her urban odyssey, chose to reveal what, if anything, they knew about her personal or family history.[7] She was, it seemed, a woman without a history or a past, a figure who existed almost out of time. Given a public image as a result of her tragic and untimely demise, Mary was constructed in everybody's image but her own. And it is this disjuncture between the invisibility of her past in the city and the weighty history of her forebears that makes Mary's tale meaningful. Hers is a tale of modernity and modernization; a story about the loss of patriarchal authority, disruption in family life, and the social transformation occasioned by the rise of modern urban culture. Simultaneously, it is a parable about the shift from an older, more private, and more linear Puritan heritage centered around family, town, and religion to one figured around the crowd—that group of relatively independent men and women who sought work, friendship, and community within the context of an urban, secular culture.

As if to underscore this issue of identity and individuation, the question of the identity of Mary Rogers, both real and imagined, became an essential aspect of the "Mary Rogers tragedy." In this regard, even the identification of Mary's body was problematic; although it was identified by her friend Arthur Crommelin for the Hoboken coroner, the issue of positive identification was uncertain. In fact, the certainty that allowed the initial judicial procedures and burial to go forward gave way almost immediately to doubts about whether or not the body had been correctly identified; whether or not it really was that of Mary Rogers. The *Herald*, in the first of many descriptions it offered to the public of the corpse, commented that because "so much violence had been done to her . . . her features were scarcely visible" and her face and forehead "appeared to have been battered and butchered to a mummy."[8]

As time wore on and Crommelin's initial identification faded from immediate memory, this identity became even less secure. When the body was disinterred almost three weeks later and returned to the Dead House in New York City, it was "in order that the deceased might be more fully identified by some of the witnesses"; but, noted the paper reporting the procedure, "decomposition had already taken place, and no trace of the once 'beautiful cigar girl' could be recognized in the blackened and swollen features."[9]

By the end of August the problem of Mary's identity had moved to yet another level as the possibility arose that Mary was not Mary at all:

> Speculative opinions have been advanced by some that the girl has not been murdered: that the body found was not sufficiently identified as hers: and that her sudden disappearance is owing to some other cause of death. The proof of her identity, however, particularly by means of her clothes, is sufficiently established in the minds of the municipal and Police authorities, to dissipate the seemingly delusive hope of her surviving. And although incredulity may still disbelieve, and fancy conceive that she is not numbered with the dead, yet the evidence is satisfactory to our mind that she has been brutally murdered; and that time, the revealer of secrets, will yet bring the authors of the horrible deed to light."[10]

These issues of identity were not only persistent, they were at the center of the case and would be examined over and over again in different ways. Initially, however, there were several immediate questions. The first concerned the physical identification of the corpse: Who was the young girl whose body was so "battered" and "bruised" that its features were "scarcely visible"? How, in the context of a crowded metropolis like New York, a "world of strangers" where violent death was just becoming a routine police matter, did one identify a body—an anonymous individual? In an age of developing medical and forensic practice, was it possible to determine the cause of death (and perhaps events that preceded it, including the possibility of rape) through the physical evidence of the corpse alone? From these other questions followed: should the details of this physical identification, especially since they involved the body and perhaps sexual violation of a young woman, be disclosed to the public; and, finally, presuming that this death was not accidental or suicide, could some unknown murderer be identified and caught?

Beyond these relatively objective issues of identification loomed the larger and more abstract problems of identity: Who was Mary Rogers, what was the nature of her life, and what unusual set of circumstances led her to meet such a violent and awful death? As Poe understood, the conundrum of her death and of the mystery her death became was ultimately to be discovered in the mystery of her life: The problem of identity lay with discovering or identifying Mary herself. But solving the riddle of Mary's identity was complex; it bespoke a larger and symbolic crisis of individual, gender, and class identity in the early modern city. And it was in the peculiar way Mary's death coincided with and addressed larger problems of social and self definition in nineteenth-century culture that made this particular story of this particular girl so compelling.

Of Mathers and Rogerses

Mary's history begins not in nineteenth-century New York, but on the eastern shores of colonial Connecticut. There, well situated on the coast, midway between the key cities of New York and Boston is New London, a thriving port surrounded on three sides by a series of New England towns and villages nestled along the banks of the Connecticut River. Just south of the town of New London, where the river meets the sound as it flows from the northernmost corners of this second New England colony, lies the small town of Lyme.[11] It was to these two settlements that Mary's forebears—the Mathers, the Rogerses and the Waits—came in the seventeenth century, counting themselves among the region's first and foremost settlers.

Like much of coastal New England, the New London area had a mixed economy. Farming, trade, and craft formed the essential economic elements in a place where the productivity of the land was always uncertain and from early on insufficient to support a rapidly expanding population. It was not uncommon for residents to work a bit at each, farming what they could from the land and selling any reasonable surplus, perhaps transporting goods and people up or down or across the river, or working in the region's skilled trades like tanning. Still others sought cash selling liquor, molasses, or nails, running grist or flour mills, or overseeing taverns, boardinghouses, and inns. Over the years trade flourished, a natural consequence of the area's excellent location and the expanding requirements of the colony's growing local communities. Indeed, from the end of the seventeenth century trade provided an extensive merchant and shipping community with a lucrative and expanding source of income. By the close of the eighteenth century, New London and its neighboring towns of Groton and Mystic had become major shipbuilding centers, known especially for their production of large sea-going vessels. At the same time New London emerged as a major American center for foreign commerce, sending Connecticut-built ships carrying foodstuffs and a variety of small manufactured goods to the South (especially to the port of Charleston, South Carolina) while others sailed directly from New London for Europe and the West Indies.[12]

Phebe Wait, the woman later identified as Mary's mother, was born in Lyme on November 23, 1778, the seventh and last child of Lowen Wait and Zeruiah Caulkins Wait—a family whose names figure in all the early chronicles of the town. Phebe was baptized in Lyme's First Congregational Church and just before her eighteenth birthday, on November 8, 1795, she married another parishioner. Born in 1770, her new husband, Ezra Mather, was the second son of Eunice Miller Mather and Jehoida Mather and a direct descendant of Richard Mather, whose uncle and great uncle were Increase and Cotton Mather, respectively, the reigning figures of Puritan culture and staunch defenders of religious orthodoxy. The Lyme Mathers were a large clan and a dominant presence in the town.[13]

Like their parents, Phebe and Ezra Mather remained in Lyme, retained their membership in the First Congregational Church, and appear to have lived within the time-bound traditions of their church and community throughout the course of their marriage. Ezra, a merchant and investor, rode the crest of expansion in the post-revolutionary period. In 1807 he moved his family into a new house and, judging from their furnishings and possessions, they ranked among the community's elite members. Their household had the comforts of a settled, ample domesticity. They slept on feather beds covered with linen sheets, bedecked with feather pillows, woolen blankets, and calico covers, all of which sat on high-posted cherry bedsteads. Other furniture included cherry bureaus, a cherry desk, fancy chairs, and cherry stands. Their dining-room table was draped in linen cloths and held a service of china, silver tea set, and silver spoons. And Ezra himself dressed well in new Holland shirts, Marseilles vests, and, on occasion, velvet pantaloons and silk stockings. In his pocket he carried a silver watch.[14]

In addition to his house and its surrounding land in Lyme, Ezra owned an additional land parcel in Old Saybrook across the Connecticut River that he let out to his father, and part of a city lot valued at one thousand dollars on Pearl Street in New York City. He had also invested in several local enterprises—extending notes for considerable amounts to his fellow townsmen and kin. His own inventory of commercial goods—rum, fabric, foodstuffs, building supplies—was considerable, evidence of a diverse and prosperous trade.[15]

Together Ezra and Phebe Mather had five children, roughly two years apart—conforming to the usual pattern of birthing in New England families. Their first child, Ezra, was born in October 1797, followed by their one daughter Phoebe A. in 1799, Orlando in 1802, Robert in 1804, and Frederick in 1808, the only son to marry and carry on this branch of the family name.[16] In their marriage and family life Ezra and Phebe Mather fit into the demographic patterns of life in other, similar New England towns. Writing of Andover, Massachusetts, Philip Greven found that, like Phebe, one-third of the women in Andover's second generation married before the age of twenty-one, while, like Ezra, the average marriage age of men of the same generation tended to be much higher—twenty-seven.[17]

The marriage of Phebe and Ezra was relatively short. In 1807 Ezra took sick and on February 12, 1808, at the age of thirty-eight, he died. In anticipation of his death, "being weak in Body, but of sound mind and memory," Ezra Mather wrote his "Last Will and Testament" through which he clearly intended to provide for his widow, his three living sons, and his only daughter, Phoebe A. According to the provisions of this will, Ezra left to his wife the considerable household furnishings and a note for ninety-five dollars that he held against his brother-in-law, George Wade (his sister's husband), "as her own and proper estate." To Phebe he also gave, for "such time as she shall remain my widow" for her maintenance and the "support, maintenance & education of my children," the use and improvement of his house and adjoining land, together with the interest accruing on his personal estate. If, however, Phebe married before the children, "each & every of them," attained the age of twenty-one years, Ezra stipulated that the house and land should be either sold or leased out by the executors as they judged most beneficial to the interests of the children. The profits from such sales or rent, Ezra continued, should be invested in Bank Stock or loaned, with the provision that land and security worth double the sum loaned be held. Ezra clearly intended that his assets be used to support his widow and children, but it was also clear that his obligation to Phebe would cease entirely should she remarry. At that point, according to the will, the estate was to be sold off and divided according to the following provisions: His three sons, Ezra, Robert, and Frederick, were to divide one-fourth of the estate equally, while the remaining three-fourths were to be equally divided "between my sd sons,& my Daughter Phebe—to them their own forever." And, to his "Honored Father," Ezra expressed his "wish and desire" that the piece of land near Saybrook Ferry as well as a small note be uncollected, and allowed for his father's use for the "rest of his natural life."[18]

This will shows how the world Ezra and Phebe Mather inhabited was in many ways typical of settled New England town life at the turn of the nineteenth century. The probate and land records describe a society heavily defined by family and kin; one in which business, friendships, and family life were overlapping dimensions in a relatively enclosed social order. Members of the community married each other (two of Ezra's siblings married members of the Wade family), and the marriage, baptism, and burial of children and family members continued for generations within the same congregation. Professional and skilled work was provided by neighbors and kin; Dr. Noyes tended Ezra when he was ill and a relative on Phebe's side built coffins, first for Ezra and again for his father, Jehoida, just two years later. It was a world still defined by some degree of deference and the careful fulfillment of obligation. Even through the illness that marked his final days, Ezra was careful to provide not only for his children—their maintenance and education, as he put it—but to ensure that his aging father was guaranteed the use of his land and loan for the rest of his life.

But if Ezra's world was in many ways regulated and contained and measured, it was simultaneously expansive, reflecting Ezra's considerable commercial and entrepreneurial skills and interests. In evidence of this were not only his holdings and investments but his concern that they be properly attended to after his death so as to be secure and yield their fullest. And there was his investment on Pearl Street, suggesting his acquaintance with the urban world of New York's commerce and development. From the records Ezra left emerges an energetic and aspiring man who, had he lived, would have continued to enlarge his domain, moving into the next century with optimism by taking hold of the opportunity offered by the coming of the modern age.

No doubt Ezra's considerable assets and his careful planning provided Phebe and her children with an adequate income. Phebe retained the house and land and two years later, in 1810, she is listed in the census as a head of household with her three youngest children still living at home. Only her oldest child, Ezra, is absent from this household compilation and at the age of thirteen he was likely to have left home, either for work or schooling.[19] However, six years after Ezra's death, in 1814, Phebe remarried, to Daniel Rogers, a man eleven years her junior. In accordance with the provisions of Ezra's will, Phebe relinquished her right to the house at that time and deeds of sale indicate that it was sold. Phebe and Daniel Rogers acknowledged their settlement with the estate, and since married women could not hold property, this marriage marked the end of Phebe's hold on what was bequeathed to her by her first husband.[20]

Phebe's second husband is difficult to measure; unlike Ezra Mather he did not leave a sheaf of written records from which we could reconstruct any part of his life and his relative anonymity in the extant records contrasts markedly to others of his own family. Daniel was the fifth child of Amos Rogers and Sarah Phillips Rogers, of New London and Lyme, respectively. Like the Mathers, the Rogers clan figured prominently among Connecticut's early settlers; James Rogers had arrived in America in 1635 at the age of twenty, was an associate of Connecticut's founder, John Winthrop, Jr., and settled in New London in the late 1650s. He acquired considerable property, establishing himself as a successful baker, furnishing goods for seamen and colonial troops, and in time became the port's largest trader. Apparently this success also afforded him considerable influence and a prominent place in New London's civil and ecclesiastical affairs. The Rogers family proliferated, giving rise to what New London's chronicler Frances Caulkins has called a "great throng" of descendants who would be intimately bound with the history of New London.[21]

The son of James, John Rogers, founded the religious sect known as the "Rogerenes," Connecticut's first dissenting group. There were two waves of intense Rogerene insurgency, almost one hundred years apart: the first occurred after John Rogers underwent a conversion experience in 1674 that led him to develop the sect's theology; the second, led by his grandson, in the 1760s. During the first period Rogers gathered a considerable following (much of it from his own large extended family as well as other disaffected individuals within the community), propagated his doctrines throughout New England, and wrote a significant body of religious literature in which he argued his beliefs and decried the erroneous ways of the established church.[22]

The Rogerene theology emerged out of the seventeenth-century dissenting tradition of the Baptists and the Quakers—in fact, they were often referred to as Quaker-Rogerenes. Their beliefs were wide-ranging and in many significant ways extremely progressive, pointing toward a more liberal and tolerant view not only of the church but of social life as well. They were strongly anti-sabbatarian, against the abjuration of the priesthood and the practice of a salaried ministry, favored the preaching of women, adult baptism, and the primacy of direct inspiration. And they contested civil law and practice as well, denouncing all links between church and state, questioning traditional views of marriage, proclaiming the legitimacy of polygamy, and maintaining that healing should occur without the aid of medical practice.[23] Because of their belief in the indwelling spirit of Christ, Perry Miller called them "Antinomians in modern dress," but they shared more with Anne Hutchinson and her followers than this.[24] For like the early Antinomians, the implications of their beliefs were in several significant ways egalitarian (not the least of these being the prominent role of women in their group) and, like the Antinomians, they struck at the very heart of those beliefs and practices that served to maintain the ecclesiastic and social order of church and state alike.

Although Rogerene creeds challenged the essence of New England orthodoxy and church organization, it was their aggressive and outlandish public behavior that brought them notoriety. The purpose of their charivari-like behavior was to wreak havoc on the town streets, in the churches, and in the courts, thereby discrediting Puritan orthodoxy.[25] Disagreeing with the Sunday sabbath, they disrupted religious services, publicly proclaiming their own "offenses" of working on Sunday. Protesting the idea of a salaried ministry, James Rogers and his wife "assaulted the constable for he was rolling away a barrel of beef that he had distrained for the minister's rate, threw scalding water upon him and recaptured the beef." And, seldom civil or quiet, they would come "into the most public assemblies nearly or quite naked, and . . . behave in a wild and tumultuous manner, carrying out, and charging the most venerable minsters with lies and false doctrines." Once, on being charged, John Rogers used the opportunity to cry out against the court "till at length a number of his followers, of both sexes, turned their pipes and screamed, roared, shouted and stamped to that degree of noise, that it was impossible to hear the clerk read."[26] And, of course, this sense of the group as scandalous as well as blasphemous was no doubt reinforced by the active role of women in the disturbances themselves.

The troublesome activities of the Rogerenes abated with the period of the Revolution and by the time of our story social conflicts surrounding the Rogers family had ended.[27] But their legacy of dissent and disorder, sexual mayhem, and the carnavelesque, anticipated the cultural struggles that took shape around one of their descendants, Mary Rogers, who becomes, in a sense, the bastard daughter of both the Mather and Rogers traditions.

Daniel's family had a more legitimate side as well: They were prominent in New London's shipbuilding and mercantile community. Daniel's father, Amos Rogers (1755–1820), was a successful carpenter and builder (he built New London's famous Ryan House on Truman Street) and proprietor of a lumber and brick yard at Pequonnock (where he lived on the old family land). It was his son, Moses Rogers, Daniel's older brother, an early adventurer and expert in steam navigation and an associate of Robert Fulton, who brought this old family its final fame and recognition while simultaneously pushing into modern times.[28]

After her marriage to Daniel in 1814, it is hard to understand what happened to Phebe and her once substantial family. The land and probate records indicate a flurry of activity during the year of their marriage and again in 1824 involving a series of land sales between Daniel Rogers and the Mather children. At least until 1830 Daniel and Phebe retained their residency in Lyme. However, considering the conspicuous absence of evidence from this period and the series of events that followed in the next eleven years, it is clear this family somehow lost its grip and its established place within the New London and Lyme communities. The names of Daniel and Phebe, for example, cease to appear in the local records of any sort, including church records and even family genealogies. In a family so well chronicled as the Connecticut Rogerses, it is striking that we know so little about Daniel and even less about his marriage to the widow Phebe Mather.[29]

Mary Rogers, the subject of this particular tale, was born in 1820, probably in Lyme, Connecticut, although the circumstances of her birth are inexplicably murky. Records chronicling the births, baptisms, and deaths of all the other Mather and Rogers births are extant in a variety of public and private sources. Evidence of Mary's birth alone is absent.

By 1820 Phebe would have been forty-two years old, and while Mary could have been a result of the union of Phebe Mather Rogers and Daniel Rogers, they had no other children before the sixth year of their marriage (Phebe's earlier births with Ezra Mather were the customary two years or so apart). At the end of the eighteenth and the beginning of the nineteenth centuries, the rates for illegitimacy and premarital pregnancy escalated dramatically, underscoring the even more dramatic changes in family and community generally, including their decreasing control over the social and sexual behavior of the younger generations.[30] In the year of Mary's birth, Phebe's second child by Ezra Mather, Phoebe A. Mather, would have been twenty-one. And, like all of Phebe and Ezra's children, save one, Frederick, Phoebe Mather never married. My suspicion is that Mary Rogers was not the child of Phebe and Daniel Rogers, but that she was her grandchild, the illegitimate child of her daughter, Phoebe Mather, and that Mary was taken in by Daniel and Phebe Rogers to be raised, according to common practice, as their child. If this calculation is correct, Mary Rogers would have been a direct descendant of the Mather line.

After 1829 Phebe Rogers's life must have been extremely difficult; three of her four children by her first marriage to Ezra Mather died in the five years between 1829 and 1834, including her only daughter, Phoebe Mather, in 1830. Around 1834 her second husband, Daniel Rogers, was killed in a steamship explosion on the Mississippi, leaving Phebe twice widowed and with only two surviving children—Ezra Mather who lived until 1855 and Mary Cecilia Rogers.[31] And it was sometime during this period, between 1834 and 1837, that Phebe Wait Mather Rogers decided to leave New London County and come to New York with the adolescent Mary.[32]

Most likely the family losses of the 1830s propelled Phebe to leave what she had always known and move with her putative child, Mary Rogers, in the late 1830s to New York City. Even within the relatively protected context of New England town society, women alone in the early nineteenth century had an increasingly hard time. Maintaining a farm was difficult and few women had the necessary skills to survive on their own by other, less traditional, means. In addition, women like Phebe and Mary Rogers were caught in large-scale societal changes over which they had little control. Even by the time of the Revolution, the traditional two-pronged economy of farming and trade was giving way to laissez-faire capitalism and the development of manufacturing, making it difficult even for intact families to retain family farms and traditional modes of life. The cohesiveness of the New England family was already yielding to accelerated patterns of family dispersion, geographic mobility, and significant social dislocation, making the experience of this particular family more typical than unique. As production of all sorts (but especially the domestic production of food and clothing) once centered in the family, moved rapidly out of the household and into the marketplace, women's traditional roles and economic functions were dislodged. Throughout the eastern seaboard women began the long-term process of shifting their economic lives from the home to the public sphere. For many in early nineteenth-century New England communities this meant migrating to the new textile and manufacturing towns like Lowell or Lynn, or making a decision like Phebe Rogers to move to an even larger city such as New York or Boston that offered greater employment possibilities.[33]

By the time of their departure from Connecticut, travel between the two port cities was a relatively routine matter. After 1815 it was possible to avoid a lengthy coach trip and go more swiftly by one of the routine steamships that traveled Long Island Sound. But the ease of the journey probably did little to ease Phebe's decision to leave; surely this decision was made in the hope that a new and very different life awaited them. As two women alone, Mary and Phebe did not have many choices in the 1830s, but they did have some. Whatever Phebe's family and social status may have been earlier in her life, her need to support herself and Mary apparently became an overriding concern by the late 1830s. By the early nineteenth century the city was filled with such women seeking work and an existence outside the definitions of traditional family life.

The disjuncture between these two social worlds—the relatively enclosed social space of Lyme and coastal New England and the wide open culture of New York, the nation's "Grand Emporium"—was enormous. The transition between these two worlds was not, of course, caused by distance, or even by the distinctions between town and city life. It was part of something much larger—the development of a modern urban culture that would, sooner rather than later, transform even Lyme itself. Living when they did, Mary and Phebe experienced these cultural transformations directly. For Phebe especially the contrasts must have been extreme, even overwhelming, if we are to believe the descriptions of a grieved and withdrawn woman characterized as the "old lady" who received the news of Mary's death: from the comfortable and relatively secure sphere of an elaborate family life, to the life of a Nassau Street boardinghouse inhabited by the denizens of lower Manhattan culture. Ironically, it was also a world the ambitious Ezra Mather, merchant and investor, had, in more ways than one, helped to create.

From this point on, Mary's story as it comes down to us both begins and ends. From here the private Mary, essentially hidden from history and left out of the written records, is replaced by the emergence of a very public persona. As we have seen, this new identity derived its meaning from the unique urban culture of New York City in the late 1830s and early 1840s; the city's social geography and the precarious situation of women within it gave Mary's life and death its larger meaning and cultural significance.

The Beautiful Segar Girl

To understand Mary Rogers's identity during her short life in New York is to locate her within antebellum urban culture. Within this context she actually has multiple identities: the vulnerable daughter of a poor respectable widow fallen on hard times, the pregnant and presumably abandoned victim of a melodramatic seduction tale, the dangerous woman associated with the city's thriving commercial sex industry. Each of these identities conformed to a familiar narrative, almost an archetypal social script, about women in antebellum cities. But transcending these projected narratives (most of them defined by and intended for the emerging urban middle class) and even making them possible, was the reality that Rogers had been stripped of the protective patriarchal identity once usually axiomatic for women in earlier generations.

In New York, with its "crowd of strangers," the culture of her past had little or no meaning; Mary was a *feme sole*, a woman without the protection of father, husband, or family and therefore outside the relatively fixed categories of class and social position associated with an earlier and more stable time. Without a proper home, a complete family, and middle-class prospects of marriage, Mary became one of the new "working women"—most of them young and unmarried—who sought employment in the transitional economy of the city. Her new roles—as cigar girl, boardinghouse keeper—not only placed her within typical early nineteenth-century female occupations, but also within the emerging female working-class culture of the 1830s and 1840s.

Although Phebe and Mary retained connections to kin (at least one of Phebe's sisters lived on nearby Jane Street), city life represented a distinct break from the past. In releasing men and women from traditional roles and associations, from families with roots and histories such as the Mathers and Rogerses, the city substituted new roles based instead on neighborhood and street life, the interplay of the workplace, and the new freedoms of public places of entertainment. Once in the city Mary not only found a means of supporting herself, but new relationships that grew out of these means. Indeed, Mary's short life in New York was closely identified with the social culture of the modern city—its new patterns of daily life, work, and leisure. The distinctly urban arenas Mary worked and played in—the male world of Anderson's tobacco shop, the newly found "kin" group of the Nassau Street boardinghouse, the "promiscuous" public places of recreation and pleasure—all were defined by this new metropolis.

The *problematic* of Mary's identity, which was initially expressed in the initial debates about her body and in the fascination that her death occasioned, transcended a specific interest in Mary herself. It was rooted in a larger problem of the transformation in social and sexual roles occasioned by this new urban culture. In both its private and public dimensions, Mary's persona derived its meaning and significance from the way it was emblematic of the new and precarious status of women of all classes in the emerging city.

It is important to note that the New York in which Mary and Phebe arrived in 1837 had fallen on hard times. By the spring of that year the new, and once flourishing American economy had "fallen apart," the combined consequence of crop failure, overspeculation, and, finally, a severe financial panic. Coming after a period of rapid expansion and commercial development, this economic collapse precipitated a traumatic and long-lived depression that left as many as one-third of the city's workers unemployed and vastly increased the misery of the city's poor and lower classes.[34] But at the same time, the period of crisis also signaled the transformation of the city's economy; New York had always been a commercial center, from here on it became an industrial one as well. New systems of work were already marking the inexorable process of industrial development, and the influx of new sources of capital and entrepreneurship after the collapse stimulated manufacturing. By 1860 the city was the nation's largest manufacturing center and its representative symbol of modernity. One feature of this economic development was that the traditional and more regulated systems of production based around systems of apprenticeship and regulated markets gave way to less regulated forms consistent with the rise of market capitalism. Another was that this new economic growth depended heavily on the wage labor of women who were a primary source of unskilled or semi-skilled work. Significantly, the crisis of 1837 exacerbated the decline of rural economies already underway, hastening the exodus of thousands like Mary and Phebe to urban areas and swelling the population of the unprepared cities. The influx of such native-born migrants changed the demography of all metropolitan centers. New York's population surge, however, was nothing short of astonishing; the once relatively compact and homogenous city mushroomed unexpectedly into a large urban metropolis. Two-thirds to four-fifths of this growth was the result of domestic immigration and the newcomers were overwhelmingly young and frequently female, with a significant cohort of people, like Phebe Rogers, over the age of 55.[35]

The largest proportion of these new women workers were employed in domestic service (a consequence of the expansion of the middle class), but thousands, especially those who were young and unmarried, flocked to the trades that marked the new economy, where they were a source of unorganized, cheap labor, especially in the new unskilled or semi-skilled trades where women's wages were roughly one-half to one-third of men's. Women worked in a wide variety of trades, but as milliners and cap makers, shirt sewers, straw braiders, and mantua makers, they became the backbone of the flourishing garment industry that outfitted the expanding population of the city. For those women working outside the hundreds of small workshops, other forms of labor, both inside and outside the home, provided a means of survival. Thousands more performed outwork at home under an elaborate and especially exploitative subcontracting system; still others worked as laundresses or, like Phebe and Mary Rogers, took in boarders.[36] Saleswork was distinct from other forms of women's work. "Public and exposed," in the words of the popular writer Ned Buntline, it carried with it certain sexual connotations. Even after the Civil War, Virginia Penny pointed out, such work was believed to be "dangerous," making women subject to "demoralizing influences" and susceptible to "corruption."[37]

Population growth and industrialization left antebellum class relations constantly in flux. Once again, the year 1840 serves as a significant point of transformation. In a diary entry for that year Philip Hone could still note that he had attended a "Fancy Ball" that "occupied the minds of the people of all stations, ranks and employments." While earlier urban culture was characterized by vast differences in wealth and status, city residents nonetheless enacted their work, daily routines, and even recreational activities within shared territory; however, after 1840 these areas were increasingly segregated by class distinctions.[38]

The theater serves as an extended metaphor for the changing character of class relations. Although they were spatially divided into the familiar three tiers (with prostitutes and their clients and African Americans in the infamous third tier), until the 1840s the theater itself was a cultural space that brought together the full range of the city's citizenry. Within a short time class distinctions intruded into this shared city space; in 1849 the Astor Place theater riots cast two famous Shakespearean actors into the symbolic spokesmen of class difference, disrupting the city's uneasy calm and signaling that henceforth even Shakespeare would be played by different actors, in different styles, to different social groupings in different theaters. Distinctions of social status, employment, and ethnicity would eventually come to segregate broad areas of the city's social life, defining public spaces and demarking urban zones. With time, residential and work areas became increasingly distinct; the wealthy moved away from the noisy and crowded downtown, and places of leisure, from beer gardens to brothels, were marked both by the sorts of entertainment they offered and by the accoutrements of their social settings.[39]

Working-class culture was of course complex and multidimensional, reflecting the ethnic and cultural diversity of this ever-increasing urban class stratification. But its most well-chronicled aspect was so-called Bowery culture, centered around the Bowery itself. A broad avenue cluttered with workshops, boardinghouses, and taverns, it featured the famous Bowery Theater, after 1849 the center of working-class entertainment. Mary's lover, Daniel Payne, was a denizen of Bowery culture, as no doubt were several of the other Rogers boarders as well. Payne had indicated in his deposition concerning his whereabouts on the evening of Mary's disappearance that he had joined the grand promenade down the Bowery.

This culture was epitomized by the Bowery B'hoys and G'hals and more specifically by two stock characters of contemporary theater and fiction, Mose and Lize. Brash and outspoken, these two colorful characters were clothed in a fanciful approximation of polite dress and provided a refreshing and striking counterpart to the restrained constructions of middle-class respectability. Mose, a working-class dandy, was featured in black frock coat and high hat, and the characteristic long greased curls that designated him a "soaplock, or rowdy."[40] But if the young men who flocked to the Bowery and gathered about shops like Anderson's were occasionally like Mose, Lize, his female counterpart, bore little resemblance to Mary. Lize dressed in bright, almost garish clothing and she was brash and outspoken in her manners, showing little regard for emulating the polite discourse or mannered behavior of middle-class sentimental culture; Mary Rogers was a cut above, her polite costuming and "pleasing manners" setting her off from the working-class culture of the Bowery. At the same time, however, Mary did not fit the prescriptive codes for the proper and polite world of the new middle class, so wonderfully detailed in Karen Halttunen's work, *Confidence Men and Painted Women*. Here proper female behavior was marked by sincerity, emotional transparency, and understated self-effacement, all intended to reveal the genteel woman's sincerity, her rejection of artifice.[41] Caught between "the highly respectable families" of her ancestry and the unrestrained culture of the city, Rogers's identity was problematic precisely because it was fluid, defined by her sexuality rather than by the usual signs of dress and manners that fixed social position in the metropolis.[42]

Using ideas of presumed sexual behavior as a means of determining social rank was an important adjunct of class identity in antebellum America. Bourgeois codes of domesticity delineated a world sharply divided between public and private, between men and women, and between the home and the world. Domestic ideology vested women in the roles of wives and mothers with a special moral authority that at once detached them from the marketplace and assured them a protected zone within the home. In this gendered division of social space women of the middle classes established a sanctuary for themselves beyond the parlor walls; protected areas within their domain included those governed by affective emotions, religious values, and morality. Placed safely indoors, such women were presumably protected from the social and sexual behavior of men that took place within the arenas associated with public culture. The home became the de-eroticized counterpart of the dangerous city.[43]

In banishing sexuality from the household, American Victorians guaranteed it a new importance in the world outside—in the male domain of commerce and public life. Antebellum writers turned the public arena into a charged erotic domain resurrecting an older, even biblical, identity of the city as a female and eroticized zone. From this rude dichotomy significant social assumptions arose that linked female sexuality to the world of the streets and to the lower classes associated with those streets, thereby connecting sexuality to notions of class and equating public displays of it (in dress and demeanor) with degradation and social deviance. While male public culture was still associated with some degree of diversity, with the intermingling of "men of all classes," the same was not true for women. George Foster made clear the distinction between men and women in certain kinds of public spaces: "The oyster bars," he wrote, featured private rooms where "men of all classes . . . reverend judges and juvenile delinquents, pious and devout hypocrites" all convened to eat "promiscuously" with women. "The women," he added, "of course are all of one kind."[44]

This social equation of female sexuality with lower-class behavior infused middle-class discussions of urban life, figuring as a constant subtext in the diverse public discourse about city life. In the new urban setting where traditional categories and identities were dismantled and new ones assembled, there was much concern with the nuances of social definition and differentiation. Indeed, one feature of this emerging culture was its urge to identify and classify the myriad aspects of city life and a vast descriptive literature arose to meet this new social preoccupation. Guides and physiologies, often replete with illustrations, scrutinized and mapped the areas of urban public life, detailing the entire range of urban customs, institutions, and curiosities, simultaneously positioning them within some presumed hierarchy of respectability. Boardinghouses, restaurants, theaters, and even brothels, all were carefully described and cataloged by contemporary observers like Asa Greene, George Foster, and, somewhat later, George Ellington, thereby mapping the new social and spatial terrain of the city in an attempt to order it and make it comprehensible and accessible.

A similar and related discourse arose specifically about urban women. Almost a subgenre of the antebellum descriptive literature, this work was sometimes presented in specific works or articles on "The Women of New York." But in the 1830s and 1840s, it was more likely to be lodged within more general works of urban literature—the city guidebooks, newspapers, dime novels, and in the extensive antebellum discourse of benevolence and social reform. But whether couched in the emotive language of sentimental reform or the often misogynist texts about sin and sexual danger, this literature voiced a profound sense of bewilderment and curiosity at the newfound lives of urban women. By ascribing social value to sexual behavior, this literature provided yet another highly useful code for classifying and thereby organizing and controlling an apparently chaotic urban landscape. In this rush to comprehend and to control, a set of social scripts focused around sexuality emerged, scripts that tied sexuality and its expression to outward signs of social position and class and left women relatively few options.[45]

By the 1840s the literature of social benevolence reflected this new sexual preoccupation. To be sure, beginning with women's evangelical benevolence early in the nineteenth century, the construct of the fallen woman had bound class and sexual identity together but it had little of the scope and condemning power of this new literature. Early nineteenth-century private charity was figured around a construct of the "deserving poor" woman as a "silent retiring sufferer," or a woman "reduced from comfortable circumstances"; later private charity took a less beneficent view of the female poor, seeing them as threatening and debased, outside the pale of respectability and just one step away from vice and sin.[46] The potential danger the poor represented, which in men was largely seen in terms of crime, was for women increasingly identified in terms of sex. Indeed, although we do not know the exact nature of Phebe's reduced circumstances, she might well have fit the earlier ideal of the respectable but indigent widow fallen on hard times who in an earlier age might have been the recipient of gracious charity; however, Mary, one generation later, fit the portrait of the working girl whose sexual behavior placed her beyond the purview of respectability, even one step away from prostitution.

Underlying these coded assumptions of female behavior and respectability lurked the omnipresent spectre of the prostitute who, within the context of the developing bourgeois attitudes toward women, female sexuality, and city life, emerged as society's most potent symbol of female sexuality. Possessing what so-called virtuous women were not permitted—sexuality and a relative degree of public freedom (expressed in dress, demeanor, and even domestic furnishings) in its expression—the prostitute threatened to break traditional boundaries and remove the restraints from passionate appetites, sexual and otherwise, that bourgeois respectability disallowed. Because in reality most prostitutes were "working women," often of the immigrant and lower classes, they were also economically and socially distinct from middle-class domestic culture. Thus associated as they were with all that was outlawed—sex, money, and the world of the streets—they became more than any other socially marginal group, pariahs.[47]

What can best be termed social hysteria over prostitution moved into the foreground of urban life in the 1830s and 1840s. There was on one account a real basis for this concern. By all accounts prostitution increased dramatically, if only proportionally to the rise in the city's population; yet in the minds of many contemporary observers it had reached epidemic proportions. Prostitution took many forms by the 1840s. Ranging from the Walnut Street bawdy houses to the high-class brothels in the city's downtown, it was a recognized feature of city life, and would remain a constant source of discussion, contention, and eventually legislation. Nevertheless, what is curious is not that prostitution increased so dramatically in the evolution of the altered social and economic relations of antebellum New York, but that it became such a preoccupation in accounts of nineteenth-century urban life, often eclipsing all others. Clearly, the prostitute provided a major vehicle for contending with urban social disorder insofar as that disorder was identified with sex, women, and forbidden or unsanctioned desires. Simultaneously, the fear of urban disorder and forbidden behavior was focused on women already on the social margins. Once again issues of sex and sexual danger melded with the notion of the dangerous city, just as the city heralded the arrival of a heterogenous and cosmopolitan culture.

There is no evidence that Mary Rogers was a prostitute. Nevertheless, her working roles as tobacco girl and boardinghouse keeper placed her within the world of working- and lower-class women, on the borderline of respectability. Indeed, Rogers's open availability and sexuality made her a representation of the eroticized culture of the metropolis. Known for her relationships with men, her "fascinating manners," Mary embodied a combination of the potentially threatening woman who was erotically provocative, and at the same time vulnerable because she lacked the protection of a traditional position as wife and mother. Mary's fate told what could happen to women who were sexual and whose sexuality and relative "freedom" allowed them to live outside the protected domestic sphere at the same time as it reiterated the danger to women—so important in the development of nineteenth-century bourgeois culture—of male power and sexuality. Related as it was to a wide set of social concerns such as the consequences of downward social mobility, the precarious position of women, and the dangers of female sexuality, Rogers's death served to focus attention on urban violence and its link to the sexual danger implicit in the new urban center.

Of Tobacco Shops, Sporting Culture, and Boardinghouses

Mary's identity, linked as it was with the relatively open sexual codes identified with the city, was further shaped by her relationship with the tobacconist John Anderson, a man only eight years her senior and a rising entrepreneur. When Mary and Phebe arrived in New York from New London in late 1837, they went to live with Anderson. This may have been because he had some earlier association with the Mathers or Rogerses. Ezra Mather, we must remember, held a plot in downtown real estate and both he and the Rogers family were, like Anderson, involved in the southern trade. Perhaps Mary and Phebe performed do-

Figure 3–1 *This engraving from the 1848–49* Mercantile Register *of New York shows the tobacco store of John Anderson on Broadway, several years after Mary's death. (Collection of The New-York Historical Society.)*

service of some sort in exchange for board; or perhaps there was an early romantic relationship between John Anderson and Mary Rogers. Whatever its basis, this domestic arrangement ended when Anderson moved his residence from Duane Street to White Street in 1838 and Phebe removed, probably taking Mary with her, to the home of her sister, Mrs. Hayes, on Pitt Street.[48] But if Mary and John Anderson no longer shared living space, their involvement was hardly over; in 1838 Mary went to work for John Anderson, selling *segars* and tobacco at his Broadway tobacco shop.[49] The store was identified outside by a statue of Sir Walter Raleigh, the patron saint of tobacco and an apt symbol of Anderson's own connection to the southern trade. Inside, Anderson featured the comely Mary Rogers, the *Beautiful Cigar Girl* herself, hired according to the English custom, to attract an exclusively male clientele.[50] The practice of placing "beautiful young girls in cigar and confectionery stores like a brilliant luminary, to catch the butterflies of fashion that love to flutter round so attractive a center" was apparently commonplace. In one of many censorious comments about young women in public places, the *Herald* noted that one result of this practice of butterfly catching was that often "they [the girls] and not the insects are generally destroyed," the victims of the "rich rascals who buy cigars and sugar plums, gossip with the girl, and ultimately effect her ruin."[51]

Anderson's business thrived. Specializing in "fine cut" or chewing tobacco, he later made a fortune by selling what was known as *Ander-*

son's Solace Tobacco, brightly packaged in gaudy wrappers and geared to troops in the Mexican War and gold miners in California.[52] And by all accounts his store was a very popular place; its Broadway address alone, just across City Hall Park, a short hop from Publisher's Square and the city offices, would have guaranteed it a thriving business. Cigar stores, like taverns, eating halls, and even boardinghouses were gathering places, forming part of a series of ancillary sites where men hung out, spent time talking, exchanging information, and carrying out business. Anderson's also had a special reputation as the center of the lively young male sporting culture; it was a place according to one source where "the young sports around New York used to go." Here, "the gay blades of the city as well as transient visitors who lived to adopt urban manners" gathered. Mary, who was known by her common name, "brought customers."[53]

The reference to "young sports" had particular meaning in 1840s culture. So-called male "sporting culture" had several dimensions: the rowdy and often violent behavior of working-class youths and neighborhood b'hoys who organized themselves around gangs and fire companies; the stylish culture of "soaplocks," young rakes, clerks, and young men on the make; and the sleazy fringe culture characterized by publications like *The Whip, The Flash, The Rake,* and *The Libetine,* which flaunted their advocacy of prostitution and brothel culture. As an important component of the construction of masculinity in antebellum America, sporting culture served as the urban counterpart of the mythology of the frontier. Like the mythic male behavior associated with the West, this urban form championed the public display of aggression and featured an ethos dependent on rough behavior and male amusements. In the city it was often organized around different forms of "gaming"—horse racing, cock fighting, and boxing. The weekly publication, the *Sporting Life,* for example, was specifically aimed at the racing crowd, mixing news of the track and trade announcements with an odd mix of fiction and gossip.[54]

Merging an older workingman's politics with the newer club house politics of Tammany Hall, editors like George Wilkes (later publisher of the *Police Gazette*), and George Woolbridge gave this culture its literary expression in a series of short-lived publications that combined an odd mix of fiction, city notices, and gossip, all flavored with a salacious and misogynist perspective. One of these, *The Whip,* was published by George B. Woolbridge out of offices on 31 Ann Street, just around the corner from the Rogers boardinghouse. The paper's credo defined its purpose:

> Devoted to the Sports of the Ring, the Turf, City Life, such as Sprees, Larks, Crim-Cons, seductions, rapes, &c., not forgetting to keep a watchful eye on all Brothels and their frail inmates . . . a paper that every one can not fail to be pleased with, and will not relinquish until finished.[55]

The Whip featured bawdy humor, an aggressive and confrontational tone, and notices of "local color." In its regular column bannered "The Whip Wants to Know," it made explicit the connection of sporting culture to Anderson's Tobacco Shop. Criticizing Anderson indirectly for his disdainful comments about some of the "young sports" who frequented his establishment, it admonished: "Whether a certain biped of segar notoriety had not better be a little careful how he utters his imprecations against consumers of that commodity, lest he feel the force of the Whip," and "Whether the accommodating keeper of Mocha and *cheap* segars had not better stop his chuckling at any one's expense, merely to satisfy the caprices of another or he will loose [sic] a good customer."[56]

Sporting culture, though principally the domain of young clerks, was marked by its fluidity, by the ways in which it cut across class lines and incorporated a wide range of urban men who frequented the city's centers of entertainment and public culture—places like Anderson's shop. Here the world of public male culture merged with the city's demimonde and Democratic Party politics. Indeed, these political connections contributed to Anderson's success and continued to frame his world. An aggressive merchant with political aspirations, Anderson had commercial and political ties that placed him within a distinctly new and powerful subculture of the city, a world of rising young men who would in short time define the masculine ethos of urban popular politics taking form around Tammany Hall. His association with Fernando Wood, Tammany leader and future city Mayor, probably date to Wood's early years in cigar manufacture, and it was an association of significance in Anderson's career. With Fernando Wood, Caleb Woodhull, and other prominent Tammany politicians, Anderson moved in the New York circle of late Jacksonian Democrats committed to free trade, low tariffs, and state's rights as well as firm opposition to the Whig tradition of protected capitalism and support for moral reform. Identified with commercial and territorial expansion, theirs was an ideology that at least nominally asserted loyalty to labor, challenged state intervention, and argued for the viability of a free market economy. Best represented by James Gordon Bennett during the early years of the *Herald*, this political creed was characterized by nativism and an increasingly aggressive anti-feminist and anti-black ideology.[57] Through Anderson and his shop Mary became part of this newfound world of rising young men and the political ideology they created—the publishers, journalists, fiction writers, and politicians who would in short time chronicle her death, tell her story, and ultimately enact legislation in her name. The relationship between John Anderson, sporting culture, and Mary Rogers, however, was double-edged; Mary's history and brutal death were at once sentimentalized and debased through the misogynist voice of "sporting culture," and John Anderson would be forever haunted by the ghostly spectre of the cigar girl who had made known his store with its special connections and ambiance.

When John Anderson died, a delusional old man in Paris in 1881, he left a considerable estate, a mansion in Tarrytown, and a legacy of litigation, much of which turned on his past involvement with Mary Rogers.[58] It is through this litigation—a civil suit tried in the New York Supreme Court in December 1892, almost ten years after Anderson's death—that we know the impact and consequences of Anderson's involvement with Mary Rogers. The case, settled out of court, was brought by Anderson's daughter, Laura V. Appleton, in what is described as "an action in ejectment" to recover what she claimed was an undivided one-fifth share of the land underneath the Plaza Hotel, property purchased by her father years before.[59] In her effort to claim a right to this land, Appleton was seeking to have her father's will declared null and void on the ground that he was mentally incompetent when it was executed. To prove mental incompetency, Appleton's attorney, Colonel Edward C. James, assembled a history of Anderson's life and evidence of his delusional state that centered around his obsession with Mary Rogers. Anderson, it seems, had often said to a number of people that he was plagued by Mary's ghost, with whom he claimed he was able to speak. Abner Mattoon, a former Assemblyman and State Senator from Oswego, New York, and apparently a close associate of Anderson's, testified that "he said she appeared to him in the spirit from time to time," and that he "had many, *very* many, unhappy days and nights in regard to her."[60]

Further testimony was more specific regarding Anderson's past involvement with Mary and its political consequences. Another associate and business partner of Anderson's, Felix McCloskey, testified that once while walking together, Anderson pointed out Mary's Nassau Street house and "dramatically denounced it as the 'damned house' which was the cause driving him out of politics and belittling him in New York and which had kept him from advancing." He also testified that on another occasion Anderson claimed that Fernando Wood had asked him to become a mayoralty candidate but that Anderson refused, fearing that his past association with the Rogers's case might be resurrected.[61] Apparently what he feared was the information that he had been arrested and examined in connection with Rogers's disappearance, but released for lack of evidence, and that James Gordon Bennett as well as others knew this information and had used it behind the scenes in some fashion against him.[62] McCloskey further quoted Anderson as saying, "I want people to believe that I had no hand in her taking off" and he asserted that Anderson had "assured me that he *hadn't* anything *directly, himself* to do with it"[ital in text].[63] It is unclear exactly what Anderson meant by his qualifiers in this statement. If Mary had indeed died of a botched abortion, it is possible that he had helped to arrange or pay for it.

McCloskey's testimony also revealed information about another public and mysterious episode in Mary's life, an episode that made her the subject of an earlier newspaper story. On October 4, 1838, Mary apparently disappeared, and even at this early date her unaccounted absence was widely reported the next day in the city newspapers. Under the column headed *Coroner's Office*, the New York *Journal of Commerce* printed the following notice of a feared suicide:

> Coroner's Office—*Supposed Love and Suicide.*— An elderly lady called yesterday evening at the Coroner's office, and shewed his clerk a letter which had been that morning found on the dressing table of a young lady, who had a few hours before left home, since which no trace could be found of her, and her friends feared that she had committed suicide. The letter was written by a Miss Mary Cecilia Rodgers [sic], who resided at 114 Pitt Street, and was directed to her mother. In this letter the young lady took affectionate farewell of her mother, and informed her that she had left home with the fixed and unalterable determination to destroy herself. As soon as the mother of the young lady received the letter, she sent messengers in different directions in search of her daughter, but up to a late hour on Thursday evening they had not succeeded in discovering any trace of her. The young lady, it appears, had some time back attended in a store in Broadway, and while there, had been for several months paid particular attention to by a gentleman who since ceased his attentions, and left the city; and it is supposed that this circumstance had so operated upon the young lady's mind as to produce the occurrence we relate. When leaving her mother's house on Thursday morning, she was dressed in a brown satin frock, Tuscan hat and wore a small red silk handkerchief on her neck.[64]

The *Morning Herald* (which did not carry the October 5 story of her disappearance and had some of the information jumbled) reported on October 6 that the announcement was false and that "she merely went on a visit to her aunt in Brooklyn." The paper claimed that she had been away for only five hours and that the suicide note was the prank of a friend.[65]

Mary returned shortly thereafter but the reasons for her actions, like the response to her second and more tragic disappearance, received varying journalistic interpretations: that she had been abducted, that she had been seduced by a U.S. Navy officer, that the disappearance was a publicity stunt designed to bring Anderson's Segar business publicity. These same interpretations would, interestingly, be reiterated initially about her disappearance in July 1841.[66]

Another and more likely interpretation was that on this occasion, in an eerie anticipation of later events, Mary had undergone an abortion. This possibility was later validated by Anderson's own comments, once again to McCloskey, that "an abortion had been committed on the girl—the year before her murder took place, or a year and a half—something of that kind—and that he got into some trouble about it,—and outside of *that* there was no grounds on earth for anybody to suppose he [Anderson] had anything to do with the murder!"[67] What is so interesting in all this, beyond the details of the episode itself, is the convergence of the daily life of this young woman and the preoccupations of the contemporary journalistic culture; a convergence that would reach its epitome after her death several years later.

The possibility that Mary's "disappearance" at this point, as well as in 1841, was to undergo an abortion was given further validation in Poe's 1842–43 version of "The Mystery of Marie Roget," and again in his 1845 revision of the work for *Tales.* Poe quoted extensively from the notices of Mary's 1838 disappearance. In a variation of a story in the *Evening Post* he asserted that

> About three years and a half ago, a disturbance very similar to the present, was caused by the disappearance of this same Marie Roget. . . . At the end of a week, however, she reappeared at her customary *comptoir,* as well as ever, with the exception of a slight paleness not altogether unusual. It was given out by Monsieur Le Blanc (Anderson!)and her mother, that she had merely been on a visit to some friend in the country; and the affair was speedily hushed upon.[68]

Poe's thinly veiled explanation for Mary's first absence—her "slight paleness"—only enhanced the revisions added by Poe in 1845 about her second disappearance. These, it will be recalled, pointed directly to an abortion as the cause of death.

After this temporary disappearance, probably in the spring or summer of 1839, Mary Rogers left Anderson's employ and with her [grand]mother, Phebe Rogers, established the small boardinghouse at 126 Nassau Street. The men who boarded at the Rogers's house might easily have bought their tobacco at Anderson's; the world they shared was just one other aspect of urban culture organized around the ever-enlarging numbers of men living and working outside the boundaries of family and home.[69]

Boardinghouses had been a feature of New York since the latter part of the eighteenth century when the commercial expansion of the city required the development of a system of housing to accommodate the transitory nature of city life. But it was a system that grew significantly with the expansion of the urban economy and the changing work and living arrangements of the early nineteenth century. Traditional eighteenth-century work forms were based on an elaborate system of paternal labor relations that often included the housing of employees and apprentices in the residence of the master as a condition of employment. One distinguishing characteristic of the modernization of work was that home and workplace, which had been connected by this built-in system of residency, became separate realms of social life by the early decades of the nineteenth century, marked quite literally by the separation of physical space.[70]

As employers increasingly turned away from providing shelter as an aspect of employment, workers were expected to provide their own. In the context of this changing system of labor and a greatly expanding economy that featured rapid population growth and the immigration of independent individuals from far-off places, boarding took on increasing importance. It was a system that supplied many needs: housing, often in the form of room and board; work, especially to women who either took in boarders themselves or found employment as domestic servants in boarding establishments; affective relations, by providing a system of household relations that substituted for those traditionally associated with family and domestic life. In such residences, writes Elizabeth Blackmar, "the lines between family and market exchanges and as in rural communities, rents themselves, were not confined to cash payments . . . boarding continued to incorporate—if not integrate—tenants into the household with the sharing of meals and possibly other maintenance responsibilities."[71]

As with other urban social institutions, boardinghouses were designated by the degree of gentility or respectability they offered. Writing somewhat later, in 1857, Thomas Gunn published *The Physiology of New York Boardinghouses*, in which he stated that they "are many and multifarious, possessing their own idiocrasies [sic]." Among the different types were "The Fashionable Boardinghouse Where You Don't Get enough to Eat . . . The Mean Boarding House . . . The Cheap Hotel Boardinghouse, The Boardinghouse Where you are Expected To Make Love to the Landlady."[72] The Rogers establishment fit the lower end, catering to sailors and corkcutters with perhaps an occasional clerk. But within this space, Mary and Phebe formed a very different kind of household from the one at least Phebe had known in Lyme. Herein was a complex social world, one probably fairly typical of the emerging male working-class culture that defined the lower wards of the city. The men who boarded at the Rogers house were not just co-residents inhabiting a common space, but friends, acquaintances, or co-workers who shared a social world, one that fractured with the disappearance and death of Mary. Included in this group were the men already encountered in the Rogers tragedy, men who were all particularly well acquainted with Mary: Daniel Payne, the corkcutter, William Kiekuck, the sailor, Arthur Crommelin, perhaps a clerk, as well as his friend Archibald Padley. They stayed there for different lengths of time; some like Kiekuck just for a few days or perhaps a week while his ship was in port, others like Daniel Payne had lived there for just less than a year.[73] Together they were an interesting cross section of the lower social ranks, representative of men who boarded.[74]

Conclusion: Mary in the Land of Strangers

As one part of a large rural to urban migration in the second quarter of the nineteenth century, Mary and women like her had left a familiar (if no longer stable) world of family and kin for an entirely new kind of life. In this her experience was shared, even as her particular familial saga of downward mobility and family disintegration was not. Once here she supported herself and her elderly [grand]mother by entering the world of women's waged work—as a salesgirl and, finally, as a boarding-house keeper. (She may have even performed domestic work at John Anderson's during her first months in the city.) Indeed, part of what defined Mary Rogers was her ordinariness, combined with her apparent good looks, her seemingly contradictory public notoriety, and her pre-sumed sexual availability. Mary inhabited three of the significant worlds of the early city: (1) the new female working class; (2) the mixed urban culture of the port city; and (3) the essentially masculine culture of "sport," commerce, journalism, and city hall politics. She was, it seems, on the edge, marginal to the traditional grouping of family and kin, even outside the traditional categories of class and ethnicity. But she existed within a largely new social world of "strangers." Mary blended into the city with its physical and social spaces and there found an independent life where she used her sexuality to gain access to the demi-monde of the newly urban cultures. In this she no doubt experienced a new and possibly unique kind of freedom, both from her own past and family traditions and from the new boundaries of life and culture taking form within the growing city. Just as the city of the 1840s was a place where the classes still mixed, where working-class and elite culture could still share a similar social space, it was also a locus of class and cultural solidification. And, just as urban culture raised conflicting definitions of social behavior and sexuality, so the city, more than any other space, raised the fundamental dilemma of defining class boundaries. Social mobility in the city, like the sexual behavior of lower-class women, was both appealing and frightening because it served as a heightened meta-phor for the struggle of class definition and identity in the new republic.

Taken as a whole, urban women, particularly those outside the pro-tection of bourgeois family life, were caught in a singular moment. In-creasing waves of immigration brought unprecedented numbers of them, especially young women separated from their families, into New York City; changing economic patterns made work available to them, especially in the newly expanded service and manufacturing sectors of the economy, but that work was underpaid and undervalued; simulta-neously, new sexual codes emerged that disassociated female sexuality from bourgeois discourse and family life and associated it with venality, danger, and most of all working-class culture. Mary (and even Phebe) were caught in this morass; young, single, outside the pale of traditional domestic life, and associated early on with men, availability, and sexual freedom, Mary epitomized all the dangers of city life.

At least in her relationships with men, Rogers seems to have crossed some of the social and class boundaries taking form in the new republic. The men with whom she associated formed a composite of the class composition of the city: a corkcutter, a clerk, a sailor, a prosperous shopkeeper and future real estate tycoon, a naval officer, and a politician's son—these were her friends, lovers, and potential murderers. Taken as a group these men raised the specter of an urban, commercial society that operated without traditional rules and regulations; a world where class identity and behavior could be bought and sold; a world where to quote Catherine Beecher, "there are no distinct classes . . . but all are thrown into promiscuous masses."[75]

Despite her vocations as a cigar girl or boardinghouse keeper, Rogers, at least in terms of her dress, style, and ambience, identified with middle-class women of the day. But her relationships with men of all classes placed her outside traditional class boundaries. Her ability to transcend class was due in large part to her beauty, sexuality, and availability. This freedom was her ticket out of the working-class world of the city. It placed her as an outsider inside of a particular subculture of the city. But in transcending class and emerging bourgeois codes, Rogers ironically encountered danger and ultimately death.

4
THE "PUBLIC PRINTS,"
THE BODY OF
MARY ROGERS,
AND THE VIOLENCE OF
REPRESENTATION

It is equally intended, for the great masses of the community—the merchant, mechanic, working people—the private family as well as the public hotel—the journeyman and his employer—the clerk and his principal.
James Gordon Bennett, editorial statement in
the first issue of the New York *Herald* (1835)[1]

There was now a partial glow upon the forehead and upon the cheek and throat; a perceptible warmth pervaded the whole frame; there was even a slight pulsation at the heart. The lady lived; and with redoubled ardor I betook myself to the task of restoration. I chafed and bathed the temples and the hands, and used every exertion which experience, and medical reading, could suggest. But in vain. Suddenly, the color fled, the pulsation ceased, the lips resumed the expression of the dead, and, in an instant afterward, the whole body took upon itself the icy chilliness, the livid hue, the intense rigidity, the sunken outline, and all the loathsome peculiarities of that which has been, for many days, a tenant of the tomb.
Edgar Allan Poe, "Ligeia" (1838)[2]

The body, several times tortured, provides the synthesis of the reality of the deeds and the truth of the investigation, of the documents of the case and the statements of the criminal, of the crime and the punishment. It is an essential element, therefore in a penal liturgy, in which it must serve as the partner of a procedure ordered around the formidable rights of the sovereign, the prosecution and secrecy.
Michel Foucault, *Discipline and Punish* (1975)[3]

A wood engraving, probably executed some years after her death, depicts the dead body of Mary Rogers in the shallow waters along a rocky and wooded Jersey shore. Mary's voluptuous and unmarked body floating languidly figures prominently in the foreground, out of proportion to the rocks and trees. She seems asleep rather than dead or drowned: a poetic, sleeping beauty, ready to be awakened. This image, typical in style of the wood engravings featured in contemporary press and pamphlet literature, offers a marked contrast to the verbal descriptions of the destroyed and violated body of Mary Rogers that appeared in the penny press. But whether depicted as the beautiful maiden or as the destroyed corpse, the imagery of Mary deprived her of all poetry and privacy, making her dead body into an image of pollution and putrefaction, a symbol of all that was fractured and fractious in the city's body politic.[4]

The Rogers's boardinghouse was located on Publishers Row, just one block south of Printing House Square, at the epicenter of the city's thriving publishing industry. Nassau Street and its environs, as one contemporary has reminded us, was the city's "brain, ever pulsating with the beating of a printing engine."[5] Within a few steps of the Rogers's residence were the offices of most of the city's major newspapers and publishing houses, as well as the headquarters of reform and evangelical publications. The veritable explosion of print culture from the mid-1830s was the consequence of several converging factors: the vast expansion of the reading public, transformations in the processes of literary production and reproduction (quite literally the ways in which information and images were collected, transmitted, and disseminated), and the acknowledged position of New York as the nation's center of journalistic and literary culture. Between 1840 and 1860 printing and publishing firms constituted the fastest growing industry in the city, giving rise to a generation of new professional journalists, engravers (like Mary's neighbor, the falsely accused wood engraver and illustrator, Joseph Morse), and storytellers. These men would turn Mary's death into news stories, novels, and graphic images; indeed what became the story of Mary Rogers was the created product of this new popular, rapidly expanding, commercial culture.[6]

The newspapers followed events through the fall of 1841 and again, after the new disclosures, in the fall of 1842. Their accounts provided the basis for all subsequent versions of the story. From these "public prints" the disappearance and death of Mary would be refigured as narrative in novels, pictures, and poetry, narrative that employed a melodramatic and sensational vocabulary to address the new diverse urban readership. And from these same prints, the story made its way to the hinterlands and was reinvented again for vastly different audiences in cities and towns throughout the nation. Here was mass culture in formation; a story with a very specific set of local references, became, through the new media, one of the means by which Americans came to know and experience the modern city.[7] As we will see, central elements

MARY ROGERS' RESTING-PLACE.

Figure 4-1 *This engraving, probably executed some years after her death, depicts the romanticized dead body of Mary Rogers in the shallow waters along a rocky and wooded Jersey shore. From George Walling,* Recollections of a New York Police Chief *(1890). (Courtesy, American Antiquarian Society.)*

of these texts, but especially of the early newspaper reports that formed the basis of all subsequent accounts, were the detailed discussions of Mary's life, depictions of imagined events around her death, and always elaborate descriptions of her murdered body. With Mary herself serving as an extended metaphor for the city, these narratives entered into discussions of sexuality and private life and provided through discussions of Mary's history, her imagined death, and even her tortured body, a means to explore the body social and the body politic. From the Rogers story the press created an event, actually several events, and infused them with urban politics and the politics of gender. A new press, in the midst of finding a popular language to address its new and diverse audience, adopted a discourse of sensation that depended on images of death, of sexual violation, and the decomposition of the female form.

Inherent in the stories the press invented were three distinct narra-

Figure 4-2 *Woodcut (1842) entitled "View of Tammany Hall" depicts the Democratic Party headquarters as well as the offices of several newspapers (The* Tattler, Brother Jonathan, *the* Sun) *that made the Mary Rogers story famous. These buildings were just down the block from the Rogers boardinghouse on Nassau Street. From* Historical Collections of the State of New York. *(Collection of The New-York Historical Society.)*

tives: the "Tragedy of Mary Rogers," the "Murder of Mary Rogers," and the "Mystery of Mary Rogers." Mingling elements of melodrama, sensationalism, and mystery, the press codified three central tropes of modern urban culture in their narratives of Mary Rogers, making her a unifying feminine subject who embodied all three at once. As a tragic narrative, her death was used to show the triumph of evil over good in the perpetual war between the competing forces of urban life; as a narrative of violent death, her story provided titillation at the same time as it provoked fear, rage, and cries for retribution; and, as a source of mystery, her death inspired literary quests for detection and understanding. Through these narratives of Mary the metropolitan press also refigured itself as a unique and complex agent of cultural mediation, becoming the medium through which a diverse readership probed and itself detected the city, examining the private lives and sexual habits of a young woman of the city, scrutinizing her friends and lovers, and through the vivid descriptions of Mary's tortured corpse, witnessing the full exposure of the female body, once simultaneously pure and provocative and now in all its ruin and decay. The "public prints" had become what their name implied: the means of reproduction of private images for public consumption.[8]

Although my focus is not so much with the differences among newspapers, either in terms of mode of representation or political viewpoint, party and political identity did figure prominently in how the Rogers story was written and utilized to profess a political agenda. James Gordon Bennett, for example, used the case as a vehicle for the law and order agenda that was part of his general indictment of city life. Nevertheless, in covering and creating the story all the mass circulation dailies created a new grammar and a new vocabulary to explain city life. And from the representations of Mary herself and the constructed narratives of imagined crimes against her, a new journalistic voice coalesced: the voice of the urban reporter. Tough, angry, voyeuristic, and deeply misogynist, this voice used the already familiar form of the crime narrative to focus on the female subject, initiating the construction of the violated and murdered woman who appeals to our prurience at the same time as she evokes our sympathy and outrage as a cliched convention of modern journalism. The accounts these newspapers offered provided a striking counterpoint to the sentimental versions of death, especially female death, associated with the genteel tradition of mourning culture. And since the journalistic significance and meaning of the Mary Rogers story was lodged in the history and politics of antebellum journalism, it is necessary to give a brief pre-history of the form itself.

The Public Prints

The rise of the popular press began in New York City in 1833 with the *Sun*, edited by the young artisan printer Benjamin Day, and the very short-lived *Morning Post*, edited by Horatio Sheppard and future *Tribune* editor Horace Greeley. Challenging both an older newspaper tradition and the elite commercial culture for which it spoke, the new penny papers, so called because of their one-cent price and unique method of distribution (newsboys hawked them on the street), challenged the established papers like the *Commercial Advertiser*, the *Courier and Enquirer*, or even the party-affiliated *Evening Post*, which relied on a small upperclass, subscription-bound clientele. The new papers proliferated, enlarging readership, soliciting local advertising, and offering a significantly different kind of "news" to a new urban audience—the "public." Within four months of its first issue the *Sun* boasted a circulation of about 4000, equal to the leading paper in New York and the nation, the *Courier and Enquirer*, and by the next year it could claim a circulation of 8000.[9] Unlike the traditional papers, which contained partisan political editorials, mercantile reports, some national news (usually reproduced from reports or news items made available through the post office's free-exchange system), and occasional serialized fiction or reviews, the new penny papers were at least nominally nonpartisan (this changed quickly), contained no mercantile news, and focused on national and local issues. As early as 1837, Asa Greene, a contemporary journalist and city chronicler, wrote that the four major penny dailies had a combined circulation of 50,000 and a readership of twice that many. Were it not for their low price, he noted, many people "would be entirely destitute of any species of reading, or of any information in relation to public events."[10]

Significantly, the principal figure in both the rise of the new urban journalism and the creation of the Mary Rogers story was James Gordon Bennett, the audacious and ever controversial editor of the New York *Herald.* Bennett, whose journalism became synonymous with the antebellum commercial press, was the most controversial publicist of his day, the ridiculed and despised symbol of sensationalism and libelous reporting. Walt Whitman, who worked as a compositor, journalist, and writer during these years described him as a "reptile marking his path with slime wherever he goes and breathing mildew at everything fresh and fragrant." Whitman's loathing for Bennett was untempered and unremitting. He considered him a "midnight ghoul, preying on rottenness and repulsive filth; a creature, hated by his nearest intimates . . . bearing the consciousness thereof upon his distorted features, and upon his despicable soul; one whom good men avoid as a blot to his nature—whom all despise, and whom no one blesses." This venom for Bennett is not surprising. For if Whitman represented the democratic impulse of the mid-nineteenth century city, its open and embracing aspects, Bennett exemplified the perversion of the Whitmanesque ideal of inclusive urban community.[11]

A Scottish Catholic who had emigrated to America in 1819, Bennett already had extensive experience in journalism when he started the *Herald* with his own capital in the spring of 1835. In the *Herald* he created a unique personal and highly political organ that espoused the brash tenor of Jacksonian populism and expansionism combined with the distinctly urban politics of Tammany Hall. Like John Anderson, Mary's employer and friend, Bennett rose through the Tammany ranks. He worked for Tammany as early as 1829, and within two years was a member of the Democratic Committee for the important First Ward. As a committed Jacksonian, he had written propaganda for Andrew Jackson's 1828 campaign, scripting the scathing attacks on the Second Bank that became Jackson's campaign hallmark. Later he supported the independence of Texas (and of course its annexation), and backed the period's most bellicose nationalistic and expansionist impulses. In Bennett the conservative and reactionary aspects of an early populist tradition found their most forceful advocate and ideologue. "It would appear," said Bennett, "that the Anglo Saxon race is intended by an overruling of Providence to carry the principles of liberty, the refinements of civilization, and the advances of mechanic arts though every land, even those now barbarous." Over the years his politics continued to be racist, antiabolitionist, and profoundly misogynist; his ideology, despite its idiosyncratic and sometimes unpredictable turns, was essentially a deeply rooted and aggressive conservatism, one that grew out of and spoke for the nativism and nationalism of mainstream Jacksonianism.[12]

"I am, and have been a pedler [sic] . . . not of tapes and laces, but of thoughts, feelings, lofty principals [sic], and intellectual truths," declared Bennett, boldly defending his position as a successful purveyor of information in a society where ideas and principles had already become the stuff of commerce.[13] Indeed, Bennett's business acumen—his ability to solicit advertising and attract readership—quickly made his venture a success; in two years he boasted a net worth of $100,000 and a circulation of 11,500, the largest of any American newspaper. Bennett had succeeded in exploiting the diversity of the new urban scene to create and market a city newspaper to a new urban audience. "It is equally intended," he wrote in the paper's first editorial, "for the great masses of the community—the merchant, mechanic, working people— the private family as well as the public hotel—the journeyman and his employer—the clerk and his principal."[14]

To accomplish this mission Bennett redefined the "news." To the usual economic and political news the *Herald* added strongly partisan editorials, personal and often libelous portraits of politicians and editors, news about the city itself, and endless sagas of murder, suicide, and seduction. The sensational text, stories of the lurid, the racy or the violent, such as the narrative of Mary Rogers, became a mainstay of the *Herald* which, in turn, set the style and tone for other city papers. In fact, by the early 1840s even the mercantile press was forced to accommodate the new trends in journalism, covering more foreign and local news, city notices and stories like Rogers's death. Intrinsic to this conception of the news was a particular view of urban life that was presented as intensely chaotic, capricious, and unpredictable, even illegible. Thus, with a city regarded as both morally bankrupt and sexually dangerous, crime stories provided useful metaphors for the urban experience.

The emphasis on crime in the news of the city was derived from two sources: the extensive and often subterranean popular crime literature and the many accounts of crimes culled directly from the police and courts of the city's criminal justice system. The roots of the first, much of it heavily religious or moralistic, were in the literature of Grub Street, The *Newgate* Calendar, and the broadsheets of late eighteenth- and early nineteenth-century American street literature. An extensive crime genre flourished throughout the antebellum period, featuring the trials of atrocious criminals or the gallows confessions of well-known murderers. Often disseminated in cheap pamphlets and sold through itinerant agents or street hawkers, these publications were the products of American-based printers who invented them from popular trials and sensational events; others, like those produced by Orestes Barclay and A. R. Orton, were admittedly fiction.[15]

One account of the Rogers death, published by Barclay in 1851, was marketed as *A Confession of the Awful and Bloody Transactions in the Life of Charles Wallace, fiend-like Murderer of Miss Mary Rogers*. It consisted of a lengthy imaginative chronicle of how Wallace strangled her in a jealous rage "until her cheeks assumed a purple hue," and included a depiction of Rogers on the cover, as well as a crude illustration of his atrocious act as the frontispiece. Another example of this genre, *The Tragic Almanack, 1843*, published by C. P. Huestis, a publisher and engraver with offices virtually adjacent to Mary's residence, featured a romantic depiction of Mary in the dramatic moment of being thrown off the Jersey cliffs by two top-hatted gents. No text accompanied this image that formed the cover of the issue (see Figure 2-1, p. 26).

Collections of these crime narratives such as *The Record of Crimes in the United States* or the later *Lives of the Felons* also proliferated, and in 1845 this tradition was codified in tabloid form by George Wilkes in the *Police Gazette*. The *Gazette* popularized both old and new crime stories; it specifically addressed the Rogers story as part of its ongoing crusade against abortion and abortionists. By the late 1840s violent crimes and stories of dangerous criminals were often part of the literature of adventure that took the form of the short novel in widely available, cheap pamphlet form. These commercial and highly popular works not only chronicled tales of felons, "rogues and fiends," as David Papke refers to them, they told stories framed within a social and moral universe where good and evil were clearly defined. The depiction of the violent and the erotic was, of course, an enduring aspect of peasant culture; these newly garbed versions were in many ways recreations of older forms, refigured for commercial distribution and consumption.[16]

Crime news itself emerged as a distinct aspect of urban reporting; it grew with the penny press and rapidly became a mainstay of these urban dailies—usually cataloged in easily recognizable columns headed as "City intelligence" or "City News." The police courts, the center of the city's already overwhelmed and chaotic criminal justice system, provided a constant source of free information, especially, as Steve Jaffe has pointed out, for the new papers forced to seek cheap new sources of information and news. In the gritty halls of the city's evolving system of criminal justice one saw repeatedly enacted the entire range of urban crime, from prostitution and disorderly conduct to theft, from abortion to murder. Early reporters such as George Wisner (the *Sun*) and James Attree (the *Herald*) invented careers for themselves as "crime reporters," turning court procedures into urban chronicles and adventure tales. Crime stories represented an opportunity to present the daily life of the streets, to forefront the tangled lives of ordinary folk, and to introduce sexual and salacious content into a legitimate public forum. Whether

Figure 4-3 *An example of the sensational pamphlet literature that circulated after Mary's death, this woodcut was the title page of* The Confession of the Awful and Bloody Transactions in the Life of Charles Wallace, The Fiend-Like Murderer of Miss Mary Rogers . . . , *published by E. E. Barclay in 1851. (Collection of The New-York Historical Society.)*

MURDER OF MISS MARY ROGERS.

Figure 4-4 *A crude woodcut illustration depicting the fictive person of Charles Wallace in the act of strangling Mary Rogers.* From The Confession of the Awful and Bloody Transactions in the Life of Charles Wallace . . . *(Collection of The New-York Historical Society.)*

pandering to assumed popular taste for sexual and violent content, or as a reflection of editorial predilection, sensational style and texts like the Rogers murder became a major aspect of so-called popular journalism. Crime stories provided an enduring link between vernacular and street publications (often underground or outlawed) and the legitimate press. As such, they offered a unique and important cultural form that bridged distinct urban social worlds, integrating them into new forms of commercial culture. At the same time, crime news served as an indirect means of political expression, thereby wedding the often voyeuristic and misogynist voice of the crime reporter to urban journalism.[17]

Because crime stories usually concerned those who either because of class or social status were on the periphery of respectable society, the press had considerable latitude to explore areas once considered beyond the purview of public discourse. In the process, traditional boundaries between private and public were discarded or even, as in the narratives of the Rogers death, inverted. Cast as news, narratives of private life moved to the forefront of the new public prints. As we have seen, the disclosure of private information was a central aspect of the press coverage of the Rogers story; the investigation of Mary's death legitimized an investigation of her life. In fact, beginning in the fall of 1838 when her first disappearance received the attention of the press, her life had been an object of public display. At that time the banner in the Coroner's column boldly announced: SUPPOSED LOVE AND SUICIDE and the text told a story of a disappearance, a suicide note, and unrequited love. Mary, the paper said, in prose quite similar to that which would be used two and a half years later, "had left her mother's house on Thursday morning . . . dressed in a brown silk frock, a Tuscan hat and . . . small red silk handkerchief on her neck." The notice told of her work at Anderson's, and of the "particular attention by a gentleman."[18] Well before her more famous and final disappearance, Mary was a source of mystery, romance, and imagined tragedy all appearing in the penny press.

In the summer of 1841, after the dead body had been the subject of an autopsy, the press probed more deeply into the mysterious and enticing story of Mary's imagined life. This time, with the ending well known, the press embarked on an urban mystery tale of dangerous romance, complete with repeated violations and impassioned pleas for revenge. As narratives, these descriptions were visual and dramatic, engaging the reader directly in the daily affairs of a woman about town. Words replaced experience for readers who moved directly into Mary's final hours as she fled through city streets (the *Post* provided her most likely route on the afternoon of her disappearance), was accosted in theater alley, or carried off to Hoboken via the Hudson River Ferry. Furthermore, the circumstances of Mary's family life—her widowed mother, disappeared adventurer father, sailor brother, and boarding-house friendships—rendered Mary into an urban type, familiar to readers used to urban novels and the popular physiologies. Speculation about Mary's leisure activities referenced public houses, ferry rides, and Hoboken excursions and revealed the newfound world of public urban recreation. But most interesting of all were the speculations about Mary's romantic and sexual life—her many beaux, her possibly notorious sexual history with its possibility of abortions, and her sexually independent and distinctly urban life style. In this version Mary's story conforms to the traditional tales of fallen women, tales especially engaging because they facilitated discussions of worlds hitherto unexplored in bourgeois commercial culture—the sexual and dangerous world of the lower classes.[19]

The disclosure of private life was not, of course, reserved for Mary alone. While readers participated vicariously in the endless quest for an unknown killer, they were delighted to read of the exploits of a series of young men. Thus, as we have seen, the press published the confession of the wood engraver, Joseph Morse, who told the details of his adulterous affair, and they printed the words of his girlfriend who (in his defense) recounted the story of their night in bed. The sailor, William Kiekuck, recounted in the press his amorous outings in the Five Points.

And the details of the final agonizing hours of Daniel Payne, Mary's inebriated and suicidal lover, were recreated and retold, further extending the ongoing saga of the "Mary Rogers Tragedy." Published under provocative banners such as THE MURDER OF MARY ROGERS—AN INQUEST ON DANIEL PAYNE, HER LOVER, or AN ARREST OF SUSPECTED MURDERER, the press generated a sense of urgency and danger and mystery about the case. But the newspapers would take this inversion of public and private discourse one step further to an area that earlier had been sacrosanct: descriptions of Mary's unclothed and destroyed corpse soon became a prominent feature of the early press reports.

   The Rogers death was not the first major crime to receive this kind of journalistic attention. In 1836 Helen Jewett, one of the city's most famous prostitutes, was allegedly axed to death by her paramour, Richard P. Robinson, in the exclusive brothel of Rowena Townshend on Thomas Street in lower Manhattan. Robinson, a nineteen-year-old clerk, who went by the alias Frank Rivers, was said to have killed Jewett after an assignation. After allegedly slashing her to death, he set her body and room afire, and hastily exited out the rear downstairs door. The son of a prominent Connecticut family, Robinson was quickly indicted for the murder, tried in a widely attended trial, and eventually acquitted. As many of its recent chroniclers have pointed out, the case was important in that it contained within it a variety of complicated social and political subtexts. Robinson was both championed and reviled as a representative of the new promiscuous male youth culture of the city. Supported at court by young men who donned what came to be called "Frank Rivers" caps (Robinson had assumed the name of Rivers), he was in turn reviled by the respectable classes who saw Robinson as a representative of the new "sporting" urban males whose sexual style and flamboyant attitude flew in the face of conventional society.[20]

   In his book, *Objectivity and the News*, Dan Schiller argues that the origins of crime reporting was at the outset intimately connected with the history of urban antebellum class relations, specifically the working-class doctrines of republicanism and equal rights. Schiller maintains that the trial of Robinson occurred at the same time that several significant political trials were underway, most notably the trial of twenty journeymen tailors for conspiracy to prevent wage reductions in New York City in 1836. Judge Ogden Edwards (grandson of Jonathan Edwards and a Whig politician) presided at these trials as well as in the Robinson case and was to hand down his decision on the tailors the same day as the Jewett trial began. These two events intertwined, Schiller argues; the political anger and energy from the tailors' case overflowing simultaneously into rage at the murder of the young and beautiful Jewett, who became a representation of justice and republican virtue, and defense of the clerk Robinson, whom many believed was accused to cover the tracks of the brothel's more wealthy and famous patrons. Thus, argues Schiller, "It is perhaps not entirely fanciful, to entertain the idea that the Liberty invoked by these journeymen may have been personified by Helen Jewett, the beautiful prostitute, the goddess, whose foul murder was being investigated under the stewardship of the reviled Edwards."[21]

The case was widely covered by the press. Benjamin Day, editor of the *Sun*, investigated it extensively and was convinced of Robinson's guilt; James Gordon Bennett, perhaps paid by either Robinson's family or his prominent merchant employer, assumed the role of Robinson's advocate. In so doing Bennett brought both the *Herald* and himself considerable attention, and allied himself with the defense of the male sporting culture associated with Robinson. The *Herald*'s reporting, however, broke new ground—introducing an unprecedented level of sexual content into the daily press and anticipating the treatment of the Rogers death, five years later. What developed from Bennett's involvement was a curious intermingling of Republican political ideology and sexually explicit and provocative reporting.

By the time of the Rogers death in 1841, the city and its political climate had changed dramatically; the depression of the late 1830s had been weathered, radical working-class politics were, at least for the moment, under wraps (coopted by Jacksonianism and muddled by the politics of immigration and race). As a result, a conservative rather than a radical political message unfolded in conjunction with the Rogers death. Although the press continued to identify itself with the notion of a democratic public, and against privilege and wealth, it no longer proclaimed the political legitimacy of the working classes with quite the same rhetoric or authority. With the threat of labor radicalism sorely diminished, the press had clearly separated itself from its once more idealistic rhetoric, and replaced it with a different vision, one that was heavily melodramatic, feared rather than welcomed the democratic impulses of the new urban culture, and contended with what it perceived as social mayhem by a Manichaean or dualistic structuring of the urban social world. And by 1841 James Gordon Bennett was weathering a personal political controversy of a very different sort—the so-called "moral wars" waged against him by a coalition of city editors.

Through the *Herald* Bennett had not only transformed the content of the daily press by incorporating the sensational and salacious, he also had taken on the established church and every other New York City editor (and most politicians), audaciously insulting them and their reputations. In May 1840, he attacked Parke Benjamin, then editor of the *Evening Signal* as "half Jew, half infidel, with a curse of the monster," claiming that the disabled editor had been crippled due to a "curse of the Almighty." He railed against the Catholic Church, urging it "to come forth from the darkness, folly and superstition of the tenth century"; he inveighed against his former editor Webb, by then editor of the *Courier and Enquirer*, and against Mordecai M. Noah, one-time newspaper man, Tammany comrade, and briefly (in 1841) state judge.[22] Benjamin and Webb led the retaliatory battle against him, the latter describing him as a "moral pestilence" whose paper was a "disgusting obscenity." Joined by many other city editors (and several from elsewhere as well), the attack on Bennett was framed, perhaps not surprisingly, in moral rather than political terms, and employed the language of sin and disease. The goal of those who initiated the attack was simply to kill the *Herald* and silence Bennett by getting advertisers to withdraw their business and public distributors to refuse to sell the paper. Bennett, of course, was indefatigable, the attacks only incited him to more outrageous stories and heavier accusations against the city's money, power, and information elite who had tried to shut him down. It was against the background of these controversies that Bennett seized and marketed the "tragedy" of Mary Rogers.

It is hard to imagine a better story for Bennett's counterattack. Inherently sensational, the Mary Rogers saga was a tale of mystery and betrayal as rich as the Helen Jewett murder. Moreover, because Mary was not a prostitute but rather a Nassau Street neighbor, and because her death, unlike Jewett's, involved several unsolved riddles, it inspired the exploration of different issues. And the cast of characters in the drama—the suspects, Mary's friends, and family—all came from a world wholly familiar to Bennett. John Anderson, Mary's former employer and friend, was, like Bennett, a Tammany man (in fact Bennett may have shielded Anderson from notoriety); and, as I have already suggested, Anderson, like several of the Mather and Rogers relatives, was involved in commerce with South Carolina, Bennett's early territory. And perhaps because the death never came to any formal resolution, or even to trial, it provided Bennett with an opportunity for exploiting its inherently salacious content and thereby recapture readership lost as a result of the "moral wars." Bennett also used it to set the tone and style for "city news," and simultaneously as a vehicle for attacking the entire criminal justice system and city administration. A tale of a young woman's death was Bennett's perfect opportunity to create a major media event and regain his position over a city that had tried to shut him down. With Mary's story and Mary as the basic text, all areas of city life, as well as Mary herself, became available for investigation and exploration.

The Tortured Body and the Violence of Representation

While the Mary Rogers tragedy was the invention of the *Herald* and the other mass circulation dailies—especially the *Tribune,* the *Post,* the *Sun,* and the *Courier and Enquirer*—both the constructions of the event and the particular depictions of Rogers herself were more than the product of the misogynist politics of antebellum journalism. Or, more specifically, the violence of representation characteristic of this journalism provided a language with which to explore the cultural text that Rogers had become. With Mary as both the subject and the object of the journalist's words, the narratives of her life, death, and physical remains incorporated the culture's hostility toward women, while simultaneously using that misogyny as a mechanism for exploring the social, political, and sexual issues that the Rogers case aroused. The meaning of the Mary Rogers story, the significance of Rogers herself as an imagined female subject, and the cultural significance of violent death as a topic of narrative, thus serve as clues toward understanding the violence of representation characteristic of the press reports.

To understand this element of the representation of the Rogers story it is helpful to remember Poe's famous statement from his essay "The Philosophy of Composition," written a few years after "Marie Roget": "The death of a beautiful woman is, unquestionably, the most poetical topic in the world."[23] Although it seems a quantum leap from the political and mundane concerns of Bennett's *Herald* to Poe's poetics, in different ways, and for different purposes, both Poe and Bennett were drawn to the destroyed female form as a topic for composition. In this shared focus both men drew from and simultaneously challenged their culture's sentimental version of death and mourning; indeed, each used the Rogers death as a means to challenge the sentimental tradition they both (for different reasons) abhorred. But whereas Bennett eroticized the destroyed body, violating it repeatedly through his words, Poe chose the stance of analytic distance and literary detachment, mocking the likes of Bennett with their taste for what he called "busy bodyism."[24]

As Karen Halttunen and other recent historians of American culture have shown, the culture of mourning in Victorian America, against which Poe and Bennett were reacting, was an elaborate affair. The death of the loved person constituted one of the most important social rituals; it involved extended public and private displays of grief and carefully defined symbols designating the relation of the bereaved to the deceased. Characterized above all by the managed expressions of emotion, it stressed restraint rather than release and focused on the attenuation of the feeling of grief over the finality of death. To effect this, the artifacts of death—locks of hair, bits of clothing—were used to indicate the connection between the living and the dead. (In the classic death scene of this time, Little Eva in *Uncle Tom's Cabin* distributed locks of her hair to the congregation assembled to witness her death.) Mourning art itself constituted a major form of cultural and artistic expression: jewelry featured elaborately woven strands of the hair of the deceased, while paintings with well-understood iconography imaged their social world.[25]

The public mourning of Mary Rogers orchestrated by Bennett and the other captains of the penny press provided an interesting counterpoint to these traditional rituals. On the one hand they reiterated (and re-presented) the culture's obsessive preoccupation with the details and artifacts of death and dying, as well as with the personal remains of the deceased; indeed, Arthur Crommelin, Mary's friend and former boarder who identified her body, brought back a lock of Mary's hair and pieces of her clothing to her bereaved mother, Phebe Rogers. On the other hand, the death of Mary was not a sentimental affair. And in striking contrast to the traditional shrouding and masking of the body of the deceased in traditional mourning culture, the body of Mary Rogers, tortured and destroyed, was fully exposed and displayed, an icon of her life and of the "tragedy" that had befallen her.

As Poe understood and made clear in "Marie Roget," vivid descriptions of Rogers's dead and destroyed body were a central and continuing aspect of the newspaper stories, her death allowing what was not permissible in life—the full physical exposure of the female form. Presenting Rogers as a corpse, a female body no longer private, but instead totally exposed, the necrophilic descriptions of Mary with lace petticoat strips around her neck and blood leaking from her mouth, were pictorial, dramatic, and erotic. Through her destroyed body three tropes of nineteenth-century Western culture converged: the danger and riddle of femininity with the mystery of death and the mystery of the city.

The first visual description was provided by the *Herald* on August 4 and depicted an undoubtedly fabricated scene of "discovery." Designed to draw the reader into the scene itself, the "discovery" of the body became a spectacle that transformed the reader into a viewer:

> When we saw her, she was laying [sic] on the bank, on her back, with a rope tied around her, and a large stone attached to it, flung in the water. The first look we had of her, was most ghastly. Her forehead and face appeared to have been battered and butchered, to a mummy. Her features were scarcely visible, so much violence had been done to her. On her head she wore a bonnet—light gloves on her hands, with long, watery fingers peering out—her dress was torn in various portions—her shoes were on her feet—and altogether, she presented the most horrible spectacle that eye could see. It almost made our heart sick, and we hurried from the scene, while a rude youth was raising her leg, which hung in the water, and making unfeeling remarks on her dress.[26]

Mary's identity here was already fading; "battered" and "butchered," her features were "scarcely visible" because "so much violence had been done to her." She was, however, still clothed, and the particulars of her gloves, bonnet, shoes, and torn dress served as visual reminders of her past life. A later description of her corpse, taken from the *Post*, chronicles the changing attitude toward her as she progresses from the "loveliest of his work" to a "decomposed mass of putrefaction," an object of disease, "corruption," and pollution:

> The body of this unfortunate girl was yesterday, at the request of our city authorities, disinterred and brought from Jersey to this city, and

deposited in the dead house in the Park. And difficult would it be for the most imaginative mind to conceive a spectacle more horrible or humiliating to humanity. There lay, what was but a few days back, the image of its Creator, the loveliest of his work and the tenement of an immortal soul, now a blackened and decomposed mass of putrefaction, painfully disgusting to sight and smell. Her skin which had been unusually fair was now black as that of a negro. Her eyes so sunk in her swollen face as to have the appearance of being violently forced beyond the sockets, and her mouth which "no friendly hand had closed in death," was distended as wide as the ligaments of the jaws would admit and wore the appearance of a person who had died from suffocation or strangulation. The remainder of her person was alike one mass of putrefaction and corruption, on which the worms were revelling at their will. . . . The remains even of her dress, in which she had been buried, were already so discolored and half rotten, as to render it almost impossible to be identified, and was so impregnated with the effluvia from her person, that scarcely any person would venture to touch or examine it.[27]

The description is striking in its specificity, in the way it turns Mary's body into an object of humiliation, horror, corruption, and, most of all, putrefaction, and how it associates her once beautiful murdered body with disgust, blackness, and race; her skin, it notes, is "black as that of a negro." Through her body Mary had become representative of three dreaded specters of nineteenth-century American culture—sex, race, and disease. She had become an untouchable.

Unusual or suspicious deaths were routinely investigated by the city coroner, the results were tabulated by the month and filed with the court of General Sessions. Generally, the reports were brief, establishing an official cause of death. Beginning with the penny press in the 1830s, the papers took such information and reprinted it, thereby providing an interesting source of city news, particularly when the deaths were strange or even accidental. Rogers's death, of course, occasioned coroner's investigations; the most important one was carried out by Richard Cook, the coroner for Hoboken, New Jersey. On August 15, almost three weeks after the death, the New York Acting Mayor Purdy and Dr. Archibald Archer, coroner for New York, examined Cook. The contents of this interview, which included details of the autopsy report, were made publicly available through the *Herald* in question and answer form under the banner THE MURDER OF MARY ROGERS—EXAMINATION OF DR. COOK BEFORE HIS HONOR THE MAYOR, AND THE CORONER, DR. ARCHER. The publication of such a detailed and visually explicit testimony was unusual, perhaps even unprecedented. Through it Mary is still, as in earlier descriptions, a spectacle, a violated and violent sight; but she has also become the object of scientific investigation. Ironically, the final destruction of Mary's body, the ultimate violation, is carried out not by her killers but by the coroner's lancet. Furthermore, the report is chilling not only in its use of scientific investigation but in how it employs medical discourse to create narratives. Significantly, no hint is made of any abortion procedure, only a faint and disingenuous statement that there was "no hint of pregnancy."[28]

The *Herald* said that Cook "surmised that Mary fainted; and that before she recovered her murderers tied a piece of fine lace trimming, tight round her neck, which prevented her breathing again." He ascertained that "she had not been smothered, but he was unable to determine whether or not she had been drugged." He testified the following about the state of the body:

> The face when I examined it was suffused with dark blood—bruised blood. There was frothy blood still issuing from the mouth. . . . Her face was swollen, the veins were highly distended. . . . The blood was so much coagulated that it was with difficulty I could get it to follow the lancet at all. . . . There was an echymose mark about the size and shape of a man's thumb on the right side of the neck, near the jugular vein, and two or three echymose marks on the left side resembling the shape of a man's fingers which led me to believe she had been throttled and partially choked by a man's hand. Both arms were bent over on the chest; and were so tight and stiff that we had to use some force to straighten them—. The right hand was clenched, and the left hand was partially open but rigid. . . .

> [It appeared] as if the wrists had been tied together, and as if she had raised her hands to try to tear something from off her mouth and neck, which was choking and strangling her. . . . There was excoriation of the left wrist in the form of two circles around it, as if a rope had been tied around it, once or twice. . . . The hand had been tied, probably, while the body was violated, and untied before she was thrown into the water.

> There was considerable excoriation upon the top of the back and both shoulder bones, and excoriation also at the bottom of the back. This was produced [Cook thought] by the young girl struggling to get free, while being brutally held down on her back, to effect her violation; and therefore, that this outrage was effected while she was laid down upon some hard substance, a hard board floor, the bottom of a board, or something similar. It convinces me fully that the outrage was not effected on a bed.

> The dress was much torn in several places. The outer dress was torn in this way: a long slip, say a foot wide, was torn up from the bottom of the frock to the waist, but the *piece was not torn off*; it was wound three times round the waist and secured by a sort of hitch in the back. The dress immediately beneath the frock, and between the upper petticoat was made of fine muslin; a piece was torn clean out of this garment, about a foot or 18 inches in width; this piece was torn very evenly and with great care, commencing at the bottom of the garment. This same piece was afterwards tied round her mouth, with a hard

knot at the back part of the neck; I think this was done to smother her cries, and that it was probably held tight round her mouth by one of her brutal ravishers. . . . I consider that her hat was off her head at the time of the outrage, and that after her violation and murder had been completed, it was tied on.

The piece of fine lace trimming I before spoke of. This for some time escaped my attention. I observed a crease round the neck . . . passing my hand behind her ear, I accidentally felt a small knot; and found that a piece of lace, which I supposed to have been the trimming of her lace collar, *was tied so tightly round her neck as to have been hidden from sight* in the flesh of the neck; *this was tied in a hard knot under the left ear.* This would have strangled her.[29]

The *Herald* goes on to note that the rest of Cook's testimony was "of such a nature that it cannot be given in detail." It related to the appearance of the body, which enabled the doctor "to state positively that the poor girl had been brutally violated." He said that "previous to this shocking outrage, she had evidently been a person of chastity and correct habits; that her person was horribly violated *by more than two or three persons.*"[30]

In reading this description the reader becomes privy to the drama of Mary's actual death—to the scene of violation, strangulation, resistance, struggle, and finally death. Through the physical evidence of Mary's destroyed remains, the press conveyed the story of "a horrible murder," inviting the reader to share in the drama of Mary's final moments. And implicit in the coroner's report of the physical evidence, which the press reprinted, was the impression that the coroner's scientific evidence indicated a particular set of events, even an accurate reenactment of the crime. Indeed, a highly dramatic rendering of the events was constructed from these pieces of medical evidence: Mary had been "throttled and partially choked by a man's hand"; her wrists had been tied together in a way that suggested struggle—"as if she had raised her hands to try to tear something from off her mouth and neck which was choking and strangling her"; she had been gagged with a piece of her own clothing "tied round her mouth, with a hard knot at the back of her neck," done, he surmised, "to smother her cries," and that "it was probably held tight by one of her brutal ravishers"; that in order to effect her violation she had been "brutally held down on her back," and that therefore this "outrage was effected while she was laid down upon some hard substance, a hard board floor, the bottom of a board . . . the outrage was not effected on a bed." Thus, from the same coroner's report, it was suggested that Mary, for her part, was tied, gagged, held down, raped by several men, then strangled to death, after which her body was tied again and thrown into the water. Mary, in turn, according to this scenario, struggled, screamed, and resisted in a way that brought yet even more abuse and violence on her body.

Mary's physical body was not only discovered and subjected to detailed and public examination, but once buried it was exhumed, reexamined, and buried once again.[31] As we have seen, at each stage of this drama vivid descriptions of her corpse were presented through the press; lurid and detailed, they enfold a tale of horrific abuse first by the murderers and secondarily by the press. Just as the authorities had exhumed the actual physical body, so the press exhumed the imagined body in a process that recreated, reenacted, and redefined the act of murder and its symbolic public meaning. Indeed, the further process of defining and narrativizing the event through the penny press (reiterated in the commentary of contemporaries, Poe's story, etc.) initiated the self-reflexive cycle of verbal exhumation of what had become the cultural remains of Mary Rogers. Here, in death, the mutilated body of the beautiful maiden was now, through the written word, available to all.

The Press Invents the Death of Mary Rogers

Through the press Mary Rogers herself had become a violent and erotic text. Her story pushed at the boundaries of contemporary social discourse while it simultaneously indulged fantasized notions of the erotics of city life and the erotics of death, both significant aspects of antebellum sentimental and popular culture. Underlying the presentation of the Rogers story and the vivid descriptions of her destroyed body, and making them possible, were complex narratives constructed around the imagined persona of Mary Rogers. In the press (especially the *Herald*) two primary and oppositional representations took form: The first depicted Mary as the once beautiful maiden, the symbol of virginity and nature destroyed by the forces of evil at the heart of the modern city; the second inverted this initial construction and projected Mary herself not as the innocent victim, but as the personification of the dangerous city. As either youthful maiden or sexual transgressor, she served a political purpose and facilitated highly melodramatic narratives.

Melodrama, the critic Peter Brooks has written, "comes into being in a world where the traditional imperatives of truth and ethics have been violently thrown into question, yet where the promulgation of truth and ethics, their installation as a way of life, is of immediate, daily, political concern." "It takes," he continues, "as its concern and raison d'etre the location, the expression and importation of basic ethical and psychic truths. It says them over and over again in clear language, it rehearses their conflicts and combats, it reenacts the menace of evil and the eventual triumph of morality made operative and evident." And while the political content may vary—be conservative or revolutionary in its social implications—it is "in all cases radically democratic, striving to make its representations clear and legible to everyone . . . melodrama becomes the principal mode for uncovering, demonstrating, and making operative the essential moral universe in a post sacred era."[32]

As told through the press, the story of the disappearance and death of Mary fits Brooks's conception of melodrama well. Written in plain style, the chronicle was enacted and reenacted as a way of expressing a set of assumed ethical, moral, and even political issues that revolved around the modern city and the place of women within it. The event was used to define social questions, to pose them in public contexts, and even to order (by disordering) the social space of the urban land-scape. It did so in a language that was both "clear and legible" and that at least attempted to posit a moral script for a presumably democratic audience. Representations of women (in this case Mary herself) were a critical aspect of this script that proclaimed an angry public message about social and moral disintegration in the antebellum city. The Rogers tragedy in particular provided an important center for these gendered constructions of social and sexual life. Insofar as these dualistic narratives of Rogers were melodramatic, they conformed to an already generalized social ambivalence about women and their relationship to urban public life. Played out first in the penny papers and later in cheap mystery novels, they expressed beliefs that saw women—or at least those whose sexual or class identity placed them beyond the margins of respectability—as both the source of urban social disorder and sexual danger and at the same time those most endangered. This was of course a modern and urban transmogrification of the mythological and literary representations of woman as both innocent and demonic, angel and whore.[33]

The first version of Mary—the one initially characteristic of the press dispatches—presented her as the beautiful and innocent maiden, a symbol of virginity and even nature in the harsh landscape of Gotham: "A young and beautiful girl," wrote the *Herald*, "has been seduced from her home."[34] Cast as the virtuous maiden, Mary became an extended metaphor for an older and presumably lost ideal of civic virtue and organic unity in the urban landscape. Bespoiled, even violated, and ultimately destroyed by elements of city life, Mary and her death provided a way of naming and identifying the sources of urban danger. Paramount, for example, were the assertions that she had been killed by one of the infamous gangs that plagued the city. This construction of Mary as virtuous victim rationalized the law and order and anti-abortion crusades of the 1840s that followed in the wake of Mary's death.

The other theories about Mary's death—that she was killed by one of her lovers or friends, or even that she died as the result of an abortion—projected narratives about the city that were similar in that they emphasized its implicit and furtive violence. But these constructions also shifted the discussion's tenor and focus. While the city was still indicted as the locus of danger and sexual violence, this version of events constructed Rogers herself as the signification of the city and the dangers it contained. Here, of course, she was neither virtuous nor innocent; "The Beautiful Cigar Girl" was the temptress behind the counter, the sexually compromising working girl, the *grisette*,* the young woman who was known for her male lovers and an earlier abortion. Herself the source of social and sexual danger, her life served as a challenge to bourgeois structures of sexual morality and order. The cautionary tale embedded in this narrative was not only about the city itself, but about the dangers of sexual freedom and unrestrained or undisciplined female sexuality. Encoded here was an altered or revised narrative of Mary's life, one that implicitly legitimized the voyeuristic dramatizations of the imagined acts of rape and murder carried out against her and the obsessive preoccupation with her destroyed remains.

Identified with the working class, single, sexually available, and apparently independent, Rogers raised middle-class fears about the dangers of city life to such an extent that she becomes therefore not the *victim* but the *danger* of the modern metropolis. In this sense she gave voice to another version of the cautionary tale; the fate of Mary Rogers—her death by murder, perhaps preceded by rape or abortion—told what might happen to women who were sexual and whose sexuality allowed them to live outside the domestic sphere. For while Mary's fate made her a victim supposedly of her own behavior, it more importantly reiterated the danger to women—so important in the development of nineteenth-century urban bourgeois culture—of male power and sexuality, or, more precisely, of murderous male sexuality that their own female sexuality could unleash. Rogers thus embodied a combination of the potentially threatening woman who was both sexually free and also totally vulnerable, unleashing an array of violent fantasies and feelings toward women of all classes, feelings that were, however, made permissible by the notion of the outlaw sexuality of lower-class women. Central here were the discussions of Mary's actual body, a corpse inscribed with the sexual politics of antebellum culture.

Insofar as the city is a gendered and feminine space, the female body serves as a metaphor for the urban. This thesis is elaborated in an essay by the French critic Christine Buci-Glucksman who argues that in the works of Walter Benjamin the female form serves as an allegory for the modern city: representations of the feminine doubling with representations of the urban.[35] Thus, while the alive and fertile female body suggests organic unity, so the destruction of that body, its death and decomposition, signifies the break-up of civilized culture, the disintegration of that social body, the modern city. Thus Mary, her death, and the destruction of her body, served as a constant reminder of the disintegration of the idea, perhaps mythic or nostalgic, of the city as an organic, unified, social space. Destroyed by the forces of evil inherent in the modern city, Rogers's putrefying corpse served as a prolonged allegory about urban fragmentation and social decay.

* *Grisette* is a French term for a shop girl of "easy virtue." Poe refers to Mary Rogers as a "grisette" throughout "Marie Roget."

Another interpretation of these images is suggested by Foucault. In *Discipline and Punish*, he speculates about the place of ritual in and the relationship between the uses of the body and notions of power in traditional judicial procedures. He speaks of the symbolic importance that the ritual of displaying the body of the condemned (what he calls the "tortured body" exhibited in procession) had for the public. "This display," he tells us, served three principle functions: (1) it made the guilty man the herald of his own condemnation; (2) it duplicated the scene of the confession by establishing the public execution as the moment of truth, thereby revealing the truth to the public of an otherwise private act; and (3) it "pinned the public torture on to the crime itself." "The body," according to Foucault, "several times tortured, provides the synthesis of the reality of the deeds and the truth of the investigation, of the documents of the case and the statements of the criminal, of the crime and the punishment."[36]

The death of Mary Rogers allowed no such public expiation. There was no criminal to be publicly condemned and no trial where people could quite literally bear witness to the event. And there was no formal resolution. Instead we have only the chronicles of the discovered body and of the imagined event, chronicles that recreate and narrativize in press columns, novels, and other written texts the crimes against the body. And in these chronicles the body of Mary Rogers figures as the critical and defining element, a body presented in the form of a corpse, a body inscribed with a mysterious life and the details of an unusual and brutal death. It is a body that serves, in this more modern context, all these traditional roles and rituals described by Foucault at once. And if for a moment we return to the two melodramatic paradigms posited above, we might for argument's sake say that Mary herself had become by the early weeks of August 1841 both the victim and the criminal in the case. Thus, the display of Rogers, and particularly the display of her body in public discourse, served as a kind of public spectacle, not unlike that discussed by Foucault. Mary's body, indeed her "very tortured body," served as a substitution for the replay of the event itself; the torture of her body through the textualizing and the telling of the event served the dual functions of reenactment and expiation.

But the differences here are as important as the similarities. Rogers was not only the victim and the criminal, she was also female and her "crime" was sexual transgression. Thus the descriptions, the texts, become not only a replacement for the reenactment of the crime, but of the punishment as well. Through the descriptive assaults on her body, a body already inscribed with crimes and punishments, Mary becomes the unifying force. Through her death, her life became a public text, and her body, verbally assaulted, became the mechanism for contending with three culturally significant riddles: death, femininity, and the city. It was a triangulated riddle inspiring detection and exploration and seeking resolution.

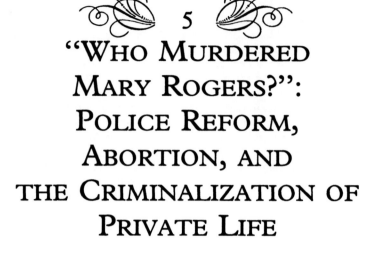

5

"WHO MURDERED MARY ROGERS?": POLICE REFORM, ABORTION, AND THE CRIMINALIZATION OF PRIVATE LIFE

The recent awful violation and murder of an innocent young woman—the impenetrable mystery which surrounds that act—the apathy of the great criminal judges, sitting on their own fat for a cushion bench—and the utter inefficiency of their police, are all leading fast to reduce this large city to a savage state of society—without law—without order—and without security of any kind. . . . In one emphatic word, New York is disgraced and dishonored in the eyes of the Christian and civilized world unless one great big, one strong moral movement be made to reform and reinvigorate the administration of criminal justice, and to protect the lives and property of its inhabitants from public violence and public robbery. Who will make the first move in this truly great moral reform?

New York *Herald* (August 12, 1841)[1]

While many suppose that crime is on the increase in a ratio greater than our increase of population, it is gratifying to find that the data furnished, fully sustains the contrary.

N.Y. District Attorney (1841)[2]

Where is Mary Applegate's child? Where's the thousand children murdered in this house? . . . Who Murdered Mary Rogers?

National *Police Gazette* (February 28, 1846)[3]

CONSTANCE Shirley, a character in Ned Buntline's 1848 novel, *The Mysteries and Miseries of New York*, is horrified when she reads in the morning *Herald* that a body "has been found in the water." It is the body of Mary Sheffield, also known as "The Beautiful Cigar Girl," and one of the novel's central characters. The newspaper asserts that Mary had been the victim of "ill treatment and murder by a gang of rowdies at Hoboken." But Buntline soon reveals to Constance what his readers already know: that "the marks of violence upon her [were] inflicted not by a gang of rowdies, but by a hag: a she devil, an abortion of her own sex, one of whom it would be blasphemy to call a woman, [the abortionist] Caroline Sitstill." Sitstill, Buntline's readers also knew, was a stand-in for Madame Restell, the period's most infamous abortionist. In this novelization the fictive Mary Rogers has died from an abortion, a "still and lost treatment" intended to end her unwanted pregnancy, the result of a seduction by Constance's own father, the prosperous merchant, Albert Shirley.[4]

In an extended appendix to this same curious book, which is part urban mystery story, part conservative social tract, Buntline appends a lengthy discussion of urban crime and social conditions, replete with the text of the 1845 New York City Police Reform Act. Buntline, already a well-known novelist and adventurer, had the advantage of hindsight; by then there was little doubt that Rogers's death was neither the work of "rowdies" nor of an individual assailant, but instead the consequence of a failed abortion. However, in blending issues of policing and social reform, Mary Rogers, and Madame Restell, all within the frames of a popular urban novel, Buntline displayed an unusual (and uncharacteristically) synchronistic understanding of his own time; in melding these disparate issues—the death of the "beautiful cigar girl," the law and order crusades of the 1840s, and the crisis over abortion—Buntline directs us to the social and political issues that contextualize the Rogers story.

Of course, these convergences had already been enacted in "real life." In the summer of 1841 Mary's disappearance and death were played out against two important issues: (1) an ongoing but increasingly rancorous and highly politicized debate about urban crime and the need for police reform; and (2) the trial (the first of many) and conviction of Caroline Restell for an act of criminal abortion. Four years later, in 1845, the legacy of Mary Rogers's death and the attacks on Restell yielded two important pieces of legislation, both inspired by fears of sexual danger: (1) the Police Act, which modernized New York City's policing system; and (2) the Abortion Law, which criminalized that increasingly widespread practice.[5] The first used the rhetoric of sexual danger to transform the premises of policing; the second attempted to control nonprocreative sexual activity by criminalizing a commercially available and popular form of birth control. Like anti-abortion crusades in modern times, this attempt to police women's sexual conduct indicated strong hostility to the changing social and sexual lives of women. Interestingly, both pieces of legislation were predicated on assumptions of assault against the female sexual body; in the case of police reform, the presumed rape and murder of Mary Rogers; in the issue of abortion,

Figure 5–1 *The cover page of the* Wonderful Trial of Caroline Lohman, Alias Restell *(1847) featured the infamous New York abortionist. The trial report chronicled her prosecution under the 1845 New York State abortion law for second-degree manslaughter. (Courtesy, American Antiquarian Society.)*

the presumed assault against the fetal body and the probing of the female body. And finally, drawing on both the legacy of Rogers's death and the public spectacle of Madame Caroline Restell, the state turned to new forms of surveillance as aspects of the body politic to "prevent" criminal danger to the social body.

In this chapter I hope to show both how and why these issues, which twice intersected in 1841 and again in 1845, were inspired by and reflected in the saga of Mary Rogers and the public meaning of her death. Recent work in critical legal history suggests that during this antebellum period the use of the law and the authority of the state both underwent significant transformation. The law, writes Morton Horwitz, was no longer an "eternal set of principles," but rather an "instrument of policy" used to effect social change. And, in a parallel trend, Lawrence Friedman has shown that the body of criminal law, especially the state criminal codes, increased dramatically as legislation was enacted to control and curtail behavior and influence social interaction.[6] As a result of these changes, many of the traditional assumptions about the locus of power and authority were redefined, particularly those limning the boundaries between individual privacy and the state. The Mary Rogers case provides a significant marker in this larger societal transformation. Coming at a critical juncture in the city's political and social history, it served as a catalytic event, propelling issues of criminal justice and social policy forward and transforming the terms in which they were presented and made popular. The death of Rogers and the sexually violent nature of the crime facilitated a shift in the tone and direction of earlier debates over urban crime and punishment. By the mid-1840s, new policies were in place, not the least of which was the restructuring and reform of the police system intended to "prevent" rather than merely "detect" crime, and new laws were enacted (as well as older ones enforced) that moved the agencies of the state more intrusively into private life. As an unsolved crime of sexual violence, the Rogers case encouraged the enactment of new legislation and underscored both the legitimacy and the utility of the public surveillance of private life.[7]

My intention is not to argue causation, to claim that Rogers's death itself resulted in police or abortion legislation (although in both cases the connections were astonishingly immediate and direct) but rather to suggest how these larger social and political issues converged around the Rogers story, both infusing it with meaning and connecting it to ongoing debates about social order and sexual danger. Furthermore, to show how these issues were aspects of something larger—"a multiplicity of discourses" about the body, sexuality, privacy, and the state.[8]

Policing the City: The Case of Police Reform

On the evening of August 11, 1841, a controversial meeting initiated by James Gordon Bennett and attended by Tammany figures among others was called to "take measures for procuring the arrest and conviction of any or all those concerned in the . . . murder" of Mary Rogers. Chaired by William H. Attree, the *Herald* crime and city reporter and editor infamous for his aggressive investigative reporting, the group proclaimed its alarm and horror at the circumstances connected with the "shocking murder of Mary Rogers." Calling themselves, the "Committee of Safety" (they were also known as the "Committee of Twenty"), they condemned the current police practice of resolving only those crimes for which a reward was offered and simultaneously authorized the collection of subscriptions toward such a reward for the Rogers death. Perhaps more important, they encouraged local vigilantism and empowered the committee "to act in aid of public authorities . . . to take such measures as they shall deem proper . . . to effect the detection of the murderer or murderers."⁹

The next day the *Herald* reported on the meeting (as did the other city papers) and included a vituperative editorial on the "Administration of Criminal Justice." It was an extraordinary statement, even for Bennett, a lengthy and emotionally charged jeremiad on law, order, and morality in the city. The statement reiterated the sentiments expressed in the manifesto of the "Committee of Safety," the attack on the police, the plea for vigilantism, etc., and claimed that "the state of criminal justice in the city had reached such 'utter degradation' and 'complete demoralization' that it was now time for the "country to take the subject in their own hands." It was, of course, the "awful violation and murder of an innocent young woman [Mary Rogers]" that excited this declaration. "Petty officialdom," Bennett claimed, pursued "petty crimes," while the "blood of Mary Rodgers [sic] [was] crying for vengeance from the depth of the Hudson." The city was fast falling into a "savage state, a place without law—and without order of any kind." "New York," he told his readers, was in "one emphatic word . . . disgraced and dishonored in the eyes of the Christian and civilized world." Employing the language of disaster, he issued a plea for a movement of moral reform to protect the lives and property of its inhabitants from "public violence and public robbery." Other papers followed suit. In response to Rogers's death, *The Commercial Advertiser* had already declared that "New York remains the most unprotected city against crime in the United States, if not in the whole civilized world." By the middle of August even the whiggish *Tribune* argued that current police system was "vicious" and "deplorably defective" and in need of "immediate, energetic reform."¹⁰

Two weeks after the August 11 Tammany meeting, William Seward, Governor of New York, responding to considerable public pressure from the press and elsewhere, offered a "reward of Seven Hundred and Fifty Dollars . . . [to be] paid to whoever shall give information resulting in the conviction either in this state or the state of New Jersey, of any person guilty of the said crimes." He issued the following statement:

> Whereas Mary C. Rogers, a young woman residing in the city of New York, was lately ravished and murdered in the said city, or in the portion of the state of New Jersey contiguous thereto; and whereas the efforts made by the police of the city of New York to discover the

perpetrators of these crimes, have as appears from the public record, proved altogether unsuccessful; and whereas the peace and security of society require that such atrocious crimes should not go unpunished: And I do hereby enjoin upon all magistrates and other officers and ministers of justice, that they be diligent in their efforts to bring the offender or offenders to condign punishment.[11]

These public declarations and rewards were indications of the way the Rogers affair became a major component of what had already emerged as a crisis over crime and the administration of criminal justice in the city. For several years an intensely political controversy had been raging over the need for police reform and the revision of urban policies and practices.[12] At issue was the extent to which the city itself had changed in the first half of the nineteenth century (the result of the rise in population and immigration, the growth of class and social segregation that came to dominate city life); the degree to which increased crime, both real and imagined, had become a factor in contemporary urban debates; and the reality that older systems of criminal law and policing had become outmoded and obsolete. The dark jeremiads about the state of law and order in New York issued in response to the Rogers murder were therefore rhetorical flourishes to a more fundamental debate about social order in the "Republican Metropolis." As such they added an important dimension to a large and sometimes hysterically pitched rhetoric about the proliferation of crime and vice in the growing city. They also helped to focus that urban discourse on women, and on issues of gender and sexual conduct.

Despite this rhetoric of imminent social decay and danger, violent death was relatively uncommon in New York during this period. In 1841 there were only two convictions for murder, a figure consistent with urban murder rates generally for the 1830s and 1840s.[13] Why then did this exceptional case of violent death come to serve as the set piece in a crisis over criminal justice? In part, the explanation lies in the manipulation of public opinion by those who held a specific vision and agenda for the city. More generally, it reinforced a sense shared by many that the city was a place of random violence where violent death, especially the violent death of a known and beautiful woman, was the logical extension of urban decay. Above all, the death of Mary Rogers joined the discourse of urban social and class disorder (a response to the radical workingmen's politics and urban riots of the 1830s) to the discourse of sexual danger. This in turn buttressed arguments for new approaches to urban crime, particularly insofar as those arguments focused on forms of surveillance as a mechanism for preventing crime. Connecting sexual danger and the fear of crime was, of course, nothing new. The city's reputation as a place of vice and sin was well secured by the 1830s, as was the belief that vice and sin were the first steps toward a criminal life.[14]

Concern over the policing of the city, however, was relatively recent.

Through the early decades of the nineteenth century traditional methods of policing were generally considered effective. Based on eighteenth-century practices, the mayor had functioned as the chief police officer in charge of fires, riots, and "other breaches of the peace." Underneath him were constables and marshals whose responsibilities were essentially to "maintain order, quell riots, act as court officers, and bring criminals to justice." The activities of marshals and constables were supplemented by those of a night watch that was expanded considerably between 1790 and 1830. These men, known as leatherheads (because of their helmets), were ordinary citizens who held other jobs during the day and supplemented their wages by serving on a night shift in one of the three watch districts in the city. Marshals had common law duties and (unlike the watchmen) the basic powers of police officers, but they had no uniforms and their responsibilities were essentially to maintain public order and execute arrest warrants issued by a magistrate. They did not receive regular salaries but were compensated for their services according to a fee schedule established by the state legislature and often supplemented by privately offered rewards.[15]

It was, however, a system that had become highly politicized and led inherently to much abuse, often leaving important crimes, such as murder, undetected. The *Tribune* articulated the issue in this way: "Can we blame the officer who, on learning a great crime against life has been committed and another against individual property, starts on the track of the latter where a reward is offered, and leaves the former where there is none?"[16] Expressing the same sentiments about the inaction and "supineness" on the part of the police, Bennett asserted that "Not a step will be taken without a reward—and if they possess a clue to the mystery, still they would keep the secret intact, like a capital in trade, till the public indignation has raised a sum sufficient as a reward for bringing the facts to the light of day."[17] In short, many agreed that as the system stood, the police could "*only discharge their public duties at the sacrifice of their private interests.*"[18]

These views were supported by a series of reports commissioned by the city on the extent of urban crime. Again, written against the background of the turbulent decade of the 1830s, these generally reflected the belief that the city was in a state of disintegration and moral decay. Echoing this widely held belief, one such report noted the rapid growth of the population and maintained that "crime has increased at a ratio far greater than the increase of population during the same period," and that the escalation could be expected only to continue. The report used "complaints to the police" as evidence of increased crime, a shaky criteria, insupportable by modern standards.[19] Other, less outspoken perspectives on crime suggested a somewhat different picture, such as a report filed by J. R. Whiting, the District Attorney of New York in January 1842, less than six months after Mary's death. Written at the request of the city's Common Council, the report consisted of the "Sta-

tistics of Crime in this City for twelve years last past." It contained five
tables enumerating the "indictments, trials, recognizance to answer,
persons discharged, cases settled and complaints not acted upon for
each year and month" in the Courts of Oyer and Terminer and General
Sessions. Mr. Whiting was a man of relatively few words and his statement on the meaning of these statistics was brief and to the point:
"While many suppose that crime is on the increase in a ratio greater
than our increase of population, it is gratifying to find that the data
furnished, fully sustains the contrary."[20]

Whiting had been in the midst of the Rogers case until it was gently
shelved in the fall of 1841 and thus the timing of his report was critical.
Moreover, the report was itself a modest and relatively reasoned statement compared to most penned on the subject of urban crime. Its conclusions were clear and straightforward: serious crimes, notably crimes
of murder, had not increased disproportionately to the rise in population. By implication, the Rogers case, insofar as it was a murder, was
an anomaly and not a representative crime.

Those who took a position similar to Whiting's included Mordecai
Noah, who had been appointed an associate judge by Governor Seward
in 1841 and argued not for increased policing but for changes in the
criminal justice and court system that would streamline court procedures. A report of the Grand Jury assembled in 1842 by the Court of
General Sessions to consider the large number of complaints coming
before the Police reaffirmed this position. It argued that these cases were
"exceedingly numerous," but that many were also "trivial and unimportant," with a large proportion of the charges being for "personal
assault, unmarked with circumstances of much criminality, and scarcely
deserving the grave consideration of being passed upon by a Grand
Jury." The Jury was referring to the large number of petty crimes
brought before the police and the lower judiciary, mostly by ordinary
citizens. These cases were clogging the criminal justice system and providing evidence for the presumed increase in urban crime.[21]

Indeed, if the rhetoric of social danger characterized the public and
political discourse of the Rogers affair, it proved an interesting contrast
to the more mundane workings of the city's police and criminal justice.
For the masses of ordinary men and women involved in the "trivial
complaints" clogging the city's overtaxed judiciary system, the meaning
of such cases was quite different. Looked at from their perspective,
rather than that offered by the advocates of the new law and order, mid-
nineteenth-century urban crime seemed not so much frightening or dangerous or even symptomatic of larger social chaos, but rather the stuff
of everyday life in a crowded city. And stripped of rhetorical embellish-
ments, the annals of urban crime suggest far more about human interaction in close urban spaces rather than any inherent social danger.

At the lowest level of the judiciary, the Police and Magistrates courts
and the Court of General Sessions, we see what was identified as crim-

inal behavior as it must have touched men and women like those who lived at the Rogers house and gathered at the local taverns and coffee houses of Nassau Street. The range of cases that came before the lowest levels of the judiciary in New York (and that to this day fill boxes in the New York City Municipal Archives) tells us much about the quality and concerns of daily life in the early city. Although it is always risky to presume normal behavior from the chronicles of deviance, one is nevertheless struck by the accounts of daily life these sources present. From the records of complaint and criminal cases, an elaborate picture emerges of urban community life—of densely populated neighborhoods, of complex living arrangements in crowded small domiciles. In these neatly folded and tied reports of the police and District Attorney are endless tales of everyday existence—of petty disputes, small crimes, sexual transgressions, and domestic life. They depict a community that had found many ways of expressing anger and redressing its grievances large and small. And it is in the context of these cases that the Mary Rogers affair becomes both situated and contextualized. The criminal cases for 1841 yield the troubled stories of her friends and neighbors, of her presumed assailants, and even of Madame Restell, the woman indirectly held responsible for her death.[22]

Placed against the context of these cases, Mary's death was both an exceptional and an ordinary event. It was exceptional because of its unusually violent character, and ordinary because of the way it melded both literally and figuratively with the life of the street; indeed, it echoed themes indicative of less celebrated crimes of its time and place. Again, the saga of the falsely accused wood engraver illustrates this point. Morse, it will be remembered, after he returned from his outing with young Mary Haviland, and before he fled the city and was arrested in Rogers's death, had an altercation with his wife, Martha, a fight played out on the street in full view of the neighbors. As a result of this dispute, Martha, her ear torn, her face battered, swore out a charge of assault and battery against her husband, a charge she later withdrew.[23]

Martha used a common charge; assault and battery was by far the most common complaint and subsumed within it were a variety of different charges. A sampling of such cases in the police court records for the period around Mary's death includes fights between neighbors, accusations of petty theft, claims of domestic violence, and charges of rape and infanticide. Take, for example, the case of Mary O'Shea, who claimed that on June 22, 1841, she was assaulted by Ann Sullivan, "who struck [her] several blows and bit her hand and kicked her, and knocked her about." This altercation was actually part of a larger inter-family dispute; an accompanying complaint was made by her husband, Michael O'Shea, who claimed that Andrew Sullivan "challenged [him] to a fight." This event, like most of its kind, took place in public, probably on the street, determined by who appeared as witnesses: fellow boarders Michael and Catherine Kinney, who lived at the same address on 182

Second Street, as well as neighbors Margaret and Michael Riley and John and Mary Smith, who lived in the next house at 184 Second Street, in addition to several neighbors from adjacent Third Street, Thomas and Ann Kilbride and Catherine Grady.[24] We do not know what issues were at the bottom of this fight, but the magistrate, exercising his power to mete out justice as he saw fit, eventually dismissed the case. It is likely that the opportunity to bring it before the authorities provided some help to the aggrieved, if not a belief that justice had been done. Fights like this between women were not unusual, and appear with regularity among the police records. For example, Elizabeth Goldsmith, a "spinster," swore out a complaint against Sarah Eldridge, claiming that she "struck deponent several blows with her fist, seized her by the hair of her head & forced her down & beat her head on the stair—and otherwise abused her."[25]

To the modern reader these disputes were direct, physical, and very rough. Neighbors struck, bit, and hit each other; they tore at noses and ears and hair. Generally, however, the fights did not result in death. Such extreme consequences of private disputes appear to have been relatively rare; when they occurred they were usually the result of a barroom fight gone out of control, a chase that resulted in a fall, or a blow that proved fatal. Many complaints were issued by wives against husbands, evidence not only of domestic violence, but that women, particularly those of the lower classes, saw the criminal justice system as offering at least some solutions to their plight. Maria Kierman of 18 Watt Street swore out a complaint against her husband, claiming that he was "in the practice of getting intoxicated & abusing" her, and that on January 31 "he struck her."[26] Sometimes a friend or neighbor would corroborate a wife's complaint against her spouse, such as in the claim made by Elizabeth Ann Allen against her husband, Francis. In this case, Oliver Weed, a cordwainer of 20 13th Street, swore that he knew Francis Allen and Elizabeth Ann Allen, his wife—and that "Francis [had] abandoned" his wife "& utterly neglected & refused to provide any thing in and of her support for three weeks now last past, although abundantly able to support his . . . wife."[27]

Other complaints were more serious, such as the complaint of attempted rape by Mary Farrell against William Bolton, a crime prevented by the attention of neighbors who heard her cries in the yard.[28] And still others were tragic and poignant, such as the charge of infanticide against Ann Sexsmith whose newborn baby was found dead by her boardinghouse keeper. Sexsmith, a twenty-year old unmarried umbrella maker, was said to have given birth to a 6 ½ pound child secretly and alone in her room. Several witnesses testified in court, as did two doctors who had examined the child shortly after its death. Ann Sexsmith herself refused to testify (other than stating her name, age, and occupation), and the case was ultimately dismissed.[29]

Whether or not such extant records, the bulk of them confronting the criminal justice system, were proof that crime was actually increasing is even now difficult to measure. Determining crime rates, especially for the early part of the nineteenth century, is a task fraught with difficulty, both because of the lack of consistent and reliable data and because of the quixotic meaning of those numbers that are available. There is no way to simply say that crime per se was increasing. Nineteenth-century record keepers tended to lump all types of crime together in their statistics and often failed to differentiate between complaints, arrests, and convictions, or to distinguish between crimes as widely divergent as assault and battery and homicide. And while the total number of convictions did rise, most were for minor crimes (petit larceny, assault, and battery) and not for more serious ones such as rape or murder. Moreover, shifting attitudes toward social behavior and deviance, especially from the middle classes, as well as changing definitions of crime, altered the kinds of arrests made and determined what crimes warranted arrest and even the extent of further criminal action. Thus, it is difficult to determine to what extent increased arrest, prosecution, and conviction numbers are indicators of accelerated crime or merely reflections of the refinement of judicial procedures and increased social intolerance of certain patterns of behavior.[30]

Nevertheless, by the time of Mary's death, the idea that crime was rampant, that the city was dangerous and out of control, and the way this belief became fixed in the public consciousness was more important than any statistically proved reality. It was this sense of social mayhem that one picks up in the rhetoric about crime that filled the pages of the press and led to endless committee reports and legislative proposals on the state of the city's system of criminal justice. What is important is that many people *thought* that crime was increasing, that they believed the city was becoming more dangerous, that their tolerance of prostitution, bawdy houses, and even public drunkenness was lower, and that women and men, particularly of the middle classes, thought that new methods of policing would make their city safer and more orderly. These perceptions, which blended the fear of crime and social danger with political considerations, and which were aided and encouraged by the press and political battles, facilitated the transformation in policing and even the revision of criminal law.

As I suggested in my earlier discussion of the penny press, following Mary's death the tenor and intensity of the rhetoric of crime and danger increased dramatically, suggesting how a sensational crime expressed both the specific agenda of those who demanded enhanced policing, and the more generalized fear and discontent of others. The Rogers murder was a particularly useful device in fostering hysteria over crime and social disorder. Masking other concerns, the unsolved and particularly sensational death seemed evidence enough of a "savage state of society—without law—without order—and without security of any kind."[31]

By the late 1830s there was already strong agitation not only for changes in the degree of policing and *how* the city should be policed, but for a restructuring of the entire city system, perhaps along the English model. The creation of the Metropolitan Police in London in 1829 offered a viable alternative. As the first modern system organized to prevent crime by a system of all-day and night patrols, the London Police differed significantly from the later New York version of a police force, but provided the framework for policing a large urban area.[32] However, the discussion about policing was not only a debate about the severity or extent of crime, but more fundamentally about new notions of privacy, surveillance, and the control and preventability of criminal behavior.

Those urging police reform for New York City argued that the current system emphasized the post facto "detection" of crime, rather than prevention. "The principal object of the Criminal Courts and Officers of the Police Department has been the detection of crime when committed, and the arrest and punishment of offenders when discovered," read an 1837 Aldermanic report. It argued that "other measures would now be adopted, to prevent as far as may be, the commission of crime as well as to secure its detection and punishment."[33] A later report of the city's Committee on Police Watch and Prisons written after Mary's death, and in anticipation of police reform, reiterated this point: that the "prevention of crime [was] more to be desired than even the arrest of the offender."[34]

The emphasis on prevention was not to be confused with the efforts of social reformers to prevent crime by restructuring the social conditions that created it. On the contrary, no such system of benevolent reform was anticipated or urged by those who advocated a new system of policing; instead, they sought a new police authority based on enhanced surveillance.[35] The aim, in short, was to "suppress the licentiousness and vices" that, they maintained, resulted in crime. This concept of prevention through surveillance evolved instead from the ideology of 1830s evangelical reformers. Drawing on an even earlier and essentially religious tradition, such reformers linked crime to sin and believed both in the significance of individual agency (and therefore the possibility of reform through individual moral regeneration) and in the social consequences of individual behavior.[36]

Issues of sexual conduct were at the heart of moral reform, both in the 1830s when it focused on prostitution and later when that focus became more diffuse. In the anti-prostitution crusades of the late 1830s, led first by moral reformers and then legislators, concern about sexual conduct fused with anti-crime campaigns; vice and crime were regarded by many not only as intimately connected, but as constituting a cause-and-effect relationship. It was in the extended discussion of moral reform that sexual conduct (more than other forms of vice like drinking or gambling) became the arena in which new attitudes about the relationship between private and public behavior were forged and initiated into public policy. In 1837 a proposed "Act for the more effectual punishment of Crime in the City and County of New York" outlawed houses of prostitution, gambling houses, and houses of assignation, or any other "disorderly house"; an additional provision of this act criminalized the sale of "obscene books, paintings or prints" and authorized any Constable or Marshall "to enter such house . . . and take possession of all such books, paintings or prints."[37] Subsequent reports stressed that the laws were defective because they did not punish adultery and seduction, nor did they restrain theaters, and other places of public amusement, "from allowing known prostitutes from being received as part of the audience, and in public view."[38] This report (and others) stopped short of urging the control of prostitution through licensing or other forms of regulation, but still saw issues of sexual conduct as the most important source of criminality.

How much this all had directly to do with the death of Mary Rogers is hard to determine, but clearly the public response to the event created an atmosphere of fear and danger, increasing receptivity to police reform and affirming the need for preventive legislation. The Police Reform Act was finally passed by the New York State Legislature when the Democrats assumed power and went into effect in spring 1845. The new law reflected current concerns about urban law and order, but it was also restrained, providing a framework for prevention instead of an aggressive plan of action. It divided the city into day and night patrol districts by ward, prescribed the number of policemen in each, stipulated the requirements for office (including residency in the same ward, if possible), and determined lines of police authority. It professionalized the police force, bonded the officers, assigned them specific duties, and specified a system of salaries to replace the controversial system of rewards. In short, it modernized the police system and attempted in some moderate way to develop a plan to cope with the needs of a rapidly growing city. Significantly, the restructuring of the police also codified surveillance as an aspect of public policy. Reasserting the old concern with sexual conduct and the places where they believed vice took place, the new law charged the police to report "all suspicious persons, all bawdy houses, receiving shops, pawn broker shops, junk shops . . . gaming houses, and all places where idlers, tipplers, gamblers, and other disorderly and suspicious persons congregate."[39]

Accompanying this new conception of policing, and following the guidelines of the earlier reports on crime, were several new additions to the criminal codes, some just proposed, others passed into law, that criminalized activities previously outside the purview of the state and attempted to regulate the public places within which illicit behaviors presumably took place.[40] A series of acts (which were never passed) mandated incarcerating and fining of brothel keepers and their clients.[41]

Ultimately, and with the help of women's rights activists, laws were enacted that criminalized adultery and seduction—providing punishment for the offending parties and those involved in the "abduction" of young females for the purposes of prostitution. Two proposed laws (also never passed) attempted explicitly to control the free movement of city residents: the first called for the "full and correct register of all persons removing into and out of the Ward . . . wherein shall be mentioned the names, age, height and place of birth"; the second, which reverberated with the memory of Mary Rogers, would have required boardinghouse keepers (as well as keepers of hotels, lodging, houses, and inns) to provide lists of their inhabitants on police request.[42] But perhaps the most important addition to the criminal codes was the 1845 Abortion Law, it too shadowed by the ghost of Mary Rogers.

Policing Sex: The Case of Madame Restell

The same July of Mary's death, a controversy was underway in the Court of General Sessions. Ann Lohman, usually known by her professional name, Madame Restell, was tried for "administering to Ann Maria Purdy certain noxious medicine . . . [and] . . . procuring her a miscarriage by the use of instruments, the same not being necessary to preserve her life."[43] After a very well-publicized trial, the jury convicted Restell of abortion, still a misdemeanor, and she was remanded to prison for one year, a term she never served. This case was Restell's first, one of many "show trials" intended to curtail the lucrative and highly controversial practice of abortion. Concern about the proliferation and commercialization of the practice was significant by the early 1840s; by 1845 that concern was codified in the first of two laws further criminalizing abortion by making it an act of manslaughter. The connection between Restell and Rogers was never proven; but whether Mary received either of her two likely abortions from Restell or any of her associates or not (it was rumored that Restell had a network of abortion establishments, including one in Hoboken), Restell, the abortion issue, and Mary Rogers were inextricably linked in the press, through popular publications like the *National Police Gazette,* which began publication in 1846, and novels like Buntline's *Mysteries and Miseries of New York* that depicted some aspect of the Mary Rogers story. But the links between Rogers and Restell were also more subtle and profound; the passage of the 1845 law against abortion was passed in the State Legislature with the help of Frederick Mather, prominent New York attorney and Mary's Connecticut relation. Moreover, the extended persecution of Madame Restell was based on extensive surveillance, surveillance carried out against women's sexual conduct in the name of crime prevention. The history of abortion has usually focused on the late nineteenth and early twentieth centuries and been figured around the purity campaigns of Anthony Comstock. Ironically, Comstock, who began his career with actions against Restell in the 1870s, used surveillance and entrapment to arrest and indict her in 1874. This indictment and the trial that followed led to Restell's sensational suicide. Thus, the abortion trials of the 1840s that occurred around the period of Mary's own abortion and death were a dress rehearsal for later waves of intense anti-abortion activity.[44]

By the early 1840s abortion had become a significant social and political issue, replacing prostitution as *the* public issue of debate concerning sexual conduct, and becoming a lightning rod in what was already emerging as a contest over privacy and women's sexual rights. Like the earlier crusades against prostitution, those against abortion attempted to condemn and control women's sexual behavior, particularly insofar as that behavior reflected widespread changes in women's lives and sexual practice. Placed within the repressive urban political climate of the 1840s, the attacks on abortion and abortionists gave voice to those who most feared those changes and their consequences. The intensity of the campaigns, expressed especially in the vilification of Madame Restell, was evidence of both the social importance of abortionists and the extent to which they represented a new form of imagined social and sexual danger.

By the 1840s, abortion, long a traditional means of controlling fertility, was both widely and openly practiced in the city. As both James Mohr and Carl Degler have shown, it was also extensively commercialized—well advertised and highly lucrative—and increasingly utilized by women as a means of controlling family size, regardless of marital status, class, or ethnic background.[45] "In the heart of the metropolis," intoned the *Police Gazette*, "she [Restell] holds her bloody empire . . . Her *patients* are of three classes, and her treatment has an equal scope."[46]

In general, as James Mohr argues throughout his book, abortion laws, both before and after 1845, were rarely enforced. Those who were singled out for attack by anti-abortion zealots tended, like Restell, to be female practitioners working outside the medical profession. Frequently highly visible, partially because of their advertising but also as a result of the attacks on them, these women plied their trade in open war with a culture requiring privacy on matters pertaining to female physiology and sexuality. As the story of Mary Rogers constantly reminds us, the transition from a rural to an urban culture brought vastly increased independence for women, changing sexual mores, and altered notions about family size and domestic life. Ironically, while New York derived much of its negative reputation as a city of vice and sin, the reality was that this new urban culture had fewer mechanisms than rural cultures for incorporating illegitimate children or even accommodating large families. Reinforcing these cultural contradictions, emerging bourgeois codes were intertwined with elaborate and highly restrictive codes of sexual behavior that translated into attempts to control nonprocreative sexual activity, particularly, but not only, outside of marriage. Of course, the technology of contraception lagged far behind social need, and repressive ideology declared matters of contraception and abortion contraband, even criminal.

The abortion practice of Restell thus provided an open and therefore highly controversial statement that social transformation had outfaced the institutional means of contending with those changes. Moreover, the extended attack on abortion and its practitioners served not only as a way of attacking the trade itself, but the social changes it represented. Ironically, the extended discourse around the abortion issue allowed a culturally legitimate means of discussing issues of sexual practice, and even of giving them public exposure.

In the anti-abortion crusades of this antebellum period a new term was coined, *Restellism*, which referred to an entire range of issues associated with women, sex, and the mystery of the female body. Most specifically, it referred to all nonprocreative female sexual behavior. Said one contemporary physician in an extended attack on Restell: "Madame Restell offered to those who would not control their appetites, impunity." "First," he claimed, "there were her powders as a preventive; if these failed, as without the greatest care they might, there were the monthly pills to overcome obstructions; and if these were unsuccessful . . . there, as a last resort, was an asylum in the house of Madame Restell—private delivery, and a hired nurse; powerful drugs to produce abortion, or the use of mechanical means to bring about a premature delivery."[47]

Restell herself became an inseparable component of this period's discourse about abortion. The quintessential anti-type of domestic literature and mid-nineteenth-century social ideology, she was depicted as brash, vulgar, audacious, and duplicitous, a woman, "tricked out in gorgeous finery." Always reviled, she was known alternatively as "madame killer," a "she devil," a "hag," and the keeper of a "bloody empire." Even after the Civil War, her notoriety was no less dramatic; she continued to inspire attacks unprecedented in the annals of urban culture and crime literature. Urban guidebooks devoted whole chapters to "The Wickedest Woman in Town," or "The Wickedest Woman in New York." Indeed, in the cautionary tales about the sexual danger of the early city, Restell, often a companion and adjunct of the figure of the "sensuous seducer," was the evil villain, the wicked witch. Pictorial images of her vividly illustrated this construction, featuring her as a grotesque hag, and, in the case of the *Police Gazette*, a witch with bat wings holding a dead baby.[48]

At least for the early years, it is hard to tell how much of her public persona was self-defined and how much simply the result of her public demonization. While she attained great wealth, drove teams of white horses through the city streets, and lived in fabulous mansions, her or-

THE FEMALE ABORTIONIST.

Figure 5-2   *This illustration from the* Police Gazette *(March 13, 1847) reflected the popular demonization of Madame Restell, depicting her holding a bat with a dead baby in its jaws. (Courtesy, American Antiquarian Society.)*

igins were humble. Restell was born Anna Trow in Painswick, England, in 1812. The daughter of a farm laborer, she married the village tailor, a man named Henry Sommers, and together they emigrated to New York in 1831. Two years later Henry died of typhoid fever, leaving Anna widowed with a young daughter. She supported herself working as a milliner, and in 1835 married Charles Lohman, a compositor (who, according to one account, worked for the *Herald*). It is unclear where Restell learned her trade (she claimed the tutelage of a French uncle) but in the 1830s she assumed her nom de plume (French-sounding pseudonyms were common for abortionists) and began practicing as a midwife and abortionist. By 1838 she advertised widely in the local papers, marketing her pills to "remove obstructions" and "powders to Prevent conception" at five dollars a packet. Restell also kept a lying-in hospital at her house at 148 Greenwich Street, a fact corroborated by extensive information from women who had given birth under her protection. More well known was Restell's increasingly controversial abortion practice; she performed abortions at various stages of pregnancy, including after the point of quickening, and by means of medicinal and mechanical methods available at the time.[49]

Restell and her second husband worked as a team. Under the pseudonym A. M. Mauriceau (after the late seventeenth-century French physician, Francois Mauriceau), Charles Lohman is credited with a popular medical advice book for women, *The Private Woman's Medical Companion*. First published in 1847, two years after the passage of the new abortion law under which Restell was later indicted for manslaughter, the work appeared under the copyright of her brother, Joseph Trow, and may well have been written by Restell herself. It was a frank and comprehensive treatise on women's reproductive health; included were sections on pregnancy, menstruation, miscarriage, and infertility. Mauriceau urged women to know their bodies and take charge of their own reproductive health. Further, he presented an open plea for information and knowledge, arguing that only "prejudice or ignorance thinks that if men and women acquired the knowledge whereby to improve their condition as social and moral beings, guard against disease and preserve their health, that *perhaps,* it might lead to immorality and vice."[50]

The Private Woman's Medical Companion was blasphemous in several ways. It offered homeopathic remedies for specific complaints and medical conditions, advocated self-treatment or treatment by midwives or other non-professional "physicians," and thus publicly confronted the medical establishment at precisely the moment when it was seeking to close its ranks through professionalization. (The American Medical Association was founded in 1847.) More sensationally, it preached the benefits of contraception, arguing that "control" over the "instinct of reproduction, would be salutary, moral, civilizing." To these ends, Mauriceau claimed to know one Dr. M. M. Desomeaux's "Preventive to Conception," the "great discovery by which pregnancy could be prevented." This preparation, he informed his readers, could be purchased from him by mail for $10 per packet.[51]

Contrary to most accounts, Mauriceau did not advocate abortion after quickening, maintaining that it was only to be used as a "last resort" to terminate a pregnancy. He did, however, claim that in its early stages (presumably before quickening) what he called a "miscarriage" could be effected with ordinary care and "attended without any danger." He concluded with the point that a "skilled and practiced obstetrician will impart no pain," and again provided his address should such services be required.[52] The information in this work, a blend of contemporary free thinking and popular medical practice, was neither strikingly new nor original. Nevertheless, it went well beyond other contemporary American marriage manuals and clearly broke prevailing codes in its use of descriptive language, in its insistence on the value of open information about sexuality and reproductive health, and in the noticeable absence of moral prescriptives concerning sexual behavior.

The actual assaults on Restell began in 1839. In April she was arrested on a charge brought by William Purdy who claimed that Restell performed an abortion on his wife, Anna, who survived the procedure, but died later in April 1841; in August she was charged again when a young woman, Ann Dahl, claimed that Restell had sold her pills intended to induce abortion. The charges in the Dahl case were dropped, but based on the Purdy complaint Restell was arrested and her case brought to trial on July 14, 1841. The trial ended on July 20, precisely at the time of the first penny press stories of Mary Rogers's disappearance.[53] Moreover, the cast of public officials in the Restell case was the same that investigated Rogers's disappearance and death: Justice Merritt, who oversaw the Rogers investigation, had taken the original affidavits against Restell from Purdy and his wife; and Judge Mordecai Noah, accused of insufficient action against suspects in the Rogers affair (and Bennett's bete noir), presided over the case when it came to trial. (On July 19, during the trial, Noah served Bennett with three counts of libel.)[54] Like Mary Rogers, Ann Maria Purdy sought an abortion, and, like Rogers, Purdy died, a death the prosecution sought to prove was the result of an abortion performed by Restell. Unlike Rogers, however, Purdy survived beyond the procedure and in fact lived until April 28, 1841. Immediately after Purdy's death the authorities moved in on Restell and arrested her. (Restell was actually at Purdy's deathbed, suggesting a more protracted and complex relationship between the two women.) Restell was charged with two counts, both misdemeanors: "Administering to one Ann Maria Purdy certain noxious medicine drug or substance unknown—she being at the time pregnant but not quick child—thereby procuring her miscarriage by the use of instruments— the same not being necessary to preserve her life, and not having been advised by two physicians to be necessary for such purpose."[55]

The charge against Restell was based on provisions established in 1829 stating that abortion after quickening (the point at which life could be detected) was an act of manslaughter or, in the event of the death of the mother, murder. (There were, however, provisions for therapeutic abortions, to save the life of the mother.) In the case of abortion of an unquickened fetus (unless necessary to preserve the life of the mother), a convicted abortionist could receive imprisonment for up to one year, and/or a fine not exceeding five hundred dollars.[56]

When the Purdy case came to trial before Judge Noah in mid-July, it was well covered by the press; the *Herald* printed most of the trial's transcript, complete with commentary on the witnesses.[57] As a public event and spectacle it contained many of the same elements of the Mary

Rogers saga that would fill the same pages in the coming weeks. Unable to keep Purdy's controversial deathbed statement attesting to an abortion by Restell out of the court proceedings, the defense tried to impugn Purdy's character as well as that of her husband. Restell's attorney also protested the legalities of the procedures and claimed entrapment, a claim that would be used more effectively in a later abortion trial against Restell. After Judge Noah admitted Purdy's statement as evidence, the jury convicted Restell and she was remanded to prison. Restell appealed and was granted a new trial, but the charges were mysteriously dropped.[58]

Two other important trials against Restell, both in the 1840s, were linked to the death of Mary Rogers. In 1846 a Philadelphia woman, Mary Applegate, swore a complaint to Mayor William Hevemeyer against Restell. Applegate claimed that she had been seduced and made pregnant by a lover who arranged for her to deliver the child at Restell's on the promise that this would end his responsibility in the affair. The young woman went to Restell's, arriving a month before she was due and remaining until she delivered a healthy girl. Applegate insisted that she refused to allow the child to be put out for adoption. However, she claimed that after the child was sent to a wet nurse she never saw the child again, and thus she charged Restell with baby stealing.[59] The case, again well publicized in the press (this time the *National Police Gazette* published Applegate's affidavit), was used to incite mob action, not unlike that of the 1830s brothel riots. An account written somewhat after the event asserted that it "created the wildest public excitement." A crowd that had gathered in a hall on Cortland Street apparently took to the street and began heading in the direction of Restell's Greenwich Street residence. The police were dispatched and met the mob:

> There was at once a shout to clean out the police and tear down the house. Some of the more excited of the mob advanced upon the officers of the law, but the latter closing their lines solidly, defied the rioters. Not only that, but five of the most demonstrative were seized, disarmed of their clubs, and incontinently marched off to the station house. This determined act on the part of the police, undoubtedly saved [Restell's] the house from destruction and themselves from rough handling and defeat.[60]

Commenting on the crowd and the event, *The Police Gazette* claimed that "Curses loud and deep upon Restell and her coadjutors were rife amid the crowd, and cries of 'Haul her out!' 'Where is Mary Applegate's child?' 'Where's the thousand children murdered in this house?' 'Who murdered Mary Rogers?' "[61]

A year later, in 1847, a third case against Restell raised issues of privacy and surveillance. Once again Restell was charged with performing an abortion. This time it was five counts of manslaughter for "feloniously, unlawful, wickedly and wilfully performing acts intended to induce a Miscarriage of Maria Bodine, who was pregnant with a quick child."[62] In the trial, which became a theatrical event, Bodine, a young domestic from New Jersey, revealed particularly graphic details about the abortion procedures, while again, like Mary Applegate, providing an extended narrative of seduction, and betrayal. In many ways the issues were the same as in the Purdy trial: a "successful" abortion, a "seduced" woman of meager means, police lying in wait for an arrest, the failing health of the subject herself. The major difference, and it was crucial, was that the law had changed; under the new law both the abortion practitioner and the woman undergoing the abortion were now liable for manslaughter.

The 1845 Abortion Law, whose first clause was revised in 1846, reiterated the provisions of the 1829 law in most ways, but added several significant provisions. It held every person liable who prescribed (in addition to those who administered) any measures toward an abortion that resulted in the death of either the child or the mother. In the event of the death of a quick child, the charge was manslaughter in the second degree; in cases involving pregnancy prior to quickening and resulting in a miscarriage (abortion), the charge was a misdemeanor. These provisions were directly aimed at abortionists and went significantly beyond the direct active intervention required by the earlier law. Most significant was the provision of section 3 of the new law that held the woman herself, as well as the abortionist, criminally liable of a misdemeanor for the abortion, irrespective of stage of pregnancy. Although rarely prosecuted, this was the provision under which Bodine was originally arrested. While technically leaving only procedures before quickening outside the intent of the law (it was considered impossible to determine pregnancy before quickening), the law effectively outlawed abortion and declared war on commercial abortionists.[63]

With the new law in effect, the prosecution hoped to convict Restell of second-degree manslaughter. Bodine, who was twenty-six, worked as a housekeeper for Joseph Cook, a widower and cotton manufacturer in Ramapo, New Jersey, by whom she claimed she had become pregnant. Six months into the pregnancy, she sought the services of Restell. After an initial consultation and examination she claimed to have returned for the procedure, which she described in full detail to a court packed with spectators. The abortion was successful, but Bodine maintained it was accompanied by significant hemorrhaging, leaving her in frail health. Bodine also claimed that under the provisions of the 1845/46 law that made her criminally liable, she herself had been arrested after the initial consultation with Restell. Clearly, this was what convinced her to bring charges against Restell. As a result, Restell was arrested, charged, and released on bail of $10,000, a sum she provided in cash, plus an additional thousand for good measure.[64]

Restell was defended by James Brady, a prominent Tammany attorney who argued that the charge against her was the result of a conspiracy by physicians and the Mayor, whom he claimed was "the sapient father of this suit. But for him as midwife, the case would never have been born, though I fear, like some of his other labors, this case will prove a still born foetus." He also asserted that Maria Bodine's medical problems were caused by a previous condition, namely that she "was ill of a disease about which there ought not be no mawkish sensibility in giving it its right name." Lastly, he charged that Bodine was of dubious reputation: "I am instructed to say and to prove, that at an early period of her life she gave herself up to this licentious course of general and promiscuous concubinage, and so precocious was she that at a very early term of comparative youth so thoroughly corrupt and abandoned had this girl become that she had destroyed her health, her character, and family reputation."[65]

Brady did not attempt to prove Restell innocent of practicing abortion, nor did he ever contend Bodine's claim that she had been a client. Instead he sought to prove that Restell had been set up from the start. "We intend to show," he said, "that an officer had been directed to watch these premises, to follow visitors, take down the names and residence, and preserve the memorandum," and that an "officer was placed on guard to watch all who went in or out of Restell's house." Nothing less, he said, than a "system of espionage was carried on by the public authorities for the purpose of gaining positive evidence against the prisoner."[66] Brady also questioned the role of public opinion and the methods of the prosecutors: "Never," he said, "had a prisoner more legal obstacles thrown in the way of her defense—no papers, no information, no affidavits had been afforded her. It was more an attempt to sacrifice an individual to the bad passion of the multitude than the administration of pure justice." His client, he continued, had "been hunted down like a poor deer by ravenous wolves." In particular, he singled out the role of the press, "that mighty but misused power [that had] "pronounced a verdict of guilty against her before the trial."[67]

Unable to prove manslaughter, the jury went for a lesser charge and found Restell guilty of a misdemeanor, "for administering to a pregnant woman . . . any medicine or drug . . . with intent to procure . . . miscarriage."[68] On conviction she was sentenced to one year in the penitentiary on Blackwell's Island. The judge denied both a stay of execution and a request for bail. Restell was remanded temporarily to the city jail until she was sent to serve her sentence on Blackwell's.

In the press, the courts, and even the streets, the crusades against Restell were fierce and protracted and spanned the entire length of her public career from the first charges against her in 1839 until her sensational suicide in 1878. While it is easy to identify the immediate sources of these attacks—physicians seeking to control all aspects of medical practice, pamphleteers and popular writers of salacious literature who marketed her story for profit, and agents of the state who sought to control sexual conduct through legislation—these alone do not explain the intensity of the attacks or their virulence.[69]

Rather, to understand the depth of the attack is to grasp the extent to which Restell, more than any other woman of this period, represented a direct assault on emerging nineteenth-century conventions of gender, social relations, and public display. She was an outspoken, independent, and wealthy woman who was unwilling to be silenced, and she was enormously successful. Like Bennett she was flamboyant, confrontational, and delighted in publicity; unlike Bennett, she was female. In her work and through her person she forced the open acknowledgment of changing sexual habits and practices and of the attempt by women, married or not and of all classes, to control fertility. Restell's success, coupled with the very public and detailed accounts of her practice, also made it clear that female sexuality, as well as illegitimate births, could no longer be publicly dismissed as having to do with women of the lower classes or prostitutes. By the mid-1840s Restell was clearly serving the city's (and perhaps the nation's) male and female elite, a situation underscored by the plaintiff Mary Applegate who claimed that while in residence at Restell's Greenwich Street house she "met . . . a widow from Albany who was being supported by a married man . . . who was president of one of the banks"; a Philadelphia woman who had her expenses defrayed by "one of the Congressmen"; and another client who was the daughter of a New York family "in one of the first circles." The latter had been brought to the care of Mrs. Restell by her own mother, who had been heard to say she "would rather submit to anything else, than the disgrace." Other sources similarly stressed the nature of Restell's practice and her importance in the world of fashion, where masking impropriety was more important than the transgression itself.[70]

To be sure, the indictments and public trials that were such an important aspect of the wars against Restell always involved poor women whose social reputations were considered inconsequential. Easily manipulated by the police and anti-abortion crusaders, these women were vulnerable and, as in the case of Maria Bodine, under considerable pressure from the police. But abortion was an issue that transcended class, and Restell's wealth was not simply the consequence of tending the poor. The fee for a "premature delivery" was anywhere between $20 and $100 (more for extended lying-in), well beyond the means of the average seamstress or immigrant wife of the period. The state, no doubt, cared little about Anna Purdy, Mary Applegate, or Maria Bodine—they were pawns in a larger agenda concerning women, sexual freedom, and sexual privacy.[71]

As women at the center of urban publicity, Restell and Mary Rogers would seem to share little resemblance: Rogers the vulnerable and youthful victim; Restell the dangerous and powerful woman who could control, through her own independent agency and her knowledge of women's bodies, the mysterious processes of birthing and conception. And if Mary signified the mystification of these poorly understood areas of women's private lives, Restell was the ultimate agent of demystification. But Restell and Rogers, or rather their public representations, served similar social functions. Both legitimized public narratives of private behavior and social relations; each in her own way confronted fundamentally that female behavior most socially proscribed—sex, pregnancy, and the open display of the female body. And each, again in her own distinct way, crossed the boundaries of class and gender so critical to social order in the antebellum city.

Ultimately it was George Wilkes, publisher of the *National Police Gazette*, who made the connection between Restell and Rogers explicit, thereby linking the fate of Rogers forever after in public presentation with Madame Restell. Wilkes, who targeted abortion and its practitioners in the paper's sensational stories, unsuccessfully attempted to provide closure on the Rogers death:

> We do not speak in parables. There is mystery yet to be cleared up which sent a thrill of horror and a sensation of profound excitement through the length and breadth of the land! We speak of the unfortunate Mary Rogers. Experience and futile effort have proved that we have heretofore followed a wrong trail. The wretched girl was last seen in the direction of Madame Restell's house. The dreadfully lacerated body at Weehawken Bluff bore the marks of no ordinary violation. The hat found near the spot, the day after the location of the body, was dry though it had rained the night before! These are strange but strong facts, and when taken in consideration with the other fact that the recently convicted Madame Costello [another well-known abortionist, reputed to be an associate of Restell] kept an abortion house in Hoboken at that very time, and was acting as an agent of Restell, it challenges our minds for the most horrible suspicions. Such are these abortionists! Such their deeds, and such their dens of crime![72]

Postscript: Convergent Genealogy

As if to underscore this connection between Restell and Rogers—fictive or real—we might finally argue that the 1845 Abortion Law was written in both their names. For in that critical year of 1845, a curious combination of individuals converged on the Albany legislature to create the new punitive abortion law. The passage of that law, it has been correctly argued, was the result of the combined and intensive efforts of a powerful physicians' lobby, led by Dr. Gunning Bedford. According to abortion historian James Mohr, Bedford, a Catholic, spoke as a "professional competitor of Restell, seeking to establish a specialty in the fields of gynecology and obstetrics." Within the New York State legislature the new abortion law was carefully squired through the legislative process by Assemblyman Abraham Thompson, Jr., from New York City.[73]

But a strange combination of legislators figures prominently in bringing this legislation about. Two familiar names surface in the New York State Senate and Assembly Journals for 1846.[74] The first was that of one Frederick Ellsworth Mather, a Democrat, who served for one year only, 1845, as a delegate from New York City. A New York attorney and Yale graduate, Mather was a distant cousin of Mary's. A member of the Hartford branch of the Mather family, he was of Mary's generation (born in 1815), and his offices were on Nassau Street. Surely Frederick Mather knew of the actual circumstances of Mary's death. He was, moreover, a man of some prominence; as a member of the New England Society, he was particularly identified with medical charities as well as with the New York Association for Improving the Condition of the Poor. Indeed, his connection to the medical establishment combined with this relation to Mary may explain his opportune presence as a member of the legislator at a key moment.[75]

Another famous name in the annals of anti-abortion crusades jumps out from the pages of the New York State Assembly *Journals*: C. Comstock, who served as an Assemblyman from Oneida County, and was a key member of the Judiciary Committee to which the abortion bill was referred in its course through the 1845 legislature. Comstock was not *the* Anthony Comstock, who pursued Madame Restell to her death and led the anti-vice crusades of the latter part of the century. That Comstock was not born until 1845. However, C. Comstock was a distant relation, making for what is surely an odd convergence of familial and political genealogy. And, as if to complete this absurd picture of intersecting genealogical trails, the Comstocks, like the Mathers and the Rogerses, were originally from Lyme and New London, Connecticut.[76]

6
POE DETECTS MARIE:
POE, MARY ROGERS, AND
THE BIRTH OF DETECTIVE
FICTION

*The detective novel was born in the margins of literature dealing with
"causes célèbre."*
Antonio Gramsci from *Prison Notebooks* (c. 1934–35)[1]

*I*N the opening pages of "The Mystery of Marie Roget," Edgar Allan
Poe's imaginative work based on the Mary Rogers case, Poe writes:
"I can call to mind no similar occurrence producing so general and so
intense an effect." Referring, of course, to all the intense public reaction
to the event that he termed the "New York tragedy," he concluded that
it was "the atrocity of this murder . . . the youth and beauty of the victim," and, above all, "her previous notoriety" that conspired to bring
about this "intense excitement." Far from being a detached observer,
Poe was engaged by this "intense excitement" as well as by the opportunity it offered to write an extended meditation on the death of a beautiful woman, his acknowledged favorite subject of composition. Like the
press reports on which it is based, the tale is a narrative of a violent and
sexually motivated death set ostensibly in 1840s Paris (a Paris that
closely resembles New York)—a narrative figured around a beautiful
female body that has already begun the process of decomposition. For
Poe, this body, the body of Marie/Mary, becomes both the subject and
object of an elaborate puzzle, a puzzle decoded by the "diseased mind"
of Poe's celebrated detective hero, C. Auguste Dupin. Here sex, violent
death, and the city once again converge, initiating the actual, if unack-
nowledged, unities of the modern detective genre around the actual
death of Mary Rogers. Through this literary transformation, what Lydia
Child understood as the "Tragedy of Mary Rogers" was reinvented by
Poe as the "New York tragedy."[2]

Poe's imaginative creation is a densely complicated story, over-

Figure 6–1 An 1848 daguerreotype of Edgar Allan Poe. (Courtesy, American
Antiquarian Society.)

wrought perhaps in some regards, insufficient in others, but in it own
way strangely compelling. With time, Poe's fictive "Marie" has even
superseded the "real" or historical Mary, just as Poe's recreation of the
events (if not his solution to the crime) has infused all subsequent accounts of the Rogers death. This is the consequence of Poe's unique
sensitivity to the elements from which the event was constructed—its
urban setting, its origins in journalism, and even the problematic identity of Mary herself. Poe's achievement was considerable; not only did
he invent the narrative framework through which we see the Mary Rogers story, he structured the way in which we associate violent death with
urban life as an event of intellectual rather than emotional engagement,
and as a mystery predicated on complex, but always depersonalized,
male/female relations.

The Problematic Spectacle

Poe began work on "The Mystery of Marie Roget" within a year of Mary's death and before the public disclosures of an abortion at Mrs. Loss's roadside inn. It was the second in what would be his trilogy of pioneering detective works, all set in nineteenth-century Paris and crafted around the character of C. Auguste Dupin, the model of the detective hero.[3] The tale was distinct from the other two stories in the trilogy, "The Murders in the Rue Morgue" and "The Purloined Letter," because in this work Poe tried to create a story out of an actual unsolved murder, using accounts in the contemporary press—the "public prints"—as his source for the work. Writing to the Boston publisher, George Roberts, in June 1842 in an attempt to sell the story, he declared his intention to "enter into a very long and rigorous analysis" of the "New York tragedy." His purpose, he said, was to design a literary method "altogether novel in literature"; to show that the subject [of the murder] had been "hitherto unapproached"; and, finally, to create "an analysis of the true principles which should direct inquiry in similar cases."[4] In that sense the "Marie Roget" story is *not* like "Rue Morgue" or "Purloined Letter." In the latter Poe invented the fictional detective story, while in "Marie Roget" he is inventing yet another literary form, the nonfiction fiction.[5]

Indeed, Poe added little embellishment to the public prints about the disappearance and death of Mary Rogers. The tale consists of lengthy passages drawn almost verbatim from the penny press, passages Dupin uses to reconstruct the crime as well as the imagined life of Marie/Mary.[6] He was true to the details of the New York setting and the principal characters; he merely transposed proper names and places to their fictive French equivalents. Thus Mary Rogers, cigar seller, became Marie Roget, *grisette* and salesgirl in a perfumerie; her mother, Phebe, became the boardinghouse keeper, Estelle Roget; her lover, Daniel Payne, Jacques St.v Eustache, and so on. But the changes were only nominal and thinly disguised. At the outset Poe informed his readers that the "extraordinary details which I am now called upon to make public will be found to form, as regards sequence of time, the primary branch of a series of scarcely intelligible coincidences whose secondary or concluding branch will be recognized by all readers in the late murder of MARY CECILIA ROGERS, at New York."[7] And in his final version of the story, published three years after its initial appearance, Poe provided his reader with footnote references to people, places, and newspaper sources: "On the original publication of 'Marie Roget,' the footnotes now appended were considered unnecessary; but the lapse of several years since the tragedy upon which this tale is based, renders it expedient to give them, and also to say a few words in explanation of the general design."[8] Poe was actually quite concerned about the relationship between what he called real and ideal events. He wrote at least two complete versions of the work: the first published serially in Snowden's *Ladies' Companion* in November and December 1842 and February 1843; the second and revised version in his own edited collection, *Tales*, published in 1845. The changes for the revised and final version did not transform the substance of the story, only amended it while allowing for the possibility of an alternative solution—namely an abortion. Thus the version in *Ladies' Companion* speaks of "a murder perpetrated, in the thicket at the Barriere du Roule, by a lover, or at least by an intimate and secret associate of the deceased," while in *Tales* it reads: "We have attained the idea **either of a fatal accident under the roof of Madame Deluc,** or of a murder perpetrated, in the thicket at the Barriere du Roule." This, as well as other smaller changes, allowed in the later version for an abortion as the cause of death, an allowance Poe surely had to acknowledge by 1845—coincidentally the year of the new abortion law.[9]

When considered along with his 1840 story, "The Man of the Crowd," "Marie Roget" was one of four works written by Poe in the early 1840s to be set within a cosmopolitan city. With the exception of the "Purloined Letter," which takes place indoors, all these stories use the architecture and culture of the city to unfold their narratives.[10] And in "Marie Roget" and "Rue Morgue" Poe took the significance offered by the urban context one step further, developing in it the detective genre, a form generally associated with the rise of the city and the rise of mass culture. Here the older form of the gothic tale with its typically country or rural setting was replaced by the modernist conundrum of an unsolved crime of death in the city.[11] It was a form that drew much from the Victorian street literature and melodrama that Poe knew so well: the pamphleteers of Grub Street, *The Newgate Calendar* and the Penny Dreadfuls, the newer genre of the urban mystery novel.[12] But, in Poe's works, murder and mystery moved from the street to a conscious aesthetic form that was consonant with the deeper psychological themes created by the tensions of a new urban culture. In these works the tensions and dynamics are large: over the familiar nineteenth-century literary preoccupation with love and death are superimposed the battle between the irrational emotional life and the logic of intellect and, not the least, the chaos of daily life in conflict with the imposition of social order. And, most important, in these tales, and especially in "Rue Morgue" and "Marie Roget," Poe introduced the art of ratiocination or detecting: an act of intellectual finesse carried out by a male observer—the brilliant, if quirky, detective.

Despite the originality of its narrative form, in the annals of literary history and criticism "The Mystery of Marie Roget" has alternately been dismissed as of little literary value or studied for its verisimilitude—its conformity (or lack of) to the real events. The former approach has tended to regard the tale as essentially outside the canon of Poe's *oeuvre*,

as a somewhat aberrant and marginal text of detective fiction sand-
wiched between his two "important" ratiocinative works, "The Murders
in the Rue Morgue" and "The Purloined Letter."[13] The latter approach
has focused on the two separate versions of the tale (1843 and 1845)
and on whether or not Poe actually solved the crime.[14] Thus the critic
William Wimsatt argued that Poe not only solved the crime, but identified (but did not disclose) the criminal. Wimsatt accuses the naval
officer, Captain William A. Spencer (1793–1854), providing the reasons
outlined in Chapter 2.[15]

More recently, John Walsh has argued that well before the 1845
version Poe was deeply troubled about the resolution of his story. Walsh
contends that the final installment that appeared in February 1843 was
actually delayed by Poe in a frantic attempt to account for Mrs. Loss's
deathbed confession about the alleged abortion, a confession that became public just as Poe had completed the version for *Ladies' Companion*. Walsh contends that Poe, having asserted that he had solved the
crime as a murder by a single assassin, feared for his reputation, literary
and otherwise. Poe, Walsh argues, came to New York in the fall of 1842
and persuaded Snowden to postpone publication of the final installment
so that he could make changes that would conform with the new disclosures. This possibility and the conjecture that Poe not only came to
New York but that he also visited New Jersey in an attempt to get more
information, are supported, Walsh claims, by an article appearing in an
1889 edition of *Harpers Monthly*. The article offers as evidence of Poe's
presence in Jersey City the information that he visited his friend Mary
Starr Jennings, while he was "on a spree."

The problem with Walsh's thesis about Poe's revisions is quite simply the date. According to Jennings's recollection, Poe, who had been
in Philadelphia at the time, came to visit her in June 1842. If this visit
was occasioned by the Loss confession of November 1842, the timing
would of course have been off. Walsh, however, concludes that Jennings
had been incorrect about the date (it did concern an event that had
taken place over forty years earlier) and that Poe's visit had actually
occurred in the fall, not the spring of 1842.[16]

Although these speculations are interesting, the narrow way they attempt to connect the story to history misses the point, focusing on what
Poe himself might have termed the "outskirts" or the marginalia. Rather
than simply a barely fictionalized recreation of "fact," the story is consistent with the canon of Poe's literary and critical work, reflecting his
traditional preoccupation with themes of death and dying (especially the
death of women), with epistemological questions, and with a sense of
the world, particularly the urban world, as a place where order and
reason are always open to subversion by chance, danger, and destruction. The historical significance of "Marie Roget" lies not in Poe's ability or inability to solve a real crime, or in his faithfulness, or lack of it,
to the circumstances of the "real" event, but rather in his understanding

of the crime as a quintessential event of modern urban culture. In this regard "Marie Roget" is not so much an attempt (successful or unsuccessful) at crime solving, but a complementary text to the other urban stories about modernity and urban life.

Because my reading of "Marie Roget" shifts the emphasis of most approaches to the story I will consider it here in conjunction with the other Dupin tales, especially "The Murder in the Rue Morgue," as well as with "The Man of the Crowd," rather than as an isolated exercise in reportage. My purpose is to explore Poe's fictive representation of the Mary Rogers mystery as an imaginative work, suggesting how Poe's own reading of the event both defined and redefined its contemporary meaning, providing a way of reading mystery and the violent death of a woman within the context of the cityscape, inscribing gender into urban detective and mystery fiction, and ultimately, if ironically, even fulfilling his own stated purpose in creating "an analysis of the true principles which should direct inquiry in similar cases."[17]

Poe Detects the City

Edgar Poe is an unlikely urbanist. His tales usually conjure up visions of decaying mansions covered with dense green foliage, interiors with secret vaults and dungeons, dark moldy rooms wrapped in cobwebs, and far-off, almost magical, places that harken back to some earlier premodern era and sensibility. Indeed, the hectic world of an urban metropolis with its busy streets, crowded houses, and noisy entertainments seems remarkably far away from what we usually think of as Poe's imaginary landscape. Yet these urban stories, all completed by the early 1840s—the critical years in the development of modern urban consciousness—are not only located in cities but in the capital cities of the nineteenth century—London, Paris, and New York. More than mere backdrops to the tales, these descriptions are crucial to the narrative, locating us in a specific time and place. The depictions of Paris, London, or New York are visual as well as kinetic and move us to experience quite viscerally the recreated street scenes. Ironically, these urban settings are more imaginary and metaphoric than real. For while Poe lived and worked in several important American cities (Baltimore, Philadelphia, and New York), he placed his urban tales in cities he hardly knew at all. He had lived in London only as a child and had never even seen Paris. (Indeed his faulty and fanciful reconstruction of the Paris streets led Baudelaire to comment that it was unnecessary "to point out that Edgar Poe never came to Paris.")[18] And, perverse as usual, when he did choose to tell a story associated with a particular city he knew well (New York in "The Mystery of Marie Roget") he chose to "set" the story in Paris.

The works all draw on specifically urban events and situations: a man frantically moving through a dark urban crowd; the mysterious and exceptionally brutal killing of an elderly woman and her daughter in a residential Parisian neighborhood; the discovery of the murdered and abused body of a beautiful young woman in the Hudson River. These are by now sensational and familiar events that titillate with their explicit themes of violence and bodily destruction and implicit sexual overtones. In fashioning them, Poe at once confirms our sense of the modern city as a dangerous place of desolating loneliness where random violence and sexually motivated murder take place. But he also establishes the city as a place teeming with activity, discovery, and possibility—a place not only of death but also of life, sensuality, and mystery.

Poe thought seriously about the city both as a site of cosmopolitan culture and as a place in which to explore the modern psyche. Indeed, Poe's city tales are filled with the rich detail, nuances, and fearsome turmoil of urban life. Through them Poe insinuates us into the streets and neighborhoods of fictionalized but surprisingly recognizable metropolises and then uses the fictional recreations to explore the questions and dilemmas posed by the rise of the actual city and modern urban culture: the Babel-like cacophony of many different tongues, the loss of identity, the isolation of one within an urban crowd, the legibility of the city itself. Poe's relationship to the city and to modern city culture is complex and ambivalent. Yet, taken as a group, Poe's city tales raise important literary, and indirectly cultural, issues about the development of mystery as a genre, the significance of the detective as a modern hero, the use of melodrama and conundrums, and, perhaps most strikingly and graphically, the depiction of the atomized female body in modern fiction.

Poe first introduces us to the urban setting in "The Man of the Crowd," his 1840 story set in nineteenth-century London. While neither a story of ratiocination or even of murder, it is first and foremost a story of the city and establishes the urban landscape for the ratiocinative tales that follow. The story is told to us by a narrator who has just ventured out into the city streets after a long and presumably debilitating illness, and who now watches the London crowd through the window of a coffee-house. From here he observes the street scene and becomes fascinated with the frantic journey of an elderly and disheveled man whom he follows for two nights and a day through the London streets. The story presents no particular mystery to be solved and has essentially no plot; in fact, the narrator's pursuit leads nowhere. Nonetheless, through the story Poe moves us directly into the cityscape, using the crowd and the city as central characters in the narrative. Baudelaire, who translated this and other Poe tales into French, considered Poe's narrator and nocturnal wanderer a *flaneur*. Later, in his essay on the French poet, Walter Benjamin rejected Baudelaire's view: "The man of the crowd is no *flaneur*," he wrote. "He exemplifies rather what had to become of the *flaneur* once he was deprived of the milieu to which he belonged."

Benjamin, who saw the story as an important link in the development of an urban modernist tradition, noted the strong affinity Baudelaire found with Poe, an affinity that was linked to Poe's "images of big-city crowds." Poe, he tells us, captured for Baudelaire the classic example of the crowd and that crowd in turn came to represent what Benjamin called "the agitated veil" through which Baudelaire saw his own Paris.[19]

Poe's portrayal of the crowd in this story is indeed extraordinary; it takes on a life of its own, ominous and secretive, ebbing and flowing and moving with an irrepressible force and mysterious erotic power. The crowd, which is analogous to the sea with its powerful tides, is controlled by no one, but instead becomes a medium through which we come to see the city, its varied inhabitants, and ultimately ourselves. Looking through the window, the narrator introduces us to the crowd:

> But, as darkness came on, the throng momently increased; and by the time the lamps were well lighted, two dense and continuous tides of population were rushing past the door. At this particular period of the evening I had never before been in a similar situation and the tumultuous sea of human heads filled me therefore with a delicious novelty of emotion. I gave up, at length all care of things within the hotel and became absorbed in contemplation of the scene without.[20]

Our observer begins by looking at the "passengers in masses," thinking of them "in their aggregate relations." Soon, however, he "descended to details, and regarded with minute interest the innumerable varieties of figure, dress, air, gait, visage, and expression of countenance." The crowd becomes complex, a mixture of all urban types ranging from those "pointedly termed decent . . . who were undoubtedly noblemen, merchants, attorneys, tradesmen, stock jobbers" to "clerks, gamblers and the urban lowlife of peddlers, mendicants, prostitutes, organ grinders monkey-exhibiters and ballad mongers." Each type is defined by its own particular style, by clothing and the artifacts of class and occupation but also by body posture and distinguishing countenances. Among all of these, the lowlife engages him the most for they present him with "the darker and deeper themes for speculation."[21] Ironically, Poe's narrator seems to think that he can analyze this crowd by identifying various urban types. He is of course wrong. The crowd, like the city it mirrors (and ultimately like the city "mystery" of "Marie Roget"), is a text that cannot be read. Thus "The Man of the Crowd" is a story of *failed* detection, the narrator's reliance is ultimately subverted by the unpredictable forces of the modern city.

In the course of the story the narrator is taken by a particular "countenance which at once arrested and absorbed [his] attention," that of a decrepit old man who begins to move furtively through the nighttime masses. As he pursues the stranger though the dark, the narrator traverses a variety of London neighborhoods until, as the "shades of the second evening came on" and feeling "weary until death . . . he stopped in front of the wanderer gazing at him steadfastly in the face." The old man does not even notice him, and the narrator comes to understand the man of the crowd as an emblem of solitude, isolation, and inscrutability, even as he loses himself among a multitude. He is the one "who refuses to be alone." "*He is the man of the crowd,*" the man who "cannot be read."[22]

As Poe first draws it in "The Man of the Crowd," the city is a place that allowed individuals like the story's narrator, or even as I will suggest, like Marie/Mary herself, to experience a freedom of movement and possibility that would have been unknown in more provincial or traditional settings. With its complex web of streets, its patterned and varied landscapes, and its endless array of characters, the city conveyed excitement, energy, and activity. (While this activity is liberating and sexual and dangerous for Marie, it infuses the man of the crowd with a strange, albeit temporary, source of kinetic energy.) Poe thus plunges us into the realm of ordinary city scenes (the streets, the neighborhood, the crowd) and extracts from them extraordinary events—experiences that are uniquely important and symbolic and at once possible within the context of everyday life while they also transcend it. Here the ordinary flows into art and reemerges as the source of mystery, horror, and death. (This anticipates Baudelaire's conversion of the mundane and the grotesque into the artistic and the beautiful.[23]) And the city, the locus of ordinary lives and events, becomes a space that permits both freedom and confinement, interconnectedness and fragmentation, energy and excitement as well as loneliness and death.

Poe's cities are places fraught with meaning. Often regarded as evil in the context of nineteenth-century American culture, for Poe they are at best morally neutral. Thus Poe's city is potentially dangerous not just because it is the city, but because of the particular way in which it facilitates the disordering of human relationships and releases the controls of traditional society. In Poe's world the city becomes a public space in which modern men and women, operating essentially alone, create the artifacts and assume the roles of modern culture only to become the arbitrary victims of their own creations. This urban space turns into an urban wilderness, analogous in its understated and charged eroticism to the natural wilderness of the sea or the frontier. And within this urban wilderness Poe explores a set of distinctly modern themes: alienation, identity, sexuality, and the atomization of contemporary life.

Like the man of the crowd, around whom is created an aura of desperate loneliness, Poe's other urban characters—Dupin and his companion, the murdered mother and daughter in "Rue Morgue," as well as Marie Roget—all operate within city spaces as social isolates; they are individuals without traditional families or even meaningful kin relationships. When such relationships do exist, they are odd or eccentric as in "Rue Morgue" or fraught with generational discontinuity as in "The Mystery of Marie Roget." What happens to these urban charac-

ters happens to them alone, and largely because of the extent to which
estrangement and even anomie is a characteristic of modern city life.
Thus Marie Roget proceeds toward her death through familiar streets.
A known neighborhood figure, she nevertheless "might have proceeded," Poe tells us, "at any given period, by any one of the many
routes between her residence and that of her aunt, without meeting a
single individual whom she knew or by whom she was known."[24] Within
the city all these characters live within their private worlds. The city has
become the space where men and women are simultaneously alone and
members of the crowd: They are a public composed of private and
isolated souls. Poe introduces us to two pairs of such isolated individuals
and their idiosyncratic public world in "The Murders in the Rue
Morgue," the first of the ratiocinative tales.

The unnamed American narrator of the stories and C. August Dupin, the prototype of the brilliant detective hero, are at once doubles of
each other and complementary parts of some divided whole.[25] Bound
in an intense and clandestine, if only implicit, homoerotic relationship
that removes them from the social world, these two men have taken
refuge "in a time eaten and grotesque mansion [in a] retired and des-
olate portion of the Faubourg St. Germaine."[26] Dupin and his new companion ("we should have been regarded as madmen," says the narrator)
lived in "seclusion" and "existed within ourselves alone." "Enamored
of the night," they hid behind the closed shutters during the daylight
hours, "admitted no visitors" and "sallied forth" for lengthy nocturnal
walks through the streets of Parisian neighborhoods "arm and arm, continuing the topics of the day or roaming far and wide until a late hour
seeking amid the lights and shadows of the populous city, that infinity
of mental excitement which quiet observation can afford."[27] Dupin and
his close companion are city strollers—urban flaneurs—who lead us on
our journey through the city streets, using city clues to solve city crimes.
We see the city, its people, and its crimes through their eyes alone, the
studied male gaze of a deracinated intellectual and his friend providing
the lens through which we see and come to interpret this urban world.

Even in his construction of the character Dupin, Poe contended with
the psychic and spiritual fragmentation of things urban. Indeed, Dupin,
who meets Poe's own conception of a "bi-part" soul with both a creative
and a "resolvent" aspect, is a supreme example of a fragmented personality, split between reason and emotion, a man who lives in a world
dominated by his own private reveries. Dupin is riddled with contradictions and thus mirrors the fragmented aspects of Poe's urban spaces
while he simultaneously resolves their inherent chaos and random disorder. Dupin, genius, "madman," and perennial observer who lives
within the context of his own bizarre imagination, becomes our guide
to the modern city. And here Poe's sense of irony, humor, and hoaxing
is at its most brilliant and beguiling. This gentleman who leads us on

our journey through the city streets, using city clues to solve city crimes and then retreating once again behind the closed doors of his own domestic interior, is the maddest of any urban character we encounter. He is a man who cannot confront the daylight, but who "sees" through the shadows. As our urban escort and "detective," he is an urban sociologist, a man who observes the city, its people, and its happenings from the perspective of a detached observer. A true reader of the city, Dupin uses urban texts for evidence, plays with problems of knowing and understanding, and solves the most "outre" of urban events. The ultimate modern man, he watches and waits, employing reason and patience to outwit a given situation. Using clues from the material world, he proceeds to solve the crime and in so doing transforms the chaotic and incomprehensible city into a mapped-out terrain, one that in the end is reordered and reassembled for us by an *apparently* rational observer.[28]

Like any true "modern man" Dupin maintains a detached stance, but his detachment helps mask what is essentially an amoral sensibility. Able to explore the most horrific events without betraying any emotion or moral judgment, he is the ultimate voyeur, watching without participating and without engaging in the emotional or physical aspects of life itself. While others react with horror and repulsion at the murder scene and corpses in "Rue Morgue" and "Marie Roget," Dupin remains steadfastly unmoved, his passivity placing in relief the more emotional, and presumably more human, responses of others. It is in the final analysis Dupin who detects the city for us, using both scientific rationalism and romantic intuition as the "tools" of his trade. By detecting the city, Dupin appears to make sense out of its chaos, solve its mysteries, even piece its bodies back together, and bring things under control. Ultimately, he makes understandable bizarre and inexplicable events. But while Dupin may solve the crime, he merely gives the illusion of solving the more complex puzzles of city life by applying what is only an orderly veneer to a disorderly and distinctly urban world. The deepest spiritual questions of providence and life and death are beyond him.

In "The Murders in the Rue Morgue" Dupin and his companion are confronted with the newspaper account—not unlike that which will figure so prominently in "Marie Roget"—of the barbaric murder of two other withdrawn and nocturnal characters, Madame L'Espanayer and her daughter. Their bodies, brutalized like Mary's, but also dismembered, are found in, or near, their top-floor apartment house residence. Although the apartment is in total disarray, the door has remained locked, there is no sign of possible entry or exit, and no clues are found. Witnesses, however, have all heard two voices in the middle of the night: one in French (uttering the phrase "Mon Dieu"), but the other in some unidentified, foreign tongue (perhaps English, Spanish, Italian, etc.). The murder scene itself is grotesque: "The apartment was in the wild-

est disorder—the furniture broken and thrown about in all directions. . . . On a chair lay a razor, besmeared with blood. On the hearth
were two or three long and thick tresses of grey human hair, also dabbed
with blood." Of the two bodies one, that of the daughter, was found
head downward and forced up the chimney, while that of the mother
was outside "with her throat so entirely cut that, upon attempt to raise
her, the head fell off."[29] The police are dumbfounded and ineffectual
and Dupin alone is able to solve the murder.

His solution is bizarre, even humorous, for the murderer proves to
be an orangutan—a beast owned and brought to Paris by a Malaysian
sailor. Only such a creature, Dupin rapidly concludes, could have the
physical characteristics that matched the available clues: an enormous
reach and a harsh voice without language. Only this creature could have
negotiated the system of windows and alleys, and have been able to exert
the sheer physical force necessary for the brutality of this crime.

But what is important initially is the relationship Dupin establishes
early in the tale between himself, his city, and his intellectual discoveries.
For Dupin's insights are consistently and intimately related to his ability
to use his immediate landscape to solve the crime. Dupin's brilliance is
revealed early in the story as we proceed through the nighttime streets
of Paris with him and his companion. He displays an uncanny ability
to read his friend's mind—to "fathom" his "soul," an exercise he engages in by analyzing and decoding the Parisian street scene before him.
The particulars of this everyday landscape—the horses, the local characters, even the patterning of the cobblestones on the street—form for
him a series of logical association that, he infers, have their corollary
within the mind of his companion.[30] As they walk down a "long dirty
street in the vicinity of the Palais Royal," Dupin lays out his abductive
method, explaining the process by which he moved back and forth between his companion's expressions and the visual images created by the
street scene to understand the associational links that formed the content of his friend's mind:

> You kept your eyes upon the ground—glancing, with a petulant ex-
> pression, at the holes and ruts in the pavement, (so that I saw you were
> still thinking of the stones,) until we reached the little alley called La-
> martine which has been paved, by way of experiment, with the over-
> lapping and riveted blocks. Here your countenance brightened up, and,
> perceiving your lips move, I could not doubt that you murmured the
> word "stereotomy," a term very affectedly applied to this species of
> pavement.[31]

These details allow Dupin to move from the exterior and visually
specific world of Paris to the interior of his companion's mind. The
particulars of the street have become not only clues to the workings of
his intellect, but the contextual framework for comprehending the inner
life itself. This movement from the labyrinthine streets of Paris to the

labyrinthine mind of Dupin and his companion is rapidly juxtaposed with another set of external and internal worlds: that of the street with its relative or at least habitual order, and the chaos of the apartment where the two murder victims lie in total disarray.

Metropolitan urban culture also figures prominently in the resolution to this bizarre murder set in a Parisian apartment house. Deriving his proof from the "journeaux," Dupin discovers the essential clues. The paper tells him that among the witnesses were a mix of artisans and foreigners typical of a cosmopolitan city. Among these are many French men and women—a laundress, a tobacconist, a surgeon—but also a Dutch restaurateur, an English tailor, a Spanish undertaker, and an Italian confectioner. Their identity and testimony provide Dupin with the crucial information he needs: namely that each believed the voice heard in the night to be foreign, yet that it was familiar to no one.

> The witnesses, as you remark, agreed about the gruff voice; they were here unanimous. But in regard to the shrill voice, the peculiarity is— not that they disagreed—but that, while an Italian, an Englishman, a Spaniard, a Hollander, and a Frenchman attempted to describe it, each one spoke of it as that *of a foreigner*. Each is sure that it was not the choice of one of his own countrymen. Each likens it—not to the choice of an individual of any nation with whose language he is conversant— but the converse.[32]

Dupin concludes that the voice was in fact not of human origin, confirming his opinion that the murderer was not human at all, but a beast aping man. The modern apartment house with its many tongues signifies that definitively urban structure—the tower of Babel. Thus does the crime and its patently absurd resolution provide a "study" of the city in all its chaos, danger, and irrationality. And the crime leaves even Dupin at a loss; the reason he symbolizes and claims to live by has been unmasked and consequently he is left powerless. Indeed, the power of reason itself is satirized and proven absurd by the crime's ultimate solution.

Language is not the sole issue of separation in the city. In "The Mystery of Marie Roget" the city as social and intellectual space displaces the city as architectural space. Thus, while the built environment of the city is an important feature of the story, what is characteristically urban in "Marie Roget" is not the cityscape that serves as a context and point of reference, but rather Marie/Mary herself, her distinct identity as an urban woman, who is "gay but not abject,"[33] and the penny press—the "public prints"—that serves as both a subject of the narrative as well as the medium through which that narrative is conveyed. Indeed, this story is written—almost transcribed—through the press reports, just as it will be resolved through them. And while the crowd is the signifier of the urban in "The Man of the Crowd," or the apartment house in "Rue Morgue," so the press serves a similar function in "Marie Roget."

Poe even regards Marie/Mary herself as a media creation, a device that distances and depersonalized her, adding to the tale's intellectual aura. Thus, while in the actual public prints James Gordon Bennett used the death of Mary Rogers as a crime of social rather than personal violation and as a symbol of the pervasiveness of social danger in the "polluted" city,[34] Poe sees the crime as a vehicle for intellectual activity and engagement. The act of ratiocination, the conundrum, had become the essential subject. The rooting out of evil, the purging of the malefactor as a means of reclaiming social and civic order, is for Poe, ultimately of little consequence.

The Public Prints: Poe Gives a Lesson in Reading

An auratic of cool intellectuality and rationality pervades all three Dupin tales, providing an apt frame for three narratives about reading, language, and the interpretation of literary texts. In "The Murders in the Rue Morgue" Dupin reads the newspapers and "detects" the babble of many tongues. In "The Purloined Letter" the essential correspondence is quite literally before his eyes; he had only to see and read it correctly (an act accomplished by reading it upside down). And in "The Mystery of Marie Roget," the last of the urban texts, the penny press itself is at the center of the tale. In "Marie Roget," however, the act of reading moves to another level, for here Poe tries to resolve the mystery by staying completely within the frame offered by the so-called "public prints." And unlike the press clips in "Rue Morgue" that are fictive and contrived, the clips he employs here are "real." " 'The Mystery of Marie Roget' " was "composed," he reminds us, "at a distance from the scene of the atrocity, and with no other means of investigation than the newspapers afforded."[35]

Poe's own relationship to the urban press and the publishing world was always complicated. A journalist by necessity, if not always by choice, he was steeped in the newspaper culture of his period. In the 1840s his work was published in several New York City dailies, including the *Sun,* the *Mirror,* the *Dollar Newspaper,* the *Weekly Tribune,* and so on; in 1844 working as a reporter he covered the city beat in "Doings of Gotham" a series for the Pennsylvania paper, *The Columbia Spy.*[36] And in January 1845, he joined Charles F. Briggs first as an assistant and then as a co-editor, and eventually as sole editor of the *Broadway Journal,* a literary and cultural review with a strong focus on the cultural life of New York.[37] Throughout his career Poe was at the center of the expanding publishing industry and more attuned than many of his fellow writers to the vagaries of the marketplace and its effect on the entire panorama of literary production. Constantly plagued by the need to maintain a literary stance while still seeking to create a commercially viable commodity, he was at once contemptuous of the new commercial culture and desirous of the financial rewards and popularity it offered. He did, however, reserve a particular disdain for the penny press, its unabashed pandering to the masses through what he called "puffery" and its presentation of what was merely "frivolous and fashionable."[38] As stories that concern different forms of "public prints," all three Dupin tales engage in a verbal dialogue with the press, its audience, and even its reporters.

In "Rue Morgue" he specifically lambastes journalistic sensationalism. "We should bear in mind," says Dupin, "that, in general, it is the object of our newspapers rather to create a sensation—to make a point—than to further the cause of truth. The latter is only pursued when it seems coincident with the former. The print which merely falls in with ordinary opinion (however well founded this opinion may be) earns for itself no credit with the mob. The mass of the people regard as profound only him who suggests *pungent contradictions* of the general idea."[39] In "Rue Morgue" he specifically took on the mass circulation dailies as disseminators of crime news by spoofing both the form itself and its audience. Here a grizzly crime story is pushed to the limit of credibility, not only in its representation of violence, but in the bizarre solution it offers for the crime. The murderer is an ape, a precivilized (or is it more civilized) version of man who, like the human murderer in "Marie Roget," has gone amuck within the city. Originally, this ape had been captured like a slave, and brought by ship to France where a sailor "at length succeeded in lodging it safely at his own residence in Paris." Wounded, the beast was kept in seclusion, but he learned quickly the habits of its master who found it one night "razor in hand, and fully lathered . . . sitting before a looking glass attempting the operation of shaving."[40] A manlike creature without language, this ape nevertheless exhibits human characteristics. But in creating an ape-murderer Poe apes us; he plays with our thirst for violence and makes fun of our gullibility. And in the end the ape is no more than an animal brought from the wild into the artificial landscape of the city where he proceeds to adapt, literally aping men, until he commits the ultimate human/anti-human act—murder.

Whereas "Rue Morgue" echoes with allusions to the slave trade or perhaps the influx of immigrants, "The Purloined Letter," written after "Marie Roget," is concerned with a theme already raised in connection with the "public prints" in the Rogers case: the public consequences of private interactions. But in this work Poe's finger is pointed quite directly at one reporter well known for brazenly crossing the boundaries between private and public. This was of course William Attree, the crime reporter for the *Herald* who had created both the Helen Jewett and Mary Rogers stories. In a final cryptic revelation at the end of the work, Poe has Dupin utter these coded words regarding the Minister D_ _ _ _ :

"I knew, he would feel some curiosity in regard to the identity of the
person who had outwitted him, I thought it a pity not to give him a
clue, He is well acquainted with my MS., and I just copied into the
middle of the blank sheet the words—
                    —Un dessein si funeste,
            s'il n'est digne d'Atree, est digne de Thyeste.

They are to be found in Crebillon's Atree."[41]*

The reference here is double edged: to Prosper-Jolyot de Crebillon's
(1674–1762), *Atree and Thyeste,* and to the horrific Greek tale of betrayal,
incest, and murder on which it is based, but also to William Attree, a
reporter whose own "MS" as well as his "MO" were widely known to
the denizens of Nassau Street. Attree, Poe need not remind us, belonged
to the "house" of James Gordon Bennett.

Poe's interest in the press extended well beyond it as an object of
ridicule and satire. He was fascinated with the way the contemporary
press served as an instrument of communication and a disseminator of
public knowledge. In this, his engagement of the press itself as a literary
subject was consistent with his ongoing preoccupation with how we
come to know what we know and with how we translate and interpret
our worldly experiences. In "The Mystery of Marie Roget" he explores
just how widely divergent individual or private readings of "public
prints" can be.

At the opening of "Marie Roget" the narrator informs us that after
solving the case set forth in "Rue Morgue," he and Dupin had removed
themselves from the social world: Dupin had "relapsed into his old habits of moody reverie," and the narrator, "Prone at all times, to abstraction, readily fell in with his humor." They continued to occupy their
chambers in the Faubourg Saint Germaine, "gave the Future to the
winds and slumbered tranquilly in the Present, weaving the dull world
around us into dreams." Two years have presumably been spent in these
reveries, but they are presently aroused by the events which the narrator
proceeds to recreate—the story of the disappearance and presumed
murder of the "young, beautiful and notorious" Marie Roget. As readers we are provided with a brief, if unrevealing, synopsis of Marie/Mary's
family history, an account of her earlier disappearance, as well as the
news of her recent absence and the discovery of her corpse floating in
the Seine. And we are told that the inability of the police to solve the
mystery of her death has led G—— (the inadequate Police Prefect of
the three detective tales) to seek Dupin's aid. Dupin accepts the case
and promptly sends his companion to procure from the Prefecture, "a
full report of all the evidence elicited, and, from the various newspaper
offices, a copy of every paper in which, from first to last, had been

---

* "So baleful a plan, if unworthy of Atreus, is worthy of Thysestes."

published any decisive information in regard to this sad affair." These materials—police reports and newspaper accounts (the public prints)—are Dupin's evidence, the city texts through which he will solve the crime. And unlike the man of the crowd, the man whom Poe identifies as "er lasst sich nicht lesen"—he who does not permit himself to be read—these texts, the public prints, are *legible* to the careful reader.[42]

The narrator recounts that several individuals were arrested and discharged and that "a thousand contradictory rumors were circulated, and journalists busied themselves in suggestions." Included "among these rumors and suggestions," he continues, was "the one that attracted the most notice . . . the idea that the corpse found in the Seine was that of some other unfortunate" and not Marie at all. (Here Poe locates the *subject* of identity, of Marie, of the killer, of the reason for her death; but more important he addresses identity as an ontological problematic, an issue I address below.) At this juncture in the tale the narrator turns directly to what he calls "literal translations," key passages from *L'Etoile* (*Brother Jonathan*), *Le Commercial* (*N.Y. Journal of Commerce*), and *Le Soleil* (*Evening Post*). These focus on three separate aspects of the case: the literal identity of the body (whether it was Marie's); whether or not she was killed by a gang; and the questions about the actual site of the murder—whether the clothes discovered in a woodland spot near Madame DeLuc's (Mrs. Loss's) roadside inn were put there afterwards. The texts of the newspaper accounts the tale provides are lengthy and discursive; seldom do they pertain to only one issue, but instead, like the actual prints, they jump from point to point in an associative and seemingly haphazard manner.[43]

The narrative then shifts to Dupin. He proceeds with a lengthy discourse in which he first rebuts the premises offered by the narrator's newspaper selections, and, second, provides some selections of his own, explaining their particular significance: "I will examine the newspapers more generally than you have as yet done. So far, we have only reconnoitered the field of investigation; but it will be strange indeed if a comprehensive survey, such as I propose, of the public prints, will not afford us some minute points which shall establish a direction for inquiry."[44] In dismissing the evidence gathered by the narrator, Dupin expounds at length on the behavior of drowned bodies (when and how and under what conditions they rise, on how the body might be identified) and concludes, therefore, that the body found was Marie's. He goes on to refute the idea that Marie was abducted and murdered by a gang, and dismisses *L'Etoile*'s discussion of the woodland spot as the site of the death in the same breath that he accuses the paper of behaving like a "parrot"—a reference to the way the paper "merely repeated the individual items of the already published opinion."[45]

At this juncture Dupin moves to what he calls "other investigations" and turns away from what he terms the "interior points of this tragedy . . . [to] . . . concentrate . . . upon its outskirts." "Not the least usual error," he says, "in investigations such as this, is the limiting of inquiry to the immediate, with total disregard to the collateral or circumstantial events."[46] Dupin now offers his own selection of the "public prints" and these consist of quotations of a very different, and only apparently, insignificant sort. Two of these concern Marie/Mary herself, her previous disappearance and reappearance, and the information that during that week she was "in the company of a young naval officer, much noted for his debaucheries," a man with whom she was supposed to have quarrelled. Another one of these selections concerns the dismissal of Mennais (Payne) as a suspect in the case, while yet another reiterates the theory that Marie was the victim of a gang of blackguards. The remaining two selections are more obtuse. The first tells of the death of a young girl who while on an outing with her family across the Seine (Hudson) was seized by a gang, "carried out into the stream, gagged, brutally treated, and finally taken to the shore at a point not too far from that at which she had originally entered the boat with her parents." The second tells of a boat found floating on the Seine that was towed by a bargeman to the barge office. The next day, the paper noted that the boat had disappeared.[47]

Dupin now turns to this evidence and concludes the following: that Marie/Mary went off with the same individual with whom she had disappeared three years earlier: that she intended to elope with him; that the clothing was placed there many days after the murder; that Mary was murdered by a "fatal accident" or a lone assassin and not a gang; and that the assassin was a "swarthy" naval officer. "Let us sum up," says Dupin in Poe's final version:

> We have attained the idea **either of a fatal accident under the roof of Madame Deluc, or** of a murder perpetrated, in the thicket at the Barriere du Roule, by a lover, or at least by an intimate and secret associate of the deceased. This associate is of swarthy complexion. This complexion, the "hitch" in the bandage and the "sailor's knot," with which the bonnet-ribbon is tied point to a seaman. His companionship with the deceased, a gay, but not abject young girl, designates him as above the grade of the common sailor. . . . The circumstance of the first elopement, as mentioned by *Le Mercurie*, tends to blend the idea of this seaman with that of the "naval officer" who is first known to have led the unfortunate into crime. [**"We are not forced to suppose a premeditated design of murder or of violation. But there was the friendly shelter of the thicket, and the approach of rain— there was opportunity and strong temptation—and then a sudden and violent wrong, to be concealed only by one of darker dye."**][48]

Thus, through the series of deductions based on selected accounts, Dupin solves the first part of his mystery. He has shown his ability to solve the crime by a flamboyant demonstration of his abilities in reading. But as Poe's ambivalent title suggests, the mystery is not the mystery of the crime, or, as is the case with "The Man of the Crowd," the mystery of the city alone: it is the mystery of Marie.

Landscaping the Female Body: The Mystery of Marie Roget

Insofar as "Marie Roget" is an extended meditation on the death of a "girl young, beautiful and notorious"—a beautiful woman—it serves as an antinome to Poe's other works on the same subject.[49] Without the effusive display of emotion, the mannerist, almost decadent, eccentricities of expression that characterize "Ligeia" or "Eleanora," the story is both anti-romantic and unsentimental. It features none of Poe's familiar conceits on the subject of female death. Absent are the intimate deathbed scene, reanimation, the funereal architecture of tombs and cemeteries, the experiences of bereavement and mourning. And what Edward Davidson, referring to Poe's scenic representations of death and dying, calls Poe's verbal landscape of death is replaced by the landscape of the city, with its apartment houses and labyrinthine maze of streets.[50] Replacing the language of sentiment, Poe turns to the language of rationalism and scientific observation: instead of the "foliage of many thousands of forest trees" that encase the young lovers in "Eleanora," or the "dim and decaying city by the Rhine"[51] that shrouds the fading Ligeia, we have the watery grave of the Seine and the "polluted" streets of Paris. In this tale Poe approached the subject of female death, not with longing and desire, but with disengaged, depersonalized detachment and dispassion. The death of a beautiful woman has become the subject of an elaborate riddle: a conundrum figured around a corpse. Just as the hard landscape of the city displaces the lush landscape of the country, so reason displaces sentiment in this unique tale of violent female death. And while the "public prints" serve as the agency of Poe's reconstruction of events, so the body itself become the subject of the story's central riddle: the *mystery* of Marie Roget.

Poe first approached violent female death as an issue of rational analysis in "The Murders in the Rue Morgue." Here the two women had been attacked with a "ferocity brutal," their destroyed and even dismembered bodies battered beyond recognition, signaling a "butchery without motive," "a grotesque horror" "absolutely alien from humanity." The body of Mademoiselle Camille L'Espanayer still "quite warm" bore the marks and bruises of her recent struggle with her attacker: "Upon the face were many severe scratches, and, upon the throat, dark bruises and deep indentations of finger nails, as if the deceased had been throttled to death." But the worst violence was reserved for the mother, "the old lady." (This term is used to refer to both the mother in "Rue Morgue" and Marie's own mother, Estelle Roget. It was also the term

THE MYSTERY OF MARIE ROGET.—*Page* 130.

Figure 6-2 *Illustration of boaters fishing the body of Marie Roget out of the River Seine. From an English version of Poe's stories,* Tales of Mystery, Imagination and Humour, *published in London in 1852. (Courtesy, American Antiquarian Society.)*

Arthur Crommelin used to refer to Phebe Rogers after Mary's death.) In a paved yard the police come upon her corpse, "her throat so entirely cut that, upon an attempt to raise her, the head fell off. The body, as well as the head was fearfully mutilated—the former so much so as scarcely to retain any semblance of humanity."[52]

In "Marie Roget" Poe retreats from the horrific descriptions that run through "Rue Morgue," but his description here is even more chilling because of its false scientism, its feigned detachment. It is interesting that given the opportunity to expound on the body (even to quote the more lurid passages of the penny press), Poe chose, almost perversely, a stance of emotional distance. Marie, in other words, seems to hold for Poe little of the compelling attraction of a Ligeia, or the other creations of his own vivid imagination. In confronting the "real" signified by Marie, Poe retreats; the "ideal" remains for him a much more compelling erotic subject. In thus becoming the subject of rational analysis instead of the object of feeling, Marie/Mary has become a physical rather than a spiritual body, and ironically less erotic. Faceless and nameless, she is once again, as in the newspaper chronicles, a decomposing mass. For this re-presentation of the body Poe had only to revise the already published coroner's report, leaving out the drama of the crime's imagined reenactment featured in the original. Poe's revised version is as follows.

> The face was suffused with dark blood, some of which issued from the mouth. No foam was seen, as in the case of the merely drowned. There was no discoloration in the cellular tissue. About the throat were bruises and impressions of fingers. The arms were bent over on the chest and were rigid. The right hand was clenched; the left partially open. On the left wrist were two circular excoriations, apparently the effect of ropes, or of a rope in more than one volution. A part of the right wrist, also, was much chafed as well as the back throughout its extent, but more especially at the shoulder-blades. In bringing the body to the shore the fishermen had attached it to a rope; but none of the excoriations had been effected by this. The flesh of the neck was much swollen. There were no cuts apparent, or bruises which appeared the effect of blows. A piece of lace was found tied so tightly around the neck as to be hidden from sight; it was completely buried in the flesh, and it was fastened by a knot which lay just under the left ear. This alone would have sufficed to produce death. The medical testimony spoke confidently of the virtuous character of the deceased. She had been subjected, it said, to brutal violence. The corpse was in such condition when found, that there could have been no difficulty in its recognition by friends.[53]

From this dry adaptation of the actual coroner's report of the body, Poe proceeds to describe Marie's/Mary's costume, or those objects that adorn and mask the physical body: her dress, lace, muslin slip, bonnet. Moreover, as Poe reveals, these commodities signify both Marie's social class status ("gay but not abject") and her presumed easy availability ("her previous notoriety"), as well as the commodification of the sexual act itself. Even more than the physical body with its marks and bruises, they are clues toward solving the crime. More important, they are clues to the *mystery* of Marie/Mary herself, clues to her *identity*. "Nothing," Poe informs us, "is more vague than impressions of identity." Thus, as the subject of a pseudo-scientific investigation, what Poe impishly called, "busy-bodyism," the adorned but faceless body of Marie provides the vehicle for Poe to ponder the story's central problematic—the question of identity. In "Marie Roget" the ontology of identity has replaced the ontology of death, a subject Poe ironically approaches through the landscape of the decomposing physical body of the already dead Marie.[54]

Poe begins by confronting identity as an issue of physical identification: "The body" he tells us, "must be distinguished from that of any other murdered female." But once again Poe moves quickly from the body's distinguishing characteristics, hair, skin, and feet, to what covers the body: Mary's many effects—garters, shoes, bonnets, and petticoats. And ultimately he needs both the body and its costume to establish her identity with any certainty. "They [the garters] alone, would have established her identity. But it is not that the corpse was found to have the garters of the missing girl, or found to have her shoes, or her bonnet, or the flowers of her bonnet, or her feet a peculiar mark upon them, or her general size and appearance—it is that the corpse had each and *all collectively*."[55]

One might also argue that Poe's concentration on these details, the "outskirts" [Poe's term] so to speak, rather than on the corpse itself, is an act of displacement, and a way to avoid confronting that subject that he never mentions: rape. For the critic Naomi Shor, this avoidance is critical, but as she suggests, it is not absent. Pointing to the significance of what Poe calls the "hitch"—the cloth that was looped around the body "affording *a handle* by which to carry the body"—she argues that "the hitch designates the locus of violence, while at the same time the use of the word 'bandage' attests to a wish to cover up and bind the wound. It is, in a degraded form, the veil that male authors are forever drawing over the female sexual organs, thereby creating mysteries." "The real mystery of Marie Roget," she writes, "lies hidden beneath the multiple circumvolutions of the text; the hitch is, to parody Freud, the navel of the tale."[56]

But while Poe might have veered away from confronting the fully exposed and violated body of Marie, he moved toward confronting her sexuality in other ways. The concentration on petticoats and garters are clues to this aspect of Marie's/Mary's persona. It is sexual "identity" that holds for Poe the real secrets of Mary's death. And here Poe is almost startlingly original. He gives the fictive Marie an identity of her very own, one that conforms to no preconceived formula, one that stares in the face of the creations of the popular press, and also one that gets to the heart of the issues avoided in the more popular constructions of the "identity" of Mary. For Poe, Mary/Marie is a *grisette*, a girl, "notorious but not abject," a girl with a secret life. And it is this private and secret Mary that Poe briefly conjures in order to solve the crime; the part the penny press cannot or will not uncover.

Thus is Marie's/Mary's identity tied firmly by Dupin not to Marie's death, but rather to her "life" and particularly her romantic life. For Poe argues that Marie went off willingly with a man other than her fiancé, St. Eustache. "Who, then," asks Dupin, "is the secret lover, of whom the relatives (*at least most of them*) know nothing, but whom Marie meets upon the morning of Sunday, and who is so deeply in her confidence, that she hesitates not to remain with him until the shades of the evening descend, amid the solitary groves of the Barriere du Rhoule? Who is that secret lover, I ask, of whom, at least, *most* of the relatives know nothing?"⁵⁷ Here Dupin's method is similar to the technique in "Rue Morgue" and "Purloined Letter"—to insert into a riddle a secret or unexplained presence.

Marie quite literally comes alive, not as the destroyed subject of reanimation but as a living being, as Poe endows Marie with a voice, as well as agency. Poe is unique here: no other chronicler of the case gave Mary either a voice or an intellect. Poe transforms the public Mary, Mary the victim, into a conscious, even scheming young woman. Getting into the mind of the character, reconstructing as he did earlier in "Rue Morgue," Dupin asserts:

> We may imagine her thinking thus,—"I am to meet a certain person for the purpose of elopement, or for certain other purposes known only to myself. It is necessary that there be no chance of interruption—there must be sufficient given to elude pursuit—I will give it to be understood that I shall visit and spend the day with my aunt at the Rue de Dromes—I will tell St. Eustache not to call for me until dark—in this way my absence from home for the longest possible period, without causing suspicion or anxiety, will be accounted for, and I shall gain more time than in any other manner. . . . as it is my desire *never* to return—or not for some weeks—or not until certain concealments are effected—the gaining of time is the only point about which I need give myself any concern."⁵⁸

Dupin's selected passages also contain two that refer back to Marie's/ Mary's previous elopement (her disappearance) years earlier. His point is that Marie having once gone off with a secret lover probably went off with him again, and it is this unknown man who is the swarthy naval officer, and hence the murderer in Poe's tale. But the importance of this section is not what it reveals about the killer, but what it tells about Marie. Poe's private Mary is a woman with a secret past and this past, at once romantic and illicit, demystifies Marie and thus provides the *resolution* to both the story and the crime.

The *mystery* of Marie Roget revolves around what Poe repeatedly referred to as the "question of identity." As the ultimate conundrum of the work, this mystery has several components: the identity of the body; the identity of the killer; and finally, and most important, the identity of Marie herself. Aptly, the city setting with its densely populated streets, its possibility for anonymity, simultaneously helps to define Marie and mask the identity of her killer. Marie, the *grisette*, the girl "abject but not notorious," is, like the man of the crowd, a stroller of the city streets, a girl who could use the city to disappear alone or with a companion and thus deliberately evade her mother and her fiancé.

In the final analysis Dupin, Poe's urban flaneur, can solve only those aspects of the crime that have clues in material reality. (In this he is unlike the Dupin of the other tales.) Thus, referring to the identity of the body, he notes: "The question of identity was readily determined, or should have been." "But," he reminds us, "there were other points to be ascertained." These other points—"the mystery which enshrouded" the fate of the "unhappy Mary Cecilia Rogers," like truth itself—continue to elude him. Here even reason fails. In a final confession, appended awkwardly to the revised version of the tale, Poe reminds us that resolving an imagined event, however parallel to the real one, is insufficient for revealing truth.[59]

> But let it not for a moment be supposed that, in proceeding with the sad narrative of Marie from the epoch just mentioned, and in tracing to its *denouement* the mystery which enshrouded her, it is my covert design to hint at an extension of the parallel, or even to suggest that the measures adopted in Paris for the discovery of the assassin of a grisette, or measures founded in any similar ratiocination, would produce any similar result.[60]

Poe introduced the first Dupin story, "The Murders in the Rue Morgue," with a curious epigram from Sir Thomas Browne, the seventeenth-century prose writer.

> What song the syrens sang, or what name Achilles assumed when he hid himself among women, although puzzling questions, are not beyond *all* conjecture.[61]

Borrowed from Browne's own meditation on death, "Urn Burial," the quote, with its implied references to Homer and the Roman historian, Suetonius, is an important clue to the meaning of these ratiocinative and urban tales and especially to the puzzles inscribed within them. A brief consideration of the quotation and Poe's own discourse on the act of "analysis" that follows it offers an appropriate, if inconclusive, ending to this discussion of these important works.

The quotation refers both to the mysteries associated with women and puzzling: "The song the Syrens sang" was the mysterious and compelling song of women, offered to seduce men away from their military and manly quest; similarly, Achilles, the ultimate male warrior, was hidden among women and dressed in feminine garb by his mother, in order to protect him from death in the Trojan War. In his disquisition on enigmas and conundrums and the faculty of re-solution that begins "The Murders in the Rue Morgue," Poe alludes to the strong parallel between the warrior Achilles and the analyst Dupin: "As the strong man exults in his physical ability, so glories the analyst in that moral activity which *disentangles*."[62] Dupin, who like Achilles with Petroclus is paired with a male companion, is the modern male equivalent of the ancient hero in a world where, according to Poe, ratiocination has replaced battle as the true test of male ability.

But as the passages in the beginning of "Rue Morgue" suggest, Poe is also concerned with the crossing of boundaries; both Achilles and Dupin are lured by and venture into the domain of women. And Dupin's world—the world of the modern city—like Poe's women (mother and daughter in "Rue Morgue," and Marie Roget herself) is labyrinthine, mysterious, even inscrutable: it cannot be read. Like battle in ancient times, puzzle solving, or detecting—that "moral activity which disentangles"—is a masculine act, just as the questions to be "resolved" are feminine. Moreover, the act of problem solving—ratiocination—is transmuted in Poe's schema to a sexual act; it is an activity from which the analyst, we are told, "derives pleasure" and the "liveliest enjoyment." Not surprisingly, the result, the solution, is a fusion of the masculine and feminine; they are both the "essence of method" (masculine), but are infused with that which is most feminine, "the whole air of intuition."[63]

The mystery of femininity, the connection between sex and death, the modern conundrum offered by the metropolis itself, are the themes Poe engages in these city tales. And through the creation of the fictive Marie Roget, Poe mounted the ultimate act of reanimation; he resurrected the corpse of Mary Rogers, infused her with life, agency, and especially sexuality. In this he reinvented the cultural text that Rogers had already become. But more significant he gave life to another kind of cultural invention: the mystery story figured around sex, violent female death, and the culture of the city. For some "The Mystery of Marie Roget" may fail as fiction, but through it Poe created an enduring legacy for Mary Rogers. The death of a beautiful woman had become the archetypal puzzle of modern urban life.

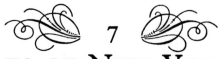

7
TALES OF NEW YORK IN
THE INK OF TRUTH:
REINVENTING
MARY ROGERS

*The author reminds his reader that he need only allude to his
event. . . . For all are familiar with the fruitless issue of the investigations
that followed her disappearance, and the deep mystery which to this hour,
envelopes, like the pall of the tomb, the whole of this painful and most
extraordinary affair.*
   Joseph Ingraham, La Bonita Cigarera; or the Beautiful Cigar Vender [sic].
A Tale of New York (1844)[1]

*I am aware that there is an air approximating so closely to entire fiction
in the accompanying tale, it seems incumbent on me to give some account
of the means by which I became possessed of a series of incidents so extraordinary.*
   Charles Burdett, Lilla Hart: A Tale of New York (1846)[2]

*Not one scene of vice or horror is given in the following pages which has
not been enacted over and over again in this city, nor is there one character which has not its counterpart in our very midst. . . . Therefore
though this book bears the title of a* novel, *it is written with the ink of
truth and deserves the name of a* history *more than a* romance.
   Ned Buntline, The Mysteries and Miseries of New York:
A Tale of Real Life (1847)[3]

TOWARD the conclusion of Joseph Holt Ingraham's *Herman de
Ruyter: Or, The Mystery Unveiled, the Sequel to La Bonita Cigarera:
Or the Beautiful Cigar Vender [sic]. A Tale of New York Life,* a handsome
young English Lord, traveling in New York, struggles to "fix and in-
dividualize" a familiar face. "Suddenly," the narrator informs the
reader, "the truth flashed upon his mind," as the young nobleman recognizes in a young woman of seventeen the face he has seen in a "portrait of a young girl at ten." They were, of course, one and the same:
"the face answered to the face as in a mirror, and their identity was

Figure 7–1 *Almost a year before Mary's final disappearance and death, The Sunday Morning Atlas anticipated the event. As part of a colorful series on New York types, "Portraits of the People," the Atlas (September 13, 1840) featured "The Cigar Girl" on its front page, complete with a wood engraving, a brief history of the occupation of cigar selling, and a short story about a missing cigar girl. The Atlas would re-issue the engraving as a depiction of Mary Rogers after her death in 1841. (Courtesy, American Antiquarian Society.)*

clear and decided." The face is that of Maria, the beautiful cigar vendor of the title and the novel's central character.[4]

As readers we already know much of Maria's history. At the beginning of this novel she was an abducted child, a girl without a remembered past, without kin, social class, or even national or ethnic identity. As she matured within Ingraham's narrative, she remained in this liminal state. The ambiguities of class, family position, and especially identity itself, continued to allude her, determining the plot of this popular novel and forming the central tension, the *mystery* of this mystery tale. Re-*solving* this "riddle of identity" simultaneously restores Maria's familial genealogy and reestablishes her especially problematic paternity as the lost child of an aristocratic British family. With patriarchy in place, class position, and even nationality reaffirmed, and order of a kind imposed, Maria is free to marry. But there is a catch: Maria's safety, her happiness, and her future wealth depend on her removal from New York and even from America. Spirited hastily away from the chaotic and dangerous streets of the "Republican Metropolis," she is returned to England, the aristocratic and presumably safer world of her birth.

Ingraham's novel, with its magical ending, suggests the narrative possibilities the Rogers story continued to hold for mid-nineteenth-century writers and readers. *La Bonita Cigarera* was one of several representations of Rogers to appear following the publication of Poe's "The Mystery of Marie Roget." Through these stories Mary Rogers not only endured by taking on an array of new fictive identities, she also became a stock character, along with Madame Restell and the ever-present "sensuous seducer" of urban popular fiction. Thus reinvented, she was the young and angelic Mary Cecilia in Joseph Ingraham's 1844 novels; the equally beatific Lilla Hart in Charles Burdett's 1846 domestic novel that is named for her; and Mary Sheffield, the victim of seduction and abortion in Buntline's 1848 city tale, *The Mysteries and Miseries of New York.* Later, jumping the cultural divide of the Civil War, she reappeared as Molly Ruciel, the seduced and abandoned cigar girl in Andrew Jackson Davis's anti-abortion tract, *Tale of a Physician: or the Fruits and Seeds of Crime.* These fictional works, expressed in a variety of literary styles— the sexual melodrama of Samuel Richardson drawn on by Ingraham, the sentimental Dickensian style of Burdett, or the dark naturalism of Buntline—reiterated once again the themes of identity, sexuality, and social order that had provided the central, recurring tropes in the history, both real and imagined, of Mary Rogers. Although history left much about Mary Rogers shrouded in secrecy and mystery, these fictions provided several alternative, and presumably more satisfactory, endings to her life.[5]

These novels were typical popular fare, characteristic of the cheap fiction intended for the new mass audience of the late 1830s and 1840s. Products of the period's flourishing popular culture industry, all but the Davis novel were originally published between 1844 and 1848 by prolific male writers close to the city's publishing world. Ingraham (1809–1860) was an enormously productive writer of cheap fiction, with over one hundred publications to his credit, written in every popular genre; Charles Burdett (b. 1815), was a reporter for the *Courier and Enquirer* in the late 1830s and 1840s who covered the city beat, but also wrote thirty fictional works, most of them sentimental and temperance novels; E. Z. C. Judson (1823–1886), more popularly known as Ned Buntline, was a notorious self-promoter and self-constructed hell-raiser in the Jacksonian mode who published several successful works about New York before he went on to invent and market the western hero Buffalo Bill; and Andrew Jackson Davis was a popular writer and lecturer, particularly interested in spiritualism and the hereditary dimensions of criminal behavior. The intertextual aspects of these works suggest that they all were close readers of "The Mystery of Marie Roget" and that they participated in an extended cultural conversation about the penny press, the conventions of commercial fiction, and the panorama of urban social life. Judson, Ingraham, and Burdett, for example, all make extensive references within the context of their novels to the penny press. Bennett himself became a stock character in cheap fiction, making an appearance in *Miseries and Mysteries*, and Judson, Ingraham, and Davis all refer, directly or indirectly to Poe's "Marie Roget."[6] It makes sense that Poe, whose career and work exemplifies the dynamic tensions between elite and popular culture, should have been a literary bridge to the production of a series of sentimental and melodramatic novels figured around the event that he, above all, made famous. Inspired by Poe's story, these vernacular texts were derived from, and simultaneously a commentary on, the popular press; like Poe's work they struggled with representations of the real and especially the urban. But here the connection to Poe ends, for while Poe was concerned with the consequences of modernity—the bifurcation of intellectual and emotional life, the stresses occasioned by the fragmentation of urban existence, the psychic dimensions of identity, the epistemology and ratiocination inspired by the event and by the city itself—the writers who followed him had other concerns.

For these popular writers the importance of the Rogers saga lay in its familiarity for the contemporary reader and in the possibilities this familiarity provided not for mimetic recreation, but for fictional reformulation. Invariably, the authors of these tales informed (and even cautioned) their readers of the closeness of their works to "real events." Buntline, for example, boldly established his intention at the outset: "Though this book bears the title of a *novel*, it is written with the ink of truth and deserves the name of a history more than a *romance*." Both Ingraham and Burdett subtitled their works: "A Tale of New York Life," while Buntline varied the theme with the subtitle: "A Tale of Real Life." Ironically, in these reconfigurations of the Rogers story, the power of "history" lay precisely in its impetus to romance; the "real events" were meaningful only insofar as they could be reinvented as fiction. As such, these stories reinvent an earlier tradition of oral narrative: each teller revised and embellished on the "real."

And it is precisely in this mix of truth and fiction, history and romance, that the significance of the Rogers story as a cultural text resides. In earlier chapters I suggested that the symbolic and representational identity of Mary Rogers reflected different and contending versions of the city itself. As dangerous woman/virtuous woman she was both the dangerous city and what was endangered. Her reinvention as a literary type reaffirms but also enlarges the scope of this typography. What happens to the Mary character within the frames of these popular novels suggests imagined visions of the future of the new metropolis and even of the democratic republic itself. Thus, insofar as the Mary character prevails, her survival infers the fragility of virtue in the disharmonious urban world. Where she dies, her death and the death of her putative child by abortion, implies the demise of an ordered, democratic society.

Of course Rogers herself remained a problematic character for writers of popular fiction. In life, as I have argued, Rogers was an independent young woman who experienced some of the new sexual freedom offered by the openness of city life, and at least in some measure melded with the working-class culture of the city. Most likely she had one, maybe two pregnancies (and abortions), and, above all, she knew her way around the town. Her male companions were representative of different urban groups—journalists, Tammany men, sailors, and workers. Through all of this the actual Rogers emerges not as the model of the sentimental heroine, but its antitype. And yet, in these popular novels, and in marked contrast to Poe's portrait of Marie Roget, she is depicted as vulnerable, virtuous, even virginal. Mary, reinvented and reimagined, became all that she was not: a sentimental, domestic, even bourgeois, heroine. Thus deeroticized, she was also demystified, and the once dangerous woman of the city was stripped of her sexual powers and reduced to a child-woman with little agency or erotic power.

What contemporary writers did with Mary Rogers, how they represented her, tells how a central historical narrative of women in nineteenth-century urban culture was not only imagined, but also evaded and reconstructed. Moreover, tracing the Rogers character through these popular works illustrates the development of a set of themes and variations on gender and class in nineteenth-century urban culture: the problematic of female sexuality that is played out in alternating vignettes of seduction and abduction, the urban landscape foregrounded as a literary subject, the class and cultural mix of the new metropolis depicted in infinite detail. More particularly, the reconfiguration of Mary Rogers provided a means of contending with a series of specific contemporary issues—the popular preoccupation with single working women, fractured families existing outside the domestic model, the availability of abortion. All these issues moved to center stage in the fictive versions of the Rogers story discussed below. As tales woven around the complex and often troublesome relationship between sex, death, and the city, these works reinvented the saga of Mary Rogers as part of a larger narrative about life in the metropolis, as one (of many) mysteries of the already mysterious city. More profoundly, the Rogers story, with its recurrent motifs of disappearance and abduction, sexual danger, loss and death, all of a beautiful woman, offers clues to the fragile and ever-disintegrating world of antebellum urban culture.

Reinventing Mary Rogers

Almost a year before Mary's final disappearance and death, *The Sunday Morning Atlas* anticipated the event. As part of a colorful series on New York types, "Portraits of the People," the *Atlas* (which published this vignette after Mary's first disappearance in 1838) featured "The Cigar Girl" on its front page, complete with a wood engraving, a brief history of the occupation of cigar selling, and a short story about a missing cigar girl. In a case of reality following fiction, both the engraving and the story plot presaged the future: the *Atlas* would reissue the engraving as a depiction of Mary Rogers after her death in 1841, just as it would retell as "news" an altered version of the fictional story.[7]

The initial *Atlas* vignette opens with a sorrowful description of a young woman, the beautiful if impoverished Ellen Somers, and her mother, sitting in an attic room pondering their desperate plight. "Times are so hard that one employer," Ellen reports, "has been compelled to discharge forty hands." Unable to find work, Ellen has one opportunity open to her: to tend the counter in a newly opened cigar store. Her mother cautions: "You would be exposed to the gaze of every creature, who, in laying out his beggarly trifle, expecting [sic] that the exhibition of a pretty girl was included in his charge, and that he had paid for the privilege of staring you out of countenance." However, after rejecting the possibility at first, the threat of starvation eventually leads her to take the position. There she encounters even more than what her mother feared: young rakes aggressively challenging her virtue. Three men in particular, "known in common parlance as gentlemen," pursue her. Two "even went so far as to bet upon who should be the happy man to make the divine creature his goddess of pleasure," while the third stood by, awaiting the result. "This" we are informed "was the crisis of the Cigar Girl's life." But Ellen's virtue held them at bay: "they hated her, while they respected her, for they felt she was a superior being to themselves." Finally, however, it is the third suitor, the "gentle, modest" Henry Wilkinson who abducts her in his coach one rainy night. Ellen pleads with him to turn back, but Henry informs her: "I have gone too far to recede. It is useless for you to oppose my wishes. What can you do?" Ellen's response reminds us of a virtuous heroine's choices in this post Richardsonian world: "I can die," she replies.[8]

But Ellen, unlike the real Mary and Richardson's Clarissa, remains undefiled and does not die. Instead, Ellen has passed Henry's final "cruel trial," the ultimate test of her virtue to determine her worthiness as his future wife. Reminiscent of some of Mary's admirers, "Henry had been struck with Ellen's manners at first." However, "it was her foiling the libertines [that] won his admiration. . . . He deemed the last cruel trial to which he put her necessary, and he gloried that she passed unsullied through the fiery ordeal." More like Richardson's earlier heroine, Pamela, Ellen returns the next morning to her distraught mother with the happy news that she has been wed. And the reader of this tale is rewarded with the story's moral lesson: "That in every station in life, in the most humble as well as the most lofty, a virtuous mind may support itself with respect and honor, may be learned from the history of the CIGAR GIRL." The sketch concluded with the cautionary Biblical homily: "Lead us not into temptation."⁹

The *Atlas* portrait reveals a striking example of the way cultural scripts provide parameters for contending with "reality." Indeed, the depictions of Mary Rogers common in the press and subsequent fictionalizations were all variations on this initial vignette. Even the story-plot anticipated later figurations in several ways: it created Mary as a virtuous working girl; it established her as fatherless, loyally devoted to a weak but loving mother; it featured an uninvited abduction: it created a struggle between male characters over the promise of Mary's virtue; and it allowed Mary, in turn, to be rewarded with marriage at the story's end for maintaining that virtue at nothing less than the peril of death. As an early version of the Rogers story, cast within a Richardsonian seduction plot mold, this particular narrative lacked several additions of the later fictionalized reinventions of Mary's history—most notably the struggle over identity. Examining these novels in the order of their publication—all of which followed Rogers's death, the publication of Poe's story, and the general acknowledgment that Mary died from an abortion—suggests how the meaning of Rogers's life and death evolved.

The first complete works to appear after "Marie Roget" were Ingraham's novels, *La Bonita Cigarera: or The Beautiful Cigar Vender* [*sic*] and its sequel *Herman de Ruyter*, published in Boston in 1844. Joseph Holt Ingraham was one of the most prolific and financially successful novelists of the period. Born in Maine, Ingraham married the daughter of a planter, settled in Mississippi, and after taking vows for the Episcopal ministry, turned his talents to popular religious fiction. In his earlier years he was a veritable one-man fiction factory (of his one hundred dime novels, eighty were written before 1846), producing so quickly that Longfellow quipped that for "this dark young man with a soft voice" the process of writing "has grown merely mechanical." He was a frequent contributor to all the important literary magazines of this period, including *Harpers, Ladies' Companion, Gentleman's Magazine* and the *Boston Miscellany*. Drawing freely from English, Continental, and American writers such as Dickens, Sue, and Poe, he epitomized the new professional hack writer who produced formula fiction duly rendered to meet the tastes and requirements of the marketplace. Less concerned with mapping the early city than other contemporary writers, Ingraham's work nevertheless features all the important elements of this early

PRICE,   CENTS.

THE

BEAUTIFUL

CIGAR GIRL;

OR,

The Mysteries of Broadway.

BY

J. H. INGRAHAM, Esq.,

Author of "The Young Ranger Hussar," "Frank Rivers; or, The Dangers of the Town," "Theo-
dore; or, The Child of the Sea." "Estelle; or, The Conspirator of the Isles," "The Surf
Skiff; or, The Heroine of the Kennebec," etc., etc.

Figure 7–2 *Ingraham's popular novel,* The Beautiful Cigar Girl, *was an urban
mystery tale figured around several parallel plots of high and low life in New York.
This cover to an 1844 edition of the novel portrays the story's heroine, Mary Cecelia,
who, after her brief tenure as a cigar girl, is restored to her aristocratic English family.
(Collection of The New-York Historical Society.)*

cheap urban fiction and most of the motifs common in fictionalized versions of the Rogers story.[10]

La Bonita Cigarera, which went through at least five editions under various titles, was essentially an urban mystery story figured around several parallel plots of high and low life in New York. It features a group of thieves who revolve around one Wilkins Wild, once a "Broadway lounger, a frequenter of theaters, billiard rooms, cafes, and gambling saloons" who "wasted" his father's fortune; his beautiful wife, Isabel, the product of a "fashionable up-town boarding school," who allowed herself to be seduced by the handsome rake Wilkins; Mrs. de Ruyter, "one of those slight elegant persons which are supposed to belong only to the purest lineage," the noble, but poor and abandoned, mother of Herman de Ruyter; the young de Ruyter, himself a wild youth with an honorable heart; a prosperous merchant, Mr. Carrol; and, of course, Maria Cecilia herself, who provides the connecting link between these otherwise disparate characters and their worlds.

Ingraham was particularly drawn to lurid aspects of urban life, no doubt because they played so well to popular taste. His earlier novel *Frank Rivers, or Life on the Town* chronicled the Helen Jewett murder in the mold of a rape/seduction tale. Unlike his Rogers novel, *Frank Rivers* is a real bodice-ripper, racy and explicit in the sexual drama it unfolds. The seduction of Ellen/Helen takes place over a series of chapters, depending on detailed descriptions and dialogue. When he turned to the story of Mary Rogers, however, Ingraham wrote not a seduction novel, but its clean-cut cousin—a captivity tale and fast-paced adventure story. The differences between *Frank Rivers* and *La Bonita Cigarera* suggest that salacious texts, acceptable in the 1830s, required toning down, even masking, in the more repressive 1840s. Here, anticipating a literary convention where rape is masked as abduction, Mary/Maria is presented not as the willing country girl seduced and abandoned, but as the innocent victim of a series of kidnappings. The story opens at the "venerable edifice of the de Ruyter family," a decaying pre-Revolutionary structure whose dilapidated state signifies the decline of a once noble Dutch farm family as well as a mythic American past; it signifies an earlier, more stable and firmly patriarchal society now gone to ruin. This noble and sturdy family heritage provides an unintended but nevertheless uncanny evocation of the decline of the Mathers and their displacement through Mary and Phebe from their patriarchal roost to the modern city. In the novel the home now sits on valuable urban land and is thus the target of modern speculators who await the demise of Mrs. de Ruyter, its impoverished owner, who in time will oblige them.

We first encounter Maria at the home of Mr. Carrol, a prosperous merchant, whose home is the object of a robbery by Herman, having been pulled into a gang of thieves led by the notorious Wild. Young Herman is bewitched by the sleeping child: "All the good and pure, and elevated feeling that had ever had being in his soul, came uppermost, communicated in his countenance as expression noble and sincere." Believing that he would be redeemed and "safest in the presence of one so pure and beautiful" he seizes her from her bed and spirits her away to his mother![11] Young Maria, "about nine or ten years of age, [and] one of those slight, elegant persons which are supposed to belong only to the purest lineage," awakens in the strange arms of Mrs. de Ruyter: "Oh, where, where have I been brought? Why have I been torn from my father? Why am I brought here? Tell me! Tell me! Save me! Save me!"[12]

Herman departs for an indefinite period, leaving Maria to be lovingly raised by his mother in a fictive mother/daughter relationship characteristic of these novels and suggestive of the unclear relationship of the actual Mary and the elderly Phebe Rogers. As the first installment ends we find Maria and "her mother" sewing and living in a tenement when Maria, now grown "fair and attractive" as well as "modest, sensible and industrious," comes across the following advertisement in the penny press: "Wanted to tend in a genteel cigar store, a young lady of prepossessing appearance and address to whom good wages will be given."[13] Thus does the abducted Maria become the "Beautiful Cigar Vender."

> The reputation of her charms, of her modesty, and of her exceeding grace in conversation, for she was alike affable to all, spread throughout the city, and 'La Bonita Cigarera,' the Beautiful Cigar Vender, became the theme of every young man's conversation. Hundreds visited there only to see her, and those who never smoke cigars, now lounged in there to purchase them, that they might behold her, who had turned the heads of half the young men in town.[14]

But as the end of the final chapter approaches, the cigar girl suddenly disappears and the narrator tells us, the morning papers declared the " 'Horrible Suspicion of Murder Most Foul.' " The author reminds his reader that he need only allude to this event in a sentence that clearly evokes accounts of the actual disappearance and death of Mary Rogers in the penny press and elsewhere: "For all are familiar with the fruitless issue of the investigations that followed her disappearance, and the deep mystery which to this hour, envelopes, like the pall of the tomb, the whole of this painful and most extraordinary affair." With this conclusion, readers are promised a further investigation of the story in the columns of the story-paper the *Yankee* under the title of "Herman De Ruyter or The Mystery Unveiled!"[15]

The novel's sequel, *Herman de Ruyter*, unmasks the true identity of the beautiful cigar girl and reveals the secrets of her past. As it turns out, she has either disappeared, relocated, or been abducted no less than three times: the first when taken from her father's carriage as a child in England; the second when her caretaker dies and leaves her in the care of a Mr. Carrol, a wealthy New York merchant; and the third when she was seized from the Carrol residence by Herman during his bungled robbery. Like Mary Rogers, Maria is a woman who has lost her past, but even more important she is without paternity. Seized from her true father whose miniature she still wears, she has moved down the social scale, falling ultimately into the loving care of a fragile woman similarly deprived of the privileges of male authority and protection. For Ingraham, republican society, contextualized in and represented by the city, is a dangerous place; it steals the past and repudiates history and the stability offered by patriarchal authority. Cast out from their natural place in the social order women like Maria and her fictive mother, Mrs. de Ruyter, are as decentered as the chaotic and unpredictable world that revolves around them. The multiple abductions of Maria thus speak of theft and a larger theft—of an ordered and virtuous society, safe from the hazards offered by the modern city. Ingraham's vision looks back to a mythic past that has been stolen, leaving social chaos in its wake.

Restoring balance to this destabilized urban world is accomplished by revealing and restoring Maria's past, reclaiming her from the unprotected zones of declassé urban women and settling her once again in ordered and protected familial and patriarchal space, a mission Ingraham suggests can only be accomplished by repudiating America altogether. Resolving his complicated story by a plot device already familiar to readers, Ingraham arranges a magical transformation for Maria at the novel's end. While tending the cigar store counter Maria, we learn, had received the attentions of a young Englishman whom, it is revealed, is Maria's cousin, the nephew of her true biological father who is English. The moment of recognition (described in the opening vignette above) leads to Maria's reclamation by her father and aunt and her return to England. And because Maria must be promptly disassociated from her working-class life,

> . . . it was decided unanimously that there should be nothing said to the proprietor of the cigar-mart, nor to any person whatsoever touching this discovery of her birth; but that she should leave with them early the next day for Boston, and at once proceed with them to England. The motive for this secrecy was to spare her own feeling, as well as those of her father in her new position, by protecting her from any allusion to her late situation as cigar-girl; it being deemed best that this precaution should be made to guard her against any reproach that might follow her into the new life before her.[16]

And so, Maria returns to England, is educated, and, in her twentieth year, marries her cousin and suitor, Sir Edward. For the reader the mystery of the disappearance of the real Mary Rogers is resolved: she is not only alive, but of noble English birth and happily married to an English Lord! She has thus even exceeded the most farfetched social possibilities that the actual Mary could have achieved in America with her Puritan lineage. As for those left behind in New York, they fare less well. Maria's rise is paralleled by Herman's fall; his moral and spiritual degeneration is followed by his early death. And for Mrs. de Ruyter, the only solution for her too is death; virtuous women without men and/or lineage have no future in the disharmonious city of the new world.

Abduction and patriarchal loss are likewise at the heart of *Lilla Hart*, Charles Burdett's 1846 novel. Like *La Bonita Cigarera*, *Lilla* is a captivity tale, a story of vanished patrimony and of patriarchal identity lost and restored. Like the Ingraham novel, the plot is figured around two women, mother and daughter, who like Maria and Mrs. de Ruyter, are without viable support in the cold and mean streets of 1830s New York. Burdett, unlike Ingraham, was self-consciously aware of his professional role as a reporter and the extent to which it positioned him to observe the scenes and incidents of city life. The city, he wrote, presented him with "all gradations of crime and its erring consequences [which] pass before him in rapid review . . . leaving impressions which even variety does not serve to efface." These "impressions" also informed his fiction writing, a calling that was for him infused with moral meaning and social obligation. Burdett steered away from the stylized sensationalism and fast-paced mystery novel, imagining himself as a writer in the sentimental tradition of social reformers such as the English writer and women's advocate Charlotte Tonna, whose books were issued in America by Burdett's Nassau Street publisher, Baker and Scribner. In keeping with this political stance, Burdett's novels, including *Lilla*, were largely morality tales of social reform, temperance, and redemption, figured around virtuous female characters.[17]

Burdett's choice of the Rogers saga is therefore an interesting one, because the fictive Lilla shares only rudimentary connections with her real-life counterpart. Without ever connecting her specifically to the cigar store or even the boardinghouse, Burdett's story creates a scenario that draws on the outward details of Mary's disappearance: the vulnerable diad of mother and daughter; the discovery of a young woman's corpse in the river; the details of jewelry as artifacts of identity; even the reclamation of a severed past. And if Ingraham's recast versions of the Mary Rogers saga were written out of a Richardsonian perspective, Burdett's invention was clearly Dickensian.

At the beginning of the novel, we find Lilla and her mother, the abused victims of an intemperate father and husband. Penniless, they are cold and hungry when the narrator, a successful city merchant named Sandford, stumbles on them in their rude tenement home on a "dismal, cheerless, and dreary" night in January in the late 1830s. Mrs. Hart, a native of Ohio, whose name underscores her character and heartland origins, possesses the "white lofty forehead, betokening intellect of no common order." Like Ingraham's virtuous women such as Mrs. de Ruyter, she is the descendent of a prelapsarian, preurban strain of innate female nobility. She was a "fine and noble-looking woman . . .

the wreck of that which womanhood might once have been." These
women are classic representations of the "deserving poor," women reduced to poverty because of sudden widowhood or crimes perpetrated
against them by unworthy or intemperate men. Death shortly takes the
intemperate husband, and the good merchant removes them to his own
warm but childless home. Shortly after, Mrs. Hart also dies, leaving Lilla
orphaned but in the Sandfords protective care.[18]

Lilla takes to life as the virtuous daughter of a good merchant. But
her new life is interrupted when she "mysteriously disappears," apparently abducted from her new home. Later, Mr. Sandford informs us,
he was "perusing the morning papers . . . [when he] . . . chanced to see
among the inquests . . . that the body of a young girl has been found in
the North River, and was left at the dead house as it was termed for
recognition." Mr. Sanford proceeds at once to the dead house, where
"lying on a rough board, placed across two barrels, and covered with
an old piece of sailcloth, was the body which . . . [he] . . . came to see."
In his one lapse of restraint in this otherwise polite novel, Burdett provides his version of a by now familiar description. The merchant and
tale's narrator recounts his encounter with Lilla's corpse:

> At my request, he [the keeper] drew down the cloth, and disclosed the
> face beneath, but it was a bloated, purple, disfigured mass, which one
> could scarcely recognize as having ever belonged to humanity. It had
> lain so long in the water, the eyes were eaten out of the sockets, and
> everything like recognition was utterly out of the question.[19]

A small gold Maltese cross, "hanging around her neck by a gold
chain . . . [and a] . . . small ring . . . on one of the fingers of her left
hand" are the talismans of Lilla's identity, which "forced [him] to believe that this was the body of . . . [his] beloved Lilla." The mystery of
her disappearance solved, Mr. and Mrs. Sandford proceed to bury and
mourn their lost charge.[20]

Of course all is not as it appears. Prior to Lilla's abduction, and in
a narrative device familiar to readers of sentimental novels, Burdett presents his readers with the nefarious Mr. Wilson, the evil merchant of the
tale (he too has a good wife and daughter, Delia) and Sandford's ma-
levolent double. Wilson, we learn, had not only arranged Lilla's disappearance, but also her murder, and was responsible for the demise of
her late father. His design was simple: to secure the inheritance of Mrs.
Hart, his own cousin.

In the end good prevails: Lilla's Christian goodness had tamed her
abductor, one George Brown, a minor criminal wanted by the police,
who merely feigned her death by exchanging her identity for that of an
anonymous, already drowned victim: "It happened that one night," recounted Brown, "in the course of my cruising, I came across a girl just
about her age, a dreadful bad girl—a drunken, quarrelsome thing. She
had died that very day from falling down stairs while she was intoxi-

cated, and her face was dreadfully bruised and battered." He stole the body, dressed it in Lilla's clothes and jewelry, and after "waiting a few days, so as to render it impossible as I thought to recognize the features, I took it one night, and getting into a small boat, pulled round into the North River, and pitched it overboard. I fixed a rope with a stone round the waist to keep it down for a while, but I cut the rope almost through, so that the workings of the water would wear it off in time . . . and when the body came up, it would not have any rope about it." Thus were the changes of identity and the discovery of the corpse accounted for.[21]

Ultimately, all is revealed and justice done. Mr. Wilson repents on his deathbed, Sandford becomes the pater familias for the widowed Mrs. Wilson and her daughter (as they had previously become for Mrs. Hart and Lilla), and Lilla, her inheritance saved, is restored to him. At the novel's end both Lilla and Delia are happily wed and the novel ends with the following moral: "It is shown that neither wealth, nor state, station, nor anything of earth, can alone confer happiness, and that wickedness in the high and great will be as surely brought to light, and bring its own rewards, as in the meanest and most abject of poor creatures, and that, sooner or later, *his sin will find him out.*"[22]

For Burdett the Rogers story offered a Dickensian narrative frame for a sentimental and bourgeois domestic novel about the power of faith and the possibilities of redemption. But undercutting this familiar moral and sentimental ending, with its socially conservative message of patience and forbearance, is a more subversive story of social instability and personal loss. Burdett has created a world of victimized women who suffer the repeated losses of husbands, fathers, family, and wealth. Lilla's survival notwithstanding, her many trials reveal more about the fragility of this real urban world for women than they do about the power of virtue. Death and poverty have a constant presence, suggesting the vagaries of social position in antebellum America, particularly as they affect women in the context of a city where the absence of extended kin leaves women alone and unprotected. The dangers they represent are symbolically transformed into plot devices of abduction and disappearance that signify the uneasy security and potential loss of identity such urban women faced in the 1840s. Lilla is not only left motherless and fatherless; she is taken away, her identity masked and exchanged. Even the melodramatic device of doubling suggests the fragility of identity: two merchants, one good and one bad, head two identical families. And like Sanford and Wilson, good merchant and bad merchant, the daughters, Delia and Lilla, are veritable mirror images of each other, as are the three adult women of the tale.

Such Dickensian moral parallels of redemption are far less inevitable in the more naturalistic works of Edward Carrol Zane Judson, known popularly as Ned Buntline. Judson, who was born in 1823 in Stamford, New York, a small rural farming community in the northern Catskill Mountains, was the son of a Masonic schoolmaster, lawyer, and author of several volumes of moral and patriotic prose. Beyond these elements of his early history, it is difficult to know what part of Judson's past was authentic and what invented. Indeed, his literary persona and alter ego, Ned Buntline, under whose name he penned much of his fiction and his "autobiography," *Ned Buntline's Life Yarn*, is a character out of his own stories. In the *Yarn*, Ned's father strikes young Ned violently in an argument over his proposed vocation, and in response Ned leaves home and hearth for a life at sea. In the *Yarn* he also recounts a subsequent meeting with his father when he again rejects his father's "power" and rightful authority over him, claiming: " *'Resurgam'* is my motto—independence my character! Farewell, Sir; you might have made me all you could have wished—now I will make myself!" The self-created image of the independent and self-made man remained Judson's creed. And like his alter ego, Judson personified the rugged individualist of mid-nineteenth-century America who sought constant adventure in the rough and often violent land of Jacksonian America.[23]

Judson, again like his alter ego Buntline, claims to have run away from home and gone to sea. Between 1838 and 1842, critical years in the history of Mary Rogers, he held a midshipman's commission in the Navy, and, after he resigned in April 1842, he most likely remained in New York City. His Navy stint overlapped with the Somers affair and may have placed him among one of the many crews on leave during the days of Rogers's disappearances. It may be pure coincidence, but Ned Buntline's ship in his *Life Yarn* is the Mary C![24]

In his subsequent career Judson was a self-alleged bounty hunter and even a murderer. He claimed to have made a remarkable escape from a mob hanging, and in 1849 he played one of his more important roles as the leader of a nativist mob in the Astor Place theater riots. He became an organizer of the Know-Nothing Party, and, after enlisting in the Union Army 1862, was discharged two years later by the War Department with a completely discreditable record.[25]

But Judson's real recognition came as the author of a wide range of urban popular tales in the 1840s and 50s. As Ned Buntline, he produced a lengthy list of popular works, among them the city tales chronicling working class life, *The B'hoys of New York* and its sequel, *The G'hals of New York*.[26] His other works included stories of adventure and romance—sea tales and westerns. In 1869 at Fort McPherson, Nebraska, he met William Frederick Cody, designated him as Buffalo Bill, and created a Barnum-like spectacle of the Wild West around this invented persona.

In Buntline's *The Mysteries and Miseries of New York*, the saga of Mary Rogers is replayed as a seduction tale, the story of Mary Sheffield, the beautiful blond cigar girl who dies of an abortion at the hands of the notorious Madame Sitstill. Unlike the story-plot of Maria that forms the narrative center of Ingraham's work, Judson's Mary saga is one of many plots that run simultaneously through this urban mystery tale. Stylistically, this work is a classic example of the urban mystery, a genre that proliferated in Europe and America in the 1840s. Modeled after Eugene Sue's *Mysteries and Miseries of Paris*, this work, like others of its kind, abounds with barely interconnecting subplots which, with their stories of gamblers and rakes, concentrate on the dark and mysterious panorama of the underworld of urban society. Urban mystery novels typically eschewed the use of a single linear narrative, figuring the world of the antebellum city through a series of simultaneous narratives involving different social groups within one shared urban space. Here the world of the new city was presented not as a single coherent whole, but rather as a vast cacophony of action enacted above, below, and on the city streets. The urban world created by writers like George Lippard or Judson was dark and labyrinthine, filled with moral precipices, worldly temptations, and characters who were seldom what they claimed.[27]

Frederic Jameson has argued that there are two paradigmatic narrative strategies of "middle-class moralizing about the lower classes": the sentimental and the melodramatic. The mystery form, he maintains, constitutes the primary expression of the latter, challenging the polite or genteel narrative, while simultaneously offering a useful form for replicating the complex and chaotic world of the city.[28] Its rhetoric of sensation and violence also made it a ready vehicle for polemics in fictional garb. Thus, in their portrayal of lower-class characters, mystery authors often encoded easily understood political subtexts within the plots. For George Lippard this political perspective was that of the radical democrat, who championed the ideals of the artisan republic and its working-class heroes against the forces of upper-class greed and corruption. For Judson, whose political stance was often masked in populist garb, this perspective was closer to that of James Gordon Bennett. Nativist and xenophobic, Judson expressed the fractious and often violent tendencies in antebellum working-class politics. Not surprisingly, his formulaic urban tale was an explicit if somewhat jumbled plea for social order, and its female characters in particular (perhaps with the exception of the prostitute Big Lize) are alternately portraits in moral vulnerability and predatory venality.

Mysteries and Miseries was composed of five separately published folios, each the requisite one hundred pages long. But Judson's chronicle was unusual because it extended the literary convention of "representations from real life" into a new dimension. The work is comprised of three distinct texts: (1) a complex fictional narrative based on "true events"; (2) a set of lengthy prefaces that precede each installment and outline the author's intent; and (3) a set of appendixes including a lexicon of contemporary urban slang, statistics on New York City crime, and official documents and reports pertaining to poverty, prostitution, and city asylums, and, most noteworthy, a reprint of the 1845 Police Act. The effect of all this is an overwhelming verbal barrage where government reports, moral tracts, and fictional narratives merge into one compendium of urban life; in Judson the boundaries between "fact" and fiction are blurred beyond distinction, and the real and the imagined cease to exist as separate and distinct aspects of literary representation or experience. More than any other figure of the time, Judson created a work that synthesizes the contemporary media: narratives and codes of urban life, fictional narratives, penny press materials, and actual laws. This strange book, which is part story, part polemic, part urban guide, serves as an unusual comment on the Rogers tragedy itself, imitating in textual form the presentation and re-presentation that melded the Rogers story to the culture of the antebellum city.

The Rogers subplot in *Mysteries* runs through all five parts of the novel, a distinction it shares with only one other story line—that of the "good" prostitute Big Lize. We first meet Mary Rogers's double within the novel, Mary Sheffield, "one of the prettiest blonds that ever poet idealized or painter pictured," as she awaits her seducer, the middle-aged, married merchant, Albert Shirley, in a house of assignation. Mary is young—eighteen or so—noble if no longer virginal, and pregnant. Shirley informs her that they cannot be married, but that he will support her and preserve her "from the danger of . . . [her] . . . present situation." Unbeknownst to Mary, he has already sought the services of the "infamous MADAME SITSTILL" who makes a "trade of murder," and "who, for a few dollars, will bind herself to destroy one life; [while] . . . in doing so often takes two." Not surprisingly, Sitstill lives on Greenwich Street, like her real counterpart, Madame Restell. By the next installment Mary, "deceived— betrayed—ruined" has already begun to fade: her cheek was pale, her eyes were sunken, her lips blue." In Book III she is in the "neat but humble" dwelling of her mother. There we find her crying and reading the Bible (the eighth chapter of St John, where deliverance is granted to the woman taken in adultery), in the company of her would-be suitor, a "thrifty artisan," who has come to propose marriage. Mary dispatches him and reluctantly proceeds to the "polluted walls of the splendid dwelling" of the infamous Sitstill. When we next meet Mary in Book IV, she is on her deathbed. "I have loved you," she tells Albert, "and I love you yet, though you have deceived, ruined and *murdered* me, soul and body." Through a swift twist of plot, Albert's wife has discovered a note telling of Mary's dire situation and has rushed to Sitstill's. Here she is quickly appraised of her husband's actions by the dying Mary herself. Confronted with his wife's knowledge and Mary's imminent death, Albert takes responsibility for his acts, proclaims himself damned, and releases himself to his wife's protection. Mary pleads with Albert to take care of her mother and to keep her from "the cold charity of the almshouse" or from becoming a "wandering beggar in the streets." She also asks that Albert bury her secretly, so as not to let the world or her mother know of her shame. In the final book, the naturalistic narrative in the tradition of

Sue, Wilkie Collins, or even Zola, comes full circle, as Albert's daughter, Constance, a double of Mary, reads in a newspaper of the discovery of Mary's body, "the beautiful 'Cigar Girl,' " again reflecting actual contemporary newspaper accounts of her supposed ill treatment and murder by a gang of rowdies at Hoboken. "Oh how horrible—she must have suffered," exclaims Constance, "I can't bear to think of it; and then her lover, a worthy mechanic, has committed suicide! Oh, mercy, it is too horrible."[29]

Other works besides Judson's focused on the issue of abortion, and particularly on the character of Madame Restell. As I noted in Chapter 5, some writers wrote elaborate stories about Restell and her practice, while others included familiar details of the Rogers tragedy in their fictional treatment of the abortion issue. Restell appears, for example, as Madame Resimer, the "Female Fiend" and evil abortionist, in George Lippard's urban mystery tales, *New York: Its Upper Ten and Lower Million* and *The Empire City*. With her infamous "red book" Resimer knows the sexual secrets of the rich and powerful of the city, and has performed an abortion on Alice, the daughter of a wealthy merchant and the victim of seduction and abduction by the duplicitous minister, Reverend Herman Barnhurst.[30]

In *Tale of a Physician: or the Fruits and Seeds of Crime*, Andrew Jackson Davis presents Mary Rogers as Molly Ruciel, the victim of the nefarious Dr. William Morte. With abortion once again as the central urban evil of the narrative, Davis has Molly die during Dr. Morte's "still and lost treatment." In this strange work, another physician and a self-appointed "New York detective," Dr. La Force DuBois, endeavors to root out evil in the city. Seeking to detect the causes of abortion and infanticide, and specifically to unmask the practice of Dr. Morte, who operates a "foeticidal" boardinghouse with a Madame La Stelle, DuBois becomes obsessed with Molly's death. The story recounts the history of Molly, "a young lady who is a celebrated beauty, and a universal favorite, and who is engaged every business day as a selling clerk in a popular down-town store." The abortion Molly requires has already been paid for by her "wealthy lover," one Jack Blake. Of course, Molly's fate is sealed; she dies during the procedure in a chapter headed by an epigram from Poe's "Ligeia": "out, out the lights—are all!/And over her quivering form / The curtain, a funeral pall,/Comes down with the rush of a storm." But Molly's death, Davis reminds us, caused unusual alarm: "Everybody in New York knows that girl" says the abortionist, "We've got a hell of a job on hand, I'll bet." Arguing that the crime must be covered up, they decide that "she must be found with every imaginable evidence of violence committed by several men." Thus, as with Mary Rogers, the body of Molly is brutalized even further, her dress is torn, her mouth gagged and bound, and she is taken across the Hudson where her body is dropped just above Weehawken. In this way, the story of Rogers was revisited in fiction almost thirty years after her death. But while the tale had lost none of its specificity, it had lost its immediacy as a story of the city, becoming a generic narrative of dangerous crimes and criminals, and a case history for Davis's spiritualistic parapsychology.[31]

Inventing History

As a cross section of popular fiction about the 1840s city written by men, these popular novels offered different representations of Mary Rogers and her story. Featured as a character in virtually all the popular story types—the Richardsonian urban captivity tale of James Ingraham, the sentimental reform novel of Charles Burdett, the sensational naturalistic mystery of Ned Buntline, the post-Civil War crime narrative of Andrew Jackson Davis—Mary's continued presence provided an enduring topic of interest and entertainment, underscoring her representational importance as a young woman in the city and as a poor working girl. And while these novels share much in terms of their intended audience and their modes of literary production and distribution, they nevertheless differ significantly in their depictions of Mary and the ideological premises that underlay their respective narratives. It is precisely the differences among these works that make their use of the Rogers narrative so interesting. As a stock character in the vast panorama of city life, Mary's imagined history provided a means by which contemporary writers contended with different and often conflicting interpretations of women, sexuality, and urban life.[32] Foregrounding the Mary Rogers narrative within these popular texts gives us a perspective not only on this set of Rogers novels, but by extension on this fiction in general. It is a perspective that forces questions about gender representation, identity, and sexuality into the center of analysis, thereby shifting other interpretive perspectives in the process. Reflecting on the Rogers narratives thus suggests the complex ways in which issues of sexuality, gender, and personal and social identity were interwoven with the configuration of the modern city and perhaps even the idea of the American republic itself.

All the works depict Mary herself as a noble, refined, beautiful, and impoverished young woman. At some point in these narratives she is also fatherless and living alone in poverty with a mother who is either biological or adopted. In most of the works, poverty forces her to seek work. In some she is abducted and returned; in others seduction is substituted for abduction and she is doomed to death. Yet within them all are two contrasting scenarios or metanarratives for her character: (1) her forced abduction and loss of identity, followed by a magical and transforming ending in which this identity is recovered and she is rewarded with wealth and eventually marriage to her social and moral equal; or (2) her seduction and pregnancy followed by a harrowing abortion, spiritual redemption, and finally death. The choice of one plot over the other reflected the author's own attitude toward and representation of the 1840s city, as well as his larger vision for the republican metropolis. No doubt, it also reflected changing times, increased fear of the consequences of immigration, and heightened anxiety about women and sex.

Contemporary literary theory points to several different perspectives on popular antebellum literary culture. David Reynolds has argued for the importance and influence of what he calls the "subversive imagination" of popular culture on the period's other literary tradition: the works of what has traditionally been identified as the American Renaissance.[33] Feminist criticism, most notably the work of Nina Baym, Jane Tompkins, and Cathy Davidson, has concentrated on the place of the popular sentimental novel, and on what Nina Baym defines as women's fiction (works written by and for women in which a heroine typically overcomes enormous obstacles to survive and prevail) for understanding the history of nineteenth-century women's culture. More recently, literary theory and cultural criticism have focused on the implicit ideological significance, or political meanings, encoded within the narratives. Inspired by Raymond Williams, Stuart Hall, and Fredric Jameson, Michael Denning has argued persuasively that the cultural meaning of cheap fiction resides in the "mechanic accents," the "relations between popular fiction and its working class audience." Denning maintains that nineteenth-century working-class culture was dominated by a single tale, "a master plot" that was made up of "nationalist" and "class-inflected" stories of the American Republic, its origins, and the threats against it. The gender narratives embodied within these texts, he maintains, are an aspect of this larger metanarrative.[34]

As a seduction plot, the Rogers narrative, as I have suggested, fits into a long and important literary tradition, dating back to Samuel Richardson, who created its models in *Clarissa* and *Pamela*. Recently, critics have seen the traditional ritualized contest in these works between an aristocratic seducer and a virtuous bourgeois heroine as a political struggle, a contest between class and power enacted over sex. But the seducer in the saga of Mary Rogers is never aristocratic; in the abortion plots the seducer is typically a prosperous merchant or rake, and in the abduction stories he is usually a lower-class lackey acting in the service of a merchant or, in the case of Ingraham, of professional thieves. This reaffirms Denning's argument that in American works the political meaning of the classic seduction narrative has to be read within its own historical context.[35]

In America where the rape/seduction plot is often part of a crime narrative, its meaning resides, argues Denning in his discussion of George Lippard, in the "emerging class conflict between merchant, manufacturers, and mechanics, between capital and labor."[36] Within this interpretation, Rogers is cast as the virtuous working girl who in fending off the potential seducer embodies the struggle of the new re-

public and its artisan-mechanic class against corruption in the form of
the seducer. But while Mary Rogers embodied a version of the noble
working girl, her salvation in these works is distinct from other contemporary novels featuring working-class heroines. Instead of salvation by
a mechanic-hero, Mary's salvation, when it occurs, is magical and transforming: she finds wealth, family, and sometimes aristocratic identity.
A class-based interpretation of the Rogers plots decenters the primacy
of gender and sexuality by privileging the class narrative over the gender
narrative, thereby oversimplifying the ambivalence about the Rogers
character typical of all these works. The point, of course, is that as
ideological problematics in nineteenth-century America, class and gender were inseparable. The Rogers story, with either of its two alternative
endings, is a seduction plot; but its meaning resides in how it forefronts
issues of gender within the context of urban social life and culture and
even within the republican concern with social class, personal identity,
and individual worthiness.

Tension and evasion, expressed in awkward plot twists and stiff dialogue pervade all the Rogers novels, signifying that Rogers herself remained a difficult character for popular writers. For at the same time
as they sentimentalize and deeroticize Mary Rogers, these works, with
their dark portrayals of female poverty and vulnerability, also contain
important subtexts that effectively subvert their magical endings. The
fragility of women's economic and social position in the new city un-
derlies all of these narratives, reiterating the very real vulnerability of
women in the capitalist city. Whether in *La Bonita Cigarera, Lilla Hart,*
or *Mysteries and Miseries of New York,* the world of women is one of
grinding poverty, social isolation, and constant danger at the hands of
predatory men. Left to suffer the exigencies of life in an unpredictable
and dangerous world, these women remind readers, past and present,
of the inability of the new society to care for its most valorized subjects—
women and children. Moreover, in the city of these fictions, danger is
not so much endemic as it is gender specific.[37]

Sentiment, if it leaves these women vulnerable, is nevertheless a female virtue, reaffirming one of the major tropes of antebellum culture.
The ability of women like Maria and Mrs. de Ruyter, Lilla and Mrs.
Hart, and even Mary Sheffield, to generate warmth and Christian charity within their fragile domains reaffirmed the essential division between
public and private spheres, between the affective but fragile spaces of
women and the rough-and-tumble male world of the marketplace. Indeed, all these works encode an ideology of male power and destruc-
tiveness. It is a power rooted in greed, both sexual and economic, and
capable of bringing untold suffering and destruction to undeserving
women. Ever endangered by the threat of repeated abductions, deceit,
and murder, these women are never safe, even in the most protected
settings. Indeed, it is the possibility of assaults—assaults threatened and/

or carried out by evil men—that initiates these narratives and propels the plot. And in subjecting vulnerable women to repeated abductions, these novels tell of a social world where assault by men (sexual and economic) has become normative behavior. Indeed, violence against women is so powerful that it threatens not only individual identity, like that of Lilla, but familial and cultural identity as well, making the knightly males who save Mary in these works seem marginal, negligible, and powerless. When and where the Mary character prevails, she does so only after suffering untold loss and deprivation.

Insofar as the fictive representations of Mary Rogers signify versions of the city and the republic, so her fate within the novels suggests some larger collective social destiny. In *La Bonita Cigarera*, Mary, like the nation itself, is of English ancestry. In her magical and Cinderella-like transformation at the story's end she reclaims this non-American identity and is rewarded with her paternal fortune. At least for Ingraham, genuine order was not possible within New York; for him the new world offered little hope. In Burdett's urban world things are less clear-cut. Here the future of the new world, and particularly the new city, is the subject of a battle. Lilla is caught between two merchants, one good, one evil. As the object of this contest, her fate tells of the possibility for justice and virtue in the competitive world of the capitalist city. It is a battle royal, a battle that will end with the demise of one party or the other. At the end of *Lilla*, the Cinderella myth prevails; Lilla is returned, she receives her legacy, and, with the evil merchant undone, she dies. But even here hope is muted. The survival of Lilla notwithstanding, we are reminded that Lilla is still without real kin. The future of good is ambiguous; Mr. Sandford, the virtuous merchant, and his wife are themselves childless. The virtuous republic may be without an heir.

If both Ingraham and Burdett lament the passing of worlds lost, Judson has neither nostalgia nor hope. His naturalistic city is the nightmare vision of the republican metropolis. Here the world of the city is gone horribly awry, a place where capitalism has run amok. The death of Mary following her seduction and abortion underscored the violence of his configuration of the city. Like that of James Gordon Bennett, his proto-naturalistic vision suggests the finality of the loss of innocence, the dooming of the republican metropolis and its permanent replacement by a world where order can be restored only through repressive government intervention. Judson's city is ultimately beyond redemption; here the dangerous classes are in power, ruling from below, aided and abetted by the corruption of the merchant class itself. It is one such morally corrupt merchant who seduces and abandons his cigar girl lover and arranges her fatal abortion; the rape-seduction of Mary Sheffield is thus just one of many violations in a world where violation is the normative mode of personal interaction.

Conclusion: Tales of New York

As tales of the city cast around different versions of the Mary Rogers story, each of these novels speaks to a particular version of urban life at mid-century. Perhaps more significantly, they use the city to project different and often contending visions for the future of American society. In all of them—the Richardsonian story of Ingraham, the sentimental and Dickensian novel of Burdett, the heavily naturalistic and overdetermined sagas of Judson and Davis—the city itself is at the center of the story, the elaborate architectural presence of the imagined city overwhelming all the individual human narratives contained within it, just as the "real" city seemed to overshadow all within its domain. In these invented urban spaces place overwhelms narrative, the force of history overrides character and human sentiment, and Mary becomes the pawn in a larger drama about urban life and the promise, or lack of it, of a new modern America.

Cast as Maria, Lilla Hart, or Mary Sheffield, these imagined Marys are analogs of the city itself—its youth, innocence, and fragility. What happens to the fictive Mary within these stories provides a way of enacting scenarios for both the city and the new republic. As we move from Ingraham's anachronistic work to Burdett's tale of benevolence and reform and finally to the chaotic and irrepressible urban panorama of Judson, hope for the city—its viability as a diverse and liveable urban space—diminishes until it is lost entirely in the dark and dreaded city of Judson.

In a sense, these popular stories compose a literary tryptic, a set of nineteenth-century New York stories, each containing its own imagined and highly cinematic narrative of a popular fable of modern city life. In Ingraham's anti-urban tracts, *The Beautiful Cigar Girl* and its sequel *Herman de Ruyter*, lineage and birthright prevail as the youthful and virginal Mary, born of an earlier time and place, is returned unscathed to her ancestral home, the imagined pastoral England. In Burdett's *Lilla Hart*, Lilla is a classic version of a domestic heroine whose Christian virtue not only ensures her own safety, but also holds the power of redemption for those with whom she comes in contact. A true Dickensian heroine on the order of Little Dorrit or Little Nell, Lilla's suffering empowers and ennobles her. Burdett's reform vision, however, is not utopic; it is tempered by his own consciousness of the uneasy tension between the gentle bourgeois city of merchants like Mr. Sanford and the implied and lurking danger of the forces of greed and violence represented by the alliance of immoral merchants like Mary's evil uncle and his proletarian lackey. Unlike Ingraham's Maria, Lilla is returned to New York and allowed to remain within the city. But her tenancy is limited and protected; she will reside in an urban space analogous to those newly created residential zones like Gramercy Park, which in their exclusionary settings are within the city but insulated and protected from the dangers they harbor.

And finally, in the jumbled and anarchic world of E. Z. C. Judson, the city is both illegible and chaotic. Here the abortion scenario, which dooms both his character Mary Sheffield and her progeny, offers no hope for the future. Mary's demise is inevitable not so much because of her lack of virtue or even her inability to fend off her seducer, but because she is so totally defenseless against the forces of evil and disorder that have taken possession of the city. In this urban nightmare there are no protected spaces left, no means short of police rule and authoritarian control by which innocence and virtue can be protected. In the form of the sensuous seducer, the city itself becomes the ravisher and destroyer, and, as Judson constantly reminds us by interspersing his fiction with urban tracts, only newfound sources of external control—increased policing, anti-immigration laws, repressive legislation—can reimpose order on this dystopic metropolis.

The sexual motifs of assault and abduction are of course not unique to Judson; he only gives them their most violent and dangerous incarnation. In fact, as I have argued, they pervade all these works, although the resolution of the sexual drama is keyed to each author's political stance and urban vision. Thus in Ingraham's anachronistic Richardsonian script, Mary is inherently virtuous; her virtue is innate, a product of her noble lineage. She repels naturally and effortlessly the constant (if implied) assaults on both her body and her character. Even her brief tenure as a cigar girl leaves her unmarked and able to reassume the social position that is her birthright. For Burdett, once again it is the moral power of Lilla's Christian heart/Hart that enables her to reject the possibility of moral and sexual assault. But for Judson (and to a lesser degree for Davis) the Mary character is powerless to reject sexual aggression, and hence she is seduced, impregnated, and doomed to death. Her death, however, is not the result of the seduction or even of her pregnancy, but of one more violent assault on her body: a forced abortion. This brings us back, once again, to the curious issue of abortion as a trope, a recurrent motif of antebellum cultural representation. For if these last depictions of Mary Rogers (unlike the others) cast her as the victim of abortion, then the question emerges: who or what is the aborted or stillborn child of the beautiful cigar girl, the urban grisette?

In Judson's bleak urban vision, abortion marks the end of innocence for the virtuous republic and is a metaphor for civic death. Drawing on all the prior versions of Mary Rogers—the English daughter of a nobleman, the native-born daughter of the American heartland, the daughter of a poor urban widow—Judson creates a version of Mary Rogers that is at once the most familiar and the most despairing; she is the pregnant and abandoned working girl, doomed to die. And the death of her unborn child signals both the loss of hope for the future and the willful failure of the dream of an ordered democratic republic—a republican Metropolis.

EPILOGUE

*I*N his fictional confection, *Invisible Cities*, Italo Calvino describes cities as mental constructs built of signs and images, and defined by an allusive combination of fantasy, memory, and desire. In particular, the description of his imagined, antique urban space, Zaira, has much to tell the contemporary historian, who, moving in the shadowland between the present and the past, attempts to recapture the pulse of yet another city through one of its own tales of memory and desire. The city, Calvino says, does not consist of those things easily measured or counted: "how many steps make up the streets . . . the degree of the arcade's curves . . . the kind of zinc scales [which] cover a roof." Rather, the city consists of *relationships between the measurements of its space and the events of its past,* with "relationships" defined by the connections between small gestures, events, and nuances that connote the tenuous meanings of everyday life: "the height of a lamppost and the distance from the ground of a hanged usurper's swaying feet; the line strung from the lamppost to the railing opposite and the festoons that decorate the course of the queen's nuptial procession." Continuing, Calvino shows how these relational signs are represented and given meaning through narrative: "The rips in the fish nets and the three old men seated on the dock mending nets and telling each other for the hundredth time the story of the gunboat of the usurper, who some say was the queen's illegitimate son, abandoned in his swaddling clothes there on the dock."[1]

The story of Mary Rogers, like the story of the queen, has been recounted for the "hundredth time." Yet it remains allusive, infinite in its recapitulations. The ever-youthful Mary comes to us in much the same way as she did to her own contemporaries, as a discovered body of uncertain identity, defined by the physical remnants of her existence (a torn dress, a piece of lace, a handkerchief, a parasol) and a web of relationships, real and imagined. And in spite of the tools of modern historical analysis, the circumstances of her life and her death still remain conjecture. We will never know for certain whether her death was an accident of the abortionist's knife or an act of deliberate malice. Why her body was discarded in the Hudson, and by whom. Who, we continue to wonder, was her "real" mother, and what were the details of her birth? Indeed, her story reminds us, the study of history remains an act of detection on the illusive body of the past.

As narrative, the story of Mary Rogers is at once a tale of family decline, urban migration, and societal transformation. It is also, as I have argued, the source of many subsequent narratives told by different tellers, in different vocabularies, for different audiences and for different purposes: in the often confrontational and voyeuristic language of the new penny press that found in a violent sensational story the stuff of city news; in the political rhetoric of city officials, lawmakers, and politicians who, in constructing a language of sexual danger, rationalized new forms of legislation; in the imaginative reconstruction of Edgar Poe who found in this "real story" the material for an imaginative work of detection; and in the rougher voices of a series of popular novelists, who, drawing on Poe's original tale, used the event to work out a series of narratives about sex, class, and urban culture in the genre of the urban mystery story.

Rogers's story remains compelling at least in part because it retains its aura as a story of the city, offering fragments of life in New York at a moment both recognizable and distinctly foreign. The 1840s city was a place of wonder and terror, a labyrinthine urban space, crowded and kinetic, and teeming with the activity that defines it to this day. With Rogers we hasten through that city—walk down Nassau Street and ferry across the Hudson on a hot summer day. Through her we encounter a group of urban characters—the quintessential newspaperman, James Gordon Bennett, the entrepreneur, John Anderson, the wood engraver, Joseph Morse, the boarder and corkcutter, Daniel Payne, and (the most colorful of all) the abortionist, Madame Restell. And just as the so-called mystery of Mary Rogers still echoes with the mystery of the urban, so the city retains its essentially 1840s feminine identity—seductive, dangerous, and powerful.

But if the story of Mary Rogers tells some dimension of the history of the city and especially of the still problematic relationship between women and cities, it does so through a narrative of sexual violence, marking the point at which the saga of violent female death became a critical, even defining, aspect of modern urban culture. Here death, mystery, and sexuality were bonded, not for the first or final time, but in a new and significant way. For just as our national culture was solidifying, becoming simultaneously expansive in its economic enterprise and more repressive in its social and sexual attitudes, the subject of violent female death became an aspect of mass commercial culture. And whether eroticized through descriptions of a corpse or fantasized into fairy tales about heritage and wealth, the essence of the story as a narrative of sexually motivated assault remained the same. In the sense then that Poe first articulated and Foucault later defined in theory, Rogers was in death, if not in life, a sexual subject.

The persistence of this narrative, or some variation of it, is disturbingly, even overwhelmingly, apparent today. Indeed, as I write these concluding pages, the latest saga of the violent death of a beautiful woman—that of Nicole Brown Simpson—has overtaken every media source in America. The connections to the Rogers case may seem remote, not the least of which is that the setting is suburban rather than urban. (Or is Los Angeles, as the film *Blade Runner* suggests, the quintessential contemporary city?) But the recreations of the crime, its narrativization in the press and on the television screen, and the public thirst for information about the lives of those involved, bring to mind many eerie similarities. And despite the wonders inspired by the new technology of videotape and instant replay, the narratives are horribly familiar: the descriptions of the body at the scene of death that reenact an imagined scene of love and violent death, the detached medical language of the coroner, the chase scene through the city for a suspected killer, the published apologia of the prime suspect. These are not so different from those that followed the discovery of the body of Mary Rogers over one hundred and fifty years ago. Even the descriptions of the crime seem scarcely less bizarre than those written by Edgar Poe. And, as in Poe's detective tales, issues of race intertwine with visions of sex, violence, and urban chaos, reiterating once again that violence, especially sexually connected violence against women, is an enduring aspect of our culture as well as a constant source of public entertainment, spectatorship, and voyeurism. Poe's trope about the death of a beautiful woman as the finest subject for composition has, over time, become commonplace, just as the retelling of such events has become a mainstay of our contemporary culture.

The Rogers saga retains its character as a modern tale, not only in its representation, but also in the ways that it raises more substantive contemporary issues as well: the significance of rape as a tactic of personal and political oppression, the sexual freedom of women, the place of women in public life and culture, and the controversy over the right to a safe and legal abortion. All these remain at the center of public and political debate, just as the role of the state in private life has become a central social question of our time.

On a recent visit to Italy I was constantly reminded that cities themselves are composed of layers of civilization: the medieval church constructed on the Roman temple, the eighteenth-century civic building built over the ruins of a Renaissance edifice, the twentieth-century tenement erected over the site of an earlier, more modest, dwelling. Even the modern highway often rings the ancient city wall. In contemporary New York this traditional pattern of layering takes on different proportions, as our preoccupation with the modern tries, with more or less success, to obliterate the past. But if the shadow cast by the twin towers now overwhelms the landscape of Mary's old neighborhood south of City Hall, the block on which she lived retains much of its original architecture, if little of its character. And, ironically, the towers themselves offer the total panorama so sought after by antebellum illustrators and dioramists. The view these nineteenth-century artists longed for, but could only imagine, offers a miraculous perspective on a city that still has the capacity to amaze. From high, New York seems both incredibly dense and anarchic, and simultaneously bound and contained. It continues to defy control and inspire with its possibility.

Calvino ends his vignette about Zaira with a fitting conclusion to this book. Because the city soaks up memories and, like a sponge, expands, so a description of the city as it is today should contain all the city's past. However, he cautions, the city "does not tell its past, but contains it like the lines of a hand, written in the corners of the streets, the gratings of the windows, the banisters of the steps, the antennae of the lightning rods, the poles of the flags, every segment marked in turn with scratches, indentations, scrolls."[2]

NOTES

Introduction

1. *Lilla Hart: A Tale of New York* (New York: Baker and Scribner, 1846).

2. For recent studies in French cultural history see especially: Corbin, *Les Filles de noce: Misère sexuelle et prostitution (19 et 20 siècles)* (Paris: Aubier Montaigne, 1978); Corbin, *The Foul and the Fragrant: Odor and the French Social Imagination* (Cambridge: Harvard University Press, 1986); Davis, *Fiction in the Archives: Pardon Tales and Their Tellers in Sixteenth-Century France* (Stanford: Stanford University Press, 1987); Darnton, *The Great Cat Massacre and Other Episodes in French Cultural History* (New York: Basic Books, 1984); Darnton, *The Literary Underground of the Old Regime* (Cambridge, Mass.: Harvard University Press, 1982); Muchembled, *Popular Culture and Elite Culture in France, 1400–1750* (Baton Rouge: Louisana State University Press, 1984).

For a useful collection of the works of Antonio Gramsci see *Selections from Cultural Writings*, ed. David Forgacs and Geoffry Newell-Smith (Cambridge, Mass.: Harvard University Press, 1985). The works of Michel Foucault that have been most useful for this book are: *The Archeology of Knowledge* (New York: Pantheon Books, 1972); *Discipline and Punish: The Birth of the Prison* (New York: Pantheon Books, 1977); *The History of Sexuality: An Introduction* (New York: Vintage Books, 1980). Works by Barthes especially useful here include: *S/Z* (New York: Hill and Wang, 1974); *The Pleasure of the Text* (New York: Hill and Wang, 1975); *Camera Lucida* (New York: Hill and Wang, 1981). Although the focus of Walkowitz's recent study, (Chicago: University of Chicago Press, 1992) is late Victorian London and her concerns more explicitly political than mine, she treats many of the issues of sexual violence, narrative, and representation considered here in a different place and time. For relevant feminist theory see especially: Scott, *Gender and the Politics of History* (New York: Columbia University Press, 1988); Mulvey, *Visual and Other Pleasures* (Bloomington: Indiana University Press, 1989); and Tompkins, *Sensational Designs: The Cultural Work of American Fiction, 1790–1860* (New York: Oxford University Press, 1985).

For work in American cultural history see especially: Levine, *Highbrow/Lowbrow: The Origins of Cultural Hierarchy in America* (Cambridge, Mass.: Harvard University Press, 1988); Smith-Rosenberg, *Disorderly Conduct: Visions of Gender in Victorian America* (New York: Oxford University Press, 1985); Halttunen, *Confidence Men and Painted Women: A Study of Middle-Class Culture in America, 1830–1870* (New Haven: Yale University Press, 1982). Two recent collections of essays in culture history are: James Gilbert, Amy Gilman, Donald M. Scott, Joan W. Scott, eds., *The Mythmaking Frame of Mind: Social Imagination and*

American Culture (Belmont, Ca.: Wadsworth Publishing Company, 1992); and Richard Wightman Fox, Jackson T. Lears, eds., *The Power of Culture: Critical Essays in American Culture* (Chicago: University of Chicago Press, 1993).

3. Foucault, "Preface" to *The History of Sexuality,* Volume II, in Paul Rabinow, ed., *The Foucault Reader* (New York: Pantheon, 1984), 333–339.

4. Fredric Jameson, *The Political Unconscious: Narrative as a Socially Symbolic Act* (Ithaca: Cornell University Press, 1981), 9.

Chapter 1

1. Graham Swift, *Waterland* (New York: Vintage Books, 1982), 107.

2. Lydia Maria Child, *Letters from New York* (New York: C.S. Francis & Co., 1845), 32.

3. Child, *Letters,* 30–32.

4. Child, *Letters,* 31–33.

5. Just one month after Mary's death, the coroner held an inquest "on the body of an unknown female, aged about 20, who was found afloat in the water at the foot of King street, having been in that water a very short time. She was dressed in a calico frock with small purple figures; a muslin under garment: a common ring on the third finger of the left hand, and was without shoes, stockings or hat. Verdict, found drowned. Her body will be kept till noon this day in the dead house for identification." New York Evening *Post,* September 2, 1841.

6. The verdict, recorded at the Clerk's office in the county of Hoboken and signed by the magistrate and thirteen jurors, was simply that she "came to her death by evident signs of violence on her body committed by some persons or persons unknown." New York *Herald* and Newark Daily *Advertiser,* July 31, 1841. On August 16, 1841, the New York *Herald* stated that "Mary Rogers was brutally violated by six, or possibly, eight ruffians . . . [the proof] was unfit for publication." The lengthy details of the coroner's report were published by the *Herald* on August 17, 1841, and are discussed below.

7. *Herald,* August 2, 4, 6, 1841; New York *Tribune,* August 6, 1841; Newark Daily *Advertiser,* August 2, 1841.

8. *Herald,* August 12, 1841.

9. Seward's proclamation was widely printed in the newspapers on September 2, 1841.

10. George Walling, *Recollections of a New York Chief of Police* (New York, 1888), 28. Walling notes that "Such men as Gen. James Watson Webb, Gen. Scott, MM Noah, James Gordon Bennett, Fenimore Cooper, Washington Irving, N.P. Willis and Edgar A. Poe, were acquainted with the dainty figure and pretty face where they bought their cigars."

11. Philip Hone, *The Diary of Philip Hone,* ed. Alan Nevins (New York, 1936), 555.

12. Modern accounts include: John Walsh, *Poe the Detective: The Curious Circumstances Behind "The Mystery of Marie Roget"* (New Brunswick: Rutgers University Press, 1968); Raymond Paul, *Who Murdered Mary Rogers* (Englewood Cliffs: Prentice-Hall, 1971). Both of these focus on Edgar Allan Poe's reading of the events and contain the text of his story, "The Mystery of Marie Roget." Another retelling is in Irving Wallace, *The Fabulous Originals* (New York: Alfred A. Knopf, 1955). An excellent summary of the events is contained in the notes

to Edgar Allan Poe, "The Mystery of Marie Roget," in Thomas Ollive Mabbott, ed., *Collected Works of Edgar Allan Poe: Tales and Sketches, 1843–1849* (Cambridge: Harvard University Press, 1978), 715–788. A careful reading of the contemporary newspapers in light of Poe's story is in William Wimsatt, "Poe and the Mystery of Marie Roget," *PMLA*, 56(1941): 230–248. Less comprehensive older accounts include: Charles E. Pearce, *Unsolved Murder Mysteries* (New York: Frederick Stokes Co., 1924), 225–245; Will M. Clemens, "The Tragedy of Mary Rogers," *Era Magazine*, 14:450–463; Thomas S. Duke, *Celebrated Criminal Cases of America* (San Francisco: James H. Barry Co., 1910), 577–582; Edmund Pearson, "Mary Rogers and a Heroine of Fiction," *Vanity Fair*, 21(1929): 59, 110, and the same in his *Investigation of The Devil* (New York: C. Scribner's Sons, 1930), 177–185; Winthrop D. Lane, "The Mystery of Mary Rogers, *Colliers*, 85(March 8, 1930):19, 50, 52; Russel Crouse, *Murder Won't Out* (Garden City, N.Y., Doubleday & Co., 1932), 52–74. For a more recent version see Amy Gilman Srebnick "L'Assassinat et le mystère de Mary Rogers: Sexualité, crime et culture au milieu du dix-neuvième siècle dans la ville de New York," *Mentalités: Histoire des cultures et des sociétés*, ed. Robert Muchembled, 3 (Paris: Imago, 1989), special issue on *Violences Sexuelles*, ed. Alain Corbin: 113–134.

13. Edward K. Spann, *The New Metropolis: New York City, 1840–1857* (New York: Columbia University Press, 1981). Descriptions of the city during this period abound. In addition to Spann see Charles Lockwood, *Manhattan Moves Uptown: An Illustrated History* (Boston: Houghton Mifflin, 1976). For an overview of contemporary observations of the city see Bayard Still, ed., *Mirror for Gotham New York as Seen by Contemporaries from Dutch Days to the Present* (New York: University Press, 1956). Important contemporary accounts include: Junius Henri Browne, *The Great Metropolis: A Mirror For New York* (Hartford: American Publishing, 1869); Charles H. Haswell, *Reminiscences of an Octogenarian of The City of New York* (New York: Harper & Brothers, 1896). The works of the astute observer George Foster are particularly rich for the 1840s. They include: *New York in Slices, by an Experienced Carver. Being the Original Slices Published in the New York Tribune* (New York: W. F. Burgess, 1849); *New York by Gaslight* (New York: DeWitt and Davenport, 1850); *New York Naked* (New York: DeWitt and Davenport, 1850).

14. M. Christine M. Boyer, *Manhattan Manners: Architecture and Style, 1850–1900* (New York: Rizzoli, 1985), 11, 15–17.

15. A good recent summary of New York City growth during this period is contained in Diane Lindstrom's excellent essay "Economic Structure, Demographic Change, and Income Inequality in Antebellum New York," John Hull Mollenkopf, ed., *Power, Culture, and Place: Essays on New York City* (New York: Russel Sage, 1988), 3–23, especially 14–18. As Lindstrom and others have pointed out, urban growth was of course typical of this period nationally, but New York's population and economic output grew at markedly faster rates than any other city. New York, in fact, just about doubled the national rate of population growth. In 1800 the population was 33,131; by 1810 it had jumped to 119,734, by 1820 to 156,0566, by 1830 to 242, 278 and by 1840, on the eve of Mary's death, to 391,114; twenty years later on the eve of the Civil War it was a staggering 1,174,779. Immigration, both domestic and foreign, accounted for this surge, as the decline of rural agricultural economies at home and abroad led to extensive outmigration, especially among the younger generations. From the second decade of the nineteenth century on the better part of this population

growth was female, and, like Mary and Phebe, tended to be either under the age of twenty-five or over fifty. There are no complete figures on immigration or on the respective rates of domestic and foreign immigration into the city. See Robert Ernst, *Immigrant Life in New York City, 1825–1863* (New York: King's Crown Press, 1949); Marcus Hansen, *The Atlantic Migration, 1607–1860* (New York: Harper & Row, 1961 [1940]; Richard Stott, *Workers in the Metropolis: Class, Ethnicity, and Youth in Antebellum New York City* (Ithaca: Cornell University Press, 1990), 70–73. Also useful is Diane Lindstrom's, *Economic Development in the Philadelphia Region, 1810–1850* (New York: Columbia University Press, 1978).

16. Harris, *Humbug: The Art of P.T. Barnum* (Chicago: University of Chicago Press, 1973), 38.

17. Child, *Letters*, 13–17. For a discussion of Child's perception of the 1840s city see Stuart Blumin, "Explaining the New Metropolis: Perception, Depiction, and Analysis in Mid-Nineteenth-Century New York City, *Journal of Urban History* 11(1968): 9–38.

18. Child, *Letters*, 2; George Lippard, *The Empire City,; or, New York By Night and Day. Its Aristocracy and Its Dollars* (Philadelphia: T. B. Peterson & Brothers [1850], 1864), 42.

19. Lippard, *The Empire City*, 42; Foster, *New York in Slices*, 52.

20. The literature on antebellum urban disorder is extensive. For a discussion of the early period see Paul A. Gilje, *The Road to Mobocracy: Popular Disorder in New York City, 1763–1834* (Chapel Hill: University of North Carolina Press, 1987). Other useful sources include: Joel Tyler Headley, *The Great Riots of New York, 1712–1873*, Thomas Rose and James Rodgers, eds. (New York: Arno Press, 1970). Studies of particular urban riots include Peter Buckley, "To the Opera House: Culture and Society in New York City, 1820–1860" (Ph.D. Diss., SUNY Stony Brook, 1984).

21. The literature of visions and versions of the city is extensive. Recently, Gail Kern Paster explored the dialectic version of the city, the way in which "the idea of the city contains its own antitype" in her *The Idea of the City in the Age of Shakespeare* (Athens: University of Georgia Press, 1985). See also William Sharpe and Leonard Wallock, who note Carl Shorske's idea that because America had no medieval or Renaissance experience with urban life our conceptions had their origins in the nineteenth-century notion of the city of vice, thereby limiting the urban vision and relegating it to a fairly narrow and basically negative range. "From 'Great Town' to 'Nonplace Urban Realm': Reading the Modern City," in William Sharpe and Leonard Wallock eds., *Reading the Modern City: Essays in History, Art & Literature* (Baltimore: Johns Hopkins University Press, 1987), 1–50. The best overview of the dialectic of dark city, light city is still in Raymond Williams, *The City and the Country* (New York: Oxford University Press, 1973), especially 214–247.

22. The history of prostitution during this period is well covered in Timothy Gilfoyle's recent work: *City of Eros: New York City, Prostitution and the Commercialization of Sex, 1790–1920* (New York: W.W. Norton, 1992). For a discussion of the social geography of the commercial sex industry, see especially 29–54.

23. Lippard, *Empire City*, 42; Child, *Letters*, 19; Melville, *Pierre; or, the Ambiguities* (New York: Library of America [1852], 1984), 276. On recent discussion of cities as feminine see Gail Pastor, 4–5; and Christine Buci-Glucksmann, "Cat-

astrophic Utopia: The Feminine as Allegory of the Modern," *Representations*, 14(Spring, 1985): 220–229.

24. The event was covered extensively by all the New York City papers and reprinted from these throughout the East Coast. Most useful are the accounts in: the New York *Herald*, the New York *Tribune*, the *Commercial Advertiser*, *Brother Jonathan*, the New York Evening *Post*, and *The Morning Courier and the New York Enquirer*. As I comment in Chapter 4, newspapers outside the city adopted the story, reprinting dispatches from the New York papers. Cast as city news, the story took on another life in towns and rural areas around the new nation.

25. Edgar Allan Poe, "The Mystery of Marie Roget" was originally published in Snowden's *Ladies' Companion*, 18(November, December 1842 and February 1843: 15–20, 93–99, 162–167; and in Poe's own edition, *Tales* (New York: Wiley & Putnam, 1845), 151–199. A fuller discussion of "Marie Roget" and Poe's other detective stories is contained in Amy Gilman, "Edgar Allan Poe Detecting the City," in James Gilbert, Amy Gilman, Donald Scott, Joan Scott, *The Mythmaking Frame of Mind: Social Imagination and American Culture* (Belmont, Ca.: Wadsworth, 1992), 71–90.

26. Most important among these are: *The Beautiful Cigar Vender [sic], and Its Sequel, Herman de Ruyter. Tales of City Life, Founded on Facts* (New York: Williams Brothers, 1849); Charles Burdett, *Lilla Hart: A Tale of New York* (New York: Baker and Scribner, 1846); Edward Zane Carol Judson [Ned Buntline], *The Mysteries and Miseries of New York: A Story of Real Life* (New York: Berford & Co., 1848); and his *Three Years After: A Sequel to Mysteries and Miseries of New York*, n.d.; Andrew Jackson Davis, *Tale of a Physician: or The Seeds and Fruits of Crime* (Boston: William White & Company, 1869). See also *The Confession of Charles Wallace* (New Orleans: E.E. Barclay & Co., 1851).

27. On the history of New York City police reform see Wilbur Miller, *Cops and Bobbies: Police Authority in New York and London, 1830–1870* (Chicago: University of Chicago Press, 1977); James R. Richardson, *The New York Police: Colonial Times to the Present* (New York: Oxford University Press, 1970). On the history of abortion law see James C. Mohr, *Abortion in America: The Origins and Evolution of National Policy* (New York: Oxford University Press, 1978); Carl Degler, *At Odds: Women and the Family in America from the Revolution to the Present* (New York: Oxford University Press, 1980), 210–248; and Cyrus Means, Jr., "The Law of New York Concerning Abortion and the Status of the Foetus, 1644–1968: A Case of Cessation of Constitutionality," *New York Law Forum*, XIV, No.3 (Fall 1968): 419–426, especially,441;443–444; 449; 454–456; 454–463. For the important legislation concerning this period's abortion see *New York Revised Statutes* (1829), Pt. IV, ch.1, tit.2, sec.9; *New York Revised Statutes* (1852), Vol. II, Tit. II, Art.I, Sec. 6, num. 8 & 9, p. 847; Tit. VI, Sec. 21,22, p. 876.

28. See Michel Foucault, *A History of Sexuality: An Introduction* (New York: Vintage, 1980), 34, 11.

29. For a discussion of narrative see Laura Mulvey, *Visual and Other Pleasures* (Bloomington: Indiana University Press, 1989), x.

Chapter 2

1. New York *Herald,* September 28, 1841.

2. The best description of individual streets is still I. N. Phelps Stokes, *The Iconography of Manhattan* (New York: Robert H. Dodd, 1918).

3. George Foster, *New York in Slices* (New York: DeWitt and Davenport, 1850), 98.

4. George Lippard, *The Empire City* (Philadelphia: T. B. Peterson & Brothers, 1864 [1850]), 42.

5. The Aymar family had considerable real estate holdings in the area. Peter Aymar's ownership of the house, often incorrectly regarded as owned by Phebe Rogers, is documented in New York City Municipal Archives, Tax Assessment Records, 2nd Ward, 1840, 1841.

6. The manuscript for the 1840 Federal Census for New York City, Second Ward, p. 11, line 22, lists Phebe Rogers as the head of household at 126 Nassau Street. Included in the household listing were seven individuals: 2 males, ages, 20–30; 2 males ages 30–40; 1 female child, under 5; 1 female, age 20–30 (Mary Rogers); 1 female, age 50–60 (Phebe Rogers).

7. *Herald,* August 12, 1841.

8. Foster, *New York in Slices,* 98.

9. "The Mystery of Marie Roget," *Collected Works of Edgar Allan Poe: Tales and Sketches, 1843–1849,* ed., Thomas Ollive Mabbott (Cambridge: Harvard University Press, 1978), 749–750.

10. *Herald,* August 12, *Tribune,* August 12, *Post,* August 12, 1841.

11. Foster, *New York in Slices,* 99–100.

12. *Post, Herald,* August 12, 1841.

13. *Post, Herald,* August 12, 1841.

14. New York *Sun,* July 27, 1841.

15. *Herald,* August 12, 1841.

16. New York *Evening Post,* August 13, 1841; *Herald,* August 13, 1841. *Sun,* August 13, 1841.

17. Valentine's, *Manual of the City of New York, 1841* lists the ferry crossings and schedules.

18. Samuel Dexter Ward, "New York City in 1842," *New York Historical Society Quarterly Bulletin* 21(1937): 114.

19. *Tribune,* July 27, 1841.

20. *Post,* August, 13, 1841.

21. *Post,* August 13, 1841.

22. The *Herald,* July 31, 1841, reported the initial inquest as the second item in a column headed simply: "Inquest at Hoboken." By August 4, 1841, the *Herald* had moved the story to a more central space and devoted a full column to a description of the body. The press coverage is discussed more fully in Chapter 4.

23. On August 17, 1841 the *Herald* printed, in question-and-answer format, the New York City Mayor's interview with the Hoboken coroner, Dr. Richard Cook. The New York City coroner, Dr. Archibald Archer, was also present at the interview but his participation was not recorded.

24. *Herald,* August 17, 1841.

25. *Herald, Post,* August 13, 1841.

26. New York City Municipal Archives, Register of Deaths, City of New York, Borough of Manhattan, Volume 12.

27. *Post* August 16, 1841.

28. *Herald,* August 8, 1841.

29. This statement was part of the set of depositions reported in the newspapers on August 13, 1841. See the *Herald, Post,* and *Tribune* for that date for the verbatim testimony. The Newark Daily *Advertiser* summarized the accounts.

30. The *Tribune,* August 19, 1841, issued a disclaimer concerning reports that Crommelin had been arrested: "We know Mr. Crommeline [sic] who is a highly respectable man, and know that *he has not been arrested,* and that no such charge is now entertained, or has ever been brought against him."

31. *Herald,* August 6, 1841.

32. *Post,* September 13 1841; *Tribune,* September 14, 1841.

33. *Herald,* October 10, 1841.

34. *Herald,* October 10, 1841.

35. Walsh, *Poe the Detective,* 37. The accounts of Payne's death were in the papers of October 10, 1841. This account is excerpted from the *Herald* of that day, which reprinted verbatim the depositions of twelve individuals given before the Mayor. These included statements from his brother John Payne, Crommelin, Mrs. Loss, friends of Payne, and Dr. Cook, the Hoboken coroner. The *Newark Daily Advertiser,* October 9, reported that Payne had committed suicide, that his throat was cut, and that a note was found in his pocket. The *Advertiser* of October 11, 1841, contained a discussion of Payne's day prior to his death.

36. *Herald,* August 10, 1841.

37. *Courier* August 5, 1841; Newark Daily *Advertiser,* August 6, 1841.

38. *Post,* August 13, 1841; and *Herald,* August 13, 1841. The quote about the Five Points is taken from the *Herald.*

39. It is also possible that Morse may actually have boarded with either Payne or Crommelin at an earlier time. All this information and quotes taken from *Tribune,* August 8, 1841.

40. *Tribune,* August 18, 1841.

41. *Tribune, Herald,* August 18, 1841. The full text went as follows:

On Sunday, the 25th of July, I met a young lady about noon, in Bleecker Street near Morton Street. She was dressed in black: I had met her before, and persuaded her to go with me to Staten Island. We went there; to the Pavilion; and had some refreshments and I kept her mind employed till after the last boat departed. I then persuaded her to agree to pass the night with me and to sleep in the same room. She did so; I tried to have connexion with her in the night but did not succeed. On Monday morning I came to the city with her, and left her in good friendship at the corner of Greenwich and Barclay Street. This was past 11 A.M. I have not seen her since. I don't know her name. I think she lives in Morton Street with her mother. I think the house where she lives has a brass plate on the door, with cyphar letters on it. I don't know the name on it. Her name might be Mary Rogers. If it is I had no hand in murdering her! as I left her in good feeling. Her hair was rather light. Her complexion light. I think her eyes brows were rather dark. She was slender made; of very genteel appearance; rather tall and thin; she told me she was seventeen years old; she had a very long delicate hand, but no rings on her fingers. She said she was going to board at the Seminary at Staten Island. This is all I know about her.

42. *Herald*, August 20, 1841. Haviland's testimony was reported in question-and-answer form.

43. Their altercation was overheard by their neighbor, Mary Haviland (whose room abutted that of the Morse's and who no doubt heard all through the boardinghouse walls), who testified on August 18 as a witness for Mrs. Morse and corroborated her story. She said that she

> saw Joseph Morse from 55 Greene Street, his place of residence and . . . that Morse did not return to his place of residence until about ten o'clock in the evening of July 26th, that he abused his wife by calling her improper names and deponent heard a shuffling between Morse and his wife, and Morse and his wife went out of the house about an hour after he came in, and shortly after they went out deponent heard Mrs. Morse screaming on the corner of Broome and Greene Street that Morse tore part of his wife's earring out, struck her and then ran away, leaving his wife there, & [that she] . . . has not seen him since that time—that Mrs. Morse was not intoxicated, and . . . [she] . . . thinks Morse was not intoxicated.

New York City Municipal Archives, Police Court Records, Box 7457.

It is also possible that the Morses had been having marital difficulties for some time and that Martha's decision to go to the police was one way of legitimizing a later claim against him for abandonment.

44. Recorded by the Court of General Sessions, August 21, 1841. New York City Municipal Archives, Police Court Records, Box 7457.

45. Bail was initially posted by his two of Morse's friends, a wood engraver and a stereographer. On August 21 his lawyer, Robert Stevenson, presented a writ of habeas corpus "for the production of the body of Joseph W. Morse." But pending all these inquiries, and because of the fact that "that there was no other complaint against . . . Joseph Morse but the one of Assault and battery" Justices Taylor and Palmer released him. That same day Martha dropped her charges against her husband and asked that the court discharge him from custody. The court officially dismissed the case, without the payment of any costs, on September 16, 1841. For Joseph Morse, however, the case remained alive and he continued to try and clear his name and reputation, keeping the story alive in the daily press.

46. The argument about the unidentified sailor hinged on an 1847 letter from George Eveleth to Poe in which Eveleth asked if "the naval officer had been discovered?" Poe responded that "The naval officer, who committed the murder (the accidental death arising from an attempt at abortion) confessed it; and the whole matter is now well understood—but, for the sake of relatives, I must not speak further." From this John H. Ingraham concludes that the implicated officer was Spencer. Wimsatt maintains that this also conforms with the story line in Andrew Jackson Davis's novel, *Tale of a Physician* in which a wealthy rake and Marie's lover, Jack Blake, pays for abortion and flees to Texas. For further discussion of this see Ingraham, *Edgar Allan Poe*, Vol. I (London, 1880), 235. Eveleth's letter is contained in *Letters from George Eveleth to Edgar Allan Poe*, ed. T. O. Mabbott (New York: New York Public Library, 1922), 15.

Poe's response is in "Letters of George W. Eveleth," ed. J. S. Wilson, *Alumni Bulletin of the University of Virginia*, 27 (1924). For a discussion see William Kurtz Wimsatt, Jr., "Poe and the Mystery of Mary Rogers," *PMLA*, 56(March, 1941): 230–248, especially 247–248.

The Somers mutiny drew the concern and considerable consternation of James Fenimore Cooper who took up the cause of the young dead seaman, maintaining that his civil rights had been violated at the hand of arbitrary authority. See Cooper, *The Cruise of the Somers illustrative of the Despotism of the Quarter Deck; and of the Unmanly Conduct of Commander Mackenzie* (New York: J. Winchester, 1844); and U.S. Courts: Court Martial (Mackenzie). *Proceedings of the Naval Court Martial in the Case of Alexander Slidell Mackenzie*, to which is annexed an elaborate review by James Fenimore Cooper (New York: Henry G. Langley, 1844). A fascinating analysis of the Somers mutiny is contained in Michael Paul Rogin, *Subversive Genealogy: The Politics and Art of Herman Melville* (New York: Alfred A. Knopf, 1983), 79–85.

47. Alan Nevins, ed., *Diary of Philip Hone* (New York: Dodd, Mead & Company, 1936), 555.

48. *Post*, September 29, 1841. The paper added: "Finnigan when arrested wore a ring which is said to have been identified as one belonging to Mary Rogers. The Bee says that he is one of the gang who about a year since committed a gross outrage upon a young girl in this city."

49. *Herald*, August 16, 21, 1841.

50. *Herald*, September, 17, 1841. "There were a much larger number of fire rowdies, butcher boys, and soap-locks, and all sort of riotous miscreants over at Weehawken, and almost all of them armed with sticks. A great many of them came in row boats to the rum hole on the mud bunk; and two boats in particular, one with six and the other with nine desperadoes in them landed."

51. The full text went as follows:

They were all mildewed down hard through the action of the rain and stuck together from mildew. The grass had grown around and over some of them. The silk and the parasol were strong, but the threads of it were run together, within the upper part where it had been doubled and folded was all mildewed and rotten, and tore on its being opened. The white linen handkerchief had a corded border round it, and was mildewed also, so was the scarf. This and the petticoat were crumpled up as if in a struggle. The pieces of her frock torn out by the bushes were about three inches wide and six inches long. One part was the hem of the frock, and had been mended; the other piece was part of the skirt, not the hem. They looked like strips torn off, and were on the thorn bush, about a foot from the ground. The petticoat, shawl, & c. were full of little bugs, called by the Dutch, kellerasbe, that is, in English, cellar jackase, an insect that always gets into clothing lying in wet places.

Upon further search the Hoboken coroner, the Mayor, and the District Attorney "examined the ground" and found "three pieces of dress which had belonged to Mary, besides other evidences of murder— traces of blood—and the rails of the fences down to the water's edge,[which] had been removed or broken down, so as to take the body, when the poor girl was dead, to the river." *Herald*, September 6, 1841.

52. *Herald,* September 24, 1841.

53. The *Flash,* a sporting sheet edited by Charles G. Scott, John Vandewater, and William Snelling, offered this opinion publicly as early as October 13, 1841.

54. The full text of the statement was as follows: "On the Sunday of Miss Rogers (*sic*) disappearance she came to her house from this city in company with a young physician who undertook to procure for her a premature delivery.—While in the hands of her physician she died and a consultation was then held as to the disposal of her body. It was finally taken at night by the son of Mrs. Loss and sunk in the river where it would be found. Her clothes were first tied up in a bundle and sunk in a pond on the land of James G. King in that neighborhood; but it was afterwards thought that they were not safe there, and they were accordingly taken and scattered through the woods as they were found. The name of the physician is unknown to us, nor do we know whether it was divulged or not." *Tribune,* November 18, 1842. Reprinted in the Newark Daily *Advertiser,* November 18, 1842.

55. *Morning Courier and New York Enquirer,* November 12, 1842. The full text of Gilbert Merritt's deposition went as follows:

State of New Jersey Hudson Co.—Personally appeared before me a Justice of the Peace of said Country, Gilbert Merritt, who duly sworn before me, deposeth and saith:—that in the month of July 1841, he(this deponent) as a magistrate held an inquest on the body of Mary C. Rogers, at Hoboken, in said County of Hudson, who this deponent believes was murdered; and this deponent further saith that from information he has obtained and facts in his possession, he verily believes that the murder of the said Mary C. Rogers was perpetrated in a house at Weehawken, called "The Nick Moore House" then kept by one Frederica Loss, alias Kallenbarack (now deceased) and her three sons, to wit: Oscar Kellenbarack, Charles Kallenbarack, and Ossian Kellenbarack, all three of whom the deponent has reason to believe are worthless and profligate characters; and this deponent further saith, that he has just reason to believe that the said sons and their mother, kept one of the most depraved and debauched houses in New Jersey, and that all of them had a knowledge of and were accessory to, and became participators in the murder of said Mary C. Rogers, and the concealment of her body.

                                                                    Gilbert Merritt

Sworn and subscribed the 14th of November, 1842

56. Newark Daily *Advertiser,* November 19, 1842.

57. Newark Daily *Advertiser,* November 18, 1842; reprinted from the *Tribune,* November 17, 1842.

58. Hone, *Diary,* 555.

Chapter 3

1. *Collected Works of Edgar Allan Poe: Tales and Sketches, 1843–1849,* ed. Thomas Ollive Mabbott (Cambridge: Harvard University Press, 1978), 415.

2. John Rogers, Sr., "An Epistle to the Church Called Quakers [1705]," in *The Rogerenes: Some Hitherto Unpublished Annals Belonging to the Colonial History of Connecticut* (Boston: Stanhope Press, 1904), 345.

3. Walt Whitman, *Leaves of Grass and Selected Prose*, ed. John Kouwenhoven (New York: Random House, 1950), 102–103.

4. Herman Melville, *Pierre; or, the Ambiguities* (New York: Library of America, 1984 [1852]), 268.

5. George Lippard, *The Empire City* (Philadelphia: T.B. Peterson & Brothers, 1864 [1850]), 42; Edgar Allan Poe, "Man of the Crowd," *Collected Works: Tales and Sketches, 1831–1842*, ed. Thomas Ollive Mabbott (Cambridge: Harvard University Press, 1978), 507; Whitman, "Crossing Brooklyn Ferry," *Leaves of Grass*, 127.

6. George Simmel, "The Metropolis and Mental Life," *The Sociology of Georg Simmel*. trans. Kurt Wolff (New York: The Free Press, 1950), 409–426; Lynn Lofland, *A World of Strangers: Order and Action in Urban Public Space* (Prospect Heights, Ill.: Waveland Press, 1985 [1973]), especially 3–23; Richard Sennett, *The Fall of Public Man: On the Social Psychology of Capitalism*, (New York: Vintage, 1978), 47–49.

7. I have found only one correct suggestion of Rogers's origins in New York and Connecticut papers: The *Tribune* of August 26, 1841, reprinted the following from the *New-London Gazette*: "Miss Rogers whose tragic fate deeply interests the community, was a native of New London, and was connected with highly respectable families still residing there."

8. *Herald*, August 4, 1841.

9. *Tribune*, August 12, 1841; Newark Daily *Advertiser*, August 24, 1841; *Courier and Enquirer*, August 23, 1841; *Tattler*, August 23, 1841.

10. The paper continued: "A foolish story was yesterday started that she had returned to home and friends; but no one could tell how or whence the rumor came abroad, and that it was almost universally believed to be a hoax, or some device of an enemy to put the authorities off their guard." *Tribune*, August 24, 1841.

11. The original town of Lyme eventually became Old Lyme. I have held to the original name, although many of the records are cataloged under "Old Lyme." State and local histories useful for reconstructing the history of the area include: Richard L. Bushman, *From Puritan to Yankee: Character and the Social Order in Connecticut, 1690–1765* (Cambridge: Harvard University Press, 1967); Frances Manwaring Caulkins, *History of New London, Connecticut from the First Survey of the Coast in 1612 to 1852* (New London, Privately published, 1860); Bruce C. Daniels, *The Connecticut Town: Growth and Development, 1635–1790* (Middletown, Conn.: Wesleyan University Press, 1979); Benjamin Tinkham Marshall, A.M., D.D., ed., *A Modern History of New London County Connecticut* (New York: Lewis Historical Publishing Company, 1922); Richard Purcell, *Connecticut in Transition: 1775–1818* (Middletown, Conn.: Wesleyan University Press, 1963); Bruce Stark, *Lyme Connecticut: From Founding to Independence* (Privately printed, 1976).

12. Bushman, *From Puritan to Yankee*, provides the best general discussion of this period of Connecticut's history. For a discussion of the economy see especially 83–103; Daniels, *The Connecticut Town*, traces the settlement and expansion of this area provides evaluations of land quality and the characteristics of local populations; on the economic history of the areas also see Purcell, *Connecticut in Transition*, 74–77. Later, by the early 1800s, whaling would make the town and its surrounding areas prosperous. This as well as all other aspects of New London's history are chronicled in Caulkins, *History of New London*.

13. Phebe is often incorrectly identified as a descendant of the Wade family, also prominent in Lyme during this period. These genealogies have been compiled from the following: *Connecticut Vital Records; Second, Third, Fourth, Fifth and Sixth Census of the United States, 1800–1850*, Manuscript schedules for New York City; *Sixth Census of the United States*, 1840; Vital Records of Lyme Connecticut to the end of the year 1850, transcribed by Verne Hall and Elizabeth Plimpton (Lyme, Conn.: American Revolution Bicentennial Commission, 1976); Samuel G. Drake, *Memoir of the Rev. Cotton Mather, D.D. with a Genealogy of the Family of Mather* (Boston: Antiquarian Book Store, 1851); Horace Mather, *Lineage of Rev. Richard Mather* (Hartford: Lockwood & Brainard Co., 1890); John Mather *Genealogy of the Mather Family, 1500–1847*, (1848); James Swift Rogers, *James Rogers of New London Connecticut and His Descendants* (Boston, published by the compiler, 1902); Daniel Rogers MS, 4 vols., New London County Historical Society; John Cassan Wait, "Some Branches of the Wait Family of New England," Typescript, New York Public Library; Family History Center of the Church of Jesus Christ of Latter-Day Saints.

14. This information is derived from the following records in the Connecticut State Library; Estate of Ezra Mather, Lyme, 1808, New London Probate District, file 3491. The extensive probate records of Ezra Mather include: "The Last Will and Testament of Ezra Mather, February 12, 1808"; "An Inventory of the Estate of Ezra Mather, Late of Lyme, Deceased"; and an additional inventory filed by his executors as "The Estate of Ezra Mather late of Lyme, deceased," Rockwell and Smith, Executors. The file includes receipts for distributions and a variety of miscellaneous documents recording transactions carried out for the estate by its executors. Additional related information is contained in Land Records for Lyme and New London; Records of the First Congregational Church of Lyme.

15. "The Estate of Ezra Mather . . . ," Rockwell and Smith, executors.

16. Ezra (10/11/97–5/6/55), Phoebe A. (2/27/99–12/22/30), Orlando (3/3/04–1806), Robert,(3/3/02–2/34), and Frederick (10/5/08–1830). This information is derived from the Family Resource Records of the Church of Jesus Christ of the Latter-day Saints, records for Connecticut. Note that a change in spelling distinguishes Phoebe Mather's name from that of her mother, Phebe Wait Mather Rogers.

17. In writing of Hingham, Massachusetts, Daniel Scott Smith writes that white women could expect to bear a child, on the average, every twenty-eight months, and that, assuming both partners lived a normal life span, on average such women bore between five and seven children before they completed their childbearing years. Philip J. Greven, Jr., "Family Structures in Seventeenth Century Andover," in Michael Gordon, ed., *The American Family in Social-Historical Perspective* (New York: St. Martin's Press, 1983), 140–142. See also Alexander Keyssar, "Widowhood in Eighteenth-Century Massachusetts: A Problem in the History of the Family." *Perspectives in American History* 8(1974): 81–119.

18. "The Last Will and Testament of Ezra Mather." Ezra's grave stands with that of this parents in the cemetery of the First Congregational Church, Lyme.

19. Third Manuscript Census of the United States, 1810.

20. "Receipt of Dan Rogers to Executor of Ezra Mather," April 12, 1814. Probate Records, Estate of Ezra Mather.

21. Rogers early land acquisitions included twenty-four hundred acres east

of the Connecticut River that he held with Col. Pyncheon of Springfield, several hundred acres in the Great Neck land at Mohegan known as Pamechaug farm, and several house lots in town. Caulkins, *History of New London*, 201–202.

22. In addition, many other family members were known to have allied themselves with other dissenting groups, especially the Baptists and Seventh Day Adventists of Rhode Island. The history of the Rogerenes deserves more serious attention. Accounts of their beliefs and practices are contained in: Caulkins, *History of New London*, especially 201–221; Marshall, *A Modern History of New London*, I, 284–285; and, John Rogers Bolles and Anna B. Williams, *The Rogerenes: Some Hitherto Unpublished Annals Belonging to the Colonial History of Connecticut* (Boston: Stanhope Press, 1904), which contains a history of the sect and selected Rogerene writings.

23. Marshall, *A Modern History . . .* , I, 284; Caulkins, *History of New London*, 201–221; Perry Miller, *The New England Mind, From Colony to Province* (Boston: Beacon Press, 1961), 448.

24. Miller, *The New England Mind*, 448.

25. From the 1670s on they were locked in battle with the New London ministry, especially that of Gurdon Saltonstall. In this they fit into a tradition of dissent and religious enthusiasms in New England, a tradition made most famous in New London by James Davenport and his followers who in 1743 preached a similarly boisterous, anti-clerical and separatist position. See Harry S. Stout and Peter Onuf, "James Davenport and the Great Awakening in New London," *Journal of American History*, 71(December, 1983): 557–558.

26. The publicly sexual and openly physical nature of their behavior was underscored by John Rogers's own sexual history—he was twice scandalously divorced and charged with bestiality. These quotes are contained in Benjamin Trumbull, *A Complete History of Connecticut, Civil and Ecclesiastical*, II(New London: H. D. Utley, 1898), 20.

27. Marshall, *A Modern History*, 285.

28. Even Amos's death spoke to the family's creative and entrepreneurial spirit; in 1820, at the age of sixty-five he drowned in a squall in the waters between Pequonnock and New London while sailing a yacht crafted in Russia and "curiously built without the use of nails" and brought to America by his son Moses.

Moses Rogers began to play with the possibilities of steam travel by taking the *Phoenix* (the first full-sized steamer built by John Stevens, "an inventor of versatile genius" and early settler of Hoboken) out into the open ocean while making its routine voyage between Sandy Hook and Delaware. According to Robert Albion, the historian of New York port, Rogers tried, without success, to get Wall Street and South Street backing to develop steam navigation for transatlantic travel. Support was forthcoming instead from a firm based in the southern cotton port of Savannah, Georgia, and with that help Rogers designed and oversaw the construction of the *Savannah*, a full-rigged steamship, intended as an experiment to initiate transatlantic travel by steam navigation. The ship, which was actually built in New York City, made its maiden voyage in 1819 to Liverpool in twenty-two days, from whence it went to Copenhagen, Stockholm, and even St. Petersburg. As the first transatlantic trip by steam, the ship and its captain were celebrated by royalty and nobility in all their ports of call. The success of this voyage prompted the formation that same spring, of the "Ocean Steam Ship Company," a firm established for "constructing and employing steam ships in navigating the ocean." Moses Rogers, however did not live to see the fruits of his labor, for he died just two years later, in 1821, one year after Mary's birth, of yellow fever in South Carolina.

Other Rogerses also made their marks. Thomas Rogers (1792–1856) left Connecticut to settle in Paterson, New Jersey, and would become that nineteenth-century industrial city's most famous inventor and one of its most successful businessmen and entrepreneurs. In 1822 with John Clark he brought iron industry to Paterson with the establishment of the Danforth Locomotive and Machine Company and years later another of his enterprises, the Rogers Company, produced the first of Paterson's line of railroad engines. Yet another New London born Rogers cousin, also named Daniel Rogers (1780–1839), reached stature of a very different sort. He was an attorney who settled in New York City and made a career of bringing criminal and legal proceedings into public view as editor of the *City Hall Recorder*. This Daniel Rogers died in 1839—two years before Mary's death. Had he lived just a few years longer, it is more than likely that our knowledge of the Mary Rogers saga might have been a very different tale. On the history of the Rogers family see also J. S. Rogers, *James Rogers of New London Connecticut, and His Descendants* (1902); Caulkins, *History of New London*, 652–654. On John Stevens see *John Stevens*, An American Record (1928); Robert Albion, *The Rise of New York Port* (New York: Charles Scribner's Sons, 1970 [1937]), 314.

29. R. B. Wall, a New London reporter writing in 1910, suggests that Daniel had been a heavy drinker and the ne'er-do-well son of his respected parents. He also writes that in keeping with his family's talents, Daniel developed the principle of dry dock for ships but never received due credit for the invention. His wandering and drinking habits, Wall claims, led him to Mississippi where he was eventually killed in a boat explosion. The New London *Day*, July 10, 1919.

Daniel and Phebe do show up in the Lyme population census for 1830 under Daniel's name, although Wall, who has other aspects of the Mary Rogers history completely jumbled, also writes that Daniel and Phebe lived as boarders in the house of Daniel's brother, Captain Stevens Rogers, in New London.

30. Daniel Scott Smith and Michael Hindus, "Premarital Pregnancy in America 1640–1971: An Overview and Interpretation," *Journal of Interdisciplinary History*, 4(Spring 1975): 537–570.

31. Daniel Rogers appears in the manuscript schedule for Connecticut, *Fourth Census of the United States, 1830. Longworth's Directory* for 1840–41 lists Phebe Rogers as the widow of Daniel.

32. It is likely that Phebe's two surviving sisters were already here as well as her oldest and only surviving son, Ezra Mather.

33. Alice Kessler-Harris, *Out to Work: A history of Wage-Earning Women in the United States* (New York: Oxford University Press, 1982), 20–29.

34. On the crisis and ensuing depression see Samuel Rezneck, "The Social History of an American Depression, 1837–1843," *American History Review* 40(1935): 663–76; Sean Wilentz, *Chants Democratic: New York City and the Rise of the American Working Class, 1788–1850* (New York: Oxford University Press, 1985), 299–301. The statement on unemployment is from Wilentz, 299.

35. On economic growth and demographic patters during this period see Diane Lindstrom, "Economic Structure, Demographic Change, and Income Inequality in Antebellum New York," John Hull Mollenkopf ed., *Power, Culture, and Place: Essays in New York City* (New York: Russel Sage, 1988), 3–23. For

the demographics of age and sex see "Age-Specific Migration Rates and Sex Ratios for New York County," Table 1.6, 16.

36. By 1860, 27 percent of the city's manufacturing labor force was female, a number that does not account for the thousands of women employed in the sweated trades that were an important adjunct to the manufacturing trades. Outside industry, women flocked to the expanded service sectors of the economy, working as laundresses, boardinghouse keepers, and especially in domestic service. And while in the nation as a whole 10 percent of women worked for wages, in New York almost one-third of the female population were so employed. On women's work during this period see Lindstrom, "Economic Structure . . . , 11–14; Kessler Harris, *Out to Work*, 20–72; Christine Stansell, *City of Women: Sex and Class in New York 1789–1860* (Urbana: University of Illinois Press, 1987 [1982]), especially 105–129. On women in manufacturing see Amy Gilman Srebnick, "True Womanhood and Hard Times: Women and Early New York Industrialization, 1840–1860 (Ph.D. Diss., SUNY Stony Brook, 1979).

37. Kessler-Harris, *Out to Work*, 139–141. On laboring women generally as sexual prey see Stansell, *City of Women*, 26–27. Interestingly, Penny's lengthy entry on saleswork includes a discussion of French saleswomen and "semptresses." *How Women Can Make Money, Married or Single* (New York: Arno Press, 1971 [1870]), 125–133; quote, 125.

38. *The Diary of Philip Hone, 1828–1851*, Alan Nevins, ed. (New York: Dodd Mead & Co., 1927), 462.

39. On the social segregation of urban culture see Larry Levine, *Highbrow, Lowbrow: The Origins of Cultural Hierarchy in America* (Cambridge, Ma.: Harvard University Press, 1990). A discussion of the Astor place theater riots is contained in Peter G. Buckley, "To the Opera House: Culture and Society in New York City, 1820–1860" (Ph.D. Diss., SUNY Stony Brook, 1884); and "The Case Against Ned Buntline: The 'Words, Signs and Gestures of Popular Authorship,' " *Prospects: An Annual of American Culture Studies*, Vol. 13, ed. Jack Salzman (New York: Cambridge University Press, 1988), 249–272.

40. Soaplocks disparagingly referred to one of the rowdy groups credited with Mary's death. For a contemporary description of a "Soaplock," see the *Sunday Morning Atlas*, April 5, 1841.

41. Halttunen, *Confidence Men and Painted Women: A Study of Middle- Class Culture in America, 1830–1870* (New Haven: Yale University Press, 1982), 67–91.

42. Working-class culture is discussed in Stuart Blumin, *The Emergence of the Middle Class: Social Experience in the American City, 1760–1900* (Cambridge: Cambridge University Press, 1989), 216–218; Stansell, *City of Women*; Elliot J. Gorn, " 'Good-Bye Boys, I Die a True American ': Homicide, Nativism, and Working-Class Culture in Antebellum New York City, *Journal of American History*, 74(1987): 388–410; and *The Manly Art: Bare-Knuckle Prize Fighting in America* (Ithaca: Cornell University Press, 1986); Wilentz, *Chants Democratic*, 257–271. On Middle-class culture and behavior see Blumin, *The Emergence of the Middle Class*; Halttunen, *Confidence Men and Painted Women*, especially 92–123; and, for a general discussion of the topic, Richard Sennett, *The Fall of Public Man: On the Social Psychology of Capitalism* (New York: Vintage Books, 1978).

43. The 1840s, notes Mary Ryan, was the "rough benchmark in the gender geography of public urban space." From here on, women (presumably middle-class women) were left "mingling in the old public realm of informal sociability or newly ensconced in their Victorian domiciles, but barred from the formal

public spaces newly opened to men." Ryan, *Women in Public: Between Banners and Ballots, 1825–1880* (Baltimore: Johns Hopkins University Press, 1990), 68. What Ryan does not account for, however, is the class based assumptions underlying this dichotomy of urban space.

44. Foster, *New York by Gaslight* (New York: DeWitt and Davenport, 1850), 9.

45. See, for example: Henri Junius Browne, *The Great Metropolis: A Mirror of New York* (Hartford: American Publishing Co., 1869); George Ellington, *The Women of New York: or, The Under-world of the Great City* (New York: The New York Book Co., 1869); Marie Louise Hankins, *Women of New York* (New York: Marie Louise Hankins Publishing Co., 1861); James D. McCabe [Edward Winslow Martin], *The Secrets of the Great City: A Work Descriptive of the Virtues, Vices, the Mysteries, Miseries and Crimes of New York City* (Philadelphia: Jones Brothers & Co., 1868); McCabe, James, Jr., *New York by Gaslight* (New York: Crown Publishers, 1984 [1882]).

46. For a more extensive treatment of the changing construction of the female poor see, Amy Gilman "From Widowhood to Wickedness: The Politics of Class and Gender in New York City Private Charity, 1799–1860," *History of Education Quarterly*, 24(1984): 59–74.

47. As many have pointed out, Victorian ideas about prostitution were intimately bound with what Ruth Rosen refers to as "class, gender and racial systems." The prostitute served a socially and politically important role in upholding already existent class and gender divisions. As Rosen reminds us, singling out one group of degraded women provided a constant and visible reminder to other women to live within expected boundaries. Simultaneously, the prostitute upheld the double standard and polarized images of women as angels or whores. Moreover, the "association of prostitution with lower-class, immigrant and non white populations served to divide women from one another and to justify the low ranking of these populations in the social hierarchy." Ruth Rosen, *The Lost Sisterhood: Prostitution in America, 1900–1918* (Baltimore: Johns Hopkins University Press, 1983), 6–7. On this topic generally see also Barbara Meil Hobson, *Uneasy Virtue: The Politics of Prostitution and the American Reform Tradition* (Chicago: University of Chicago Press, 1990); and, most recently, Timothy Gilfoyle, *City of Eros: New York City, Prostitution and the Commercialization of Sex, 1790–1920* (New York: W.W. Norton, 1992). Stansell, *City of Women* discusses the working-class view of prostitution, 178–179.

48. Longworth's *New York Directory* for 1838–39 lists Phebe Rogers, "widow of Daniel," at the home of John Anderson on 155 Duane Street. Her name is absent from the 1839–40 *Directory*, but reappears in 1840–41 when her address is listed as: boardinghouse 126 Nassau Street.

49. The first *Directory* listing for Anderson is in 1837–38. At that time his business ("segars") address is listed at 321 Broadway, his home as indicated above. By September 1841, Anderson's store moved to 2 Wall Street. An advertisement in William Porter's *Spirit of the Times*, September 4, 1841, indicates that Anderson also had a store at Saratoga Springs, New York, near the race track.

50. The *New York Times*, November 26, 1881, says that Anderson was born in New York and apprenticed in business before entering the tobacco business. Samuel Copp Worthen writes that he was born in Boston, and migrated to New York where he worked as a laborer, first in a wool pulling plant and then as a

bricklayer. Worthen claims that he was set up in the cigar business by Asa Pritchard, a master bricklayer. Worthen's information is based on extensive testimony chronicled below. See "Poe and the Beautiful Cigar Girl," *American Literature*, 20(1948):306.

51. *Morning Herald* October 8, 1838.

52. *Times*, November 26, 1881; Worthen, "Poe and The Beautiful Cigar Girl," 306–307.

53. Quoted in Worthen, "A Strange Aftermath of the 'Mystery of Marie Roget,' " *Proceedings of the New Jersey Historical Society*, 60(1942): 121. A similar description ("the gay blades of the city as well as transient visitors who likes to adopt urban manners gathered") is contained in "Poe and the Beautiful Cigar Girl," 306. See also Walling, *Recollections of a New York Chief of Police* (Montclair, N.J.: Patterson Smith, 1972 [1877]). The information that the shop was popular among writers remains undocumented in nineteenth-century sources. More modern accounts have depended on the undocumented commentary in *Murder Won't Out*, 56. *The Sunday Morning Atlas*, September 13, 1840, featured a vignette on the "Cigar Girl." The picture accompanying the story was reputed to be an image of Mary Rogers and was used to depict her after her final 1841 disappearance. The piece contains the comment about the "recently adopted practice of hiring pretty girls as clerks in cigar stores for the purpose of attracting the 'men about town.' " Following the essay was a brief history emphasizing the danger of such employment. See my discussion of the *Atlas* piece in Chapter 7.

54. On male sporting culture see Gilfoyle, *City of Eros*, 92–116; Pat Cline Cohen, "Unregulated Youth: Masculinity and Murder in the 1830s City, *Radical History Review*, 52(1992):33–52; Herbert Asbury, *The Gangs of New York* (Garden City: Garden City Publishing Co., 1927); Elliott J. Gorn, " 'Good-Bye Boys, I Die a True American': Homicide, Nativism, and Working-Class Culture in Antebellum New York City," *Journal of American History*, 74(September, 1987): 388–410.

55. *The Whip and Satirist of New York and Brooklyn*, June 18, 1842.

56. *The Whip and Satirist of New York and Brooklyn*, June 18, 1842. Because of its advocacy of prostitution as a legitimate aspect of male recreation, sporting culture is often associated with violence against women, particularly prostitutes. Both Timothy Gilfoyle and Pat Cline Cohen have connected the murder of the prostitute Helen Jewett by her paramour Robinson to the legitimation of sexually associated violence. See Gilfoyle, *City of Eros*, 92–101; Cohen, "Unregulated Youth . . ." and "The Mystery of Helen Jewett: Romantic Fiction and the Eroticization of Violence," *Legal Studies Forum*, 17(1993): 133–147.

57. For a discussion of party ideology during this period see Amy Bridges, *A City in the Republic: Antebellum New York and the Origins of Machine Politics* (Cambridge: Cambridge University Press, 1984), especially 24–33.

58. The details of this story are contained in Worthen's two articles: "Poe and the Beautiful Cigar Girl," *American Literature*, 20(1948): 306–312; and "A Strange Aftermath." Worthen's "Poe and the Beautiful Cigar Girl" cites an early and important article by W. K. Wimsatt, "Poe and the Mystery of Mary Rogers," *PMLA*, 61(March, 1941):230–248, and Wimsatt responded in "Mary Rogers, John Anderson, and Others," *American Literature* 12(1950): 482–484. Subsequent treatment of John Anderson has been based on these earlier articles.

59. Worthen, "Poe and the Beautiful Cigar Girl," 305.
60. Worthen, "A Strange Aftermath," 122.
61. Worthen, "A Strange Aftermath," 121–122; see also "Poe and the Beautiful Cigar Girl," 309–310.
62. Worthen, "A Strange Aftermath," 121–122.
63. Worthen, "A Strange Aftermath," 122.
64. New York *Journal of Commerce*, October 5, 1838; The *Morning Herald* contained the same story on October 7, 1838. See also rthe *Spectator*, October 11, 1838; the *Weekly Herald*, October 13, 1838.
65. This notice contains the first reference to Rogers as the "Beautiful Cigar Girl." *Morning Herald*, October 6, 1838.
66. A full account of this event is chronicled in Walsh, *Poe the Detective*, 11–15. See *Commercial Advertiser*, October 5, 1838; the *Morning Herald*, October 6, 1838; the New York *Journal of Commerce*, August 26, 1841. The possibility of a hoax or publicity stunt was indicated in the *Tragic Almanack*, 1843.
67. Worthen, "A Strange Aftermath," 122. As Worthen points out, it is unclear from these comments exactly *how* directly involved Anderson was with this first abortion. And, while McCloskey's dates do not exactly fit, it is likely that the first abortion did coincide with Mary's October 1838 disappearance.
68. Poe, *Works*, 753.
69. By 1840, both the city *Directory* and the manuscript census indicate that the Rogers women were renting the building at 126 Nassau Street. The building was built originally by James Aymar an early developer, and passed eventually to Peter, probably his brother. By 1840 Peter Aymar owned 126 and 128 Nassau as well and four years later he had also acquired 130 and 132 and a larger building at the corner where Beekman and Ann Streets intersected. When the tax listings consolidated their listings in 1847 Aymar also owned 134 and 136 Nassau Street. According to John Walsh, the building at 126 was torn down in 1852. He also notes that by 1885 the property has been acquired by William Vanderbilt who combined the land with several additional lots and erected an eight-story building there. See Walsh, *Poe the Detective*, 83, fn. 24. It is likely that many of Peter Aymar's buildings were let out to be run as boardinghouses, not unlike the one run by the Rogerses around 1840. In fact, most of the buildings adjacent to the Rogers building were similar establishments—in 1841 numbers 122, 124, and 128 were also occupied by widows, most likely earning their living by providing residences for some of the thousands of inhabitants in lower Manhattan who "boarded."
70. These changes were characteristic not only of New York but of industrializing economies in smaller cities as well. In Rochester, New York, for example, workers had typically lived under the roofs of their masters, taking meals and sharing in some degree of family interaction. But by the mid 1830s, writes Paul Johnson, "Masters had separated their families from their work, and there is evidence that the change was bound up with a new concern with privacy." By 1834, Johnson continues, "the social geography of Rochester was class-specific: master and wage earner no longer lived in the same households or on the same blocks." Instead of one shared social world, at least two, if not three, now existed each corresponding to a distinct socioeconomic group and each with its own amusements and customs of social life. Johnson, *A Shopkeeper's Millennium: Society and Revivals in Rochester, New York, 1815–1837* (New York: Hill and Wang, 1978), 53. Mary Ryan, writing of social life in Utica,

New York, tells a similar story. Her concern is with locating a similar break in social life, especially insofar as these changes affected the privatization of family and domestic life. See her *Cradle of the Middle Class: The Family in Oneida County, New York, 1790–1865* (New York: Cambridge University Press, 1981).

71. Elizabeth Blackmar, *Manhattan for Rent, 1785–1850* (Ithaca: Cornell University Press, 1989), 67.

72. Thomas Gunn, *The Physiology of New York Boardinghouses* (New York: Mason Brothers, 1857), 15.

73. New York Evening *Post*, August 12, 13, 1841.

74. Richard Stott describes a "boardinghouse ethos" referring to the male youth culture that bonded in these residences. His sample of residents in wards two, four, and seven in 1850 suggests that the Rogers house was fairly typical in its social composition. Of 698 residents, 533 were unmarried males, and of these most were skilled workers. See his *Workers in the Metropolis: Class, Ethnicity, Youth in Antebellum New York City* (Ithaca: Cornell University Press, 1990), 372.

As we have seen, the men who boarded at the Rogers house were particularly well acquainted with Mary and because of this they became the principal subjects in the case. At least two—Crommelin and Payne—were romantically involved with her; and Mary's choice of lovers led both Crommelin and Padley to leave the house. Even Kiekuck mentioned that he had been to see Mary in July. And if the world of the cigar store brought Mary in contact with the mixed social world of male leisure and "sport," boardinghouse culture centered her in the downtown cultural world of working-class daily life and recreation.

75. Catherine Beecher, *A Treatise on Domestic Economy* (New York: Shocken, [1841] 1971), 17.

Chapter 4

1. New York *Herald*, May 6, 1835.

2. Thomas Ollive Mabbott, ed., *Collected Works of Edgar Allan Poe: Tales and Sketches, 1831–1842* (Cambridge: Harvard University Press, 1978), 328. "Ligeia" was first published in 1838.

3. Michel Foucault, *Discipline and Punish: The Birth of the Prison* (New York: Random House, 1979), 47.

4. This image appears in George Walling, *Recollections of a New York Chief of Police* (Montclair, N.J.: Patterson Smith 1972 [1877]), 28. I have been unable to locate the original source.

5. Foster, *New York in Slices* (New York: DeWitt and Davenport, 1850), 98.

6. In 1836 steam power was harnessed to the single cylinder Napier press, and in 1846 the four cylinder Hoe or "lightning press" quadrupled the rate at which copy was reproduced. On the technical history of the newspaper see especially Alfred McClung Lee, *The Daily Newspaper in America: The Evolution of a Social Instrument* (New York: Macmillan, 1937), 116–117; Frederic Hudson, *Journalism in the United States from 1690–1872* (New York, 1873); Frank Luther Mott, *American Journalism* (New York: Macmillan, 1941). The history of the newspaper revolution and the Jacksonian press is extensive; see especially James Crouthamel, "The Newspaper Revolution in New York, 1830–1860," *New York*

History, 54(1964):91–113; and, most recently, Alexander Saxton, *The Rise and Fall of the White Republic: Class Politics and Mass Culture in Nineteenth-Century America* (London: Verso, 1990), 95–108. Readership and the class politics of the penny papers are addressed in Michael Schudson, *Discovering the News: A Social History of the American Newspaper* (New York: Basic Books, 1978), especially 3–60; and Dan Schiller, *Objectivity and the News: The Public and the Rise of Commercial Journalism* (Philadelphia: University of Pennsylvania Press, 1981). Gunther Barth treats the rise of the penny press as an aspect of modern city culture in *City People: The Rise of Modern City Culture in Nineteenth-Century America* (New York: Oxford University Press, 1984), 58–109.

Like everything else about New York, its literary scene was multidimensional and constantly in flux. By the beginning of the 1840s an older literary elite, ruled by Irving, Cooper, and the *Knickerbocker* group, was displaced by the rising lights of the self-identified "Young America," what Thomas Bender refers to as the first generation of "American free intellectuals, men and women from a variety of social backgrounds, who assumed a new and self conscious identity, even an intellegensia." This discussion is developed in Bender's history of the period's literary culture, *New York Intellect: A History of Intellectual Life in America* (New York: Alfred A. Knopf, 1987), this quote, 156.

7. The issue of cultural transmission and the development of mass culture is developed in Andrea J. Tucher, " 'Froth and Scum:' Truth, Goodness, and the Axe-Murder in the First Years of the New York Penny Press"(Ph.D. Diss., N.Y.U., 1990).

8. This idea refers back to Walter Benjamin's classic essay, "A Work of Art in the Age of Mechanical Reproduction," Hannah Arendt, ed., *Illuminations* (New York: Schocken Books, 1969), 217–252.

9. Crouthamel, "The Newspaper Revolution," 95.

10. Asa Greene, *A Glance at New York* (New York: A. Greene, 1837), 132–133. Greene's point about readership refers to his assertion that each paper was read by at least two different people. His estimate is probably very modest.

11. On the history of James Gordon Bennett and the New York *Herald* see James L. Crouthamel, "James Gordon Bennett, the New York *Herald* and the Development of Newspaper Sensationalism," *New York History*, 54(July, 1973): 294–316; Douglas Fermer, *James Gordon Bennett and the New York Herald: A Study of Editorial Opinion in the Civil War Era, 1854–1867* (New York: St. Martin's Press); Isaac Pray, *Memoirs of James Gordon Bennett* (New York: Stringer and Townsend, 1855). Whitman's description of Bennett is from the New York *Aurora, 1842* and is quoted in David Reynolds, *Beneath the American Renaissance The Subversive Imagination in the Age of Emerson and Melville* (New York: Alfred A. Knopf, 1988), 174.

12. From 1835 until a fire destroyed the building in 1841 the *Herald* was located on Ann Street; thereafter (until 1867) its headquarters was the *Herald* building at Nassau and Fulton streets. Bennett's politics are well covered in Crouthamel, "James Gordon Bennett," and Fermer, especially 13–43. Bennett's early biography is derived from Fermer, 13–17, and Pray. Although Bennett's Tammany affiliations are well recorded, Bennett's name does not appear in any of the membership lists or minutes of the Tammany Society. Other names, however, did figure prominently, among them John Anderson, Mordecai Noah, Philip Spencer. See MS, "Membership of The Society of Tammany and Columbian Order in the City of New York," Kilroe Collection, Columbia Uni-

versity. The quote from Bennett is from the *Herald*, July 17, 1843, and is taken from Crouthamel, "James Gordon Bennett," 310.

13. Pray, *Memoirs*, 267.

14. The *Herald* enabled Bennett to amass a personal fortune and live a flamboyant life that completed his enduring image as a powerful bully and ill-mannered intruder into the already faltering world of old New York money, politics, and power. The statement about the worth of the paper and its circulation is from Crouthamel, "James Gordon Bennett." The quote is from the first issue of the *Herald*, May 6, 1835.

Most historians of journalism agree that the formation of a new reading public made possible the print revolution of the nineteenth century and the transformation of the newspaper from a sheet of editorial and opinion to one of so-called objective news and facts. Historians, however, disagree over the social and political identity of this new public. In his *Discovering the News*, Michael Schudson credits the expansion of democracy and the development of what he sees as a new, largely middle-class market. Dan Schiller offers a more historical and convincing argument maintaining that, at least initially, this new public was largely composed of the urban working classes—especially the skilled artisans and tradesmen (and no doubt women as well) who sought sources of public information. He argues that the new penny press combined a sharp business and commercial sensibility with the idiom of republicanism, the rhetoric of "equal rights, enlightenment and political independence," borrowed from the radical labor press that flourished in the 1830s, to develop a newly defined and more broad-based metropolitan press. In attacking the old party papers and the upper classes as well, the new penny papers were able to gain the following of this urban market and forge a new conception of the news. But the anger and bluster of a James Gordon Bennett contained little of 1830s radical working-class politics; its bravado gave voice to a far different social vision, one that saw the world and especially the world of the nineteenth-century city in Manichaean and religious notions of good and evil, dark and light, sin and retribution.

15. Daniel Cohen's recent work, *Pillars of Salt, Monuments of Grace: New England Crime Literature and the Origins of American Popular Culture* (New York: Oxford University Press, 1993) offers an excellent history of this genre. See also Karen Halttunen's essay, "Early American Crime Narratives: The Birth of Horror," in Richard Wightman Fox, Jackson T. Lears, eds., *The Power of Culture: Critical Essays in American Culture* (Chicago: University of Chicago Press, 1993), 67–102.

16. On the history of crime literature see Daniel Cohen, *Pillars of Salt: The Transformation of New England Crime Literature, 1674–1860* (New York: Oxford University Press, 1992); and Halttunen, "Early American Crime Narratives." Reynolds, *Beneath the American Renaissance*, surveys the development of the genre, emphasizing its relation to "high culture," 169–210. See also David Ray Papke, *Framing the Criminal: Crime, Cultural Work, and Loss of Critical Perspective, 1830–1900* (Hamden, Ct.: Archon Books, 1987); especially 21–32. Thomas McDade, *Annals of Murder: Bibliography of Books and Pamphlets on American Murders from Colonial Times to the Present* (Norman: University of Oklahoma Press, 1961) is a useful bibliography. On the history of crime news see Crouthamel, "James Gordon Bennett," 303–310; and Schiller, *Discovering the News*, who covers the history of the *Police Gazette*, 96–178. The history of so-called "Lurid Literature" is treated in Thomas McDade, "Christian Brown," *New-*

York Historical Society Quarterly, 1968; and Thomas McDade, "Lurid Literature of the Last Century: The Publications of E. E. Barclay," *Pennsylvania Magazine of History and Biography,* 30(October, 1956).

17. On the history of the reporter see Steven Harold Jaffe, "Unmasking the City: The Rise of the Urban Reporter in New York City, 1800–1850" (Ph.D. Diss., Harvard University, 1989). On the reporter James Attree, see Patricia Cline Cohen, "Unregulated Youth: Masculinity and Murder in the 1830s City," *Radical History Review,* 52 (1992): 33–52.

18. *Morning Herald,* October 6, 838.

19. For an exposition of this see Peter Brooks, "The Mark of the Beast: Prostitution, Melodrama, and Narrative," in *Melodrama,* Daniel Gerould, ed. (New York: New York Literary Forum, 1980), 125–140.

20. On the Helen Jewett murder see Patricia Cline Cohen, "Unregulated Youth"; and "The Mystery of Helen Jewett: Romantic Fiction and the Eroticization of Violence," paper delivered at the AHA, 1992; Crouthamel, "James Gordon Bennett . . . ," 303–309; Gilfoyle, *City of Eros,* 92–98; Schiller, *Discovering the News,* 58–65; Tucher, "Slime and Froth," 164–177.

21. Schiller, *Discovering the News,* 65.

22. On the history of the moral wars see Crouthamel, "The Newspaper Revolution," 97–100; and Pray who as a sympathetic biographer argues for Bennett, *Memoirs of James Gordon Bennett,* 264–268 (this quote, 97). Tucher casts doubt on the significance of the moral wars, "Slime and Froth," 218–270.

23. David Galloway, ed., *The Fall of the House of Usher and Other Writings* (New York: Viking Penguin, 1986), 486. This essay first appeared in *Graham's,* April 1846.

24. Seen within the larger perspective, Poe places the Rogers story within the frame of contemporary social attitudes toward death, and, more specifically, the cultural construct of the death of a beautiful woman, rather than only within the more narrowly defined history of antebellum journalism. In regarding women and death as the principal topics for art, Elizabeth Bronfmen reminds us, Poe was "articulating a culturally prevalent aporic attitude to death, to feminine beauty, and to art." This point and others about the convergence of death and femininity as cultural tropes are developed in her work, *Over Her Dead Body: Death, Femininity and the Aesthetic* (New York: Routledge, 1992), 62. For a good discussion of the erotic representation of death in American literature and especially in the works of Edgar Allan Poe, see Edward Davidson, *Poe: a Critical Study* (Cambridge: Harvard University Press, 1964), 106–121.

25. See Halttunen, *Confidence Men and Painted Women* (New Haven: Yale University Press, 1982), 124–152. Other relevant discussions that develop the connection between middle-class women's culture and the preoccupation with death can be found in Ann Douglas, "Heaven Our Home: Consolation Literature in the Northern United States, 1830–1880," *American Quarterly,* 26 (1974): 456–476; and Nancy Cott, *The Bonds of Womanhood* (New Haven: Yale University Press, 1977), 126–159.

26. *Herald,* August 4, 1841.

27. *Post,* August 12, 1841. The same vocabulary was offered by the *Tribune,* although in a somewhat more restrained version: "By order of Acting Mayor Purdy," the paper said, "her body was yesterday disinterred, in order that the deceased might be more fully identified by some of the witnesses; but decom-

position had already taken place, and no trace of the once 'beautiful cigar girl' could be recognized in the blackened and swollen features." *Tribune*, August 8, 1841.

28. *Herald*, August 17, 1841.

29. *Herald*, August 17, 1841.

30. *Herald*, August 17, 1841. Pregnancy would have been indicated by the presence of a corpus luteum. Other conclusions drawn from the forensic evidence alone could not have been substantiated and were, in some cases, not even logical conclusions. It would, for example, be impossible to know how many violations had occurred or by how many men. (Only recent medical science has enabled different semen types to be identified.) Her "chastity and correct habits" would have been impossible to determine and inconsistent with the physical evidence of rape.

31. Rogers was buried initially in Hoboken after her body was identified. It was later exhumed and returned to the New York City Dead House for further identification. *Herald*, August 12, 1841; *Tribune*, August 12, 1841; and the *Post*, August 13, 1841.

32. Peter Brooks, *The Melodramatic Imagination: Balzac, Henry James, Melodrama, and the Mode of Excess* (New York: Columbia University Press, 1985), 15.

33. For a discussion of this cultural dialectic see Nina Auerbach, *Woman and the Demon: The Life of Victorian Myth* (Cambridge: Harvard University Press, 1982). Mary Ryan, *Women in Public: Between Banners and Ballots, 1825–1880* (Baltimore: Johns Hopkins University Press, 1992), 58–94, discusses this theme in terms of the social geography of urban space.

34. *Herald*, August 2, 1841.

35. Christine Buci-Glucksmann, "Catastrophic Utopia: The Feminine as Allegory of the Modern," in *Representations*, 14(Spring, 1986):220–29.

36. Michel Foucault, *Discipline and Punish*, 43–44.

Chapter 5

Abbreviations Used

BAD	*Documents of the Board of Aldermen of the City of New York*
BAP	*Proceedings of the Board of Aldermen of the City of New York*
DAP	*District Attorney Indictment Papers*, Court of General Sessions, New York City
NYCMA	New York City Archives and Record Center
PCP	*Police Court Papers*, New York City

1. New York *Herald*, August 12, 1841.

2. "Report of the District Attorney, with Statistics of Crime in this City for Twelve Years Last Past," *BAD*, vol. viii, no. 57 (1841–42):409.

3. *National Police Gazette*, February 28, 1846.

4. Ned Buntline [Edward Zane Carrol Judson], *The Mysteries and Miseries of New York: A Story of Real Life* (New York: Berford & Co., 1848), Book V, 68–70.

5. *By-Laws and Ordinances of the Mayor, Alderman, and Commonality of the*

City of New York (New York, John S. Voorhies, 1845), 546–550; *Revised Statutes of the State of New York*, 1852, vol. 2, 847.

6. Morton J. Horwitz, *The Transformation of American Law, 1820–1860* (Cambridge: Harvard University Press, 1977), 30; Lawrence M. Friedman, *A History of American Law* (New York: Simon and Schuster, 1973), 508–509. In *The Transformation of Criminal Justice: Philadelphia, 1800–1880* (Chapel Hill: North Carolina Press, 1989). Allen Steinberg traces the history of private prosecution and the centralization of the criminal justice system in Philadelphia. He argues that in the course of the nineteenth century, the disempowerment of the ordinary citizen and the increased powers of the state were consequences of judicial reform.

In this antebellum period the number of laws on the statute books increased dramatically, totally transforming the legislated boundaries of everyday life and conduct. Included were regulatory acts which routinized commerce, sanitary provisions to guard the safety of the water supply or monitor situations of public health and the large expansion of criminal codes and punishments. Taken together they represented broad transformations of the law and the uses of the judiciary that marked this period in the quarter century before the Civil War.

7. On the history of policing generally during this period see Wilbur Miller, *Cops and Bobbies: Police Authority in New York and London, 1830–1870* (Chicago: University of Chicago Press, 1973); James T. Richardson, *The New York City Police: Colonial Times to 1901* (New York: Oxford University Press, 1970).

8. Michel Foucault, *The History of Sexuality: An Introduction*, trans. Robert Hurley (New York: Vintage Books, 1980), 33.

9. *Herald*, August 12, 1841. The *Herald* claimed that the meeting was held at the home of James Stonehall, a Tammany man whose address they listed as 21 Ann Street. In fact, the city directory lists this address as Stonehall's place of work. Both James Attree and James Gordon Bennett were also listed in the New York City directory as residing at 21 Ann. The text of the proclamation went as follows:

Whereas, the members of this meeting view with alarm and horror the circumstances connected with the shocking murder of Mary C. Rogers. They also recollect, with deep regret, that within the last few years sever [*sic*] murders have been committed in this city and neighborhood, for the perpetration of which no one has been brought to punishment. And without desiring to cast unnecessary censure upon any of the authorities, they deprecate the apeorent [*sic*] apathy that has characterized the Chief Magistrates of the States of New Jersey and New York, and the authorities of the county of New York, in not offering a reward for the arrest of any or all those concerned in the late murder—and believing that in the present inefficiently organized state of our Police Department, that little will be done towards detecting the authors or perpetrators of this awful crime without a reward.

10. *Herald*, August 12, 1841; *Commercial Advertiser*, August 8, 1841; *Tribune*, August 16, 1841.

11. *Post*, September 2, 1841.

12. For a discussion of the political history of New York City police reform see Richardson, *The New York City Police*, 37–50. As he points out, the cause of police reform was largely a Democratic issue.

13. On violent death and the city see Roger Lane, *Violent Death in the City:*

Suicide, Homicide, and Accidental Death in Philadelphia (Cambridge: Harvard University Press, 1979); Eric Monkkonen, "Homicide in New York, 1823–1989," paper delivered at Social Science History Association, annual meeting, Minneapolis, Minn., 1990.

14. On the relationship between sin and crime and its connection to urban moral reform see *Urban Masses and Moral Order in America, 1820–1920* (Cambridge: Harvard University Press, 1978), 54–107; and also David Rothman, *The Discovery of the Asylum: Social Order and Disorder in the New Republic* (Boston: Little Brown and Co., 1971), 57–78.

15. Richardson, *The New York City Police*, 18–20.

16. *Tribune*, August 16, 1841.

17. *Herald*, August, 12, 1841.

18. *Tribune*, August 16, 1841.

19. *BAD*, No. 88(1836–37), 563.

20. *Report of the District Attorney, with Statistics of Crime in This City for Twelve Years Last Past. BAD*, Vol. 8, No. 57 (1841–42), 409.

21. NYCMA, Statement of the Grand Jury, September 23, 1842, Minutes of the Court of General Sessions, 1840–1841, 355.

22. This discussion of private prosecution is based on an unsystematic but fairly thorough reading of the Police Court Records and District Attorney Indictments and accompanying docket and record books for the Court of General Sessions and the Magistrates Court located in the New York City Municipal Archives. For a discussion of the changing nature of personal prosecution during these years in Philadelphia, see Steinberg, *The Transformation of Criminal Justice*. A thorough history of rape and sexual assault has yet to be done on this period. Some discussion of the subject is contained in Christine Stansell, *City of Women: Sex and Class in New York, 1789–1860* (Urbana: University of Illinois Press, 1987[1982]), 20–28, 97–98.

23. On August 21, 1841, Martha acknowledged "full satisfaction" in the case and withdrew her charge. The complaint was officially dismissed by the Court of General Sessions, September 16, 1841. PCP, Box 7457.

24. The complaint of Michael O'Shea v. Andrew Sullivan and Richard Crane, June 22, 1841. PCP, Box 7457.

25. The People v. Sarah Eldridge, April 14, 1841. PCP, Box 7456.

26. The People v. Thomas Kierman, February 1, 1841. PCP, Box 7456.

27. The People v. Francis Allen, February 6, 1841. PCP, Box 7456.

28. The People v. William Bolton, August 30, 1841. PCP, Box 7457. One wonders whether, under other circumstances, Mary Haviland might have regarded her encounter with Morse differently. Would she have viewed his overtures as a form of assault or attempted rape? Would she have brought charges?

29. The People v. Ann Sexsmith, November 27, 1841. PCP, Box 7457.

30. For a discussion of this issue see Roger Lane, *Policing the City: Boston, 1822–1885* (Cambridge: Harvard University Press, 1967), 228–229.

31. *Herald*, August 12, 1841. The issue of class control and its significance in debates about police reform were not unique to New York, or even to the United States. On the comparative history of policing see Barbara Weinberger and Herbert Reinke, "Law and Order in the Industrial City: An Anglo-German Comparison," paper presented at the Social Science History Association, annual meeting, Washington, D.C., 1989.

32. For a description of London's Metropolitan Police and its distinction from the New York 1845 system, see Miller, *Cops and Bobbies*, 1–24; and Clive Emsley, *Policing and Its Context, 1750–1870* (London: Macmillan, 1983).

33. *BAD*, No. 88(1836–37), 562

34. *BAD*, Vol. II, No. 21(1844–45), 243–244; *BAD*, No. 53 (1844), 793. The opening words of the 1844 report read: "The system of the Criminal Department, is with few exceptions, designed exclusively and only for the arrest, trial and punishment of offenders, but not calculated sufficiently to prevent crime nor to suppress the licentiousness and vices, which lead to it."

35. This issue is briefly discussed in reference to the Boston police in Lane, *Policing the City*, 34–35.

36. Deriving their strategies for moral reform from the Scottish reformer Sir Thomas Chalmers, early nineteenth-century American evangelicals stressed the importance of surveillance as a tactical method of dealing with a densely populated metropolitan area. From the late eighteenth century, reform groups, particularly those managed and run by upper-class women, attempted to effect moral reform and prevent the spread of vice by carefully designed programs of neighborhood surveillance and household intervention. According to these plans, the city was divided into districts and agents of reform organizations visited families in an effort to root out sin and prevent further moral deterioration, especially where children were concerned. More modern ideas about policing drew on this tradition of districting (the new police law divided the city into watch districts) and the importance of surveillance. Indeed, the essence and intention of the new policing lay in the attempt to prevent crime and suppress those agencies that caused it. I have discussed this issue in an earlier article: Amy Gilman, "From Widowhood to Wickedness: The Politics of Class and Gender in New York City Private Charity, 1799–1980," *History of Education Quarterly*, 24(Spring, 1984): 59–74. More general discussions of this connection are contained in the literature on early nineteenth-century evangelicalism and moral reform, see especially discussions about social order and control in Boyer, *Urban Masses and Moral Order*, 4–64; Rothman, *Discovery of the Asylum*, 57–78; Carol Smith-Rosenberg, *Religion and the Rise of the American City* (Ithaca: Cornell University Press, 1971); M. J. Heale, "From City Fathers to Social Critics: Humanitarianism and Government in New York, 1790–1860," *Journal of American History*, 63(June, 1976): 21–41. The connection between crime and sin is also briefly discussed in Friedman, *A History of American Law*, 258.

37. *BAD*, No. 88 (1836–37), 582–583.

38. *BAD*, No. 53 (1844), 799.

39. *A Compilation of the Laws of the State of New York, Relating Particularly to the City of New York* (New York: Edmund Jones & Co., 1862), Chap. CCCII, art. I. sec. 8, 918; the same in *BAD*, No. 57 (1846), 1107.

40. See Horwitz, *The Transformation of American Law*, 30.

41. Timothy Gilfoyle, *City of Eros: New York City, Prostitution and the Commercialization of Sex* (New York: W.W. Norton & Co., 1992), 138.

42. *BAD*, No. 53 (1844), 808.

43. The original indictment in the Purdy case was filed on June 5, 1839, but was discharged. A subsequent indictment was made in 1841. See NYCMA, *Minutes of the Court of General Sessions*, 1839, 218; 1841, 626. The Minutes for 1841 alone list four other entries pertaining to Madame Restell: 215, 572, 601, 615.

44. On the general history of abortion during this period see James Mohr, *Abortion in America: The Origins and Evolution of National Policy* (New York: Oxford University Press, 1978), especially 119–146, 125–129; and Carl N. Degler, *At Odds: Women and the Family in America from the Revolution to the Present* (New York: Oxford University Press, 1980), especially 227–248. On the details of abortion law see Cyril C. Means, Jr., "The Law of New York Concerning Abortion and the Status of the Foetus, 1664–1968: A Case of Cessation of Constitutionality," *New York Law Forum* 14(Fall, 1968):411–515, especially 441–463.

Despite extensive primary sources on Restell, a modern critical account of her life and career has yet to be written. Available accounts of her life (including two recent monographs) are all drawn from the literature penned against her in the politically and emotionally charged anti-abortion crusades of the mid-nineteenth century. Accounts of Restell are included in Mohr, *Abortion in America*, 48–50, 125–128; and briefly in Degler, *At Odds*, 228. Recent monographs about Restell include: Clifford Browder, *The Wickedest Woman in Town: Madame Restell the Abortionist* (Hamden, Conn.: Archon Press, 1988); Allan Keller, *Scandalous Lady: The Life and Times of Madame Restell* (New York: Atheneum, 1981). Nineteenth-century sources that provide some account of her life include: Anonymous. *Madame Restell, An Account of Her Life and Horrible Practices, together with Prostitution in New York, Its Extent—Causes—and Effects upon Society* (New York, 1847); Rev. Bishop Huntington, *Restell's Secret Life: A True History of Her From Birth to Her Awful Death by Her Own Wicked Hands* (Philadelphia: Old Franklin Publishing House, 1897). Published trial transcripts include: George Dixon, *Trial of Madame Restell, alias Ann Lohman, for abortion and Causing the Death of Mrs. Purdy*, 1841; *Wonderful Trial of Caroline Lohman, Alias Restell with Speeches of the Counsel, Charge of Court and Verdict of Jury.* repro of Crt. of Sessions, 1846 trial for abortion on Maria Bodine. Chapters devoted to Restell in urban guides include: Junius Browne, *The Great Metropolis: A Mirror of New York* (Hartford: American Publishing Co., 1869), 582–587; Edward Winslow McCabe [Martin], *Secrets of the Great City* (Philadelphia: Jones Brothers & Co., 1868); James McCabe, Jr., *New York by Gaslight* (New York: Crown Publishers, 1984[1882]), 493–495. A detailed chronicle of Restell's suicide in addition to biographical information is contained in the lengthy obituary that was the lead story in the *New York Times*, April 2, 1878.

45. On the social implications of antebellum abortion practice, see Mohr, *Abortion in America*, 128–129.

46. *National Police Gazette*, March 13, 1847.

47. Anonymous, *Madame Restell, An Account of Her Life and Horrible Practice*, 8.

48. *National Police Gazette*, March, 13, 1847, 209. The reference to Restell as Madame Killer, *National Police Gazette*, March 13, 1847; "Wickedest Woman in the City," Browne, *The Great Metropolis*, 582; "Wickedest Woman in New York," McCabe, *Secrets of the Great City*, 420.

49. The details of Restell's biography are from the *Times*, April 2, 1878; Browder, 3–18; *Madame Restell, An Account of Her Life and Horrible Practices*, 4–5. Browder claims that Lohman was a Russian immigrant, born in St. Petersburg in 1809 of German descent. Based on evidence that Lohman frequented the Chatham Street bookstore of George Matsell where he purchased the works of

Paine, Browder asserts that he also had some reputation as a freethinker. Browder, *The Wickedest Woman*, 4.

50. Dr. A. M. Mauriceau, *The Private Woman's Medical Companion* (New York: 1853 [1847], x–xi. Francois Mauriceau (1637–1709) published *The Diseases of Women with Children* (London, 1752). The work was first published in France in 1738.

51. Mauriceau, *Private Woman's Medical Companion*, 107.

52. Mauriceau, *Private Woman's Medical Companion*, 107, 169.

53. The Minutes of the Court of General Sessions list five separate entries for Restell in 1841 alone, including a denial by the court that it had a request to squash the indictment in the Purdy case. See NYCMA, Minutes of the Court of General Sessions, 1841, 626.

54. NYCMA, Minutes of the Court of General Sessions, July 19, 1841, 215; and the District Attorney's Papers, Minutes of the District Attorney, July 19, 1841.

55. NYCMA, Minutes of the Court of General Sessions, July, 1841, 204, 210, 218. The Purdy charge against Restell, 204.

56. Prior to 1829 the common law on this subject was in effect and it was legal for women in New York to have abortions prior to quickening. *N.Y. Revised Statutes* (1829), Pt. IV, ch. 1, tit. 2, sec.9. On the specifics of abortion law see Means, "The Law of New York Concerning Abortion and the Status of the Foetus, 1644–1968," 441,443–444, 449, 454–456, 454–463. In trial the case turned on the admissibility of an affidavit Purdy allegedly gave to Justice Merritt shortly before her death, and which judge Noah finally admitted as legitimate evidence for the case. NYCMA, Minutes of the Court of General Sessions, July 16, 1841, 210. A similar course of action was used against Restell in an 1847 arrest and trial. On this occasion the alleged victim was still alive and able to describe in detail her extended relationship with Restell as well as the details of the procedure itself. At this time Restell's attorneys were more prepared and built their elaborate defense on entrapment and privacy rights.

57. *Herald*, July 15–20, 1841.

58. NYCMA, Minutes of the Court of General Sessions, July, 20, 1841, 218; *Herald*, July 20, 1841.

59. *National Police Gazette*, February 7, 1846.

60. *The Secret History of Madame Restell*, 10–11.

61. *National Police Gazette*, February 28, 1846. A lengthy description of this event, including much of the *Gazette* copy, is contained in a chapter on Restell entitled "The Mansion Built on Baby Skulls," Edward Van Every, *Sins of New York as Exposed by the National Police Gazette* (New York: Frederick A. Stokes Co., 1930), 99–104. Browder claims that the crowd was led by George Dixon, editor of the scandalous *Polyanthos*. Browder, *The Wickedest Woman*, 63.

62. NYCMA, DAP, "The People v. Caroline Lohman alias Ann Lohman alias Madame Restell," September 7, 1847.

63. 1852 Revised Statutes, Title II, Article I, Sec. 6, numbers 8 and 9, Vol. II, p. 847 and Title VI, Section 21, p. 22, 876.

64. The People against Caroline Lohman alias Ann Lohman alias Madame Restell, NYCMA, DAP, September 7, 1847. A transcript of the trial is contained in *Wonderful Trial of Caroline Lohman, Alias Restell with Speeches of the Counsel, Charge of Court and Verdict of the Jury* [n.p.:n.p., n.d.].

65. *Wonderful Trial*, 21.

66. *Wonderful Trial,* 6, 14.

67. Brady went on to attack the New York *Sun* and to cite James Fenimore Cooper's libel suit, *Wonderful Trial,* 20.

68. *Wonderful Trial,* 38.

69. The importance of medical opposition to Restell is well explored in Mohr, *Abortion in America,* 147–170; and Degler, *At Odds,* 228–233.

70. Van Every, *Sins of New York,* 100.

71. The price of abortions is from Browder, *The Wickedest Woman in Town,* 18.

72. Van Every, *Sins of New York,* 93–94.

73. Mohr, *Abortion in America,* 123.

74. *Journal of the Assembly of the Sate of New York at their Sixty-Eighth Session,* 1845, 1404, 1405. Entries on the abortion issue are indicated on 302, 324, 539, 787, 1312.

75. *New York Times,* November 10, 1900.

76. The genealogy of the Comstock family is in John Adams Comstock, *A History and Genealogy of the Comstock Family in America* (Los Angeles, privately printed, 1949).

Chapter 6

1. *Selections from Cultural Writings,* ed., David Forgacs and Geoffrey Nowell-Smith (Cambridge: Harvard University Press, 1985), 369.

2. "The Mystery of Marie Roget," *Collected Works of Edgar Allan Poe: Tales and Sketches, 1843–1849,* ed. Thomas Olive Mabbott (Cambridge: Harvard University Press, 1978), 726–727.

3. "The Murders in the Rue Morgue" was originally published in *Graham's Magazine,* April 1841 (18:166–179), and in Poe's own edition, *Tales* (New York: Wiley and Putnam, 1845), 116–150; "The Mystery of Marie Roget" was originally published in Snowden's *Ladies' Companion,* November, December 1842, and February 1843: 15–20, 93–99, 162–167), and in *Tales,* 151–199; "The Purloined Letter" was originally published in *The Gift: A Christmas, New Year, and Birthday Present,* MDCCCXLV (September 1844), 41–61, and in *Tales,* 200–218. All references to these stories in this essay are taken from Edgar Allan Poe, *Collected Works of Edgar Allan Poe,* ed. Thomas Olive Mabbott (Cambridge: Harvard University Press, 1978), 3 vols. Hereafter referred to as *Works.*

4. Poe to George Roberts, Philadelphia, June 4, 1842. In James T. Harrison ed., *Complete Works of Edgar Allan Poe* (New York,: Thomas Crowell & Co., 1902), 17, 112–113. The complete text of the letter is as follows:

The story is based upon the assassination of Mary Cecilia Rogers, which created so vast an excitement, some months ago, in New York. I have, however handled my design in a manner altogether *novel* in literature. I have imagined a series of nearly exact *coincidences* occurring in Paris. A young grisette, one Marie Roget, has been murdered under precisely similar circumstances with Mary Rogers. Thus, under pretence of showing how Dupin (the hero of "The Rue Morgue") unravelled the mystery of Marie's assassination, I, in reality, enter into a very long and rigorous analysis of the New York tragedy. No point is omitted. I examine, each by each, the opinions and arguments of the press upon the subject, and show that this subject has been, hitherto, *unapproached*. In fact I believe not only that I have demonstrated the fallacy of the general idea—that the girl was the victim of a gang of ruffians—but have *indicated the assassin* in a manner which will give renewed impetus to investigation. My main object, nevertheless, as you will readily understand, is an analysis of the true principles which should direct inquiry in similar cases. From the nature of the subject, I feel convinced that the article will excite attention, and it has occurred to me that you would be willing to purchase it for the forthcoming Mammoth Notion. It will make 25 pages of Graham's magazine, and at the usual price which would be worth to me $100. For reasons, however, which I need not specify, I am desirous of having this tale printed in Boston, and, if you like, I will say $50. Will you please write me upon this point?—by return mail, if possible. [Italics are Poe's.]

5. A modern version of this technique is the film, *The Thin Blue Line* by Errol Morris. Thanks to Tom Benediktsson for this observation.

6. For transcriptions of important passages from the contemporary press and attributions to specific newspapers see William K. Wimsatt's careful literary detective work in, "Poe and the Mystery of Marie Roget," *PMLA*, 56(March 1841): 230–48.

7. "The Mystery of Marie Roget," *Works*, 724.

8. The passage continues: "A young girl, *Mary Cecilia Rogers*, was murdered in the vicinity of New York; and, although her death occasioned an intense and long-enduring excitement, the mystery attending it had remained unsolved at the period when the present paper was written and published (November 1842). Herein, under pretence of relating the fate of a Parisian *grisette*, the author has followed in minute detail, the essential, while merely paralleling the inessential facts of the real murder of Mary Rogers. Thus all argument founded upon the fiction is applicable to the truth; and the investigation of the truth was the object." *Works*, 723.

9. A comparative text of both versions of Poe's story is contained in Mabbott, *Works*; Ray Paul, *Who Murdered Mary Rogers?* (Englewood Cliffs, N.J.: Prentice-Hall, 1971); and John Walsh, *Poe the Detective: The Curious Circumstances Behind the Mystery of Marie Roget* (New Brunswick: Rutgers University Press, 1968).

10. "The Man of the Crowd" was originally published in *Gentleman's Magazine*, 7(December 1840): 267–270; and in Poe's own edition of *Tales*, 219–228.

11. For a discussion of the genre see John G. Cawelti, *Adventure, Mystery and Romance: Formula Stories as Art and Popular Culture* (Chicago: University of Chicago Press, 1976), 81.

12. For a good discussion of this literature in England see Richard Altick, *Victorian Studies in Scarlet* (New York: W.W. Norton, 1970). Poe's satirical treatment of this literature is found in much of his writing and specifically addressed in his "How to Write a Blackwood Article," in Edmund Clarence Stedman and George Edward Woodbury, eds., *The Works of Edgar Allan Poe*, vol. iv (New York: Charles Scribner Sons, 1927), 224. A more recent treatment of Poe's rather ambivalent relationship to the new sensational literature and his uses of the mid-century irrational impulse is David Reynolds, *Beneath the American Renaissance: The Subversive Imagination in the Age of Emerson and Melville* (New York: Alfred A. Knopf, 1988), 225–248.

13. Mabbott, for example, begins his discussion of his edition of the work by saying that "This is a historical tale of historical importance, since it is the first detective story in which an attempt was made to solve a real crime. It has, I feel, enjoyed a higher reputation among general readers than it deserves." *Works*, 715. Mabbott and others have noted Dorothy Sayers's exception to this prevalent view. In *The Omnibus of Crime*, she notes that of the Dupin stories, she finds it "the most interesting of all to the connoisseur." More recently, J. Gerald Kennedy referred to the work as "that forgettable experiment in forensic narrative." *Poe, Death and the Life of Writing* (New Haven: Yale University Press, 1987), 120.

14. If literary critics have generally been among the former, writers of crime stories and bibliophiles have generally been among the latter. For discussions of the veracity of Poe's tale and discussion of his sources see especially: Wimsatt, "Poe and the Mystery of Marie Roget"; Samuel Copp Worthen, "Poe and the Beautiful Cigar Girl," *American Literature*, 20(November, 1948): 305–312; and John E. Walsh, *Poe the Detective*.

15. A native New Yorker, on leave at two key times during Mary's life—in 1837–38, and again in 1840–41. Using Navy records, Wimsatt concludes that Spencer, who resigned from the Navy in 1843, continually asked to be excused from duty on account of illness between the time of Mary's death and December 1841 when he asked to be assigned a command. On William Spencer see Chapter 2, fn. 46. Moreover, Alexander Mackenzie, Captain of the *Somers* (the ship on which Spencer's cousin was hung for mutiny), was related to the William MacKenzie family of Richmond. William Mackenzie and his wife, Jane Scott Mackenzie, adopted Poe's sister, Rosalie, and Poe remained close to the family throughout his life. Curiously, the possibility that both theories are plausible— that Mary died of an abortion and that she also had a relationship with an individual like Spencer—and not necessarily mutually exclusive has seldom been considered. Given what we now know about the connection of the Rogers family to shipping and trade, the proximity of the boardinghouse to the docks, and so on, it is likely that Mary could have been connected, romantically or otherwise, with a man like either one of the Spencers. Surely Poe, in his own inimitable fashion, had picked up on a thoroughly plausible connection, one perhaps closer to Mary's identity (and to his own) than even he may have suspected. See also Michael Paul Rogin, *Subversive Genealogy: The Politics and Art of Herman Melville* (New York: Alfred A. Knopf, 1983), 79–101, for a discussion of the symbolic importance of the *Somers* mutiny.

16. Walsh, 62–67. This information is based on August Van Cleef, "Poe's Mary," *Harper's Monthly*, 78 (March 1889): 634–640; It is quoted in Dwight Thomas and David Jackson, *The Poe Log: A Documentary Life of Edgar Allan Poe, 1809–1849* (Boston: G.K. Hall & Co., 1987), 639. Mary Starr apparently told August Van Cleef, the author of the Harper's story that:

> He came to New York, and went to my husband's place of business to find out where we lived. He was on a spree, however, and forgot the address before he got across the river. He made several trips backward and forward on the ferry-boat . . .
>
> When Mr. Poe reached our house I was out with my sister, and he opened the door for us when we got back. We saw he was on one of his sprees, and that he had been away from home for several days . . .

Mr. Poe staid to tea with us, but ate nothing; only drank a cup of tea . . . He then went away. A few days later Mrs. Clemm came to see me, much worried about "Eddie dear," as she always addressed him. She did not know where he was and his wife was almost crazy with anxiety. I told Mrs. Clemm that he had been to see me. A search was made, and he was finally found in the woods on the outskirts of Jersey City [the area where the events of the Rogers case took place], wandering about like a crazy man. Mrs. Clemm took him back with her to Philadelphia.

According to Poe's most recent biographer, Kenneth Silverman, Poe's friend Mary Starr also remarked that Poe "didn't like dark-skinned people." See *Edgar A. Poe: Mournful and Never-Ending Remembrance* (New York: HarperCollins, 1991), 207.

17. Poe to Roberts, in Harrison, *Complete Works*, vol. 17, 113.

18. Poe was more than arbitrary in fashioning the geography of Paris. See the comments of French critic E. F. Forgues reviewing Poe's *Tales* in the *Revue des Deux Mondes*, October 1846, in Mabbott, *Works*, 777, fn. 17.

19. Benjamin continued with the comment that this urban setting, depicted by Poe, has for Poe something barbaric: "discipline just barely manages to tame it." Walter Benjamin, "On Some Motifs in Baudelaire, *Illuminations*, ed. Hannah Arendt (New York: Shocken Books, 1969), 168, 172, 174. Interestingly, Benjamin's linking of this tale to the modernist tradition may be further solidified by Poe's own explanatory footnotes that were discussed above, a device that was to appear some eighty years later in T. S. Eliot's footnotes to his signal modernist poem "The Wasteland."

Robert Byers excellent essay, "Mysteries of the City: A Reading of Poe's 'The Man of the Crowd,' " in Sacvan Bercovitch and Myra Jehlen, eds., *Ideology and Classic American Literature* (Cambridge University Press, 1987), 221–246, draws on many of these same themes placing Poe within a Marxist framework, emphasizing his place in the modernist tradition.

20. *Works*, 507.

21. *Works*, 508–510.

22. *Works*, 511, 515.

23. Marshall Berman, *All That Is Solid Melts into Air* (New York: Simon and Schuster, 1982), 159–160.

24. *Works*, 749–750.

25. The issue of doubling in the Dupin stories is addressed in J. Gerald Kennedy, *Poe, Death, and the Life of Writing* (New Haven: Yale University Press, 1987),121–122; and in Barbara Johnson, "The Frame of Reference: Poe, Lacan, Derrida," in *Literature and Psychoanalysis: The Question of Reading: Otherwise*, ed. Shoshana Felman (Baltimore: The Johns Hopkins University Press, 1982), 470.

26. *Works*, 531–532.

27. *Works*, 533.

28. Edward Davidson, *Poe: A Critical Study* (Cambridge: Harvard University Press, 1964), especially 214–222.

29. *Works*, 537–538.

30. Poe was fascinated by the process of street paving as well as by the way in which ancient methods of road construction still prevailed, establishing remarkable continuity between the streets of the modern city and those of ancient Rome. See his essay, "Street Paving," *The Broadway Journal*, April 19, 1845, 1.

31. *Works*, 535–536. Nancy Horrowitz uses this key passage as an example of Pierce's abductive method. For her semiotic approach to Pierce and Poe, see "The Body of the Detective Novel: Charles Peirce and Edgar Allan Poe," in Umberto Eco and Thomas Sebeok, eds., *The Sign of the Three: Dupin, Holmes, Peirce* (Bloomington: Indiana University Press, 1983), 179–197.

32. *Works*, 549.

33. *Works*, 769.

34. Poe refers to "polluted Paris. . . ." *Works*, 760.

35. *Works*, 723. Poe also provided a reminder that the translations are "*literal*," *Works*, 731.

36. Linda Patterson Miller, "Poe on the Beat: *Doings of Gotham* as Urban Penny Press Journalism," *Journal of the Early Republic*, 7(Summer 1987):147–165. As Miller correctly points out, Poe used these pieces as a way not only to comment on city life, but quite specifically on the penny press as well.

37. The journal, which ceased publication in February 1846, was intended to be a high-quality literary review dedicated to publishing original American work. It also had a distinctly urban character, paying attention to a wide range of city events and subjects ranging from architecture to theatre and "city amusements." For a brief history of the *Broadway Journal* and the history of Charles Briggs see Thomas Bender, *New York Intellect* (New York: Alfred A. Knopf, 1987), 161–162.

38. Miller, "Poe on the Beat," 163.

39. *Works*, 738.

40. *Works*, 564, 565.

41. *Works*, 993. According to Mabbott, 997, fn. 27, the quotation is from *Atree et Thyeste* (1707) V, iv, 13–15, by Prosper-Jolyot de Crebillon (1674–1762).

42. *Works*, 724, 728–729; *Works*, 515.

43. *Works*, 731–735.

44. *Works*, 752.

45. *Works*, 751–752, 753.

46. *Works*, 751–752.

47. *Works*, 751–753.

48. *Works*, 768–769. I have adopted Walsh's method of marking the text: passages in boldface type indicate the changes Poe made in the 1845 version of the story. Material he deleted is indicated by boldface type and brackets. See Walsh, 97–143, especially, 127–143.

49. *Works*, 757.

50. For a discussion of this aspect of Poe's work see Kennedy, *Poe, Death and the Art of Writing*, 3; and Davidson, *Poe: A Critical Study*.

51. *Works*, 1831–42, 320.

52. *Works*, 538.

53. *Works*, 730.

54. "Busy-bodyism," *Works*, 747, 748.

55. *Works*, 747.

56. Naomi Shor, "Female Paranoia: The Case for Psychoanalytic Feminist Criticism," *Yale French Studies*, 62(1981): 218–219.

57. *Works*, 755.

58. In the first version of the story, this paragraph is followed by another that de-emphasizes the private and somewhat sinister ruminations of Marie: "Such thoughts as these we may *imagine* to have passed through the mind of

Marie, but the point is one upon which I consider it necessary now to insist. I have reasoned thus, merely to call attention, as I said a minute ago, to the culpable remissness of the police." *Works*, 756.

59. *Works*, 751.
60. *Works*, 772–773.
61. From "Urn Burial," Chapter V, Sir Thomas Browne.
62. *Works*, 528.
63. *Works*, 528.

Chapter 7

1. Joseph Holt Ingraham, *La Bonita Cigarera; or the Beautiful Cigar Vender [sic]. A Tale of New York* (Boston: The Yankee, 1844), 48. This novel and its sequel, *Herman de Ruyter,or Mysteries Unveiled: A Sequel to the Beautiful Cigar Vender. A Tale of the Metropolis* (Boston: The Yankee, 1844), were published under a variety of titles and title combinations. *The Bibliography of American Literature*, vol. IV, comp. Jacob Blanck (New Haven: Yale University Press, 1963), 459, notes that the full publication history has not been determined, that the order of presentation is arbitrary, and that it is possible that different forms, issued in either pink or yellow wrappers (which also served as a title page) may have been printed simultaneously from multiple settings. My page references to *La Bonita Cigarera* are from the 1844 edition; for *Herman de Ruyter*, from the combined edition: *The Beautiful Cigar Vender, and its Sequel,Herman de Ruyter. Tales of City Life, Founded on Facts.* (New York: Williams Brothers, 1849).

2. Charles Burdett, *Lilla Hart: A Tale of New York* (New York: Baker and Scribner, 1846), vii.

3. Ezra Zane Carroll Judson [Ned Buntline], *Mysteries and Miseries of New York: A Tale of Real Life* (New York: Berford & Co., 1848 [1847]), 5.

4. Ingraham, *Herman de Ruyter*, 2.

5. Andrew Jackson Davis, *Tale of a Physician: or The Seeds and Fruits of Crime* (Boston: William White & Company, 1869).

6. On Ingraham see Robert Weatherby, *J. H. Ingraham* (Boston: Twayne, 1980); F. L. Mott, *Golden Multitudes: The Story of Best Sellers in the United States* (New York: Macmillan, 1947), 306–308; and David Ray Papke, *Framing the Criminal: Crime, Cultural Work, and Loss of Critical Perspective, 1830–1900* (Hamden: Archon Books, 1987), 88–91. Works on Judson include Jay Monaghan, *The Great Rascal: The Life and Adventures of Ned Buntline* (Boston, Little Brown & Co., 1952); Peter G. Buckley, "The Case Against Ned Buntline: The 'Words Signs, and Gestures of Popular Authorship,'" *Prospects: An Annual of American Culture Studies*, vol. 13, ed., Jack Salzman (New York: Cambridge University Press, 1988), 249–252. Michael Denning includes a discussion of Judson's mystery novels in *Mechanic Accents: Dime Novels and Working-Class Culture in America* (Bristol, England: Verso, 1987), 85, 93, 106.

7. *The Sunday Morning Atlas*, September 13, 1840.

8. *Atlas*, September 13, 1840.

9. *Atlas*, September 13, 1840.

10. The details of Ingraham's life and career are covered in Robert Weatherby, *J. H. Ingraham*; Mott, *Golden Multitudes*, 306–308; and Papke, *Framing the Criminal*, 88–91. The Longfellow quote is taken from Mott, 94.

11. Ingraham, *La Bonita Cigarera*, 38–39.

12. Ingraham, *La Bonita Cigarera*, 12,14.

13. Ingraham, *La Bonita Cigarera*, 47.

14. Ingraham, *La Bonita Cigarera*, 48.

15. Ingraham, *La Bonita Cigarera*, 48.

16. Ingraham, *Herman de Ruyter*,93

17. There is no critical work to date on Charles Burdett. His published works include over 19 novels, the most famous of which are about the western hero Kit Carson. In addition to his work as a reporter, Burdett published his fiction frequently in the city newspapers. Indeed, Burdett's first acquaintance with the story of Mary Rogers may have dated to the *Atlas* story of September 13, 1841; his own story, *Pete Yerks—A Legend of Musquito [sic] Cove*, was serialized in that same issue.

18. Burdett, *Lilla* , 16.

19. Burdett, *Lilla*, 91.

20. Burdett, *Lilla*, 91.

21. Burdett, *Lilla*, 146–147.

22. Burdett, *Lilla*, 197.

23. *Ned Buntline's Life-Yarn* (New York: Dick and Fitzgerald, 1849), 19.

24. See Monaghan, *The Great Rascal*, 54; Buckley, "The Case Against Ned Buntline," 270, fn. 14.

25. This aspect of Buntline's life is described in Buckley, "The Case Against Ned Buntline," 251–256.

26. *The B'hoys of New York*; *The G'hals of New York* (New York: Robert M. De Witt, 1850).

27. For discussions of the mystery genre see Denning, *Mechanic Accents*, 85–117; Peter Brooks's discussion of Eugene Sue in "The Mark of the Beast: Prostitution, Melodrama and Narrative" in *Melodrama*, ed. Daniel Gerould (New York: New York Literary Forum, 1980), 125–140, provides an analysis of the European tradition, as does Daniel Burt's "A Victorian Gothic: G. M. W. Reynolds's *Mysteries of London*" for the English tradition, in *Melodrama*, 141–158.

28. Frederic Jameson, *The Political Unconscious: Narrative as a Socially Symbolic Act* (Ithaca: Cornell University Press, 1981), 186.

29. Buntline, *Mysteries and Miseries*, vol. I, 100; vol. II, 38; vol. III, 19–20; vol. IV, 65; vol. V, 68–69.

30. George Lippard, *New York: Its Upper Ten and Lower Million* (Cincinnati: H. M. Rulison, 1853); *The Empire City: or, New York By Night and Day. Its Aristocracy and Its Dollar* (Philadelphia: T.B. Peterson & Brothers, 1864 [1850]). The reference to "female Fiend" is from *The Empire City*, 133.

31. Davis, *Tale of a Physician*, 192, 197. The quote from "Ligeia" is on 196.

32. It is important to remember that by the time these novels were written in the mid to late 1840s, the story of Mary Rogers was well known. Her disappearance, the discovery of her body in the river, etc., were all well-traveled material for the readers of the penny press and popular novels. Readers similarly knew of Madame Restell, and the fast and loose versions of her name would have surely brought both recognition and probably a laugh from the experienced reader of these tales. A wide audience approached these fictive renderings of her life and death with appreciable knowledge of the events. In addition, these novels not only circulated among a shared clientele, but were also themselves part of an extended intertextual conversation about everything from the Rogers story itself to the restraints occasioned by the popular publication formats.

33. Reynolds defines his term "subversive" as close to de Tocqueville's idea of a democratic style. He refers to a "style of intentional narrative discontinuities, oddly juxtaposed imagery, confusions between dream and reality, and feverish emotions creating distortions of perception." *Beneath the American Renaissance*, 202.

34. Michael Denning, *Mechanic Accents*, 27, 87, 73. Denning is concerned (particularly in the mystery novel) with the "paradoxical union of sensational fiction and radical politics"(87) that they contain. He sees the plots of these tales made up of "nationalist, class-inflected stories of the American Republic, inter-related, if sometimes contradictory tales of its origins and the threats to it." (73)

35. On the political meaning of the seduction plot see Cathy Davidson, *Revolution and the Word* (New York: Oxford University Press, 1984).

36. Denning, *Mechanic Accents*, 96.

37. On the figure of the working woman in popular literature see Reynolds, *Beneath the American Renaissance*, 351–367, and Amy Gilman, " 'Cogs to the Wheel': The Ideology of Women's Work in Mid- Nineteenth Century Fiction," *Science and Society*, 47(Summer 1983): 178–204.

Epilogue

1. Italo Calvino, *Invisible Cities*, translated by William Weaver (San Diego: Harcourt Brace & Co., 1974), 10.

2. Calvino, *Invisible Cities*, 10.

SELECTED BIBLIOGRAPHY

Primary Sources

Manuscript Collections

NYC Municipal Archives

District Attorney Indictment Papers
Coroners Inquisitions
City of New York, Borough of Manhattan, Register of Deaths. Vols. 11,12,13,14
Police Court Records, 1837–1847
Annual Record of Property Assessment for Manhattan, 1840–1845
Minutes of the Court of General Sessions
Magistrate's Court Records

Connecticut State Library

Connecticut Vital Records for Lyme and New London
New London Probate District, Estate of Ezra Mather
New London Probate District, Estate of Jehoida Mather
New London Probate District, Estate of Amos Rogers
Lyme, Land Records

Miscellaneous Collections

Arents Collection, New York Public Library
James Gordon Bennett Papers, New York Public Library
Philip Hone Diary, New-York Historical Society
Daniel Rogers Papers, New London Historical Society
Tammany Society Papers, Columbia University, Kilroe Collection
U.S. Manuscript Census Schedules for New York and Connecticut, 1800–1850
John Cassan Wait. "Some Branches of the Wait Family of New England, 1904–1919." Typescript, New York Public Library.

Primary Sources: Printed

Government Records

Henry Davies, ed. *A Compilation of the Laws of the State of New York, Relating Particularly to the City of New York.* New York, 1855.

By-Laws and Ordinances of the Mayor, Aldermen, and Commonality of the City of New York, revised, 1845. New York, 1845.

Hiram Denio and William Tracy, eds. *The Revised Statutes of the State of New York.* 2 vols. New York, 1852.

Journal of the Senate of the State of New York. 67–69 Sessions. New York, 1844–46.

Journal of the Assembly of the State of New York. 67–69 Sessions. New York, 1844–46.

Newspapers and Magazines

The *Broadway Journal*
Brother Jonathan
The *Commercial Advertiser*
The *Flash*
The *Ladies' Companion*
The *Morning Courier and the New York Enquirer*
National Police Gazette
Newark Daily *Advertiser*
New London *Gazette*
New London *Day*
New York Evening *Post*
New York *Herald*
New York *Journal of Commerce*
New York *Sun*
New York Times
New York *Tribune*
The *Rake*
Spirit of the Times
Sunday Morning Atlas
Tattler

Anonymous. *Madame Restell, An Account of Her Life and Horrible Practices, Together with Prostitution in New York, Its Extent—Causes—and Effects upon Society.* New York: Privately published, 1847.

———. *Trial of Madame Restell, alias Ann Lohman for Abortion and Causing the Death of Mrs Purdy; being a full account of all the proceedings of the trial, together with the suppressed evidence and editorial remarks.* New York, 1841.

———. *Wonderful Trial of Caroline Lohman, Alias Restell with Speeches of the Counsel, Charge of Court and Verdict of Jury.* New York: Enoch and Wilkes, 1846.

Beach, Moses Yale. *Wealth and Biography of the Wealthy Citizens of New York City*. New York: The Sun Office, 1845.

Beecher, Catherine. *A Treatise on Domestic Economy*. New York: Schoken Books, 1977 [1841].

Belden, Ezekiel Porter. *New York—As It Is*. New York: J. P. Prall, 1849.

———. *New York: Past, Present and Future*. New York: G.P. Putnam, 1849.

Bolles, John Rogers and Anna B. Williams, eds. *The Rogerenes: Some Hitherto Unpublished Annals Belonging to the Colonial History of Connecticut*. Boston: Stanhope Press, 1904.

Brace, Charles Loring. *The Dangerous Classes of New York and Twenty Years Among Them*. New York: Wynkoop & Hallenbeck, 1880 [1872].

Browne, Junius Henri. *The Great Metropolis: A Mirror for New York*. Hartford: American Publishing Co., 1869.

Burdett, Charles. *Lilla Hart: A Tale of New York*. New York: Baker and Scribner, 1846.

———. *Never Too Late*. New York: D. Appleton & Co., 1845.

———. *Chances and Changes; or Life As It Is*. New York: D. Appleton & Co., 1846.

Child, Lydia Maria. *Letters from New York*. New York: C.S. Francis & Co., 1845.

Children's Aid Society. *Annual Reports*. New York, 1854.

Comstock, John Adams. *A History and Genealogy of the Comstock Family in America*. Los Angeles: Privately Printed, 1949.

Cooper, James Fenimore. *The Cruise of the Somers Illustrative of the Despotism of the Quarter Deck; and of the Unmanly Conduct of Commander Mackenzie*. New York: J. Winchester, 1844.

Davis, Andrew Jackson. *Tale of a Physician: or the Seeds and Fruit of Crime*. Boston: William White & Co., 1869.

Dixon, George. *Trial of Madame Restell, alias Ann Lohman, for Abortion and Causing the Death of Mrs. Purdy*. New York, 1841.

Drake, Samuel G. *Memoir of the Rev. Cotton Mather, D.D., with a Genealogy of the Family of Mather*. Boston: Antiquarian Book Store, 1851.

Ellington, George.*The Women of New York, or, the Underworld of the Great New York*. New York: New York Book Co., 1869.

Felton, Mrs. *American Life. A Narrative of Two Years' City and Country Residence in the United States*. London: Simpkin, Marshall, and Co., 1842.

Foster, George. G. *Celio: or New York Above-Ground and Under-Ground*. New York: DeWitt and Davenport, 1850.

———. *New York by Gas-Light: With Here and There a Streak of Sunshine*. New York: DeWitt and Davenport, 1850.

———. *New York Naked*. New York: DeWitt and Davenport, 1854.

———. *New York in Slices: By an Experienced Carver*. New York: W. F. Burgess, 1849.

Greene, Asa. *A Glance at New York*. New York: A. Greene, 1837.

Griscom, John, M.D. *The Sanitary Condition of the Laboring Class of New York, with Suggestions for Its Improvement*. New York: Harper & Brothers, 1845.

Gunn, Thomas. *The Physiology of New York Boarding Houses*. New York: Mason Brothers, 1857.

Hankins, Marie Louise. *Women of New York*. New York: Marie Louise Hankins Co., 1861.

Haswell, Charles H.. *Memoirs of an Octogenarian of the City of New York.* New York: Harper & Brothers, 1896.

Hone, Philip. *The Diary of Philip Hone,* ed. Alan Nevins. New York: Dodd Mead & Co., 1927.

Huntington, Rev. Bishop. *Restell's Secret Life: A True History of Her Birth to Her Awful Death by Her Own Wicked Hands.* Philadelphia, 1897.

Ingraham, James. *The Beautiful Cigar Vender [sic] and its Sequel, Herman de Ruyter. Tales of City Life Founded on Fact.* New York: Williams Brothers, 1849.

———. *Frank Rivers, or the Dangers of the Town.* New York, 1843.

Judson, Edward Zane Carroll [Ned Buntline]. *The B'hoys of New York: A Sequel to the Mysteries and Miseries of New York.* New York 1850.

———. *The G'hals of New York: A Novel.* New York: DeWitt and Davenport, 1850.

———. *The Mysteries and Miseries of New York: A Story of Real Life.* New York: Berford & Co., 1848.

———. *Three Years After: A Sequel to Mysteries and Miseries of New York.* New York: Berford & Co., 1849.

Lippard, George. *The Empire City; or, New York by Night and by Day. Its Aristocracy and Its Dollars.* Philadelphia: T. B. Peterson & Brothers 1864 [1850].

———. *New York: Its Upper Ten and Lower Million.* Cincinnati: H. M. Rulison, 1853.

Mather, Horace E. *Lineage of Richard Mather.* Hartford, Ct.: Press of the Case, Lockwood & Brainard Company, 1890.

Mather, John. *Genealogy of the Mather Family, 1500–1847.* Hartford: Press of E. Geer, 1848.

Mauriceau, A. M. *The Private Woman's Medical Companion.* New York: 1853.

James D. McCabe [Edward Winslow Martin], *The Secrets of the Great City: A Work Descriptive of the Virtues, Vices, the Mysteries, Miseries and Crimes of New York City* (Philadelphia: Jones Brothers & Co., 1868).

McCabe, James, Jr. *New York by Gaslight.* New York: Crown Publishers, 1984 [1882].

Melville, Herman. *Pierre; or, the Ambiguities.* New York: Library of America, 1984 [1852].

[Pray, Isaac.] *Memoirs of James Gordon Bennett and His Times.* New York: Stringer and Townsend, 1855.

Proceedings of the Naval Court Martial in the Case of Alexander Slidell Mackenzie, . . . to which is annexed an elaborate review by James Fenimore Cooper. New York: Henry G. Langley, 1844.

Poe, Edgar Allan. *Collected Works of Edgar Allan Poe.* Edited by Thomas Olive Mabbott. 3 vols. Cambridge, Mass.: Harvard University Press, 1978.

———. *Tales.* New York: Wiley and Putnam, 1845.

———. *Tales.* New York: John Willey, 1849.

———. *Tales of Mystery, Imagination, and Humour; and Poems.* London: Henry Vizetelly, 1852.

———. *Complete Works of Edgar Allan Poe.* Edited by James T. Harrison. 17 vols. New York: Thomas Crowell & Co., 1902.

Rogers, James Swift. *James Rogers of New London Ct. and His Descendants.* Boston, privately published, 1902.

Rogers, John, Sr. *The Rogerenes: Some Hitherto Unpublished Annals Belonging to the Colonial History of Connecticut.* Boston: Stanhope Press, 1904.

Sanger, William. *The History of Prostitution: Its Extent, Causes, and Effects throughout the World.* New York, 1859.

Thompson, George. *The Mysteries of Bond Street or, The Seraglios of Upper Tendom.* New York, 1857.

Tragic Almanack, 1843.

Vital Records of Lyme Connecticut to the End of the Year 1850. Transcribed under the direction of Vernon Hall and Elizabeth B. Plimpton. Lyme, Conn.: American Revolution Bicentennial Commission, 1976.

Wallace, Charles. *Confession of Charles Wallace.* New Orleans, 1851.

Whitman, Walt. *Leaves of Grass and Selected Prose,* ed. John Kouwenhoven. New York: Random House, 1950.

Secondary Sources

Albion, Robert. *The Rise of New York Port, 1815–1860.* New York: Scribner, 1970 [1939].

Altick, Richard D. *The Scholar Adventurers.* New York: The Macmillan Co., 1850.

———. *Victorian Studies in Scarlet.* New York: W. W. Norton, 1970

Arden, Eugene. "The Evil City in American Fiction." *New York History* 35(1954): 259–279.

Armstrong, Nancy. *Desire and Domestic Fiction: A Political History of the Novel.* New York: Oxford University Press, 1987.

Asbury, Herbert. *The Gangs of New York.* Garden City: Garden City Publishing Co., 1927.

Auerbach, Nina. *Woman and the Demon: The Life of Victorian Myth.* Cambridge: Harvard University Press, 1982.

Avery, Edward. *Sins of New York as Exposed by the Police Gazette.* New York: Frederick A. Stokes, 1830.

Banta, Martha. *Imaging American Women: Idea and Ideals in Cultural History.* New York: Columbia University Press, 1987.

Barth, Gunther. *City People.* New York: Oxford University Press, 1980.

Bender, Thomas. *Toward an Urban Vision: Ideas and Institutions in Nineteenth Century America.* Baltimore: Johns Hopkins University Press, 1982.

———. *New York Intellect: A History of Intellectual Life in America.* New York: Alfred A. Knopf, 1987.

Benjamin, Walter. *Illuminations,* ed. Hannah Arendt. New York: Shocken Books, 1969.

Berger, John. *About Looking.* New York: Pantheon Books, 1980.

Berman, Marshall. *All that Is Solid Melts into Air.* New York: Simon and Schuster, 1982.

Bernstein, Iver. *The New York City Draft Riots: Their Significance for American Society and Politics in the Age of the Civil War.* New York: Oxford University Press, 1990.

Blackmar, Elizabeth. *Manhattan for Rent, 1785–1850*. Ithaca: Cornell University Press, 1989.

Blumin, Stuart. "Explaining the New Metropolis: Perception, Depiction and Analysis in Mid-Nineteenth Century New York City." *Journal of Urban History* 2(1984):9–38.

———. *The Emergence of the Middle Class: Social Experience in the American City, 1760–1900*. New York: Cambridge University Press, 1989.

Bode, Carl. *Antebellum Culture*. Carbondale: Southern Illinois University Press, 1970.

Boyer, Paul. *Urban Masses and the Moral Order in America, 1820–1920*. Cambridge, Mass.: Harvard University Press, 1978,

Bridges, Amy. *A City in the Republic: Antebellum New York and the Origins of Machine Politics*. New York: Cambridge University Press, 1984.

Bronfen, Elisabeth. *Over Her Dead Body: Death, Femininity and the Aesthetic*. New York: Routledge, 1992.

Brooks, Peter. *The Melodramatic Imagination: Balzac, Henry James, Melodrama and the Mode of Excess*. New York: Columbia University Press, 1985.

Browder, Clifford. *Madame Restell The Abortionist*. Hamden, Conn.: Archon Press, 1988.

Brown, Herbert Ross. *The Sentimental Novel in America, 1789–1860*. Durham, N.C.: Duke University Press, 1940.

Brown, Richard D. *Modernization: The Transformation of American Life 1600–1865*. New York: Hill and Wang, 1976.

Buckley, Peter G. "Culture, Class and Place in Antebellum New York," in John Hull Mollenkopf, ed., *Power, Culture, and Place: Essays on New York City*. New York: Russel Sage Foundation, 1988.

———. "To the Opera House: Culture and Society in New York City, 1820–1860." Ph.D. diss., State University of New York at Stony Brook, 1884.

———. "The Case Against Ned Buntline: The 'Words, Signs, and Gestures' of Popular Authorship," in Jack Salzman ed., *Prospects: An Annual of American Culture Studies*, 13(1988):249–72.

Buci-Glucksmann, Christine. "Catastrophic Utopia: The Feminine as Allegory to the Modern." *Representations* 14(1985): 220–229.

Bushman. Richard L.. *From Puritan to Yankee: Character and the Social Order in Connecticut, 1690–1765*. Cambridge, Mass.: Harvard University Press, 1967.

Byers, Robert. ""Mysteries of the City: A Reading of Poe's 'The Man of the Crowd,' " in Sacvan Bercovitch, Myra Jehlen, eds. *Ideology and Classic American Literature*. New York: Cambridge University Press, 1987.

Caulkins, Frances Manwaring. *History of New London, Connecticut from the First Survey of the Coast in 1612 to 1852*. New London, Conn.: Privately published, 1860.

Cawelti, John. *Murder, Mystery and Romance: Formula Stories as Art and Popular Culture*. Chicago: University of Chicago Press, 1976.

Cohen, Daniel. *Pillars of Salt: The Transformation of American Crime Literature, 1674–1860*. New York: Oxford University Press, 1992.

Cohen, Patricia Cline. "Unregulated Youth: Masculinity and Murder in the 1830s City." *Radical History Review* 52(1992):33–52.

———. "The Mystery of Helen Jewett: Romantic Fiction and the Eroticization of Violence." *Legal Studies Forum* 17(1993): 133–147.

Cook, Adrian. *The Armies of the Streets: The New York City Draft Riots of 1863.* Lexington: University of Kentucky Press, 1974.

Corbin, Alain. *Les Filles de noce: Misère sexuelle et prostitution (19 et 20 siècles.)* Paris: Aubier Montaigne, 1978.

————. *The Foul and the Fragrant: Odor and the French Social Imagination.* Cambridge, Mass.: Harvard University Press, 1986.

Cott, Nancy. *The Bonds of Womanhood: "Women's Sphere" in New England, 1780–1835.* New Haven: Yale University Press, 1977.

————. "Passionlessness: An Interpretation of Victorian Sexual Ideology, 1790–1850." *Signs* 4(1978): 219–236.

Crouthamel, James L. "James Gordon Bennett, the New York *Herald* and the Development of Newspaper Sensationalism." *New York History* 54(1973): 294–316.

————. "The Newspaper Revolution in New York, 1830–1860." *New York History* 65(1964): 91–113.

Cvetkovich, Ann. *Mixed Feelings: Feminism, Mass Culture, and Victorian Sensationalism.* New Brunswick, N.J.: Rutgers University Press, 1992.

Czitrom. Daniel. *Media and the American Mind: From Morse to McLuhan.* Chapel Hill: University of North Carolina Press, 1982.

Daniels, Bruce C. *The Connecticut Town: Growth and Development, 1635–1790.* Middletown, Conn.; Wesleyan University Press, 1979.

Darnton, Robert. *The Great Cat Massacre and Other Episodes in French Cultural History.* New York: Basic Books, 1984.

————. *The Literary Underground of the Old Regime.* Cambridge, Mass.: Harvard University Press, 1982.

Davidson, Cathy. *Revolution and the Word.* New York: Oxford University Press, 1984.

Davidson, Edward. *Poe: A Critical Study.* Cambridge, Mass.: Harvard University Press, 1964.

Davis, Natalie Zemon. *Fiction in the Archives: Pardon Tales and Their Tellers in Sixteenth Century France.* Stanford: Stanford University Press, 1987.

Degler, Carl N. *At Odds: Women and the Family in America from the Revolution to the Present.* New York: Oxford University Press, 1980.

Dijkstra, Bram. *Idols of Perversity: Fantasies of Feminine Evil in Fin de Siècle Culture.* New York: Oxford University Press, 1986.

Douglas, Ann. "Heaven Our Home: Consolation Literature in the Northern United States, 1830–1880." *American Quarterly* 26(1974):456–476.

————. *The Feminization of American Culture.* New York: Alfred A. Knopf, 1977.

Douglas, Mary. *Purity and Danger: An Analysis of Concepts of Pollution and Taboo.* New York: F. A. Praeger. 1966.

Dublin, Thomas. *Women at Work: The Transformation of Work and Community in Lowell, Massachusetts, 1826–1860.* New York: Columbia University Press, 1979.

Eco, Umberto and Thomas Sebeok, eds. *The Sign of the Three: Dupin, Holmes, Peirce.* Bloomington: University of Indiana Press, 1983.

Elias, Norbert. *The Civilizing Process: The History of Manners.* Translated by Edmund Jephcott. New York: Urizen Books, 1978.

Ernst, Robert. *Immigrant Life in New York City, 1825–1863.* New York: Kings Crown Press, 1949.

Ewen, Stuart. *All Consuming Images: The Politics of Style in Contemporary America.* New York: Basic Books, 1988.

Fermer, Douglas. *James Gordon Bennett and the New York Herald: A Study of Editorial Opinion in the Civil War Ear 1854–1867.* New York: St. Martin's Press, 1986.

Foucault, Michel. *The Archeology of Knowledge.* Translated by A. M. Sheridan Smith. New York: Pantheon Books, 1972.

———. *Discipline and Punish: The Birth of the Prison.* Translated by A.M. Sheridan Smith. New York: Pantheon Books, 1977.

———. *The History of Sexuality: An Introduction.* Translated by Robert Hurley. New York: Vintage Books, 1980.

French, Warren. "A Sketch of the Life of Joseph Holt Ingraham." *The Journal of Mississippi History* 10(1955): 45–54.

———. "The Twice-Told Travels of Joseph Holt Ingraham." *American Notes and Queries* 1(1962): 51–52.

Friedman, Lawrence J. *A History of American Law.* New York: Simon and Schuster, 1973.

Geertz, Cifford. *The Interpretation of Cultures.* New York: Basic Books, 1973.

Gilfoyle, Timothy. *City of Eros: New York City, Prostitution and the Commercialization of Sex, 1790–1920.* New York: W.W. Norton, 1992.

Gilje, Paul A. *The Road to Mobocracy: Popular Disorder in New York City, 1763–1834.* Chapel Hill: University of North Carolina Press, 1987.

Gilman, Amy. " 'Cogs to the Wheel:' The Ideology of Women's Work in Mid-Nineteenth Century Fiction." *Science and Society* 47(1983):178–204.

———. "Edgar Allan Poe Detecting the City," in James Gilbert, Amy Gilman, Donald M. Scott, Joan W. Scott, eds., *The Mythmaking Frame of Mind: Social Imagination and American Culture.* Belmont, Ca.: Wadsworth Publishing Company, 1992.

———. "From Widowhood to Wickedness: The Politics of Class and Gender in New York City Private Charity, 1799–1860." *History of Education Quarterly* 24(1984):59–74.

Gorn, Elliot J. " 'Good-Bye Boys, I Die a True American ': Homicide, Nativism, and Working-Class Culture in Antebellum New York City." *Journal of American History* 74 (1987): 388–410.

———. *The Manly Art: Bare-Knuckle Prize Fighting in America* Ithaca: Cornell University Press, 1986.

Gramsci, Antonio. *Selections form Cultural Writings,* ed. David Forgacs and Geoffry Newell-Smith. Cambridge: Harvard University Press, 1985.

Greven, Philip J., Jr. "Family Structures in Seventeenth-Century Andover," in Michael Gordon, ed., *The American Family in Social-Historical Perspective.* New York: St. Martins Press, 1983.

———. *Four Generations: Population, Land, and Family in Colonial Andover, Massachusetts.* Ithaca: Cornell University Press, 1970.

Grimsted, David. *Melodrama Unveiled: American Theatre and Culture, 1800–1850.* Chicago: University of Chicago Press, 1968.

Hall, Peter. *Cities of Tomorrow: An Intellectual History of Urban Planning and Design in the Twentieth Century.* Oxford: Basil Blackwell, 1988.

Hall, Stuart. "Deconstructing the Popular," in Raphael Samuel, ed., *People's History and Socialist Theory.* London: Routledge, Kegan Paul, 1981.

Halttunen, Karen. *Confidence Men and Painted Women: A Study of Middle-Class Culture in America, 1830–1870.* New Haven: Yale University Press, 1982.
———. "Early American Crime Narratives: The Birth of Horror," in Richard Wightman Fox, Jackson T. Lears, eds., *The Power of Culture: Critical Essays in American Culture.* Chicago: University of Chicago Press, 1993.
Harris, Neil. *Humbug! The Art of P. T. Barnum.* Boston: Little Brown and Co., 1973.
Haswell, Charles A. *Reminiscences of an Octogenarian of the City of New York.* New York: Harper & Brothers, 1896.
Heale, M. J. "From City Fathers to Social Critics: Humanitarianism and Government in New York." *Journal of American History* 63(1976):21–41.
Henretta, James A. *The Evolution of American Society, 1700–1815: An Interdisciplinary Analysis.* Lexington, Mass.: D.C. Heath and Co., 1973.
Higgins, Lynn A. and Brenda R. Silver, eds. *Rape and Representation.* New York: Columbia University Press, 1991.
Hobson Barbara Meil. *Uneasy Virtue: The Politics of Prostitution and the American Reform Tradition.* Chicago: University of Chicago Press, 1990.
Hone, Philip. *The Diary of Philip Hone, 1828–1851,* 2 vol., ed. Alan Nevins, New York: Dodd Mead & Co., 1927).
Horlick, Allan Stanley. *Country Boys and Merchant Princes: The Social Control of Young Men in New York.* Lewisburg, Pa.: Bucknell University Press, 1975.
Hurwitz, Morton J. *The Transformation of American Law, 1780–1860.* Cambridge, Mass.: Harvard University Press, 1977.
Jackson, Kenneth T., and Schultz, Stanley K., eds. *Cities in American History.* New York: Alfred A. Knopf, 1972.
Jaffe, Steven Harold. "Unmasking the City: The Rise of the Urban Newspaper Reporter in New York City, 1800–1850." Ph.D. diss., Harvard University, 1989.
Jameson, Frederic. *The Political Unconscious: Narrative as a Socially Symbolic Act.* Ithaca: Cornell University Press, 1981.
Johnson, Barbara. "The Frame of Reference: Poe, Lacan, Derrida." in Shoshana Felman, ed. *Literature and Psychoanalysis: The Question of Reading: Otherwise.* Baltimore: The Johns Hopkins University Press, 1982,
Johnson, Claudia D. "That Guilty Third Tier: Prostitution in Nineteenth-Century American Theatres," in Daniel Walker Hall, ed., *Victorian American.* Philadelphia: University of Pennsylvania Press, 1976.
Johnson, David R. *Policing the Urban Underworld: The Impact of Crime on the Development of the American Police, 1800–1885.* Philadelphia: Temple University Press, 1979.
Johnson, Paul E.. *A Shopkeeper's Millennium: Society and Revivals in Rochester, New York, 1815–1837.* New York: Hill and Wang, 1978.
Kalikoff, Beth. *Murder and Moral Decay in Victorian Popular Literature.* Ann Arbor: UMI Research Press, 1986.
Kasserman, David Richard. *Fall River Outrage: Life, Murder, and Justice in Early Industrial New England.* Philadelphia: University of Pennsylvania Press, 1986.
Keller, Alan. *Scandalous Lady: The Life and Times of Madame Restell.* New York: Atheneum, 1981.
Kendrick, Walter. *The Secret Museum: Pornography in Modern Culture.* New York: Viking, 1987.

Kennedy, J. Gerald. *Poe, Death and the Life of Writing*. New Haven: Yale University Press, 1987.

Kessler-Harris, Alice. *Out to Work: A History of Wage-Earning Women in the United States*. New York: Oxford University Press, 1982.

Kett, Joseph. *Rites of Passage: Adolescence in America, 1790 to the Present*. New York: Basic Books, 1977.

Ketterer, David. *The Rationale of Deception in Poe*. Baton Rouge: Louisiana State University Press, 1979.

Keyssar, Alexander. "Widowhood in Eighteenth-Century Massachusetts: A Problem in the History of the Family." *Perspectives in American History* 8(1974): 81–119.

Lane, Roger. *Violent Death in the City: Suicide, Accident, and Murder in Philadelphia*. Cambridge, Mass.: Harvard University Press, 1979.

——. *Policing the City: Boston, 1822–1905*. Cambridge Mass.: Harvard University Press, 1967. .

Laquer, Thomas. *Making Sex: Body and Gender from the Greeks to Freud*. Cambridge, Mass.: Harvard University Press, 1990.

Lee, Alfred M. *The Daily Newspaper in America*. New York: Macmillan Co., 1937.

Levine, Lawrence. *Highbrow/Lowbrow: The Origins of Cultural Hierarchy in America*. Cambridge, Mass.: Harvard University Press, 1988.

Lindberg, Gary. *The Confidence Man in American Literature*. New York: Oxford University Press, 1982.

Lindstrom, Diane. "Economic Structure, Demographic Change, and Income Inequality in Antebellum New York," in John Hull Mollenkopf, ed., *Power, Culture, and Place: Essays in New York City*. New York: Russel Sage Foundation, 1988.

Lockwood, Charles. *Manhattan Moves Uptown: An Illustrated History*. Boston: Houghton Mifflin Company, 1976.

Lofland, H. Lyn. *A World of Strangers: Order and Action in Urban Public Space*. Prospect Heights, Ill.: Waveland Press, 1985 [1973].

McDade, Thomas M. "Lurid Literature of the Last Century: The Publications of E.E. Barclay." *Pennsylvania Magazine of History and Biography* 80(1956):452–464.

Marcus, Steven. *The Other Victorians: A Study of Sexuality and Pornography in Mid-Nineteenth-Century England*. New York: W.W. Norton and Company, 1964.

Marshall, Benjamin Tinkham, A.M., D.D., ed. *A Modern History of New London County Connecticut*. New York: Lewis Historical Publishing Company, 1922.

Masur, Louis P. *Rites of Execution: Capital Punishment and the Transformation of American Culture*. New York: Oxford University Press, 1989.

Means, Cyrus Jr. "The Law of New York Concerning Abortion and the Status of the Foetus, 1644–1968: A Case of Cessation of Constitutionality. *New York Law Forum* 14(1968):419–426.

Meyers, Marvin. *The Jacksonian Persuasion: Politics and Belief*. New York: Vintage Books, 1960.

Miller, Douglas T. *The Birth of Modern America, 1820–1850*. Indianapolis, Ind.: Bobbs-Merrill Educational Publishing, 1970.

Miller, Linda Patterson. "Poe on the Beat: Doings of Gotham as Urban, Penny Press Journalism." *Journal of the Early Republic* 7(1987): 147–165.

Miller, Perry. *The New England Mind, From Colony to Province.* Boston: Beacon Press, 1961.

Miller, Wilbur R. *Cops and Bobbies: Police Authority in New York and London, 1830–1870.* Chicago: University of Chicago Press, 1977[1973].

Miller, Zane. *The Urbanization of Modern America: A Brief History.* New York: Harcourt Brace Jovanovich, 1973.

Minnegeroode, Meade. *The Fabulous Forties, 1840–1850: A Presentation of Private Life.* New York: G.P. Putnam, 1924.

Mohr, James. *Abortion in America: The Origins and Evolution of National Policy.* New York: Oxford University Press, 1978.

Mollenkopf, John Hull, ed. *Power, Culture and Place: Essays on New York City.* New York: Russel Sage, 1988.

Monaghan, Jay. *The Great Rascal: The Life and Adventures of Ned Buntline.* Boston: Little Brown and Co., 1952.

Monkkonen, Eric. *Police in Urban America, 1860–1920.* New York, Cambridge University Press, 1981.

Most, Glenn W., and Stowe, William W., eds. *The Poetics of Murder: Detective Fiction and Literary Theory.* New York: Harcourt, Brace, 1893.

Mott, Frank Luther. *American Journalism: A History of Newspapers in the United States Through 260 Years: 1660–1950.* New York: Macmillan, 1950.

Muchembled, Robert. *Popular Culture and Elite Culture in France, 1400–1750.* Translated by Lydia Cochrane. Baton Rouge: Louisana State University Press, 1885.

Mulvey, Laura. *Visual and Other Pleasures.* Bloomington: Indiana University Press, 1989.

Olasky, Marvin. *The Press and Abortion, 1838–1988.* Hillsdale, N.J.:Lawrence Erlbaum Associates, 1988.

Papke, David Ray. *Framing the Criminal: Crime, Cultural Work, and Loss of Critical Perspective, 1830–1900.* Hamden, Ct.: Archon Books, 1987.

Paster, Gail Kern. *The Idea of the City in the Age of Shakespeare.* Athens: University of Georgia Press, 1985.

Paul, Ray. *Who Murdered Mary Rogers?* Englewood Cliffs, N.J.: Prentice-Hall, 1971.

Pearce, Charles E. *Unsolved Murder Mysteries.* London: S. Paul & Co., 1924.

Pease, Donald E. *Visionary Compacts: American Renaissance Writings in Cultural Context.* Madison: University of Wisconsin Press, 1987.

Peiss, Kathy, and Christina Simmons, eds. *Passion and Power: Sexuality in History.* Philadelphia: Temple University Press, 1989.

Pessen, Edward. *Jacksonian America: Society, Personality, and Politics.* Homewood Ill.: Dorsey Press, 1978.

———. *Riches, Class, and Power Before the Civil War.* Lexington, Mass.: D.C. Heath and Co., 1974.

Praz, Mario. *The Romantic Agony.* Meridan Books, Cleveland and New York: 1951 [1933].

[Pray, Isaac.] *Memoirs of James Gordon Bennett and His Times.* New York, 1855.

Prude, Jonathan. *The Coming of Industrial Order: Town and Factory Life in Rural Massachusetts, 1810–1860.* New York: Cambridge University Press, 1983.

Purcell, Richard. *Connecticut in Transition: 1775–1818.* Middletown, Conn.: Wesleyan University Press, 1963.

Reynolds, David. *Beneath the American Renaissance: The Subversive Imagination in the Age of Emerson and Melville.* New York: Alfred A. Knopf: 1988.

Richardson, James. *The New York Police: Colonial Times to 1901.* New York: Oxford University Press, 1970.

Rogin, Michael. *Subversive Genealogy: The Politics and Art of Herman Melville.* New York: Alfred A. Knopf, 1983.

Rosen, Ruth. *The Lost Sisterhood: Prostitution in America, 1900–1918.* Baltimore: Johns Hopkins University Press, 1982.

Rosenberg, Charles. *The Cholera Years: The United States in 1832, 1849, and 1866.* Chicago: University of Chicago Press, 1962.

Rothman, David. *The Discovery of the Asylum: Social Order and Disorder in the New Republic.* Boston: Little Brown, 1971.

Ryan, Mary. *Cradle of the Middle Class: The Family in Oneida County, New York, 1790–1865.* New York: Cambridge University Press, 1981.

———. *Women in Public: Between Banners and Ballots, 1825–1880* Baltimore: The Johns Hopkins University Press, 1990.

Saxton, Alexander. "George Wilkes: Transformation of a Radical Ideology." *American Quarterly* 33(1981):437–458.

———. "Problems of Class and Race in the Origins of the Mass Circulation Press." *American Quarterly* 36(1984):211–234.

———. *The Rise and Fall of the White Republic: Class Politics and Mass Culture in Nineteenth-Century America.* London and New York: Verso, 1990.

Schiller, Dan. *Objectivity and the News: The Public and the Rise of Commercial Journalism.* Philadelphia: University of Pennsylvania Press, 1981.

Schudson, Michael. *Discovering the News: A Social History of American Newspapers.* New York: Basic Books, 1978.

Scott, Joan Wallach. *Gender and the Politics of History.* New York: Columbia University Press, 1988.

Sennett, Richard. *The Fall of Public Man: On the Social Psychology of Capitalism.* New York: Vintage Books, 1978.

Sharpe, William and Leonard Wallock, eds. *Reading the Modern City: Essays in History, Art & Literature.* Baltimore: John Hopkins University Press, 1987.

Shor, Naomi. "Female Paranoia: The Case for Psychoanalytic Feminist Criticism." *Yale French Studies* 62(1981):218–219.

Siegel, Adrienne. *The Image of the City in Popular Literature, 1840–1870.* Port Washington, N.Y.: Kennikat Press, 1981.

Silverman, Kenneth. *Edgar A. Poe: Mournful and Never-Ending Remembrance.* New York: HarperCollins, 1991.

Simmel, Georg. *The Sociology of Georg Simmel.* Translated by Kurt Wolff. New York: The Free Press, 1950.

Sklar, Kathryn K. *Catherine Beecher: A Study in American Domesticity.* New Haven: Yale University Press, 1973.

Smith, Daniel Scott. "Family Limitation, Sexual Control and Domestic Feminism in Victorian America." *Feminist Studies* 1(1973): 40–57.

Smith, Daniel Scott and Michael S. Hindus. "Premarital Pregnancy in America 1640–1971: An Overview and Interpretation." *Journal of Interdisciplinary History* 4(1975): 537–570.

Smith-Rosenberg, Carroll. *Disorderly Conduct: Visions of Gender in Victorian America*. New York: Oxford University Press, 1985.
———. *Religion and the Rise of the American City*. Ithaca; Cornell University Press, 1971.
Sontag, Susan. *On Photography*. New York: Delta, 1977.
Spann, Edward. *The New Metropolis: New York City, 1840–1857*. New York: Columbia University Press, 1981.
Srebnick, Amy Gilman. "True Womanhood and Hard Times: Women and Early New York City Industrialization, 1840–1860." Ph.D. diss., SUNY Stony Brook, 1979.
———. "L'Assassinat et le mystère de Mary Rogers: Sexualité, crime et culture au milieu du dix-neuvième siècle dans la ville de New York." *Mentalités: Histoire des cultures et des sociétés*, ed. Robert Muchembled, 3 (1989), special issue on *Violences sexuelles*, ed. Alain Corbin: 113–134.
Stansell, Christine. *City of Women: Sex and Class in New York, 1789–1860*. New York: Alfred A. Knopf, 1986.
Stark, Bruce. *Lyme Connecticut: From Founding to Independence*. Privately Printed, 1976.
Steinberg, Allen. *The Transformation of Criminal Justice: Philadelphia, 1800–1880*. Chapel Hill: University of North Carolina Press, 1989.
Stern, Madeleine B. *Books and Book People in 19th-Century America*. New York: R.R. Bowker Company, 1978.
———, ed. *Publishers for Mass Entertainment in Nineteenth Century America*. Boston: G.K. Hall & Co., 1980.
Still. Bayard, ed. *Mirror for Gotham: New York as Seen by Contemporaries from Dutch Days to the Present*. New York: New York University Press, 1956.
Stott, Richard B. *Workers in the Metropolis: Class. Ethnicity, Youth in Antebellum New York City*. Ithaca: Cornell University Press, 1990.
Stout, Harry S. and Peter Onuf. "James Davenport and the Great Awakening in New London." *Journal of American History* 71(1983): 557–558.
Suleiman, Susan Rubin, ed. *The Female Body in Western Culture: Contemporary Perspectives*. Cambridge, Mass.: Harvard University Press, 1986.
Sundquist, Eric. J. *Home as Found: Authority and Genealogy in Nineteenth-Century America*. Baltimore: The Johns Hopkins University Press, 1979.
Taylor, William R. *Cavalier and Yankee: The Old South and American National Character*. New York: Harper and Row, 1961.
———. *In Pursuit of Gotham: Culture and Commerce in New York*. Oxford University Press, 1992.
———. "The Launching of a Commercial Culture: New York City, 1860–1930," in John Hull Mollenkopf, ed., *Power, Culture, and Place: Essays on New York City*. New York: Russel Sage Foundation, 1988.
Thomas, Dwight and Jackson, David, K. *The Poe Log: A Documentary Life of Edgar Allan Poe 1809–1849*. Boston: G. K. Hall & Co., 1987.
Tompkins, Jane. *Sensational Designs: The Cultural Work of American Fiction, 1790–1860*. New York: Oxford University Press, 1985.
Trachtenberg, Alan. *The Incorporation of America: Culture and Society in the Gilded Age*. New York: Hill and Wang, 1982.
Tucher, Andrea J. " 'Froth and Scum;' Truth, Goodness, and the Axe-Murder In the First Years of the New York Penny Press." Ph.D. Diss., New York University, 1990.

Trudgill, Eric. *Madonnas and Magdalens: The Origins and Development of Victorian Sexual Attitudes.* New York: Holmes and Meier, 1976.

Trumbull, Benjamin. *A Complete History of Connecticut, Civil and Ecclesiastical.* 2 vols. New London, Conn.: H. D. Utley, 1898.

Walling, George. *Recollections of a New York Chief of Police.* Montclair, N.J.: Patterson Smith, 1972 [1877].

Walkowitz, Judith. *City of Dreadful Delight: Narratives of Sexual Danger in Late-Victorian London.* Chicago: University of Chicago Press, 1992.

Walsh, John. *Poe the Detective: The Curious Circumstances Behind the "Mystery of Marie Roget."* New Brunswick: Rutgers University Press, 1968.

Warner, Sam Bass, Jr. *The Private City: Philadelphia in Three Periods of Its Growth.* Philadelphia: University of Pennsylvania Press, 1968.

Watt, Ian. *The Rise of the Novel: Studies in Defoe, Richardson, and Fielding.* Berkeley: University of California Press, 1967.

Wells, Robert V. "Demographic Change and the Life Cycle of American Families." *Journal of Interdisciplinary History* 2 (1971): 273–282.

Wethersby, Robert W. *Joseph Holt Ingraham.* Boston: Twayne Publishers, 1980.

Whiteaker, Larry Howard. "Moral Reform and Prostitution in New York City, 1830–1860." Ph.D. diss., Princeton University, 1977.

Wilentz, Sean. *Chants Democratic: New York City and the Rise of the American Working Class, 1788–1850.* New York: Oxford University Press, 1985.

Wimsatt, William Kurtz, Jr. "Poe and the Mystery of Mary Rogers." *PMLA* 56(1941): 230–248.

Worthen, Samuel Copp. "A Strange Aftermath of the Mystery of Marie Roget." *Proceedings of the New Jersey Historical Society* 60(1942): 116–123.

———. "Poe and the Beautiful Cigar Girl." *American Literature* 20(1948):305–312.

INDEX

CPSIA information can be obtained at www.ICGtesting.com
Printed in the USA
BVOW010305301211

279407BV00001B/7/P

Spiritual Resiliency in Older Women

For our mothers

Carlene Amelia Geske Lauchnor

and

Mary Clare Lamb Blieszner

You showed us how to be women
and you taught us how to listen for God

Spiritual Resiliency in Older Women

Models of Strength for Challenges Through the Life Span

Janet L. Ramsey
Rosemary Blieszner

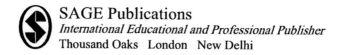
SAGE Publications
International Educational and Professional Publisher
Thousand Oaks   London   New Delhi

For information:

SAGE Publications, Inc.
2455 Teller Road
Thousand Oaks, California 91320
E-mail: order@sagepub.com

SAGE Publications Ltd.
6 Bonhill Street
London EC2A 4PU
United Kingdom

SAGE Publications India Pvt. Ltd.
M-32 Market
Greater Kailash I
New Delhi 110 048 India

Printed in the United States of America

Library of Congress Cataloging-in-Publication Data

Ramsey, Janet L.
  Spiritual resiliency in older women: Models of strength for
challenges through the life span / by Janet L. Ramsey and
Rosemary Blieszner.
       p.   cm.
  Includes bibliographical references and index.
  ISBN 0-7619-1276-2 (cloth: alk. paper)
  ISBN 0-7619-1277-0 (pbk.: alk. paper)
    1. Aged women—Religious life—United States—Case studies.
2. Aged women—Religious life—Germany—Case studies. 3. Church work
with the aged. 4. Church work with women. I. Blieszner, Rosemary.
II. Title.
  BV4445.R36 1999
  261.8'3426—dc21   98-40299

99 00 01 02 03 10 9 8 7 6 5 4 3 2 1

Acquiring Editor:	Jim Nageotte
Editorial Assistant:	Heidi Van Middlesworth
Production Editor:	Diana E. Axelsen
Editorial Assistant:	Patricia Zeman
Cover Designer:	Candice Harman

Contents

Preface

This is a book about hearty old women and about the faith that makes them strong. It is neither a typical self-help book nor a book strictly for persons with academic or clinical interests. Rather, it was written for anyone who wants to learn about spirituality and strength, about aging with the support of an ageless faith. Although we wrote this book for a wide audience, we did include many specific clinical and scholarly discussions. Some guidance on how to read the book according to your own interests is, therefore, in order.

Part I consists of an introduction to the cross-cultural research project that inspired this book. Chapter 1 is basic and important for all readers, for it states the purpose of the book and explains the topic areas that the research project was designed to explore. In Chapter 2 we review both the clinical practice and academic intellectual roots out of which our research grew. The third chapter will be of interest chiefly to our academic readers; here, we give a brief summary of the methodology used in conducting the study.

Part II is the heart of the book, for it presents both quotes and interpretations based on our long interviews with the old women. Research adventures and data from both the focus groups and individual interviews are presented in this part, followed by a discussion of the basic findings and our scholarly interpretations of those data.

Implications for general readers, clinicians, and academics are elucidated in Part III. Chapter 10 will be of particular interest to clinicians and Chapter 11, to academicians. Our Postscript describes how the research continues to affect both the old women and us in the present.

Finally, the Appendix contains the spiritual journal written by Jan Ramsey during the time she conducted the initial interviews. It includes descriptions of her personal faith journey along with insights she gained from conversations with the women.

Acknowledgements

It is our great pleasure to express thanks to the many people who helped to make this book possible. Robert Benne, Director of Church and Society at Roanoke College, Salem, Virginia, wrote a letter of introduction to Germany and thereby got our research under way. Henry C. Simmons, Director of the Center on Aging at the Presbyterian School of Christian Education in Richmond, Virginia, graciously made available to Ramsey the resources of the Center's extensive library on aging and religion and shared many useful suggestions for this project. William J. McAuley, now at the University of Oklahoma, spent much time helping with the proposal for this research.

The assistance of two parish pastors was invaluable, for they made many practical arrangements that enabled the conducting of focus groups and interviews. Heartfelt thanks to Pastor Robert Maier, of Glade Creek Lutheran Church in Virginia and Pastor Karl-Wilhelm Steenbuck, of St. Bartolomäus Kirche in Germany. Pastor Steenbuck and his wife, Frau Selma Steenbuck, not only provided important cultural and practical help on a daily basis, they also extended to us friendship and *Gastfreundschaft* (hospitality) during two visits to Wilster.

A grant from Lutheran Brotherhood helped in meeting travel expenses for this project. Dr. Gudrun Freeman, clinical partner of the first author and a native of Nüremberg, Germany, proofread Ramsey's translations of the German interviews. Karen Carter, Brethren pastor and a native of Berlin, carefully and rapidly transcribed most of the German interviews. Roswitha Jarrett, also a German American, transcribed the interview with Elisabeth on very short notice. Dr. Margaret D. Cohn read and commented on the entire manuscript. Diana Axelsen, Senior Production Editor at Sage, offered warm and encouraging support. We are grateful for all of their assistance.

Many thanks to the older women we met at workshops, our colleagues at Virginia Polytechnic Institute and State University, and especially Dr. George Hillery, who all encouraged us to write a book to share our work with others. We appreciate, too, the spiritual guidance and encouragement of our pastors and friends, Pr. Mark Radecke, Fr. Donald H. Lemay, and Deacon Michael J. Ellerbrock.

Finally, we appreciate the support of our husbands, Joe and Steve, and our children, Jason, Benjamin, Leigh, Katherine, Brian, Suzanne, and Mark, who graciously tolerated our strange schedules during both the conducting of the research and the writing of this book.

PART I

Introduction to Spiritual Resiliency

CHAPTER 1

An Invitation to Listen

You are invited to listen to Lovey. Come down a winding, single-lane country road, walk into her white frame house, and sit down in a comfortable wingback chair. Lovey is 89 years old, and she lives alone on the farm in southwestern Virginia where she and her husband raised their family. The room is filled with photographs of people—many children, some adults. You see a colorful, hand-made quilt covering the bed in the adjoining room, and your hostess tells you she'd be glad to show you others she's made. Lovey is looking out her window at the snow that has just fallen, and she is talking about her faith.

> If I get down and out and feel bad, I pray. I talk with the Lord and he takes all of that away. You don't have to sit and worry and bother about it. It's just like dying, I don't mind dying, but I don't want to die. I want to live. He made a beautiful earth here for us to live in, and we are supposed to beautify it. You just think of what all He does. Just look how pretty it is today. I look out the window and said, "Thank you, God, it is so pretty. You have decorated this whole world and it looks so pretty. It's so beautiful." Looking out, those trees are white and their limbs are all white and it is beautiful. I said, "I thank you for it and I love you."

One of the eight spiritually resilient women you will meet in this book, Lovey speaks the simple language of country folks and uses childlike words to discuss her life and faith. Although she would never describe herself as outstanding, she does know that she has unusual spiritual strength. She is perfectly comfortable talking about this gift, and there is much to be gained from listening to her.

Or meet Anna, also a remarkable older woman. Like Lovey, she lives alone and speaks readily about her spiritual life. Anna, who is 75, lives in Wilster, a small marsh town in northern Germany. When you walk up to the front door of her charming town house, you first notice the Greenpeace sticker hanging there. Then, sitting in her comfortable parlor, you smell the marvelous German coffee she has prepared. Looking around, you wonder who reads all the newspapers and books. As Anna begins to speak in her soft, sophisticated voice, you quickly learn that her life has been, in many ways, paradoxical. A member of the Nazi Party as a young woman, she now works tirelessly for her two main interests: world peace and care of the environment. Although highly introspective in her religious life, she has been politically active and was elected the first woman mayor of her town. A woman of great dignity who values gracious hospitality, she is nevertheless likely to raise unmentionable topics, such as the Holocaust, in conversations with friends who stop by for coffee and pastries. But the apparent contradictions are all part of God's way, Anna would tell you, all part of the complexities this universe, and a sign of what she calls *die Zusammenhängen* (connectedness). "Yes, the older one becomes, the more one sees that everything is connected," she often says.

The authors of this book have been, for the past two years, custodians of a collection of remarkable narratives told by Lovey, Anna, and six other spiritually resilient older women. Both of us, Jan Ramsey and Rosemary Blieszner, met and talked with the women in their homes in Virginia, in the mid-Atlantic region of the United States, and in the province of Schleswig-Holsteins, Germany. We share our experiences with you because we have found them to be of value, both personally and professionally, and because we strongly believe they can benefit you.

If you have ever wondered what it would be like to live alone someday, or if you have ever tried to comfort a new widow who feels that her life is over, the story of Lovey will inspire you. If you have ever felt guilty about mistakes you made in the past or counseled someone who has difficulty appropriating forgiveness, you will find important the narrative told here by Anna. If you work with people who are coping with serious health problems or face those problems yourself, you may wish to meet Rebecca, who lives alone at 93, is blind and partially paralyzed, yet considers herself "lucky," "blessed." If you work with families attempting to solve cross-generation problems, you may find hope in knowing Emma, whose poverty forces her to live with her adult children yet feels joyful and enthusiastic. If you would like to be more effective in grief counseling but discover your own painful losses to be a barrier, you'll want to meet Miriam, who says she is never really alone, even though she now comes home to an empty house, or Martha, who has been single all her life and who works on and manages her own farm. If you counsel caretakers or care yourself for a chronically ill spouse, you will understand Elisabeth, who lives with her disabled husband and is also a poet and gardener. Or if you have known, either personally or indirectly, the ineffable sorrow that comes after the death of a child, you will find a friend in Inge, who lost her young child in an open wagon during the terrors of World War II.

We have written this book for persons who are searching for meaning, still on their way. It was written with special affection for older persons, but it does not promise successful aging in the usual sense of that term. There is more of hope and spirit here than of "success" as it is typically understood. The stories of these extraordinary women are intended for those who value mystery and becoming over smooth answers and quick fixes, for those who look for abundance in simplicity rather than for security in things. Many people feel, at times, that their life stories have been punctuated primarily with question marks. We offer these women's narratives as signposts along the way for such acknowledged pilgrimages. They are furnished for journey makers who cannot clearly see the end of their travels but who do not wish to walk alone. In religious language, this book is written for the poor in spirit. It is an offering for those who thirst, not for the fountain of youth but for things of the spirit.

You are invited to listen to these women as you prepare for your own later years. Learn from them and from their stories what spiritual resiliency can look like, what dimensions it can contain, and how your own religious faith might be enriched. Listen, now, to women who have listened for God.

WHAT IS SPIRITUAL RESILIENCY?

If you are a professional who works primarily with older clients, you have noticed tremendous differences among the persons you see in your office. Their diversities include varying abilities to survive and to grow after experiencing life crises, and result in intriguing questions for you as a practitioner: Why is it that Mary, 79, who came to the clinic this morning, is not only facing her own breast cancer with hope and dignity but has also courageously survived the death of her beloved husband, yet this afternoon Jane, also 79 and married to an able-bodied, cheery man (who can drive at night!), seems unable to deal with a mild case of arthritis? What can explain these individual variabilities? Clearly, it is not primarily the states of their health, since Mary's problems are far more serious. Is it the quality of their marriages or the number of their friends? The proximity of their children? Their financial situation? Or have some people always had an "executive competence"[1] that enables them to cope well? What is different about them or about their situations powerful enough to explain this dramatic and enigmatic contrast?

Health care personnel, clergy, social service providers, all gerontologists doing applied work, have noticed great diversity in elderly persons' abilities to cope. Who copes best and why has become a crucial question, for if we can predict who will most successfully navigate life transitions, both prevention and treatment of emotional illness in old persons can be improved. Questions of coping and resiliency under stress are, of course, not confined to the present day nor to those who work with the elderly; since the time of Plato, they have often been a topic of inquiry.[2] Both acute traumas and everyday losses require coping skills, and clinicians working with clients of all ages and circumstances have often asked the perplexing question, "What factors predispose people to react with despair and dysfunctional behavior on one hand or with hope and functional responses on the other?" A vast body of research on coping has sprung up in response to this question (see Chapter 2).

Resiliency, then, implies an ability not only to cope with traumatic difficulties but also to respond with flexibility under the pressures of everyday life. People who are resilient have the ability to move beyond being survivors to being thrivers. It is easier to speak in metaphors when describing these strong persons. Estes talked about them as "tough little plants" that manage to send out brave little leaves anyway; she wrote of women who, their bad times behind them, put themselves into "occasions of the lush, the nutritive, the light, and there to flourish, to thrive with busy, shaggy, heavy blossoms and leaves."[3]

The term *spirituality* is sometimes a problematic one, signifying vastly different things to different persons. The term *resiliency* can also be misleading. As used in this book, spirituality refers to a lived experience that includes attitudes, beliefs, and practices that animate (give spirit to) people's lives. It helps them to reach out toward supernatural realities.[4] It also implies a varying and unique style of discipleship for which each denomination has a particular combination of themes and practices. In the Lutheran tradition, the denomination of the older women we write about here, spirituality has had the flavor of a questioning "wintry spirit"[5] and has emphasized the Word of God and the communal nature of the spiritual experience.[6] The authors of this book believe that one basic and important truth has generally been overlooked in research, namely, that spirituality means very different things to different persons. We also believe that this unfortunate omission of denominational specificity has contributed to much of the confusion and to some of the apparently contradictory findings in research on aging and religion. Therefore, even though we believe that these special women can appropriately serve as role models and inspirations across denominational boundaries, we felt it was important to work within one religious tradition. Here, we were instructed by models such as Myerhoff's work with Jewish elderly[7] and Kraus's research among older African Americans.[8] Our hope is that our work, like theirs, might be wide in its implications and broad in its applications yet also honest in its specificity. In other words, we wish to respect religious diversity while we simultaneously acknowledge that the God to whom we take different paths is understood by the wide world of spiritual pilgrims as One.

We were curious about the ways in which resiliency and spirituality might be related in the later years. But a coming together of spirit and science in our present culture is an awkward meeting, often ignored rather than acknowledged. The areas of religion and science appear far apart, in method, theory, and practice. Yet when questions of meaning arise, as they do after a crisis, our ways of knowing the world seem less significant than any assistance we can give. For example, scientists believe that precise scientific method and careful use of technology will eventually lead to knowledge capable of solving many, if not all, of life's difficulties. Religion and the social sciences vary sharply, also, over issues of agency. The social sciences seek to find ways of increasing personal control, and religion teaches that there are times when individual control ends and transcendent sources of support begin. We recognize that while we are working at the interstices of these disparate issues, they may never be totally reconciled.

WHY STUDY OLD WOMEN?

Persons aged 65 and over now represent almost 13% of the population of the United States and over 13% of the population of Germany; projections point to large increases in the aged population around the world in the coming decades.[9] However, professionals in the human service disciplines, including the area called family services, do not consistently recognize these demographic realities.[10] This field has lagged behind both in research and in providing specialized clinical education for those in occupations where this rapidly increasing age group is important, such as counseling and social work.

Research has shown that we have the potential for self-development and for psychological growth throughout our life span.[11] However, we also now know that we do not suddenly become different persons as we age, and we do not typically define ourselves to ourselves as *old*. Instead, an individual experiences a consistent sense of self throughout his or her life span.[12] Nevertheless, providers of services to the elderly need to be aware of the unique needs of this population, not because older persons are inherently different but because of the similarity of problems they face.[13] For example, persons over 65 more frequently experience stresses such as the deaths of close family members, chronic health problems, and the need to deal with an increasingly complex system of health, finances, and residential resources.[14]

In his book on aging, Henri Nouwen wrote, "There is the temptation to make aging into the problem of the elderly and to deny our basic human solidarity in this most human process."[15] Similarly, Betty Friedan noted the troubling tendency by a wide variety of professions, including scholars, social service workers, clergy, and even politicians, to view elderly persons as "problems to be solved."[16] If viewed in this way, elderly adults become merely candidates for services for the frail.[17] They are the direct objects in the sentences we create to discuss them, not subjects of their own actions. Our patronizing attitude then prevents us from viewing older persons as actors in the drama of their own lives.

Strangely, the fact that most elderly persons successfully manage the losses and challenges in their lives is overlooked in our great rush to be helpful. The truth is that most older persons do not use formal services or facilities. Most use their own resources and display a kind of mental hardiness[18] that enables them to resolve life-span transitions adequately, including adjustment to events such as retirement or even the death of a spouse.

The authors of this book are not particularly interested in older persons as problems or as objects of care. We wish, instead, to focus on successful seniors, on remarkable older persons who can serve as models of strength and resiliency. Because persons over 65 in our society are more diverse than those in any other age group, having had more time to get that way, it is important to remember that this cohort group is far more competent than implied by the ageist characterizations of the little old man or little old woman seen so frequently in the media. Resilient older adults are not passive recipients of society's charity; they are social actors, capable of helping to shape the communities to which they belong.[19] Many of them have survived multiple crises to accumulate compensatory wisdom[20] and learn spiritual strength[21] while they continue to grow developmentally.[22] This book is a response to insufficient attention to successful, resilient older persons and their wisdom.

ADVOCACY ISSUES

We hope that, as stereotypes recede, images and sounds of old people in the media will slowly improve. However, it will be some time before the overemphasis on youth in our society makes way to more age-friendly values. Perhaps when enough baby boomers are seniors, such intangibles as wisdom, experience, and a distinguished appearance will be treasured.[23] Meanwhile, women will continue to experience a double jeopardy—sexism plus ageism.

The losses of health, endurance, roles, and friendships, so typical of the later years, are not pleasant for anyone. But aging is far worse for many old women, who lag behind old men in terms of respect, influence, and power in Western society. Said feminist Baba Copper, "The old woman finds herself captured by stereotypes which drain her initiative and shatter her self-respect."[24] Evaluated throughout their lives on the basis of physical beauty, women not only face the normal challenges of the biological aging process, they find themselves anxiously fighting (and inevitably losing) a cosmetic battle.[25] Finding themselves no longer needed in the roles that gave their lives meaning, old women must discover new reasons to live.[26] Thus, beginning in middle age, women often experience invisibility, a cultural devaluing that prevents their being chosen as sexual partners[27] and results in low self-esteem. Unlike men who "develop" and whose faces show "character," women "decline" and worry about "wrinkles." Our language reflects this reality—there are no labels capable of conjuring up associations more degrading or insulting than those popular phrases referring to old women: "Why, you little old woman" or "Stop acting like a little old lady." Where else but sitting on a rocking chair, what else than knitting socks, how else than acting stupidly and naively? We have placed old females quite solidly in our imaginations, and only with difficulty will we relocate them.

Do negative stereotypes mean that it is always more difficult to grow old if one is female? It would certainly appear that, in Western culture, sexism and ageism combine forces to make aging more difficult for women. Betty Friedan spent her early years fighting sexism, but as an old woman, she found it far more difficult to endure the injuries of ageism.[28] In spite of such difficulties, spending one's life being determined by cultural values is not inescapable, as the lives and spirit of persons like Friedan demonstrate. Being completely determined by one's society is not a fate if one is conscious of other options; it becomes a choice. Feeling that one cannot enjoy the years after 60 is not inevitable if one sees a new and powerful "self within"[29] that can grow throughout a new life stage. During what some are calling the crone years,[30] it is possible to leave behind negative and humiliating popular images and embrace positive images of a late-life self.

But to do so, we must have available to us other values, other images. To engage and inspire, stories of actual people are frequently more powerful than arguments or abstract doctrines. With this book, therefore, we seek to join forces with all those who would promote corrective images of old women by offering the voices of real, old women who are strong and courageous persons, worthy of respect and emulation. We offer narratives because we believe that, in advocating for an oppressed group, one good story is worth many pages of political argument or philosophical reasoning.

THE PRECIPITATING EVENT

Like all occurrences, our research project began for more than one reason. Both authors are themselves women experiencing the process of growing older in this problematic cultural climate. Both of us wish to advocate for a new and more empowering image of older females. We both actively participate in our faith communities and believe that our spiritual growth is more important than our intellectual and professional development. We both regret that we have not always given this aspect of our lives the attention it merits. Finally, both of us are hungry for role models of successful aging, models that take into account our value systems and emphasize the spiritual over the material.

It is always interesting, however, to note the one factor that sets a complicated project into motion. In the case of our book, the precipitating event was the experience of listening to older persons themselves and attempting to reconcile what they were saying with what is so often written in gerontological journals about successful aging. What we read in the academic press focused on variables such as quality of health, extent of social support, or financial situation. What we heard from the older persons themselves was, "I couldn't have done it without the Lord."

This is particularly true when elderly people speak about personal crises. I (Ramsey) worked for six years as a nursing home chaplain and administrator. Repeatedly, the people in my facility credited their religious faith as the primary reason for their ability to cope with life stresses, including those most typical of the later years, such as health problems, the death of loved ones, or retirement-related changes. Blieszner also heard these words when she interviewed people for her friendship studies or spoke to older persons in her congregation. The frequency with which we heard "God" or "the Lord" cited as the source of strength in trouble caught our attention and created a kind of cognitive dis-ease.

We decided that research was needed to examine this contradiction. Why had the words of older persons themselves so often been ignored? Why is so much planning and teaching in gerontology and its subspecialties conducted without taking the *spiritual* aspect of resiliency into account? How might exploratory research be designed so that the voices of older persons could be heeded with the seriousness that they deserve?

THE PROJECT

The stories related here were initially part of a research project completed in 1994–1995. A feminist, qualitative, cross-cultural study was conducted in Blue Ridge, a small town in the Blue Ridge Mountains of Virginia, and in Wilster, a small town in northwestern Germany. In order to understand the ways in which women have been empowered by their religious faith to survive losses and crises in their lives, Ramsey listened to and analyzed narrative data from two focus groups and from in-depth interviews with four American and four German Lutheran women, aged 65 years and older, in these communities. I (Ramsey) also reviewed the personal journal entries and field notes that I had written during the time that I collected the data. For the taped focus groups and interviews, I solicited the participation (and informed consent) of aged lifelong Lutheran women who were members of the two parishes participating: Glade Creek, an Evangelical Lutheran Church in America congregation in Blue Ridge, and St. Bartolomäus Kirche in Wilster.

This book is a cooperative, interfaith effort by a clinician and an academic. Ramsey is a Lutheran pastor, a licensed marriage and family therapist, and a part-time gerontology instructor. In her clinical work, she specializes in chronic illness and aging-related issues. Ramsey conducted the initial interviews, analyzed the data, and wrote up the first interpretation of results. Blieszner is a professor of gerontology and has conducted extensive research in relationship issues in the lives of elderly persons. Her special area of interest has been older adult friendships. A Roman Catholic, Blieszner helped to plan the project, met later with women in both countries, and participated in the final analysis found here. We wrote this book after we had worked closely together to tease out the significant themes embedded in the interview transcripts.

The goals of this research were at once practical, academic, and personal. Our practical purpose was to allow the voices of older women to be heard so that respect for elderly women might increase and clinical work in gerontology might grow in depth and sensitivity. Our scholarly goal was to present the academy with a new model for qualitative, feminist, cross-cultural research in religion and aging built on a combination of traditional theory and innovative methods. We were also concerned with identifying themes and categories of older women's spirituality for later research, and we wished to demonstrate the importance of being specific about religious denomination and about gender when conducing research in the area of religion and aging. Finally, we sought to grow personally in our spiritual lives, as we came to know more intimately the faith experiences of outstanding women in two cultures.

The questions addressed by the women we interviewed were posed in general terms and directed to the belief systems and interpretations of faith given by the women themselves. Because we wanted to avoid preconceived categories that would skew our results, our inquiries were open-ended. We explored several general questions: How significant is spirituality in the lives of strong women, among those who not only survive but triumph over adversities? Do patterns of strength, courage, and empowerment in their stories point to a spiritual source? Do the women believe that faith in God has enabled them to gain new perspectives on the struggles of their lives, especially during times of transition? Have they reframed the story of their lives through the symbols and meaning systems of their faith? Finally, how are continuity and change related to their senses of themselves as women? Has their faith made it possible for them to come through, intact and resilient, the numerous changes they have witnessed in their public and private worlds?

A PREVIEW OF THE FINDINGS

The narratives shared here address these very questions in rich detail. They narrate faith that is alive, active, and compelling. It is multifaceted, as well. As we will show in the following chapters, although diverse in life circumstances and experiences, the participants told stories that embodied some common elements repeated again and again. For example, the women spoke often of the importance of Christian *community*, by which they meant not only their immediate social circle but also all Christians, across denominations and across the globe, living and dead. Christian community provides much of their social, emotional, spiritual, and even physical sustenance. It is, for them, both symbolic and actual, an everyday reality and also an intangible abstraction. For all eight women, the faith community was integral to their spirituality and was a vital component of their resiliency. In addition, the women talked freely and easily about their feelings and their *affective experiences*, comfortably relating emotions to their life stories and their spiritual selves. They described and demonstrated a full range of emotions, including fear, enthusiasm, courage, pain, joy, sorrow, happiness, and disappointment. Laughter was as common as tears during the interviews; forceful vocalizations alternated with sighs and whispers. There is a strong relationship between affect and belonging to the religious group for these women. They see emotions not simply as private matters but as experiences anchored in the sacred symbols, history, and daily life of the faith community. Finally, the interviews were frequently interwoven with stories of *personal relationships*. Children, husbands, parents, grandparents, nieces, pastors, and friends all appeared, disappeared, and reappeared on the stage of the women's lives as they discussed their faith. The women care deeply about other people, learn from others, appreciate other members of the community who are role models for their development, nurture and care for others when necessary, and wish their children and grandchildren to find what they have found in Christian community. They suffer when there is conflict in their families and rejoice when things go well for the special people in their lives. These three experiential elements— *community*, *affect*, and *close interpersonal relationships*—are foundational to the spiritual resiliency of the women in this study. Examining the meanings associated with these themes and observing how they are played out in everyday lives illustrate a new dimension of aging well.[31] We invite you now to listen to the words spoken by eight spiritually resilient older women, and we hope that you may gain both insight and encouragement from their lives.

NOTES

1. Giesen & Datan, 1980.
2. Pargament, 1997.
3. Estes, 1992, p. 197.
4. Wakefield, 1983.
5. Marty, 1983a.
6. Sager, 1990.
7. Myerhoff, 1978.
8. Krause & Van Tran, 1989.
9. Kinsella & Taeuber, 1993.
10. Kim, 1991.
11. Researchers who have described this phenomenon include Breytspraak, 1984, and Erikson, Erikson, & Kivnick, 1986.
12. Kaufman, 1986.
13. Kim, 1991.
14. Hashimi, 1991.
15. Nouwen, 1974, p. 17.
16. Friedan, 1993.
17. Thursy, 1991.
18. Hashimi, 1991, p. 38.
19. Hendricks & Leedham, 1991.
20. Baltes & Staudinger, 1993.
21. Birren, 1990.
22. Erikson, Erikson, & Kivnick, 1986.
23. Cockerham, 1991, p. 3.
24. Copper, 1997, p. 121.
25. Sontag, 1997.
26. Bart, 1997.
27. Sontag, 1997.
28. Friedan, 1993.
29. Pearsall, 1997.
30. Le Guin, 1997.
31. Johnson, 1998.

CHAPTER 2

Questions of Meaning, Stories of Faith

Just as there is no one way to speak, so there is no one way to listen. We listen according to categories of our own, we frame questions out of schema we have devised, and we interpret stories within a narrative context understandable only to us. Before attempting to report and interpret what we heard from the women we interviewed, we will identify the clinical and intellectual roots out of which we have grown and to which we are indebted. We will place our *selves* quite consciously within this work, disbelieving that pure scientific objectivity is achievable and confessing that the work of our clinical and academic predecessors are the raw material out of which we attempt to "find new words and create new methods."[1] We will explain how journal keeping was one tool we used to control subjectivity and to deepen personal reflection, and we will celebrate the risks we were able to take as we worked together, deepening our own relationship and bringing ourselves quite openly into this project. Calling for change in the state of the social sciences, Krieger lamented, "We are used to claiming that the experiences we describe represent external realities rather than realities of the self."[2] Here we make no such claim; we want instead to summarize the professional and personal maps that have lead us to this point on our journey. Our ultimate goal: a fresh view of spiritual resiliency; our starting place: an overlook of the scenery described by others.

One of the ways in which our clinical, academic, and personal curiosity has inevitably influenced this research is in the formulation of interview questions. Even though we tried to keep our questions as open-ended as possible, we realize that all questions raise new questions.

Critical gerontologist Jaber Gubrium has shown that the issues gerontologists pose often lead respondents to ask themselves, What *should* I think?[3] He wrote that social science research designs need to focus not only on technical aspects of communication but also on how we "conceptualize the manner by which experience is given voice."[4] Our academic roots in gerontology and our practical (for Ramsey, clinical) experiences with old people supplied us with categories with which to analyze and ultimately, to interpret, the narratives we heard. Critical gerontology in particular provided language that was sufficiently inclusive and meaning-filled, but we were also interested in how our findings fit into previous, traditional work on aging and religion.

We are convinced that prior conceptualizations of resiliency and of spiritually affected our listening and influenced the language we now use to describe what we learned from the women in this study. Intellectual honesty and scholarly vigor demand that we share our clinical, academic, and personal perspectives before we share the old women's stories.

RESILIENCY: THE BOUNCING-BACK FACTOR

As mentioned earlier, one underlying assumption in this book is that the quality of each person's life is formed by two experiences, one external and one internal: what happens to us and how we *react* to what happens to us. Some persons are emotionally overwhelmed by events that most would consider minor and unimportant—the tinge of pain in a leg, a quarrel with a spouse, the stare of a stranger. When transitions or heavy losses, such as the death of a parent or a late-life divorce, occur in the lives of these persons, they typically experience severe depression or debilitating anxiety. Others are able to go through both daily life and heavy losses and "keep on trucking"; they even appear to benefit from and be strengthened by their ordeals. Still others are somewhere in between and can survive many transitions but not every loss. This ability to survive and even to transcend adversity is often referred to as *resiliency*.[5] Like many other contemporary terms in psychotherapy, such as *systems* or *boundaries*, this word is borrowed from the world of the physical sciences. It means exactly what it sounds like: Just as rubber balls rebound after being hurled down to a solid surface, resilient people "bounce back" after life throws them against a hard reality.

According to Pargament, all attempts to explain variations in coping are rooted in a central world view, one "that sees people both as shapers and products of their circumstances."[6] Although formal scientific interest has focused on resiliency for only the last thirty years or so, there is a long history of informal interest in the subject. Plato described Socrates as a model of the composed and honest life. Many characters in world literature could be considered examples of the human ability to deal with troubles effectively.

Pargament suggested that the rapid pace of change in modern culture, along with a lack of spiritual activity, may be reasons that people are fascinated by this subject today. He wrote that our accelerated pace has "disrupted the traditional institutions of society, particularly the institution most responsible for the construction and transmission of world views—religion."[7]

Are we created with this bounce-back factor or do we develop it later? A recent article in the *Harvard Women's Health Watch* addressed this very issue. The author concluded that although some people do seem to be innately more capable of bouncing back than others are, resiliency is not simply created. It can either be either developed or destroyed by life experiences. Furthermore, as every counselor knows, "recovering from one setback makes it easier to come back from the next."[8]

Because resiliency is so important to success and even to survival, it is not surprising that psychologists have begun to devote much time and attention to investigating how the bounce-back factor can be developed and augmented. Among the characteristics that have been identified are authenticity, willingness to accept responsibility, acceptance of change, responsiveness (to the world around), self-confidence, the ability to take risks, and religious beliefs.[9] It is the latter aspect of resiliency that is the subject of this book.

The author of "Bouncing Back from Bad Times" stated, "Even in late adulthood, it's still possible to increase one's resilience." Among other suggestions given is "exercise your beliefs." "If your strength springs from religious faith, spend more time in prayer, contemplation, or meditation. Take time to enjoy art, music, literature, a walk outdoors, or any activity that elevates the spirit. Explore community service; giving to others reaps great rewards."[10] Like most writers about spiritual resiliency, this author seemingly views spiritual resiliency as principally an individual activity. Although service to others is mentioned as an afterthought, it is in solitary, meditative acts that we are presumably renewed and strengthened. Similarly, when we first talked with colleagues about this book and told them that our subject was spiritual resiliency, we found that their comments often assumed an emphasis on personal acts. As we designed this project, however, we wondered: Would this strongly individualized description hold true for the old Lutheran women we would meet? Or would Pargament's more encompassing view hold true?

CLINICAL PERSPECTIVES

Findings from cognitive-behavioral, existential, and narrative therapies have had particular impact on our perspective. Resiliency during stress implies that one has learned how to think rationally, come to terms with the meaning of one's own existence, and integrate both positive and negative life events into an ongoing life narrative. Practitioners with cognitive, existential, or narrative perspectives all raise questions of how we interpret ourselves to ourselves. How do we narrate our life experiences to our own interior audience? These theories are a good starting point for understanding resiliency; they allow us to take a confident first step in understanding the more specific phenomenon and subject of this book, spiritual resiliency.

Cognitive Therapy

A therapy often used to treat depression and anxiety, cognitive therapy is actually one component of a very effective combination, cognitive and behavioral therapies. Practitioners of cognitive therapy seek to modify a client's thoughts and perceptions about events in order to bring about healthy changes in his or her behavior. Beck, one of cognitive therapy's founders, proposed that it is not so much the activating events of our lives that disturb us as it is the catastrophic thoughts (cognitions) we have after those activating events occur. Clients are, therefore, taught to identity irrational thinking, dispute it in an ongoing internal argument, and replace it with thoughts and behaviors that are more rational and more helpful in developing an attitude of problem solving.[11] This approach, combined with appropriate modifications in behavior, is a highly effective therapy for depressed elderly people and is often maintained at follow-ups, even by clients with chronic illness or dementia.[12] Its success echoes the bounce-back factor described earlier in so far as it emphasizes the importance of the "self talk" we do in determining whether personal losses and transitions will lead to worry, sadness, and fear or to new growth, confidence, and feelings of mastery—what we call "resiliency." A resilient person, proposes cognitive therapy, is one who has learned how to *think*.

Existential Therapy

Existential therapies, including logotherapy and some family therapy models, have also been useful for the focus they place on the way individuals experience the world. What "existential" meaning does someone give to his or her life, to being itself? How does someone "frame" experiences in either negative or positive ways, leading either to despair or to well-being? Suffering does not have to have the final word, according to Victor Frankl, a Viennese psychiatrist and a survivor of the Nazi Holocaust; the "will to meaning" we give our sufferings can enable us to transcend any ordeal. The counselor using Frankl's logotherapy confronts a person with his or her life and engages with him or her in a healing process that leads to the discovery of new meaning. Frankl's personal experiences as a prisoner in Auschwitz taught him that the health of one's inner self is less dependent on external circumstance or psychological abnormality than it is the result of making a free decision. He witnessed, in that grotesque place, a fascinating process: Those prisoners who held fast to their moral and spiritual values survived emotionally intact. They filled what seemed a to be a terrifying vacuum with the discovery of beauty and with spiritual meaning. This same process, said Frankl, can help clients discover meaning through spiritual reinterpretations of suffering.[13] Similarly, family therapists with a constructivist view, including solution-oriented therapists, believe that there is no single, correct view of reality and that neither the therapist's view nor the family member's view is "correct." Therefore, they encourage clients to define their own goals and search out their own meaningful solutions.[14] For example, Gestalt therapist Walter Kempler urged family members to become more intensely aware of what they were doing or saying or feeling, more in touch with what was going on in everyday family discussions in order to look beyond the surface and to uncover and "own" the basics of their human experience.[15] The resilient person, for the existential therapist, is someone who knows how to *be*.

Narrative Therapy

Narrative therapists believe that we live in a "destoried" world[16] and, as a result, suffer an impoverishment of meaning in our lives. Feelings of emptiness and dissatisfaction, expressed especially by those in younger cohort groups, may result from what was, at first, their lost belief that objective, scientific truth would supply all the answers to life's questions.[17] When illness or other losses occur that cannot be remedied by technology, despair or at the least feelings of disempowerment can occur. Chronically ill people in particular tend to have "problem-saturated" descriptions of their lives; they have difficulties separating themselves from their illness. Thus, clients in narrative therapy are first encouraged to *externalize* their problems and create for themselves new and more meaningful life narratives. The therapist then helps them to search for exceptions, for times when they were able to manage and cope during transitions and thereby increase their levels of empowerment, responsibility, and choice. Language is framed in positive modes, such as, "When your life is better, how will that be?" Narrative therapists also help their clients identify problems that may be the property of society, not of the ill or old or "different" person who is the client. Together, therapist and client deconstruct reality and its dominant narrative and "rewrite" self-descriptions anchored in more authentic plot lines for past, present, and future.[18] For narrative therapists, the resilient person is one who has learned how to *narrate* his or her own life story.

As we began this project, categories of resiliency derived from these clinical perspectives were available to us as organizing tools, providing classifications to use in our search for resiliency. Would the assumptions of cognitive, existential, and narrative therapies be confirmed? Would we find evidence of the assumption that persons mourn not what they have lost but rather the gap between what they have and what they expect? We hypothesized that the women's abilities to accept the sometimes harsh realities of their lives would be part of their capacities to cope with limitations and with the numerous losses so common in aging. We were curious to hear the spin women would place on their narratives, and we listened for how cognitive interpretations might influence their ability to be spiritually resilient.

DEVELOPMENTAL PERSPECTIVES

A recent passage in a counseling newsletter described the ideal geriatric counselor. She or he "understands the aging process not as a problem, but rather as a life season of dramatic developmental lifework, culminating in a personal unfolding [and] bearing gifts of peace, wisdom, acceptance, stamina, perseverance, kindness, gratitude, and many others which together reflect greater clarity and heightened meaning of what came before . . . "[19] This marvelous description of appreciation for positive old age stems from the work of psychoanalyst Erik Erikson, a pioneer in the area of adult development.

Building on Freud's insight that "the child is father to the man,"[20] Erikson viewed the later years as an integral part of human growth and identified specific tasks he believed necessary for a successful completion of each life stage. In many ways, he is a conceptual grandfather to all professionals who stress old age as a positive opportunity for growth and maturity.[21] Furthermore, although not especially religious in its language, his work on human development in later life formed a bridge between purely secular approaches and most current work in religion and aging. It is precisely the developmental lifework with which spirituality intersects.

Even though the implicit age linking of Erikson's stage theory and the rigid ways in which it is sometimes employed are troublesome, Erikson's thought has an almost irresistible appeal for scholars interested in the relationship of human development and spirituality. His interest in the cultural and historic, along with the psychological, and his ability to describe the interactions of all these elements with a particular human story were especially appealing and useful in our cross-cultural, historically influenced work. His eighth stage, *integrity versus despair,* sees wisdom as the emerging strength of the latter years and was the frame of reference we frequently used to understand resilient women. Although it could be said that relying strictly on notions of age-related stages tends to limit understanding of religion and spirituality in explaining the life course, we found, in Erikson's theory, room for the centrality of a spiritual life.

INTERSECTION OF CLINICAL ASSUMPTIONS
AND RELIGIOUS QUESTIONS

Before we met the eight women we interviewed for this book, we had some expectations. Thinking in terms of resiliency, cognitive, existential, and narrative therapies and Erikson's developmental orientation, we had vague images of what a resilient old woman might be like. She would think rationally, struggle with meaning questions courageously, and sound like the author of her own story. She would surely be wise, have lived productively, and have achieved integrity over despair. Whether learning to *think* rationally, to *be* authentically, or to *narrate* constructively, she would be coping well with the losses that she was experiencing in old age. This much we expected to find.

But we began this work with much curiosity about how all of this would converge with the women's religious faith. Here we had more questions than theories, and we were interested in many unexplored issues. How would the healthy, rational thinking of these women intersect with an appreciation for the many unseen, unknown mysteries of life and death? How would they think about their unknown futures, especially the likelihood of increasing dependency if their health failed? How would their faith help them to manage their anxieties? What about the multiple losses they had faced—how would these experiences fit into quests for purpose and direction? We had no idea how questions of *being* would actually be played out in the narratives we would hear. Would the women speak in largely individualistic terms? Would they be calm, emotional, or controlled as they spoke of their spirituality? Had other people tried to write their stories for them, and if so, at what point did they become empowered to reinvent themselves and to create their own plot lines? Would their religious communities consider them wise? Would relationships with others in their faith group be primary or secondary to issues of strength and resiliency? How had they come to terms with failure and weakness, with times they had lost their way? Did they really experience God's forgiveness and truly forgive themselves, thus reaching integrity over despair?

We knew what we would *not* find. We expected that a spiritually resilient old woman would seek personal integrity and exhibit courageous honesty, so we did not expect to hear the easy story, the kind of religious sentimentality that Barnes called the "tired old plot" in which "all turns into good news at the moment the Christian meets God."[22] We were not looking for a spiritual superwoman who, with the power of God, could hurdle over the handicaps of life with a single bound. The resilient woman, we expected, has often wept but is not mourning endlessly. Our own beliefs led us to anticipate that her experiences of the gracious love of God would come first and matter most. Because she knows she is first a child of God, she would struggle for acceptance, not only of unalterable circumstances and realities, but acceptance of what she herself is. She would know first Whose she is, then who she is. The failures and losses in her life would not have become unmanageable catastrophes; they would be viewed as opportunities for growth, for increased maturity, and for trust in the promises of God. Thus, her emotional maturity would be matched by spiritual maturity. In her later years, she would have a new mindfulness, a lively sense of herself and of her story heightened through the clarity of honest, ongoing self-examination. And she would recognize in this growth through suffering something beyond her own doing; she would be able to discern a process not of reasons alone, but one of Spirit. In the words of the Christian apostle Paul, she would be "grown up in Christ."[23]

Nevertheless, we expected that each woman would have, as do we, religious questions and that she would be more seeker than expert. She would be the person with curiosity, not one who has all the answers. We expected that her peers would see her as a pilgrim, not as a disillusioned authority. But then, the questions returned. Would she be respected in her community? Would her religious honesty make her too vulnerable to criticism for leadership? Would others look to her as a model? Above all, we wondered how her narrative, including the hurts, dangers, and joys, would be placed into the larger narrative of God's love.

Even though we were interviewing Lutheran women, our many

questions cut across denominations. We decided the questions were universal, just as loss and joy and life and death are universal. And we resolved, at the onset of this project, to be as open-minded as possible in our work, so that persons of all faiths might discover a commonality with the strong old women we would meet. In so far as possible, we resisted preconceived ideas about how the women's spirituality would enable them to cope with and even transcend life difficulties. We began our project without assuming we knew how the women's ways of thinking, being, and telling their life stories would intersect with the Word, the Being, and the Story of God.

SCHOLARLY PERSPECTIVES

Early Work on Religion and Aging

Much important writing has been done on the subject we explore here, aging and religion. We are indebted to a vast array of scholars who discovered abstract categories and formed new language that was, in turn, available to us. Without those who came before us, we would have had neither the ability to recognize old people's spiritual resiliency when we saw it nor the language to describe what we saw. We briefly summarize this academic scholarship so that readers may understand the historical context within which we worked.

The area of religion and aging developed early on within the relatively young field of gerontology, as scholars attempted to answer questions about the quality of life in old age. Chiefly, they wanted to be helpful to elderly persons and their caretakers by discovering what factors might positively influence how elderly persons get through difficult times. Gerontology has had, from its inception, a strong applied thrust, and the desire to help has never been far behind when research is conducted. This is a response, in no small part, to the great *need* for help. There is no disagreement that many persons, albeit not all, experience high levels of difficulty in old age. Not only are the obvious problems related to physical health and finances present but just as crucial are problems of the spirit, problems with depression, grief, and loss. As has often been said, "Old age is not for sissies!"[24] In response, research investigating how to help people cope with stressors has always been important and popular.

But because of the diverse nature of human personality, a diversity that only increases as people age, gerontologists quite obviously could not concentrate solely on *external* influences on quality of life.

Clearly, the extensive diversity of the elderly population encompasses not only the external conditions of their lives but also how they *perceive* what happens to them. The internal is at least as significant as the external. However, as soon as researchers wished to include intangible, abstract dimensions—what could be called the *perception factor*—great complications arose. Perception is abstract; its causes are complicated and its effects varied. How does one count it, measure it, research it? Even labeling internal perception is a tricky business. Many scholars ultimately adopted the inclusive term *subjective well-being*.[25] But validity and reliability, both important in social scientific research, varied greatly from study to study. Researchers wondered if they had overlooked significant variables that were necessary to include so that more predictable, meaningful, and consistent results could be obtained. Some gerontologists questioned the research models being used, arguing that the methods employed for measuring external factors mathematically, called "quantitative research," were not appropriate for abstract concepts. Given the importance of matching the concepts under study to the investigative methods for obtaining reliable and valid results, debates about how best to assess abstractions such as perceptions and subjective well-being are likely to continue.

Because early gerontologists had noticed that old people often cited faith in God as a coping resource, they borrowed existing categories of well-being or findings about the psychology of coping to begin exploration of the intersection of religiosity and aging.[26] About thirty years ago, variables related to *religion* were added to the list of possible causes of subjective well-being in studies of people at all age levels, including old age.[27] To the surprise of many, these were immediately found to be very powerful variables. But from the start, the religiosity factor has been problematic and controversial.[28] It has been measured in many ways. First, scholars simply counted frequency of church attendance. Then, when they realized that many old people are too frail to attend services or climb the steps of the church or synagogue,[29] they added other behaviors to the list, such as watching religious TV, attending revivals, contributing money to religious organizations, and prayer. For nearly a generation, gerontological researchers "with a behavioral and quantitative cast of mind"[30] have searched for an *activity* that would somehow serve as an accurate index for religion. But as one scholar noted, they have not found it and they never will,[31] for religion is a matter of the heart, as well as head, and it produces deep thoughts, commitments, and emotions that are not necessarily reflected consistently in one's outward behavior.

Gerontologists working primarily in religion and aging have

been, of necessity, a risk-taking, courageous bunch. Even though a significant number, for example David Moberg,[32] have been interested in religious topics for years, it has been difficult, and at times even dangerous to one's academic health, to admit to a strong interest in what Jeffrey Levin called "the r-word."[33] Because the "science" in "social sciences" has been dogmatically emphasized, most people in academia have believed that it is quaint at best, and politically dangerous at worst, to focus on matters of religion. A climate of near reverence for scientific methods has led to respect for technology and for producing quantitative data. Work with abstract topics, such as faith and the meaning of human suffering, has therefore not been taken seriously. Such research is, said Levin, "mostly invisible."[34] As a result, only rare and tentative dialogues between the religious community and those working in the multidisciplined fields of gerontology have occurred. Academics, physicians, counselors, and social workers have gone one way, while clergy, pastoral counselors, and professors of philosophy and theology have gone another. Noting this situation as early as 1973 and hoping for more focus on moral issues and positive development in the later years, social psychologist Lawrence Kohlberg offered a challenge to gerontology: "Perhaps the field of aging could find some of its own most unique and deepest problems emerging from philosophic concepts rather than from the more usual concepts of biology and social science."[35] For many years, no one appeared to be listening to this challenge.

Recent Work on Religion and Aging

Kohlberg would be pleased with gerontological research since 1990. Since that time, scholarship has frequently broken with the mandate to obtain quantitatively based data and scholars have ventured into more philosophical and anthropological domains. Grounded in the methods of modern cultural anthropology, work is often qualitative and *emic*—that is, researchers seek to see the world through the eyes of differing people. To do this, they become immersed in the everyday lives of the people they study, keeping cross-cultural considerations in mind. Direct observation, participating in daily life, and recording the meanings of things, persons, and actions in the native language of the people[36] are tools that replace calculators, charts, and lists of structured questions. Such approaches give way to open-ended inquiry and to an attitude of respect for individual and group differences, including differences of gender, class, culture, religion, and ethnicity. This comparative paradigm creates an interactive process between the researcher and the participant. It is mainly descriptive and relies on people's *words* as primary data.

Listening, rather than counting, becomes the focal research activity. The humanities, rather than the statistical sciences, are the nurturing grounds for qualitative researchers. Their work is, as one scholar said, "an exciting, sometimes frustrating, but ultimately rewarding journey."[37]

The authors of this book have derived both inspiration and information from a variety of scholars working qualitatively.[38] We are particularly comfortable with a recent movement in aging research and teaching called *critical gerontology*.[39] Critical gerontologists are certainly not confined to those studying religion and aging, but their approach is highly compatible with work in this area. They are comfortable with ambiguity and with a wide range of topics, including everything from reflections on the "third age"[40] to critical perspectives on institutional adaptations to an aging society. They deny the assumption that research can ever be value-free, and they pay attention to the moral economy,[41] the political climate in which they work. Having a particular respect for the humanities, they are comfortable moving back and forth among intellectual paradigms,[42] and they theorize and practice their art along the lines of the postmodern movement.[43] We claim for our work an orientation within critical gerontology, as one application of postmodernism, because we firmly believe that there is, indeed, no single, correct view of reality. Nor is there a value-free environment in which to conduct research. Like many other gerontologists today, we are completely comfortable with approaches that raise as many questions as they answer.

We find this to be an exciting time to be writing about aging and the spirit. Past negativity toward religion is rapidly changing. Partially in response to the consistent attention that many aging persons themselves pay to religious questions and partially in response to a new respect for prayer in some quarters of the medical community, the religious dimension is gaining new focus and approval. If the highly respected *Harvard Health Letter*, for example, can print as a lead article, "Faith and Healing: Making a Place for Spirituality," then the multidisciplinary world of gerontology continues to ignore religion at its peril. Said the author of this article, "Today, the long-standing wall between medicine and religion is crumbling, due in part to the disillusionment of many Americans with what they see as high-tech, impersonal health care. Indeed, there is a growing interest among patients in simpler, holistic approaches to healing. For an increasing number of Americans and their physicians, this whole-body approach includes attention to spirituality."[44] We hope that studies such as ours will be helpful in demonstrating the value of research that investigates the connection between spirituality and the experience of growing old.

We hope, too, that as narrative approaches in therapy and research become more honored, the work of a very special anthropologist and gerontologist, Barbara Myerhoff, will be better known. If Erikson is the theoretical grandfather to this work, than we consider Myerhoff to be our methodological grandmother. It was reading about her life and work among the conservative Jewish elderly in California that inspired Ramsey to begin this project. Myerhoff's books were, indeed, a "triumph of continuity and culture," and her ability to relate "being, meaning, and narrative" has been an inspiration for the academic, clinical, and literary work of many scholars. A searcher for depth and yet a dweller in the "plain strong wool of ordinary human life,"[45] Myerhoff discovered that it is not always possible or necessary to distinguish fully between research for professional reasons and research that becomes a personal quest. Her confidence that motivations could be openly acknowledged while work remains academically sound was very helpful to us. For, as we acknowledge here, our work has been both personal quest and scholarly adventure.[46]

FEMINIST VOICES AND LUTHERAN BELIEFS

The narratives you are will read are told, as much as possible, in the voices of the women we met. We made a firm commitment to keep *listening* as the central piece of our research act; this is reflected in the numerous direct quotes we have included in this book. Having *voice*, finding one's *voice*: These are important goals for all women and particularly for older women. Our roots in feminist inquiry are summarized. Then, aware that readers will be from a variety of faith groups and wishing to respect those preferences, we review how Lutheran voices may differ from those of other religious groups. An introduction to this denomination is needed before entering the belief system of the women you will meet in the next chapter. Then, we briefly describe how we conducted the research, the methodology that structured our work.

Women's Voices

Perhaps because women's positions in religious systems are so often reflections of their status throughout society, the experiences of women have not been thoroughly studied, and their contributions to spiritual life are greatly underestimated.[47] Partially in response to this historical neglect, spirituality has recently become a popular topic in feminist writings. Past work that is relevant to this book includes conviction about the central importance of using women's experiences as a basis for knowledge,[48] the "refusal to ignore the emotional dimension of the conduct of inquiry,"[49] an emphasis on human relationships in spirituality,[50] and the ability to ask larger questions of meaning.[51]

Beginning in the late 1970s, feminists have criticized traditional theories and methods in the social sciences. They have conducted research based on personal awareness, political advocacy, and the study of female subjects. Many scholars believe that feminism has become a new world view.[52] Debates within the movement have never been lacking, however. For example, early on, inattention to ethnic women's experiences was a problem in the feminist movement. More relevant to our research is the controversy sparked by Carol Gilligan's discovery of "a different voice."[53]

Gilligan found relational aspects of women's lives to be highly important to those who are making ethical decisions. Whereas men tended to reach moral decisions based on abstract principles, women focused on their relationships and the impact of their choices on significant others. In her "Letter to Readers" in the 1993 edition of her popular book, *A Different Voice*, she wrote that she had found a tendency for women and men to make different relational errors—for men to think that if they know themselves, they will also know others and for women to think that if only they know others, they will come to know themselves. Gilligan's findings were controversial but significant, and her work has become part of an ongoing process of changing the world through attending to women's voices.

Gilligan's work seemed to imply a sharp dichotomy between the experiences of men and women, however, that has had political and personal consequence not acceptable to all feminists. Recently, Wood wrote of what she called Gilligan's "rhetorical construction of woman"; she also found Gilligan's definition of woman's nature both "inaccurate and regressive."[54] Particularly important for this study was Wood's criticism that Gilligan's book actually contains two voices, one dominant and the other muted. One is the voice of the scholar herself, the "conventional, psychological" voice of a "faculty member at Harvard."[55] The other, muted, voice is that of the women with whom Gilligan worked. Avoiding a confusion of voices has been an important challenge in our study, and our decision to keep personal, spiritual journals was one response to this potential difficulty. The journals enabled us to distinguish between the old women's voices and our own.

Although she spoke with mostly younger women, writer-psychologist Randour also listened for women's spiritual voices. In her study on spirituality and its intersection with relationships, she interviewed ninety-four women of various ages, denominations, and geographic and ethnic backgrounds, then narrated and interpreted their spiritual experiences. She also wished to discover what women's spirituality could teach about women's psychological development and expression. Randour found a strong relational element to the women's lives and spirituality. All the respondents she studied were "seekers of meaning" who found that significance frequently rose up out of every day life.[56]

> Although truth and beauty arise out of the ordinary, there is nothing "ordinary" about any one person's life. Each of us repeatedly face challenges that call into question a sense of order or coherence we once felt, but no longer do. . . It is in this ordinary and very human struggle to live with the responsibility for our freedom, the knowledge of our death, and the uncertainty about our future, that some of us find some of the time the possibilities for our extraordinary courage to strive for a coherence or wholeness in life. All of us have a story to tell. It is the story of being human, of reaching for new understandings, of appreciating mystery, and of seeking wholeness, beauty, and truth. All we need to do is to ask, and to listen.[57]

With its emphasis on listening for women's voices, seeking meaning, and telling spiritual stories based on ordinary women's lives, Randour's study has been an additional model for this project.

Other scholars who have heeded Gilligan's call to listen to women are Belenky, Clinchy, Goldberger, and Tarule. In *Women's Ways of Knowing: The Development of Self, Voice, and Mind,*[58] they interviewed women with the goal of giving them voice and honor. They described the obstacles women must overcome in developing the power of their minds. Their identification of categories of knowledge as received, subjective, procedural, and constructed was helpful to this study.

Lutheran Theology and Spirituality

"All spirituality is about roots. . . . Tradition is the common nourishing and searching and growing of our roots."[59] Certainly, persons cannot be understood apart from their roots, and if spirituality is understood as a lived experience, then it is best viewed in the context of a group's belief and history. We restricted our study to women over 65 who had been lifelong members of the Lutheran church. Although their faith sometimes varies in emphasis, the denominational heritage of both traditional Lutheran *theology* and *practice* has been an important component of the religious education and spiritual formation for all the women we interviewed.

Like all Christian traditions, Lutheran spirituality has always contained a tension between those who would emphasize more of a "heart religion" and those who are closer to a "religion of the head."[60] This becomes understandable in light of Lutheran history. Theologically, whatever unity exists in world Lutheranism today has grown out of the confessional writings in *The Book of Concord*,[61] an important document written in 1580 to articulate Lutheran theology and respond to the many differences of opinion springing up after the Reformation. It is a carefully written statement and has been one of the reasons that Lutherans feel they have strong theological roots. However, as Martin Luther, founder of the Lutheran Church, had preached, "The heart of religion lies in its personal pronouns"[62] and a well-known Lutheran movement, Pietism, responded to the obligation to pay more attention to the needs of ordinary people, especially their emotions—what Pietists called the "affective dimension of the spiritual life."[63] As you will see in the following pages, this affective, pietistic strain is alive and well today and was particularly evident in several of the German women we met.

Lutheran spirituality must also be understood as part of a larger, interfaith spirituality movement. The history of world spirituality reveals many and varying themes, including labor and prayer, service to the needy, asceticism, appreciation for the "small, daily pleasures of life,"[64] martyrdom, the reading of sacred texts, mysticism, narration, incarnationism, and narratives of personal growth.[65] Lutheranism contains many of these to a limited degree but also adds foci of its own, such as a questioning spirit,[66] an emphasis on the Word of God,[67] stress on the goodness of all creation,[68] a persistent accent on the communal nature of the spiritual experience,[69] and the primacy of the story of Jesus Christ, the gospel story of redemption and the Grace of God.[70] All of these aspects will be evident in the strong women you meet in this book.

Lutheran spirituality begins with an honest look at the human condition, including our finitude and mortality. One well-known Lutheran writer, Martin Marty, called this a "wintry" disposition. He referred to a somber but honest insistence on the reality of death and the inevitability of spiritually dry times. Wrote Marty soon after the death of his wife, "The search for a piety does not permit evasion of the central issue of life: its 'being toward death.' Every Yes hereafter has to be made in the face of 'ceasing to be' as the world ordinarily knows being."[71] The well-known writings of Joseph Sittler[72] also reflect a starkly honest, wintry mood; in his last lecture, he said, "Life is characterized by temporality, mortality, passing-ness, mutability. Life comes, unfolds, closes, and departs. That is the only kind of life we know anything about."[73] Lutherans do not ignore the difficult questions of suffering, death, and the meaning of life when they write about their spiritual journeys; they ask many Why? questions along the way. Marty wrote that people can endure any kind of How? if they can endure a Why?[74] Lutherans do not deny that the religious person can experience acute loneliness, emotional pain, and great doubt.

Lutheranism is also characterized by an emphasis on the paradoxical nature of human experience, rather than progress toward sanctification. Lutherans talk about being "sinners yet saints" and wish to hold onto a sense of awareness in their brokenness even while they acknowledge that they have a new life as followers of Christ. Wrote Paul Tillich,

> In Lutheranism the emphasis on the paradoxical element in the experience of the New Being was so predominant that sanctification could not be interpreted in terms of a line moving upward toward perfection. It was seen instead as an up-and-down of ecstasy and anxiety, of being grasped by agape and being thrown back into estrangement and ambiguity. This oscillation between up and down was experienced radically by Luther himself, in change between moments of courage and joy and moments of demonic attacks, as he interpreted his states of doubt and profound despair. The consequence of the absence in Lutheranism of the Calvinistic and Evangelistic valuation of discipline was that the ideal of progressive sanctification was taken less seriously and replaced by a great emphasis on the paradoxical character of the Christian life.[75]

Lutherans derive strength at times of crisis from the rituals and symbols of their own tradition. Recently, Lutheran pastor and gerontologist Kimble wrote of the spiritual dimension of his own personal aging. He found that family and community rituals were very real supports for coping "with transitions and crises in a universe that is saturated with a blessed ambiguity."[76]

From the very origins of this denomination, Lutheran theology has been centered on God's Word. In a work prepared in 1527, Martin Luther stressed that "everything our body does outwardly and physically is in reality and in name done *spiritually* [italics added] if God's Word is added to it and it is done in faith."[77] Lutherans have found that the stories in scripture of creation, dividedness, journeying in the wilderness, and being called to return "fit the reality of human experience with a kind of exactitude which evokes . . . constant surprise and admiration."[78] Because Lutherans believe that "the most important single thing we can do in a culture of disbelief is to worship and listen to God,"[79] there is a stress on listening and on language in Lutheran spirituality. Sittler called it a "linguistic quality"[80] and wrote of his "affection for language" in worship and the hearing of scripture:

> Coming from a tradition in which both the Biblical literature and the old liturgical life of the Church were very important, this affection for, and this invocatory character of language as a way to understanding, were early grooved in my mind . . . [81]

This love of language finds its way into Lutheran worship as prayers, hymns, scripture readings, liturgy, preaching, and the spoken words that accompany the actions of the Sacraments:

> Take and eat; this is My body, given for you. This cup is the new covenant in My blood, shed for you and for all people for the forgiveness of sin. Do this for the remembrance of Me.[82]

To Luther, the whole of creation, all its creatures, all human beings, were the "masks" of the hidden God, "in, with, and under which" He gets all His work done.[83] This metaphor is particularly helpful, said Heineken, when one wishes to know how philosophical speculation and scientific methodology might be combined. Luther's writings reveal that although redemption is primary, his spirituality also has a creation dimension. Luther's hymns, in particular, show that some of his most tender words were for God's creation: "Now let all the heavens adore you, And saints and angels sing before you . . . We gather round your dazzling light. No eye has seen, no ear has yet been trained to hear. What joy is ours."[84]

Lutheran spirituality is communally based. For a Lutheran, the foundations of the spiritual life are laid in the Christian family, where the Commandments, the Apostles' Creed, and the Lord's Prayer are learned and where the first explanations of the sacraments are given.[85] Luther believed that

> When Christians thus come together their prayers are twice as strong as otherwise. One can and one really should pray in every place and every hour; but prayer is nowhere so mighty and strong as when the whole multitude prays together.[86]

There is also a sense of oneness with the entire human family as part of God's creation. Wrote Sager,

> The Christian journey is fundamentally a communal experience, God

having fashioned us as "the people of God." A growing life with God leads us more deeply into a sense of solidarity, not only with the whole Christian Church but with the whole human family of which we are a part.[87]

Finally, there is in Lutheran spirituality a belief in the ongoing spiritual unity of the community *after death*, based on the doctrine of the church as the Body of Christ. This belief is heard in the words spoken during the Lutheran service for the burial of the dead: "Almighty God, you have knit your chosen people together one communion, in the mystical body of your Son, Jesus Christ our Lord. Give to your whole Church in heaven and one earth your light and your peace."[88]

Lutherans believe that, because we have been saved by God's work, not by our own good deeds, the spiritual initiative always lies with God. The "gracious encounters" between God and God's children, including those that occurred during this study, are gifts from God, not the result of human effort. Concerning their faith, Lutherans prefer to say "I have been found," rather than "I have found it." Spirituality viewed this way has a surprise element and offers limitless opportunities to discover life's adventures and joys. In Lutheran thought, God's purposes go beyond language, which speaks of religion as a way of coping during tough times. Wrote a retired pastor in a recent article in *The Lutheran*,

> We begin with God. Spiritual formation or nurture or sanctification— however we name it—is not about learning to live with unhappiness or how we can feel better or worse. It's about the great work God is doing: God is forming Jesus within us. This isn't done by us; it's done by God.[89]

Lutheran Practice

In practice, Lutheran spirituality has emphasized the two sacraments, Baptism and Holy Communion, and the preaching and teaching of God's Word. Lutheran worship is central to the spiritual life of the community; it is the "means by which Christ becomes truly and wholly present, really conveying the power of God's saving grace."[90] Music, including hymns, and liturgy are interwoven with the spoken word in Lutheran worship, which has kept many elements of the Roman Mass. In fact, Luther retained a "critical reverence" for the dogma, liturgical orders, and church polity received from the Western Catholic tradition.[91]

The Biblical cannon is normative for all practice of the faith[92] and the private practice of Lutheran spirituality is characterized by much reading and studying of scripture. The purpose of this Bible study is "that by it we may be confirmed in penitence, lifted in hope, made strong for service, and above all filled with the true knowledge of you [God] and of your Son Jesus Christ."[93] Prayer is to be a daily activity because it has been "commanded" by God; Luther did not understand it to be optional for Christians.[94] Prayer is the act of faith par excellence because "it is the point where the powers of darkness attack faith most sharply."[95] Wrote Luther, "Without the Word of God the enemy is too strong for us. But he cannot endure prayer and the Word of God."[96]

For a Lutheran, the doing of good works and the care of creation are also important parts of spiritual practice. They are to be understood as being in response to God's Grace, to what He has done for us through Jesus Christ; they are never to be viewed as paths to moral perfection.[97] The Grace of God is not to be taken lightly or viewed as "cheap," however, for it cost a Man His life.[98]

NOTES

1. Gilligan, 1982, p. x.
2. Krieger, 1991, p. 47.
3. Gubrium, 1993, p. 48.
4. Gubrium, 1993, p. 46.
5. Interestingly, the term "resiliency" exists in English but not in German.
6. Pargament, 1997, p. 71.
7. Pargament, 1997, p. 73.
8. "Bouncing Back from Bad Times," 1998.
9. "Bouncing Back from Bad Times," 1998.
10. "Bouncing Back from Bad Times," 1998, p. 3.
11. Goldenberg & Goldenberg, 1996.
12. Teri, Curtis, Gallagher-Thompson, & Thompson, 1994.
13. Frankl, 1969.
14. Goldenberg & Goldenberg, 1996.
15. Cited in Goldenberg & Goldenberg, 1996, pp. 146-153.
16. White & Epston, 1990.
17. Bateson, 1972.
18. For a more complete description of narrative therapy see White & Epston, 1990.
19. Johnson, 1998.
20. Aiken, 1995, p. 137.
21. Johnson, 1998, p. 11.
22. Barnes, 1991, p. 26.
23. See Paul's writing in First Corinthians, Chapter 13.
24. Kaufman, 1989.
25. George, 1990, p. 190.
26. Interestingly, some of the best early work in religion and aging was done by nurses and by members of the African American religious community, where the importance of church has never been debated.
27. Levin, 1989.
28. In his excellent recent book, Pargament (1997, pp. 407-464) showed that results in this area are often contradictory, with one study showing a positive correlation between church attendance and coping and the next yielding opposite findings.
29. Tobin, 1991, p. 120.
30. Moody, 1994, p. xi.
31. Moody, 1994, p. xi.
32. See, for example, Moberg, 1979.
33. Levin, 1994.
34. Levin, 1994, p. 11.
35. Kohlberg, 1973.
36. Sokolovsky, 1990, pp. 2-18.
37. Marshall & Rossman, 1989, p. 11.
38. See, for example, articles in the *Journal of Religious Geronotology* and

books and articles by scholars such as Payne, McFadden, and Simmons.

39. Cole, Achenbaum, Jakobi, & Kastenbaum, 1993.
40. Laslett, 1991.
41. Minkler & Cole, 1991.
42. Cole, Achenbaum, Jakobi, & Kastenbaum, 1993.
43. The term *postmodernism* describes a cross-disciplinary movement in which a powerful (modern) myth is debunked, namely the myth that technology and quantitative methodology would soon give humankind the answers to all human dilemmas. Rather, say those with a postmodern orientation, it is important to acknowledge that all knowledge is secondary to the theoretical orientation and the cultural biases of those who create knowledge. They want to deconstruct many popularly accepted beliefs that were created under the false guise of objectivity.
44. "Making a Place for Spirituality," 1998.
45. Turner, 1978, p. xv.
46. Myerhoff, 1978.
47. Sinclair, 1986.
48. Yates, 1983.
49. Fonow & Cook, 1991, p. 9.
50. Randour, 1987.
51. Langer, 1942.
52. Tarnas, 1991.
53. Gilligan, 1993, p. ix.
54. Wood, 1994, p. 62.
55. Wood, 1994, p. 65.
56. Randour, 1987, p. 226.
57. Randour, 1987, pp. 227-228.
58. Belenky, Clinchy, Goldberger, & Tarule, 1986.
59. Fox, 1981, p. 1.
60. Nelson, 1982, p. 25.
61. Lutheran Church, 1580, 1959.
62. Cited in Nelson, 1982, p. 25.
63. Holt, 1993, p. 84.
64. Holt, 1993, p. 34.
65. Holt, 1993.
66. Marty, 1983a, p. 52.
67. Sager, 1990.
68. Heinecken, 1986.
69. Heinecken, 1986.
70. Tripp, 1986.
71. Marty, 1983a, p. 53.
72. Sittler, 1987.
73. Sittler, 1987, p. 63.
74. Marty, 1983b.
75. Tillich, 1963, p. 230.
76. Kimble, 1993, p. 28.

77. Quoted in Sager, 1990, p. 25.
78. Sittler, 1987, p. 64.
79. Vaswig, 1994, p. 170.
80. Sittler, 1987, p. 60.
81. Sittler, 1987, p. 60.
82. Evangelical Lutheran Church in America, 1978, p. 90.
83. Quoted in Heinecken, 1986, p. 20.
84. Senn, 1986.
85. Tripp, 1986.
86. Quoted in Owen, 1993, p. 202.
87. Sager, 1990, p. 81.
88. Evangelical Lutheran Church in America, 1978, p. 209.
89. Vaswig, 1994, p. 17.
90. Braaten, 1983, p. 90.
91. Senn, 1986, p. 9.
92. Beintker, 1961.
93. Luther, quoted in Owen, 1993, p. 263.
94. Luther, quoted in Owen, 1993, p. 195.
95. Tripp, 1986, p. 345.
96. Cited in Tripp, 1986, p. 345.
97. Braaten, 1983.
98. Bonhoeffer, 1949.

CHAPTER **3**

Overview of Study Methods

In order to understand the ways in which women have been empowered by their religious faith to survive losses and crises in their lives, we listened to narrative data from focus groups and in-depth interviews and also reviewed Ramsey's personal journal entries, written during the data collection process. Thus our methods involved "triangulation," or making use of multiple sources of data, in order to strengthen our confidence in the identification of the themes and categories of old women's spirituality as they related to common perspectives about personal development. For those with research interests and for general readers who wishes to understand how we conducted our project, we present here a brief description of our study procedures.

CROSS-CULTURAL METHODOLOGY

From its inception, this study was designed to be cross-cultural and to include interviews and comparisons of both American and German women. Cross-cultural studies can increase understanding of what it means to be human, create new possibilities for living, and facilitate cooperation in world community. Family scholars, gerontologists, therapists, and feminists are all enriched by making more frequent use of this methodology. Many gerontologists have come to recognize that culture does make a real difference,[1] and in response, a dramatic increase in research on culture, ethnicity, and aging has occurred over the past decade. Variously referred to as "ethnogerontology" and "anthropology of aging," this new specialty area has helped scholars understand the impact of varying cultural contexts on the social interaction and physical and mental well-being encountered in old age. A central reason for working cross-culturally is, therefore, to emphasize the richness that cultural variety can bring.

SYMBOLIC INTERACTIONISM

Besides grounding the investigation in feminism and Lutheranism, we adopted the approach suggested by symbolic interaction theory. Symbolic interactionism focuses on the connection between symbols (shared meanings) and interactions (verbal and nonverbal actions and communications).[2] The world is viewed as penetrated with symbolic meaning, and the universe becomes a socially constructed reality.[3] Focus is on the inner or experiential aspects of human behavior, wherein people make reflexive use of symbols to interpret and to elicit meaning in their lives. Persons act and create worlds for themselves; they do not simply react to stimuli.[4]

Family studies scholars interested in questions of meaning have increasingly recognized the suitability of qualitative work using symbolic interactionism as its organizing domain.[5] We used it here because it is conceptually rich and uniquely compatible with the research design, with our cross-cultural framework, with our religious subject matter, and with our insistence on the research activity of listening.

THE IMPORTANCE OF A DENOMINATIONALLY SPECIFIC SAMPLE

Our selection of participants from one denomination was intentional. Each person responds to her or his spiritual impulse in a unique way and in keeping with learned tradition. Personal experience is a major determinant of the manner in which one expresses one's spirituality, along with historical era, education, age, gender, and social class. Often ignored in aging and religion research, denominational identity is also an important component, we believe, both by itself and in interaction with the foregoing factors. In designing this project, therefore, we examined spiritual resiliency within the context of Lutheranism, the specific denomination best known by Ramsey.

STUDY PARTICIPANTS

The sample selection was purposive, convenient, and theoretical.[6]

Participants in this study were Lutheran women over 65 years of age residing in southwest Virginia and northwest Germany. Fifteen women from each country attended the focus group meetings in each setting. We then chose eight women, whom we called "spiritual nominees."[7] We first observed these women within a focus group and then conferred with their local pastors, who responded to the question, "To whom would you go, among these women, if you yourself needed spiritual guidance?" Although women who could articulate their faith and talk easily were sought, being well-educated and verbal was not a requirement; depth of spiritual maturity was. These candidates were carefully screened for suitability by age, lifelong membership in the Lutheran church, and willingness to participate in a long interview. All eight spiritual nominees who were invited to complete intensive interviews agreed to do so. The interviews were conducted, the journal kept, and the original observations made by Ramsey; assistance with research design and data interpretation was given by Blieszner.

SOURCES OF DATA

Focus Groups

The Americans met in a comfortable lounge in the church basement and the Germans met in the church parish house. Location in the churches was psychologically helpful because it was a comfortable and familiar environment and because it served as a clue for the agenda, religious subject matter. The group meetings, which lasted an hour each and were tape recorded, focused on ways in which faith had been helpful in coping with life's challenges.

In-Depth Interviews

The personal interviews with the spiritual nominees lasted about 1 to 2.5 hours each; second and third interviews of the same length were conducted as needed until material was repeated, indicating data saturation. All but one were conducted in the women's homes. All were tape recorded for later transcription, verbatim, in the speaker's language. The interviews began with simple, informative questions to relax the informants and then moved on to inquiries about the significance of spirituality in their lives. The women themselves easily set the discussion agenda, expressing consistent and strong interest in spirituality. They were remarkably open in relating intimate life experiences. In the following pages we refer to the spiritual nominees from Virginia as Rebecca, Lovey, Martha, and Miriam and to those from Germany as Emma, Anna, Inge, and Elisabeth.

Personal Journal and Field Notes

A final source of data, contributing to triangulation of methods, was the use of researcher as self.[8] In qualitative research, it is important to distinguish between what are called "first- and second-order constructs."[9] In this study, first-order constructs were the basic themes that arose from the words and meanings of the women informants. Second-order constructs arose from our analytic interpretations of their words. We wished to preserve the participants' own meanings and categories but also remain sensitive to significant aspects of their experiences that might differ from our own. What has been called the "fallacy of objectives"[10] could have occurred if we had repeatedly substituted our own perspectives for those of the women. One strategy to monitor that tendency was to keep two extensive sets of notes during the time of data collection and analysis. One was a set of field notes and the other was the personal, spiritual journal of the researcher conducting the initial interviews.[11] All of these data were analyzed for categories and themes, just as were the focus group and interview data.

Journal keeping has a long tradition in spirituality, reaching back to the seventeenth and eighteenth centuries.[12] It was an important part of this project for both personal and scholarly reasons. I (Ramsey) wrote a journal while conducting these interviews because I found it useful to remove spiritual roadblocks, promote more self-awareness, and keep myself more grounded in my human needfulness. In keeping a journal, the signs of God's love in everyday life became clear to me, and the stresses of traveling abroad and listening in a foreign language seemed more manageable. Also, my own complicated motivations for the project emerged. The actual journal entries are included as an appendix to this book.

The model for my journal was Nouwen's *The Genesee Diary*.[13] This journal reports the joys and disappointments of a well-known author, Roman Catholic, and contemplative priest who taught at Yale Divinity School while I studied there. Written during the time he lived in a Trappist monastery, Nouwen's journal is refreshingly frank in its self-examinations and soul searching. His book is an example of journalizing as a spiritual discipline; it was his "response to grace."[14] Like him, I found that writing a journal was a way to experience renewed energy and spiritual refreshment. The solitude demanded by this activity was a rare experience for me, one that I found to be surprisingly conducive to growth. Said Nouwen in his popular little book, *Out of Solitude*, "But in solitude, our heart can slowly take off its many protective devices, and can grow so wide and deep that nothing human is strange to it."[15] What could be a better daily discipline for a researcher who would be meeting new women, living in their culture, and learning to listen to their voices than a time of solitude devoted to quiet reflection?

I began the journal in September, 1994, when I first began working on research questions for this project and was making arrangements for the interviews. I compiled field notes after each focus group meeting and personal interview. I wrote journal entries on and off throughout the next months, the last one in March, 1995, when I was analyzing the data I had collected. The majority of journal writing was done while I was in Germany, however. During that time, I was more intensely involved in the project on a daily basis, and I felt more emotionally and spiritually alive than I ever had before.

My scholarly reasons for keeping the journal are related to its function as a kind of window into my own inner experiences. Scholars before me, such as Kleinman and Copp, had looked at fieldworkers' feelings during the research process and argued that awareness of one's own emotions as a researcher should not be suppressed or denied. Rather, authors should openly present themselves as emotional agents, writing their own accounts of the research experience. Kleinman and Copp believed that two equally unhelpful images of the fieldworkers are the "perfectly empathic researcher and the perfectly distant writer," and they urged researchers to find ways to avoid either extreme.[16] Writing a journal was an excellent way of tracking my emotions as well as my spiritual life during this experience. My goal was to be engaged and yet separated, keeping my heart engaged but my boundaries intact, lest my subjects be distracted by feeling a need to take care of me during the interviews. Thus, journal entries included my feelings for and about the women, my speculations about them, my own spiritual issues as they arose, and my reflections on how the work itself was affecting my spiritual life. After the fieldwork was completed, the journal was analyzed for categories and themes in the same manner as the other data.

DATA ANALYSIS

Analysis of the data began with reading and reviewing, in the original languages, the focus group and interview transcripts, the field notes from participant observations, and the journal entries. We searched for categories that reflected the women's views of their spiritual lives and relationships among the data sources. The work proceeded along a stage process, modified for cross-cultural research, based on an approach suggested by McCracken.[17] Each statement was treated on its own terms, not necessarily in terms of its relationship to other statements. Next, an auditory review of the tapes was conducted to recall the unique qualities of each woman's voice, followed by additional reading of the transcripts, highlighting observed themes. Key terms in the transcripts were coded, the list of code words was refined, the transcripts were re-coded, the codes were tabulated, and the transcripts were evaluated for frequencies and more encompassing themes by use of The Ethnograph®[18] software. The last stage was a cultural and denominational interpretation of the themes and categories revealed by the analysis process.

VALIDITY AND RELIABILITY IN THIS RESEARCH

Validity in this study was enhanced by triangulation of methods, linkage of our findings to prior research, and examination of the internal coherency of the findings. Reliability is strengthened by the care and consistency with which Ramsey collected and analyzed the data and by the confirmation provided by the spiritual nominees after they read transcripts of their interviews (see Postscript, this volume).

The interviews, focus groups, and journal all highlighted, to varying degrees, the importance of community, affect, and a balance of concern with close relationships versus concern with abstract doctrine. Although the picture created by the interviews was the most complex, it is important to note that similar themes emerged independently from the other data sources as well.

Our findings are consistent overall with past research in religion and aging. What was possible here that was not possible in past quantitative work was the capturing of more subtleties in theme and more complexities in variations. This is especially true in the finding about the combination of relational and traditional elements in spirituality.

In conducting the focus groups and interviews, Ramsey attempted to be as consistent as possible and to avoid influencing the discussions in any way. For example, during the interviews, she said very little but only nodded or repeated a few words, allowing the women to talk about themes important to them within the larger framework of the interview questions.

Our insistence on honoring worlds of meaning[19] was applied in data analysis as well, which was particularly challenging when analyzing the German conversations. The German interviews were transcribed into German; then Ramsey read them in German several times before and during coding. This allowed her to hear the women's voices with sharper attention to nuances and subtleties of meaning, possible only when one works in the original language of a speaker. For both the American and German conversations, the extra time she spent listening to sections of the original tapes (both focus groups and interviews) before beginning to interpret and write about the results was also helpful in recalling the emotional tones of the interviews and groups and the personal characteristics of the women.

In addition to its efficiency, The Ethnograph® computer program fostered a high level of objectivity in data analysis and, therefore, helped rule out more rival explanations for the findings than otherwise would have been possible. Comparisons were possible across countries, by topic, and by participant. Thus, the major findings emerged out of the codings and then were evaluated in light of impressions gained from the transcriptions. We did not, for example, realize that community would be so strong a finding as it was, even though Ramsey recognized its importance during the interviews themselves. The Ethnograph® was also particularly helpful in confirming the importance of affect.

Finally, the internal consistency of the three major findings is a strong indicator of the validity of this research. Community, emotionality, and human relations are fully interwoven in the faith experiences of these resilient women. It is within community that they feel and that they experience an affective relationship with others, even as they also do the hard cognitive work of making sense of both their own life stories and their faith tradition.

THE COAUTHORS' RELATIONSHIP

One of the freeing and invigorating aspects of scholarship in the postmodern climate is that it is not only permissible, but even commendable, to work in new ways and to allow one's personal and professional lives to intersect. For the writers of this book, this coming together has included enriching interfaith experiences, grand adventures, and an enduring friendship. We first met when Ramsey was a graduate student at Virginia Polytechnic Institute and State University and

Blieszner was her *Doktor Mütter* (doctor mother), as our German friends refer to the female chair of a doctoral committee. Since then, we have worshipped together in our respective Lutheran and Roman Catholic congregations, dialogued about commonalties and differences in our belief systems, and, overall, done our part to strengthen the local ecumenical movement. We have traveled to Germany on a whirlwind trip and shared many of our daily joys and sorrows through communication by telephone, e-mail, and meetings. What began as an academic venture became a personal journey of humor and companionship. In spite of sometimes forgetting how time passes before we get down to work, we feel that we have reached a pleasant synthesis in our commitment to both a study of resiliency and a special friendship.

We share these personal matters with you, our reader, because we encourage you to experience us as women as well as writers. Not that the particulars about us are the focus of this book—the eight wonderfully strong women you will meet certainly are central. But the ways in which they touched us as human beings continues. As Rachel Naomi Remen wrote, "Anything that is real has no beginning and no end. The stories in your life and in mine do not stop here."[20] That is so true of what has happened to us—everything is continuing, especially our own journey into spiritual resiliency. May it also be so for you!

NOTES

1. Sokolovsky, 1985.
2. LaRossa & Reitzes, 1993.
3. Berger, 1967; Kimble, 1990.
4. Morse & Johnson, 1991.
5. Marshall & Rossman, 1989; Payne, 1990.
6. Strauss & Corbin, 1990.
7. We are indebted to life-span psychologist Paul Baltes (Baltes, Staudinger, Maercker, & Smith, 1995), who used the phrase "people nominated as being wise" in his research on aging and potential for lifelong learning.
8. Krieger, 1991.
9. Daly, 1992.
10. Denzin, 1970, p. 8.
11. See Appendix.
12. Holt, 1993.
13. Nouwen, 1976.
14. Sager, 1990.
15. Nouwen,1974, p. 45.
16. Kleinman & Copp, 1993, p. 54.
17. McCracken,1988.
18. Qualis Research Associates, P. O. Box 2070, Amherst, MA 01004.
19. Berger, 1967.
20. Remen, 1996, p. 331.

PART II

The Stories

CHAPTER 4

The Gracious Encounters Begin

A cross-cultural research project is not easy to organize. Before it is possible to walk into a room and get to work, many plans must be made and preparations done. We relate here only a few important aspects of our planning in order to share with you some of the excitement of organizing our international experience. The gracious help of persons on both sides of the ocean was a first step in getting organized to listen. Since Ramsey conducted the initial stages of this research, the voice in this chapter is hers.

BEGINNINGS

From the start, a sense of cooperation and community, extending across the ocean, made amazing things happen. Somewhat ironically, although this book has led primarily to stronger female relationships, it was the international friendship of two men that enabled us to get started. One night, over dinner, I asked Dr. Robert Benne, a friend who teaches religion at a local college, "Bob, do you know anyone in Germany who might be able to help me with a research project?" I explained my interest in meeting and interviewing spiritually resilient Lutheran women over 65 in two countries. I told him I had a pastor in Virginia in mind but also needed to find a Lutheran pastor in Germany who could introduce me to some old women there. Bob smiled broadly and assured me that I had asked the right person. The next day, he took time out from his many duties as department head to write to his friend and former student, Pastor Karl Steenbuck. Herr Steenbuck pastors a church in Wilster, a small town in the marshlands of northern Germany, where he lives with his wife, Selma, and their two teenaged sons. Many members of his congregation are women over 65, survivors of World War II, who, unlike most Germans, are still active in their local congregation. Bob told me that the Steenbucks both had very large hearts and were likely to help me.[1] His letter of introduction led to a very quick response. "Yes, come on over," wrote Pastor Steenbuck. He and his wife not only pledged to help me with the project but also graciously invited me to come live with them while I conducted the interviews. Suddenly, the research process accelerated rapidly.

The American pastor I was hoping would help me was kind as well. Pastor Bob Maier, whom I had known for years and whose church was just a half hour away, introduced me to the women in his parish in Blue Ridge, Virginia. Pastor Maier, who also could have found many other things to do with his time, met with me, talked at length about the old women in his parish, and offered suggestions for how to get started meeting them. Like the church in Wilster, Glade Creek has many elderly members who are lifelong Lutherans. It is about the same size as the church in Wilster and has experienced continuity in both membership and in pastoral leadership. Happily, both pastors were also well liked, for in both parishes, the affection and respect the women felt for their pastors created an entré for me that would not have otherwise occurred.

ADVENTURES ON THE JOURNEY

The work in America began with a focus group; it was easy to arrange, with Bob Maier's help, and it proceeded smoothly (see the following section). Next, I conducted the first of the four in-depth American interviews, with Rebecca. My biggest fear was that the tape recorder would not function adequately, but it did the job well. The first interview was exciting for me. Rebecca was very helpful and interesting, and I could immediately see that I was going to be the custodian of some very helpful data. A sense of excitement began to set in as I prepared for my trip to Germany.

But my fears about this portion of the research were enormous. What would the Steenbucks be like? How would I feel living in a stranger's home in a strange country? What about the women—why would they want to talk to an American they did not know and whose German they would have trouble understanding? Most of all, I worried about my competency in the language. I had studied German in high school and college, and I had spent the last months basically teaching myself a deeper vocabulary, through cassette tapes and many hours of hard work. But would I be able to follow what the women were saying and respond appropriately? Or would I make a total fool of myself in the first few minutes and be run out of town?

Soon it was time to leave. Several letters had gone back and forth between Pastor Steenbuck and me. My entire family, including husband, children, and in-laws, planned to accompany me to the airport to wish me well. But now, weather became my chief anxiety. My worst fears were confirmed when a serious ice storm occurred on December 31, New Year's Eve, the day that I was to leave. To my horror, the airport closed down for the first seven hours. But my flight, a connecting flight from Roanoke to Pittsburgh, was given a "go." My relief was enormous, for had I missed the first flight, all my carefully scheduled plans would have been in disarray.

As it turned out, I had worried about the wrong things! My luggage was lost. It did not show up on the turnstile in the airport, and when I went to bed in Frankfurt that night, after a long flight, I had no change of clothes, no cosmetics, no books. I watched some TV, hoping that the German would sink in quickly. The next morning, I took a train to Hamburg and then another to Wilster. Perhaps my luggage would be there when I arrived.

But at least the Steenbucks would greet me at the train station after my long journey. I had now been traveling for over two days and was eager to be somewhere safe and warm, with people who would be kind. When I arrived in Wilster, snow covered the ground and the red-tiled roofs on the small cottages. The village was a living picture postcard. But no one was in sight at the train station nor was there a phone! I walked across the yard to a factory and asked shyly to use their phone. Looking at me as if I had just landed from Mars, the people graciously pointed to a phone and I called the parsonage. There had been a mix-up caused by my forgetting that 7:00 p.m. is 19:00 in Europe! Pastor Steenbuck (hereafter, Karl) came immediately and warmly greeted me. Coffee and pastries and a very friendly and kind Selma were waiting. Karl told me that he was "relieved" to find that my German was adequate. Without confessing my own fears in that area, I felt far more relief than he did. He was so easy to understand, so *genau* (precise) in his pronunciation. I was to discover that this is far from a common phenomenon.

But no luggage had arrived! Inside my bags were my tape

recorders, cassette tapes, and laptop computer—everything I needed to do my research. Several days passed pleasantly, but still no bags arrived. My worries threatened to overwhelm me, and I wrote in my journal,

> I'm trying not to panic, even though the luggage has not arrived by bedtime. Inside the bags is everything I need to do my work here including cassettes recorders, translations, laptop computer. I'm telling myself that I certainly need trust, not so much God (my bad planing is not God's emergency) as German efficiency [the bags were lost in the United States, but the German airlines promise to deliver them to our door].

At 10:00 the night before the women were to come for the first focus group, the bags arrived. Everything I needed was inside, and the research adventure could really begin.

THE FOCUS GROUP MEETINGS

As I anticipated, the focus groups allowed me to capture some interesting data in a very short time. Discussions were lively in each group. In fact, in Germany, the women were *so* lively initially that *Durcheinander* (all talking at once) occurred, resulting in much confusion. Although some women were more vocal than others, all in attendance at both groups made at least one or two contributions to the discussion and no one person dominated.

The groups accomplished the two intended purposes. First, they allowed me to meet potential spiritual nominees and thus enter into the process of choosing them. Second, themes of spirituality arose from the discussions that were carried over into the private interviews later, especially in Germany. The groups discussed topics that would later emerge as most significant: affect, community, and the tension between close relationships and beliefs.

But research never turns out to be quite what is expected and, in addition to the original purposes, some unexpected findings from the group meetings occurred. It was these positive surprises that, more than anything else, convinced me of the importance of this aspect of triangulated methodology (see Chapter 3). First, the groups allowed the women to meet *me* for the first time in a less intense environment than later during the private interviews. I had wanted to check them out as prospective spiritual nominees, but I came to see that it was also helpful in reverse: They needed to check me out, to decide whether or not they would want to be interviewed and to trust me with pieces of their lives. No one refused in either country, perhaps because of this opportunity. Something that I found out after the group meeting in Germany confirmed this: Karl had misunderstood my plans for the individual interviews and had told the women, when he invited them to the focus group, that I would be meeting with *all* of them for individual interviews after the group meeting. We were able to clear that up without too much difficulty, but in the meantime, one woman he had invited did not attend the focus group because, she told her friends, she did not wish to be "interrogated." However, she met me later, at a nonresearch function, the *Alters Gruppe* (older persons' group), where I was also introduced and given an opportunity to talk about my work. After listening to my presentation there, the woman called the parsonage and requested that she be interviewed! Although that was not possible, it showed me how crucial it had been for the women to meet me first in a group setting, especially in Germany. The endorsement given me by Karl, who is highly respected and loved by everyone I met in his congregation, was no small part of this process of trust building. An additional factor was that the subject matter appealed greatly to the women; they reacted enthusiastically to the idea of being spiritual resources.

Another advantage was the opportunity the groups gave me to observe, first hand, the dynamics of the two faith communities. In Germany, this exact group had never been together before, whereas in the United States, the women frequently were together in that exact group. But in both countries, I learned much about how the women interacted, especially how they supported and nurtured one another, that was helpful both in gathering the data and later in analyzing it. As I came to see it, *in the focus groups, the women did not so much discuss community as live it.*

The groups had another advantage that I had originally seen as a potential disadvantage because it was not the recommended procedure for focus groups:[2] The members knew each other in advance. I found that knowing and being known by group members facilitated high levels of comfort, support, and trust and promoted group cohesiveness. I am not sure the discussions would have been as fruitful without the community feeling and deep levels of friendship that were present.

Finally, the German group allowed me to cast aside a stereotype. I had grown up thinking that Germans are very emotionally controlled and wear masks to hide their feelings. This thinking resulted from my childhood experiences in a Pennsylvania German community, where it definitely was *not* acceptable to show strong feelings, especially in public. This appears to be a common misconception, for just before I left on the trip, a local pastor asked me, "How will you be able to distinguish spiritual resiliency from just plain German stoicism?" Ironically, both the focus group and the interviews in Germany were more emotionally intense overall than those in the United States were; no one in Germany was the least apologetic for tears that were shed. After the focus group there, I quickly put this stereotype of stoicism aside, at least for women. Karl speculated that emotional constraint might be more typical of German men than women.

Comparing the groups yielded both differences and similarities. In America and Germany, there was much informal conversation, and laughter, and many references to church members who were not present. However, the subject matter varied between countries, resulting from differing historical and cultural experiences. Faith was the most frequently discussed topic in each group. In the United States, however, the topics appearing with greatest frequency after faith were children, teaching experiences, readings, and special people, whereas in Germany, the topics next in frequency were hard times (especially the war), the gospel, death, and questions of human suffering. It is interesting that in both groups concern for children (both their own and all children in coming generations) was central to the particular theological issues that arose.

American Focus Group

Although their attitude was friendly and positive, this group of fifteen American women got off to a slow start because they had some difficulty remembering enough facts about the women in the Bible to be able to talk about them. As I saw this occurring, I helped them remember by reading aloud a line or two about each Bible woman from a book I had brought along. That tactic helped stimulate discussion. Even though I was not particularly interested in this educational aspect of the group, the procedure I had planned to ensure consistency across countries was to use the Bible women format to start conversation in each group. Just as I had hoped, after about ten or fifteen minutes into the meeting, the American women had begun talking about their own faith issues, and we left the specific discussion of Bible women behind.

Two major findings from the United States focus group were the ability of a religious community to practice affirmation and identity building and the importance of theological reflections. The American women demonstrated how their affirmation of one another can be a community gift. Although Lutheran theology states that human abilities are gifts from God, acknowledging one's strengths publicly often contradicts cultural norms. It was difficult for most of the women in the focus group to speak of their talents. Only spiritual-nominee-to-be Martha took the risk:

> I asked the question, remember a few weeks ago when I asked the question, if any of us felt that we had a God-given talent? I was the only one that was bold enough to speak up and say that I knew I did. (Showing me an altar cloth she had hand stitched) Now you see why I said I have a connection with Lydia? [Bible woman] . . . Look at those little stitches in that hem. . . Now you don't feel like I was bold when I told the Sunday School class that I felt like God had given me talent?

Martha mentioned this because in a way her behavior went against what might be called a humility norm (actually, a misunderstanding of humility) that is particularly emphasized in southern U.S. culture: Speak humbly about oneself and do not brag about abilities and accomplishments. I was amazed at the way the women got around this norm by praising one another, thereby allowing their talents to be affirmed. By the time the hour was over, I had an excellent idea of what each woman's accomplishments were, without her ever having told me directly. Said one member of the group, "Martha, your name ought to go there [on a list of saints] for keeping flowers on the altar all the time." Another said about a group member and her husband, "They've made the wine ever since I can remember." Still another acknowledged the mentoring one woman and her husband had done for her grandchild:

> I appreciate you and G. sticking by S. until he got confirmed. He's a 17-year-old teenager now and other things come first for them, you know.

The second significant topic of conversation in this group, theological reflections, was especially interesting because of (a) Gilligan's work on the role of gender in making ethical decisions, (b) one of the German women's problem with having her baby baptized during World War II (see next section), and (c) the themes of love and forgiveness in the comments of two participants, Lovey and Martha, who would later become spiritual nominees for in-depth interviews. The discussion at first centered on sainthood, but then it turned to forgiveness, judgment, and salvation. Mary posed the question, "How do we know that we are going

to be saints when Christ comes again?" "We have to have faith,"
responded several women. But Mary was not convinced. "What about
judgment?" she asked. "The Bible says, 'vengeance is mine, saith the
Lord.' " From this point on, baptism and its relationship to salvation and,
especially, the fate of children who die without being baptized, became the
focus of the discussion. Said Mary, "But I've always been concerned
about this, too. When a little baby comes into this world, it's born into
sin. And it dies before it can be baptized."

The women went on for several minutes debating this topic. It is
interesting that they used a combination of what Gilligan would call
abstract principles and relational considerations as they talked. They
moved back and forth between relational considerations and the abstract
doctrines of forgiveness and original sin. The *combination* of these factors
confirms findings from the interviews that occurred later, that although
relationships are always present in women's thinking, it would be an
oversimplification to dichotomize their spiritual lives into categories such
as focused only on relationships versus focused exclusively on traditional
beliefs.

In retrospect, I find a sad irony in the fact that the American
women argued about the very topic that was so painfully recalled by the
German woman Inge in her life story: the proper attitude toward
unbaptized children (see Chapter 6). At no time did any American woman
suggest something so dreadful as what Inge's German pastor did,[3] but I
believe Inge's story demonstrates what can occur if *only* institutional
dogma is applied without human considerations.

In this discussion, Lovey, who would become a spiritual nominee,
made statements consistent with her loving and compassionate
personality. "That baby is helpless and can't help itself" and "the Lord
teaches if you ask for forgiveness . . . if they really in their heart have
asked for forgiveness, I believe they will get it." Similarly, Martha
insisted on an attitude of compassion and understanding, a theme that
reappeared during my interviews with her. The spiritual nominees were
not chosen because of characteristics of mercy and love alone, but it is not
surprising that these Lutheran women are persons for whom God's
forgiveness dominates over judgment, given that justification by grace is
the yardstick Martin Luther used to measure the world.[4]

German Focus Group

In contrast to the American experience, Pastor Steenbuck
attended the German group meeting with me. My field notes record how

impressed I was with the difference in cultural atmosphere upon arrival at the German focus group. Rather than casual chatter and lounging around on sofas and chairs, the fifteen German women sat at tables with purple linen cloths where coffee and cookies were elegantly served by candlelight. I felt somewhat anxious until Karl graciously introduced me and told the women, "*Selma und ich haben Jan sehr lieb gefunden.*" (Selma and I have found Jan to be very dear.) At that point I lowered my head, pleased but a little embarrassed, and several of the women said, "*Sie versteht!*" (She understands!) From that point on, I was doubly accepted as someone of whom their beloved pastor approved and as someone who understood their language.

After having coffee, we moved to another part of the room for the group discussion. When the group moved from all speaking together to speaking in turn, the room was almost too quiet for a short time. The participants soon reached a balance of animation and order, however. They were sitting in a circle, so it was easy for all to see one another and to communicate both verbally and nonverbally. As in the American group, the women soon left behind the topic of Bible women and moved on to talk about their own spiritual issues. Spiritual-nominee-to-be Inge was the first woman to speak individually, courageously sharing how she identified with Mary, the mother of Jesus, because she, too, had lost a son. I was amazed at how quickly the topic of war experiences came up (about one third of the way into the transcribed conversation); this helped to prepare me to anticipate that the topic would arise often in the in-depth interviews.

One of the most difficult problems facing both would-be Christians and practicing Christians is the question of suffering and its relationship to human sin. The women in Germany have been forced by the experience of war to face this issue in a way that has not presented itself in America, where most can reflect at a greater distance on the consequence of that dramatic episode of sin brought on by Adolph Hitler and the Nazi Party. Although this topic's importance in our conversation was no great surprise, given the horrors of that war and the Holocaust, what did surprise me was the trust the German women demonstrated by discussing this issue so openly with me, an American. Here again, the only explanation is Christian community. This bond made me an insider in a way that I did not anticipate. As my journal reflects, the concerns I had about being a foreigner before going to Germany were unwarranted.

The group discussion in Germany first moved to the topic of suffering when one of the participants, Frau P., said, "My faith helped me

very much during the war. I had . . . it was a time when I saw only death."
She related at some length a traumatic experience as a refugee, trying to
get a ride on a train out of a heavily bombed area with her small child and
old mother and being helped by a stranger. Frau P. cried openly as she
told her story, and soon another woman, Frau C., surprised me somewhat
by saying that, during her difficult times during the war, "faith did not
help at all." Communicating her pain through her bent-over body posture
and facial expression of unhappiness, she went on to say that since that
time, however, her faith has grown stronger through her experiences in the
church. Immediately, several other women jumped in and said that their
faith *had* been helpful, had helped them to get through war experiences,
including deaths of family members and the traumas of being refugees.
Frau C. continued to look pained; she soon came back into the
conversation to say that as she gets older and sees so many innocent
people suffering from terrorism and war, she finds herself again
questioning and "not getting an answer." But it was when this woman
spoke of the suffering of innocent children that the conversation became
really animated.

> But now, as I become older, genuine doubts really do arise, [as to]
> where God is, and why the innocent people must [suffer], above all the
> children who can do nothing about it. And so many questions present
> themselves to me.

Before anyone else could speak, I gave the group my "permission" to
voice their doubts publicly by saying, "That I can understand." The next
ten or fifteen minutes were fascinating, as the woman began speaking
Durcheinander (all together) again, this time with great intensity. Anna,
another spiritual-nominee-to-be, said that war is created by human beings,
not by God. I noticed she was held in high regard and appeared to have
social authority with the group, as seen by the way other women looked at
her when she spoke and then quoted her by name. Emma, also interviewed
later, participated at length and said repeatedly that Frau C. had
"formulated the question" incorrectly because she was making God
responsible for human evil. This conversation made a great impact on the
other women and on me. Both the interviews and journal entries that
followed referred back to this theme and this conversation.

   I was very pleased that Karl had been there because these women
obviously needed some pastoral and theological care as a result of the
discussion. Although he stayed out of the discussion in order to let the
research progress, at the end, Karl made arrangements with the women to

meet again soon to continue the discussion. I was impressed with his sensitive balancing of my research needs and their spiritual needs. I was also surprised by how cohesive the group had become,[5] given that this particular group of women had never met together before.

THE IN-DEPTH INTERVIEWS

In the next chapter, you will meet individually the women who are the heart of this project, the spiritual nominees. The interviews that led to the stories you will find were highly gracious encounters. Our entrance into the women's lives was more than a formal matter; it was warm and kind. The *Gastfreundschaft* (hospitality) extended us by the women we met in each country was a treasure that we did not take for granted; it was obvious in both the larger focus groups and when the eight special women welcomed us into their homes for hours of conversation. They shared not only their time, their coffee and cakes, and their hospitality, but pieces of themselves. This graciousness and trust has touched us deeply, as reflected in this entry from my journal, written after meeting Anna for the first time: "After today, I feel much more at ease, because of her graciousness, warmth and almost casual manner with me. I certainly don't feel any less in awe, however."

NOTES

1. Later, I wrote about Karl in my journal: "Karl is really a terrific pastor; he brings his theological knowledge and personal convictions into everyday situations so sensitively. I'm learning much from watching him."
2. Stewart & Shamdasani, 1990.
3. The pastor refused to bury Inge's baby because it had not yet been baptized.
4. Holt, 1993, p. 69.
5. Cohesiveness is defined as "the desire of group members to remain as members of the group" (Cartwright, 1968, quoted in Stewart & Shamdasani, 1990).

CHAPTER 5

The American Women

We now present the stories of the four American spiritual nominees in some detail, followed in the next chapter by the stories of the four German spiritual nominees. For each woman, we have provided a descriptive phrase that captures a theme of her life. Although I (Blieszner) did meet the women later, these narratives are presented in Ramsey's voice, based on her role as the initial interviewer.

REBECCA: STRENGTH THROUGH PRAYER AND THOUGHT

I'm 93 and I don't know what in the world I'm left here for. I do have a lot more problems than a lot of people, but I don't have any pain. I don't suffer at all. . . I feel like I'm lucky. I'm blessed I guess. I still believe in God, I believe in Jesus Christ the Lord. I know He is my Savior, and I'm ready to die, I think! When my time comes.

At 93, Rebecca is the oldest woman in this group and has the most extensive physical limitations. Not surprisingly, these problems were a frequently mentioned topic of conversation:

They say I broke my hip, I say my hip's way up here, but I broke my leg anyway. I was rushed to the hospital. Then I was recuperating from that and I was in a nursing home and I had a stroke on my left side. So this side is broken and this side's got a stroke on it. So that was in 1992. I've recovered enough so that I can walk with my cane.

She is legally blind, partially deaf, moves slowly, and uses a walker or cane to get around her cottage. Since 1935, Rebecca has lived alone in a small house immediately beside the church. She has attended Glade Creek Lutheran Church since it was built. Several times during the discussions, when she referred to the church, she would nod her head to signify the direction of the church building, as though its presence was very much a part of her immediate environment. She does not leave her house except for Sunday mornings when her niece and her niece's husband take her to worship.

A housekeeper comes in for a few hours daily to help Rebecca with personal care and do whatever housework is necessary. This woman was just leaving as I arrived, and I noticed that her small daughter, about six years old, went up and kissed Rebecca good-bye as they left.

Rebecca spends most of her time in a special chair, beside which she has set up a tape recorder so that she can listen to recordings for the blind. Her house is very humble, but it is also cheery, clean, and orderly.

Rebecca talked to me quietly and with great dignity. My field notes reflect my impression that she is accustomed to being listened to and respected, and, indeed, her pastor described Rebecca as the matriarch of the congregation. I found no traces of arrogance, but I did have the feeling during our conversation that she was prepared to switch roles and become my advisor if need be. At one point she said,

> Preachers need strength more so than us ordinary humans I guess.
> 'Cause you might be tempted to neglect your duty or something.

She asked me more questions about my family and personal life than any of the other nominees, even though I explained that it would be best if we talk about those things later. A religiously conservative woman, she also tried to test me several times on my orthodoxy.

> Some people . . . I've had some pastors to say that the Bible is just like a prayer. I don't believe that, Jan. It's the Word of God, and I think it's true. And I don't care how it sounds to some of these episodes in the Bible, I still believe them. Don't you?

This impression, that she wanted to teach me and was interested in being helpful to me as an faith advisor, was corroborated when Pastor Maier told me that, in fact, she has served as his spiritual advisor in the past, during times of crisis and discouragement in his life. As he put it, he might have left the ministry without her help and encouragement. However, when I insisted on being vague about my own convictions, she came to respect that position and stopped asking me questions.

Rebecca was raised in a religious farm family as one of eleven children. She has been a widow for ten years. Soon after they married, her husband became paralyzed and was unable to work.

> We just lived here and he had a stroke in 1937, which he did not recover from. That was 5 years after we were married. And we raised a little garden here. . . We canned vegetables and had vegetables to eat from the garden, all summer long.

All through the years of her marriage, Rebecca had triple responsibilities—managing the house and garden, caring for her husband, and earning a living. She had no children. Most of her relatives are deceased, except for a niece who is now in poor health herself. Rebecca is not hesitant about getting help when she needs it, but she clearly values the fact that she can still live in her own home.

Attending church weekly, reading the Bible, praying, and participating in the Lutheran sacraments are all important for Rebecca. She quoted the Bible frequently, usually from memory. She spoke of the Lutheran sacraments and what they meant to her more than any other woman did, and she was the only woman to mention the role of the Holy Spirit in prayer.

Rebecca's physical problems are the biggest challenge in her life. The doctor now has told her she may need more surgery, and she dreads the idea.

> I didn't want to have my whole body cut across. . . I think I'm too old. I believe I've got a good heart. I think my heart could stand it. I don't know. If it gets terribly bad, I may have to. I don't know what I'll do. Maybe I'll die before it gets too bad.

And it is precisely these anxieties about health that she takes to God:

> R: He sustains me day after day. I don't have to worry. I'm just like the Bible says, "The Lord looks after them." He looks after the birds so why wouldn't He look after people, if you let Him . . .
> J: So you really have a sense that God is caring for you, don't you?
> R: Yes, after I do what I have been doing, Jan. Life is no bowl of cherries. You know that.

Church attendance has always been crucial for Rebecca:

I guess outstanding would be the fact that all these years I have always gone to church. Always gone to church. . . The first Sunday in January of '41 is when we had our first service over here. And then we've been here ever since attending services regularly.

Later she said,

I don't think I ever missed . . . I hardly ever missed going to church unless the weather was really bad.

Rebecca's sense of humor is one of her gifts, and a sign that she can keep life in perspective. Speaking of how she's had so many birthdays and that some of her friends dread them, she said,

If you don't have birthdays, Miss Jan, you're dead!

Rebecca told me that as she sits and listens to her tapes, she thinks about life and God and faith. As she ponders, she often works out answers to her own questions with words from the liturgy, prayers, the Apostles' Creed (she quoted it to me at length), and the Bible. She does not always have answers to her questions, but the real bedrock of her faith is a firm belief that God is in charge of her life and of human history.

R: The Lord taught us in the Lord's prayer, "thy will be done in earth as it is in heaven." He doesn't say *on* earth. He says *in* earth. Did you ever notice that?
J: What does that mean to you?
R: It means God's will is always done, whether you think so or not. Or whether you believe it or not. It's true.

For Rebecca, ultimately it is God's power, not human belief, that determines human history.

But Rebecca's faith is not only cognitive; she also has a strong sense of God as present daily in her life.

I know He's right here. I know He's always there. It has always seemed like that to me. Even when my husband had a stroke and was laid up for forty-eight years. I never questioned God and I didn't get bitter like some people.

Prayer is Rebecca's ministry for her church community, now that she can no longer be physically active. Rebecca firmly believes that faith should be put into action and that Christians should lead moral lives. Although she talks often about evil and temptations, she sees her own life as having been mostly on track. But does not feel she is anybody special; like all of these spiritual nominees, she does not view herself as unusual in any way. And so she speaks modestly about her life.

> And then we've been here ever since, attending services regularly. Doing whatever I could. Trying to live the right kind of life. Never being anything very outstanding, I would say.

It would be impossible to overestimate how much Rebecca's faith means to her in everyday life. Blind, almost deaf, partially paralyzed, and with no close living relatives other than a sick niece, Rebecca considers herself a "lucky" woman, "blessed" by God. Through her faith, she has developed an amazing ability to search out positive ways to view *all* aspects of her situation, to accept things she can't control, and to see them as blessings in disguise. Instead of complaining about her paralysis, for example, she focused on her lack of pain.

> I don't have any pain, I'm very fortunate that way. So, I guess I'm lucky.

Being childless, she thinks of how a biological child might not have loved her as much as does the child of her day helper:

> 'Cause as I said, I never did have any children. And even if you have children, Jan, they don't love you like an outsider. You've heard how kids treat their parents haven't you?

Although bad weather can prevent her from her treasured, and only, outside activity, attending worship, she says,

> You don't do that. You don't question the nature of God. You don't. I don't like to fuss about the weather. If it's bad, I just accept it, I don't say, "I don't like this kind of weather." I hate hailstorms and sleet and snow, I wish it wouldn't happen, but I never say that. I never say that.

Through her ministry of prayer, her ability to reframe her experiences positively, her Bible study and theological reflections, and her patience with her many infirmities, Rebecca illustrates how spirituality can lead to a general resiliency that permeates all aspects of daily life. She could be described by those who do not know her well as a sad, sick, old woman living a lonely life, but nothing could be further from the truth. By her own standards, she lives a full life of connections with others and with her God, a life for which she is grateful.

LOVEY: FAITH AS LOVE AND FAMILY

The Lord did help me and I've always trusted Him. He's been faithful to me all the way through my life and still is. That's one thing that I have, it's the greatest thing on earth I have experienced, is my Lord. He has been really good. I could ask of Him and he gives it. I can feel it and receive it and it's just wonderful to live for God you know. Like things I can't get done, if I can't do them by myself, and nobody's here but me, well I'll say, "Jesus, if you'll help me it won't be hard and I'll do all I can. If you and I do it, it's not hard at all." It's just wonderful.

Lovey is 89 and lives alone in the old farmhouse where she and her deceased husband raised their family. The modest white house is down an isolated country road, about one half mile from the church. We sat in her living room to talk, a comfortable room filled with pictures of family: two children, six grandchildren, and ten great-grandchildren. In the dining room, the floor was covered with a quilt Lovey has finished sewing and is now assembling. After the interviews, she showed me about twenty other quilts she has made, and we had a Coke in the bright, cozy kitchen that also serves as her sewing room.

Family is the central theme of Lovey's life. She has close and very positive ties with her daughter and son and their families; they live nearby and stop in almost every day to see her. She says that sometimes they call and say "Get ready!" and then take her on surprise outings; these trips are obviously the special joy of her life. Lovey appears to be in excellent health and is very proud of keeping house for herself and of still being able to cook large family meals on occasion.

Like most people her age, Lovey has lost many friends and family members, and their deaths are her saddest memories.

Some [memories] are sad, of course. Mom and Dad, my brothers and sisters, there are only two of us living. There were eight in the family. Just two living now.

Her life has had many personal struggles that included early caretaking responsibilities: She was left, when she was just 16, with total responsibility for raising her family of origin.

I had my daddy's brother, an old bachelor, Uncle Bill, just as sweet as he could be. He lived with us so I had to take care of him and my daddy. Two brothers and several little sisters, [one was] near 3 years old, that was in January and Mama died in March . . . 'course it was terrible to give your mama up at that time, she was young and so pretty and sweet and everything. You know you have to take the sad with your joys.

Hard work and long hours have been part of Lovey's life, but she loves doing work and being able still to get around.

Like Rebecca, Lovey is highly respected in her congregation. She appears not to be so much matriarch as saint, a person known for her remarkable powers of faith. Miriam, another spiritual nominee, mentioned Lovey once in conversation with me, and during the focus group, the women listened to her with respect. Pastor Maier mentioned her first when we discussed possible spiritual nominees, saying, "Well, there's no question that Lovey must be on that list. She's remarkable."

Lovey is, indeed, remarkable. She speaks in the simple language of country folks and uses an almost childlike style of discussing her faith. Although she sees nothing spectacular about herself, she knows she has a gift of faith and was not at all surprised to be asked to share it with me. She talks comfortably about experiences that other people might consider shocking or at least unusual, such as her visions. When I mentioned that I would not be using people's actual names in my research reports, Lovey said, "Oh, I don't mind. Go ahead and use mine if you want to." She understands that her name matches her primary spiritual activity, loving. She talks often about her love for her family, for other people, and for God.

Lovey told me how even as a child she would take her troubles to God, but she does not complain about requests that were never granted. For example, one of the sorrows of Lovey's life has been that she never learned to read well.

I never could read very well. I was a poor reader and I wanted to read, cause I loved to hear people read and I love to try to read myself, but I never have been able to read in public or out loud. I try to read out loud when nobody is around me and it's kind of stumbling, you know.

As a child, she began to pray, privately, for the ability to read better.

L: I remember, the house had rock around it and there was a place open that we could put things under the house, maybe the lawnmower or something like that . . .

J: Sort of a secret place.

L: Yeah, and I used to crawl back in that hole and pray. I can remember praying when I was a little kid that God would help me to learn to read good so I could read in public. I can read anything and just tell it, but to read it, I wasn't much at it.

When her husband died, Lovey's grief was almost unbearable.

I thought I was going to die too, because it looked like my heart was getting bigger and bigger and I thought it was going to burst out of my body.

She told me of calling the rescue squad immediately after she found him sitting in the living room, dead. The emergency worker told her to go to the back yard and wait. It was then that she had her vision of God's presence, an experience still vivid to her today.

I hadn't thought to pray. I don't know why I hadn't thought to pray, so I turned around to go back into the kitchen. When I got to the corner of the table there in the dining room, well it just came over me to pray. And when I said, "Dear Father," He knew, I reckon, what I was going to say, because it looked like the whole house just opened up like that, roof and all. He said to me, "Don't worry, you are in my arms." You know, it all went down, my heart went back to beating like it ought to.

For Lovey, as for Rebecca, God is a very real, daily presence in life. Her only requirement for each day in the future is that God abide with humankind. When I asked her what she thought the world might be like in fifty years, she responded,

I don't know, I hope the Lord stays with us. That He doesn't forsake us and leave us alone, you know. Not be with us. Long as I live I hope He stays. Then I've got children, grandchildren, and I hope He stays with them.

She stated directly what mattered to her above all else in life:

L: The Lord is the most important thing to me.

J: Your relationship with the Lord.

L: Yes sir. That's what it is. That's the greatest thing. Nothing else comes above that.

Lovey is, indeed, well named. Her spiritual strength has grown out of her love-based interconnections with family, church family, and God. This strength enables her to live with joy and optimism. It is impossible to be with Lovey without feeling that you would like to go back to her warm home, pull out a chair, and sit down for dinner with her extended family. Best of all, to be with her is to be caught up in her vision of the world as the beautiful place that God has made.

MARTHA: FAITH AS THE POWER FOR WORK

Oh, I feel that [God's closeness] every day that I'm home. If I didn't, I don't believe I'd even feel safe enough to lay down and sleep at night. I don't know of anybody else to protect me, that's for sure. To go to bed tonight, if I think there's a cow that might be having trouble in the barn, I'll go down there by myself and sit down by him . . . I have two [calves] that are getting close [to being born]. I'm thankful that I'm able to look after things.

Martha, the only never-married woman in this study, is an unusually independent woman, aged 77, who lives on the farm where she was raised and cares for the crops, the animals, and the buildings with just a little help from her neighbors. Her house was the most isolated of any of the nominees, about five minutes' drive down a country lane off the main road leading to the church. Behind the house are other outbuildings, including a large barn and a chicken house. Animals are everywhere, including a sheltie dog, twenty-eight chickens, some cattle, and a goat. Her sister and her sister's husband live directly across the road, in a newer house. Martha's house was the family home and is very old by American standards. Before her family lived there, it had been a tavern and inn.

Although she admits that she fears little and that she loves to work, Martha would not describe herself as independent or self-sufficient; doing so would be to deny her dependence on God. She quickly corrected me when I implied she was self-sufficient because she grew her own food. She told me firmly that no one is really self-sufficient.

Martha has a very direct, blunt style. She considers her sister a bit of a whiner and said,

You've got to look at the positive side. My sister's like that, she's always got a pain. I could not live like that, I think that's part of her health problems. You can't be "anti" everything.

She also has, by far, the best sense of humor of any of the women I interviewed, and most of her jokes are at her own expense. For example, she laughs at her own workaholic personality.

> I said, well, I never sit down to rest unless somebody does come. If anyone would come by and see me sitting out in the field, they would know I was dead!

About pastors, she said,

> They talk about preachers that we've had and I said I'm not going to leave because of a preacher because I'll probably outlast him! I have, I've outlasted several.

In addition to her sense of humor, she has many talents, which she recognizes as her gifts, including the ability to manage her farm, grow incredible house plants, and do fine handwork, including knitting and cross-stitch. She sees God as the source of her ability to do work and the source of the energy to get things done. Unlike her peers (see the description of the American focus group meeting), she does not consider it bragging to mention these gifts.

> I told you that the preacher asked if any of us thought that God had given us some talents, and I was the only one that would speak up. I noticed that Bernice went and got those [the altar clothes she made] to show you. I think that a lot of the things I do are required as talents. I had Mary ask me things to pick up and repair, I put in new washers. She'll say, "What made you think you could fix that?" I'll say, "Well I don't know, but what made me think I couldn't if I didn't try?" I'm sure that if God gave us the power in the brain, that gives me the power to figure these things out and do them.

We sat in her living room for the interviews, and I was struck by how simple and spare it looked. No pictures were on the walls, and the furniture was a few pieces of antiques, including a beautiful, very old clock and a 200-year-old table. It reminded me of rooms that are reproductions of colonial days, such as those at historic Williamsburg, Virginia. Martha is clearly a practical, no-nonsense kind of woman who prefers simplicity in life. Her hair is cut short, in a boyish style; she wore sweat pants and a comfortable knit top. But she also loves beauty. After the interview, she showed me a side room filled with at least 100 African violet plants, all healthy and blooming, and the hand-smocked dresses she had made for her niece.

Martha dearly loves her dog, Spot, and was eager for me to meet him (however, he did not reciprocate and almost bit me when I leaned to pet him; all research has hazards). After the second interview, Martha, Spot, and I went out onto the front lawn, and she showed me proudly how Spot could catch a ball in midair, like a circus animal. During the interview, she became teary when she said that, if she were to die, her dog might have to be put to sleep.

Martha has grown past the judgmental, frightening God she heard about as a child from relatives. She believes in grace and forgiveness and expressed her sympathy for several persons accused of crimes. Her aunt told her once that God was in the thunder, and she laughs at herself for her former fears.

> M: I told you, it was the song on Sunday that says that God was slow to anger and all this. Somehow I can't understand, I don't believe that He ever gets angry with us because He see things go on. If He did, He could do away with us right then. He has the power to.
> J: So it's not an angry God you see?
> M: No, no. Even though I used to think He was in the thunder!

Faith is very closely tied to work for Martha, and this is a subject about which she feels deeply. However, her lifestyle is simple and, as she cares for her land and animals or sews for the church, she works not for material reward but for the glory of God. Anything else, says Martha, would be just plain "stupid."

> M: I'll tell you another one [Bible verse] I think about. Verse that says, "work while it's day, for the night comes."
> J: Tell me what that means to you.
> M: That I am supposed to stay busy at my own work or at God's work. I think that everything I do is God's work, and it reflects on me, the way I do it and the attitude I have towards my work. I feel like I owe it to God to stay busy every day. Wouldn't it be stupid for me to sit here and do nothing? Wouldn't it?

Faith is the natural energy by which Martha lives her active life and through which she has learned not to fear life or death. She told me that she ends every day sitting on the sofa, with Spot by her side, reading the Bible. More liberal in her views of scripture than Rebecca, she said she does not always understand what she reads in scripture but, rather, trusts God's good intentions for her above the literal meaning of the words.

I'll have to admit the one part of the Bible I don't understand one bit of it, I don't think, are Revelations, and I have just tried not to confuse myself with it. As long as I have faith enough to believe that I will be with God, why should I believe all this stuff about these golden candlesticks and stuff? I don't care, if I'm in my heavenly home, what it's going to be like. Anything is going to be better than what we had here. . . Was it Paul that told us that we saw dimly now? My sight is certainly dim!

Prayer, too, reassures her before she retires:

I just feel like when my day comes to an end that I need to be assured that I will be looked after and cared for another day, hopefully. But if I don't [live another day], that's not worrying me either.

This close relationship with God is something she learned as a child.

There was a blessing at every meal. As children we was taught to say our prayers every night when we went to bed, mother or daddy or Aunt C. would go with us to be sure that we did. They didn't say, "Go on up those steps and go to bed." They went up *with* us to see that we were in bed and that we said our prayers.

The significance of Martha's faith for daily life can best be understood by visualizing her at the end of her day, tired but strong and unafraid, as she closes her Bible and walks upstairs to sleep. Instead of her parents' presence, she now experiences a spiritual presence, going with her to see that she is safely in bed and that she remembers to say her prayers.

MIRIAM: GROWTH THROUGH SUFFERING

So we had it pretty hard, but I think with the help that I had, I came through it with a lot of help from everybody, and I knew the Lord was on my side. I've really been a person like that, really, 'cause I've had so much trouble in my life, and I've had a lot of joys. I feel like I've come through it with the help of the Lord.

Miriam is an attractive, white-haired woman of great enthusiasm and feeling who lives just off the main highway that goes through the town of Glade Creek. For 80 years, her life has, indeed, been filled with strong contrasts, with extremes of joys and sorrows. But my first impression, when I met her during the focus group, was, "Here is a woman filled with happiness and energy." During the interviews, I discovered the source of her enthusiasm: experiences in Christian community. I learned, however, that there was another side to her story: great sorrow arising from family tragedies. In fact, when Pastor Maier suggested her name as a spiritual nominee, he said, "Miriam is a woman who has had tremendous suffering in her life."

I visited this spiritual nominee three times and at her invitation, had lunch with her on the last visit. A widow, like Rebecca and Lovey, she lives alone in a small, white house. She told me that she and Johnny, her husband, had "a wonderful life together," but she spoke less frequently of him than of other people during the interviews. They did not have children, because her husband was opposed to the idea of adoption. Miriam's door was decorated for the season (Valentine's Day), and indoors I could see evidence that she enjoys crafts and bright colors. She also likes to be reminded of the many important people in her life. What was unusual in Miriam's living room was not the number of family photos but the fact that in her case, everyone in every photograph had died. Miriam spoke often but without self-pity of her many family losses.

> We've been such a small family and such a close knit family that when they drop one by one, it gets slimmer.

The sorrow side to Miriam's story is one of illness, accidents, losses, and deaths. First, her brother died in an accident when she was a young adult. Six months later, she lost her father, who died in her arms. Then her mother, unable to cope with the losses of both husband and son so close together, collapsed physically and mentally. The newly married Miriam was for several years her mother's caretaker, until her mother recovered and went home. That role of caretaker to her mother returned again in later years, when her mother was frail and old. Miriam's husband died in 1979, her mother died in 1986, and last year Miriam lost her sister-in-law's second husband, who had become a surrogate brother to her.

One of the most difficult periods of Miriam's life came after surgery when she was unable to walk for a time. During this time, her friend and former pastor, Pastor R., was a primary supporter. He stopped by the house every day to see how she was getting along, prayed with her, and encouraged her in her recovery. Miriam could not say enough positive things about this man and his care. The following example demonstrates how difficult it was, at times during her narrative, to decide whether Miriam was actually talking about Pastor R. or about God! To her, clearly the help and encouragement of this pastor represented the help and encouragement of God.

> I think that was the most that I felt that the Lord was really with me. 'Cause it was almost every day that I could not keep up my faith. I just felt every day that I don't know if I can go another day. He'd come back, and say, "Yes, you can!" I'd go another day and I think that's the time I felt the Lord was close to me.

The two greatest current challenges for Miriam, as the only person from her family remaining alive, are being alone and worrying about who will care for her if her health fails. Initially, just after her mother's death, being alone in the house was the primary struggle. Now that she has adjusted to that, she wonders what would happen if some of her earlier physical problems return or if new ones develop. But it is precisely these two chief worries that her faith has most directly ameliorated. To combat her loneliness, she has, first of all, a Christian community. A church leader for many years, she has served on church council, sung in the choir, taught Sunday School, and participated in the woman's group. The members of Glade Creek Lutheran are now her functional family, and she is grateful for them.

> M: We've always been interested in this church here. We've made a lot of friends over the years. Some come and go, but I love this church. I love my church friends. I don't know what I'd do without them.
> J: They are important to you.
> M: That's right. They really are. They're down there quilting this morning. I wouldn't try it with the way my back is . . .

But she did have plans, back problems or no, to join a church group that evening for a visit with residents at a local nursing home.

Another weapon in her armory against worry is Miriam's attitude of gratefulness and her incredible sense of God's daily presence in her life.

> M: Every morning and every night [I pray]. A lot of times through the day. If anything happens, I say, "Thank the Good Lord." That's just kind of my byword when it comes to a crisis that happens. You are just really upset about it, but you can still thank the Good Lord for this or for that. I think we can say "Thank you, Lord" anytime during the day when you feel like it. It is a prayer. Anything that I have, you know when I come in and I've been down, the weather's

been bad and maybe the roads are slick. I open my door and ask the Lord to take care of me and bring me home safe. I always do things like that, it means a great deal to me. I say, "Thank you" to the Lord for a lot of things that I'm doing, that worked out good. The other day, I said "Thank you, Lord, for getting this [problem] off my mind." I was so glad to get that over with, I didn't know what to do. When things are finished and you think, "Well, I've done a good job," you thank the Lord for getting you through that. "I'm glad I got that behind."

J: So it doesn't have to be the most serious matter in the world?

M: No, just anything that I feel, I got through with the Lord's help.

To deal with her other anxiety, being left without a caretaker, she trusts the purposes and plans she believes God has made for her. She remembered how her husband died quietly in his sleep and says that she hopes and prays she may die the same way.

I found him dead in the bed. I hope that will be the way the Lord takes me, but we don't have our druthers. We don't know what's best for us. You wonder sometimes if things will work out like that for you. The Lord knows your circumstances, and He knows me and I feel that He'll take care of me.

Looking back over the struggles of her life, she feels that they have served a purpose: her growth in faith.

M: I used to say, "I know how you feel," but until you've lost something like that and been through a lot of trials and troubles, you really don't know. But, I think it's all a purpose, which I know is true. And I think it hit me, Jan. I think it helped my faith to grow, I really do.

J: In what ways?

M: Well, I don't know. I feel like when I get up in the morning, I set down and do my reading, and I pray to the Lord for strength for the day, and I feel like He's with me. I can come in and undo my door and I feel like I'm not by myself. I pray every morning and say, "I know I'm lonely, and I feel like I'm by myself, but I know you're with me." And I do really feel like it 'cause I had never stayed a night by myself in my life until my mother died.

Being spiritually strong does not prevent problems or anxieties from arising, as Miriam's life shows. However, it does mean that, for her, even fear does not have the last word. When this woman unlocks the door of her house and comes in to spend another evening alone, she realizes her vulnerabilities: to illness, to loneliness, to fear. But she has such a strong sense that God is present with her, making wise and compassionate plans for her future, that she is able to go on. She not only functions in the face of her fears and grief, she laughs and works and plans ways to do good for others. Miriam worries, but she does not get stuck in her anxieties. She grieves, but she does not despair. Spiritual resiliency explains her capable lifestyle in the face of multiple losses and daily concerns.

CHAPTER 6

The German Women

We turn now to narrate the in-depth interviews with four spiritual nominees from Wilster, Germany. These interviews were conducted and transcribed in German, but the portions quoted here have been translated for the convenience of English-speaking readers. The interviews are again described by Ramsey.

EMMA: FAITH AS REFLECTIONS AND COMMUNITY

You know, sometimes in the mornings, I want to tell you about that, in the mornings when I wake up and the alarm clock rings and I think, "My Goodness, how could you manage the day?" you know. And sometimes one thinks, "How will things go?" And then I have a wonderful prayer. . . I always find that the Word is so helpful, that one, well, it's like a spring, [like] fresh water for me to drink, that makes me strong for the day.

The second youngest of the women interviewed for this project and one of the most articulate was Emma, who is 68. She has been a widow for two years and because she has no home of her own, lives with her adult daughter. She was left penniless when her husband, an artist, died of cancer. She definitely has mixed feelings about living with her daughter and grandchildren:

I have the fortune, or the misfortune, I don't know, we'll say the fortune, to live with the family of my daughter.

She enjoys them yet finds her life there tiring. She misses the peace of having her own home. Karl told me he nominated her because she can articulate her faith, is very sensitive, has survived hard times, is ready to try new things, and values her spiritual life over material possessions. All of these aspects of Emma were confirmed during the interviews. She was, in fact, one of the most spiritually impressive women I have ever met. It was an honor to come to know her and to learn from her.

Emma was the only spiritual nominee whom I could not interview in her own home. Because of her noisy young grandchildren, we decided it would be best for her to come to me, so we had our discussion upstairs in the private bedroom where I slept in the parsonage. I met with her three times because I kept hearing new and interesting things; my interview transcriptions from those meetings are the lengthiest in this project.

One of the things I noticed about Emma when I first saw her at church, at meetings, and at the focus group was that she always wore the same pink sweater. Before I knew of her financial situation, I speculated that she was simply unconcerned about her appearance. She did wear a different outfit for the first time on the second interview with me, but by then I knew that, in contrast to her more affluent friends in the congregation, she simply does not have the money to purchase an extensive wardrobe.

Emma went through a difficult period when she lost her husband, *"ein ganz grösser Schmerz, natürlich"* (a rather great sorrow, naturally). Her identity had been tied closely with his and with his work. They lived in a quiet, isolated house in the marshes where he could paint without being disturbed; they had no real friends, and their only acquaintances were customers who bought his paintings. When he died, she felt that her life, too, was over. But her children challenged her to "get a life," and she did: She became active in the local faith community, began attending worship regularly, joined a Bible group, and began calling on elderly housebound members. She now feels that her life is full and that she has actually started over on what she calls her *"Weg"* (way), a faith pilgrimage. Ironically, her husband's death became her second chance at life.

This change has not been merely emotional for her because, Emma told me, she is a person who stays level in her emotions, not someone who swings between *"die höchsten Höhen und dann die tiefsten Tiefen"* (the highest heights and then the deepest depths). It was, instead, an entire lifestyle change. But when she speaks of what it has meant to her, she is, indeed, very moved.

Emma has many memories and considers how they might relate to her faith; she shared surprisingly intimate feelings with me, such as her sorrow at her son's alcoholism, her regrets that her children do not attend church, and the pangs of sorrow she still feels when she sees retired couples together, enjoying more years than she and her husband had. She also has some regrets about her husband's death, particularly, that they did not talk more about their faith or pray together, even when he was dying.

> E: Then, when we noticed it was going that way, he knew it too, he said, "It won't last much longer, then it's past." So he knew that he must die. Then I only asked him if he was afraid. And he said, no, that he wasn't. But I was, I certainly prayed in that last hour. I was, I was with him as he died, that was wonderful. That much we can say: that was wonderful for me.
> J: Yes, yes, I believe that.
> E: That he didn't have to be in the hospital, but was at home—and then I certainly prayed. But, I didn't pray together with him. And that, that's what troubles me.

A person of deep sensitivities and high intelligence, Emma was the evangelist of this group of spiritual nominees. She has both the ability to articulate how she feels, believes, and thinks and the desire to share her spirituality with others. Whether she talked about her favorite subject, Christian community, her Bible studies, or a special person in the congregation, she was able to express succinctly how her faith relates to the rest of her life. Relistening to the tapes when I got home, I was struck, too, by the way in which she did not often need time to think before answering my questions, did not hesitate for more than a moment before speaking.[1] I attributed this ease of expression in large part to the fact that Emma speaks so often about her faith with other people that she has thought things through and found words for her feelings and beliefs. For example, she told me that when she visits an older member who might be in danger of dying soon, she brings up the subject of faith so that he or she will have a chance to think and pray. In light of her regrets about her husband's death, this makes perfect sense. Here, again, she gets a second chance.

Speaking of Holy Communion, Emma said,

We Germans are so often inclined to take everything so bitterly and earnestly. Terrible, isn't it? But, no, that one goes there with joy [to communion] and takes part in the Lord's Supper, that He is there and says to us, "Yes, I have died for you, and I have given Myself up for you," this is a joy and not so, mmm, so terrible.

In spite of all she has suffered, Emma radiates a happiness that seems to enliven the room when she is present. She refuses to be pensive and somber, even though she is decidedly pious in the sense that she studies her Bible daily and quotes scripture readily. She feels that faith brings joy and that this joy must be communicated with others. An impoverished widow, she has riches that permeate all aspects of her life, including her confidence in God's love and forgiveness, her ability to be nurtured by community, and her disciplined participation in a wide variety of daily spiritual exercises. She is a resilient woman who has not let life come to an end through grief. Rather, her strength and joy grow stronger all the time through daily spiritual devotion and through her zeal for sharing the gift of faith with others.

ANNA: FAITH AS CONNECTEDNESS

Yes, the older one becomes, the more one sees that everything is connected.

Anna was, for me, more than a spiritual nominee; she was a gift. My journal reflects that, in dialogue with her, I had strong emotional reactions that continue to this day. She was more than an inspiration and role model, she was a resolution and a homecoming. Apart from my subjective reaction, Anna is unique. Even though I resist thinking in the rather rigid categories of faith stages, I found that when I was with Anna, I kept thinking of Fowler's description of those unusual persons he said were most spiritually mature. Fowler used Erikson's model of stages and tasks to create his faith stages and model of faith tasks. About the highest level of faith development, he wrote:

Stage 6 is exceedingly rare. The persons best described by it have generated faith compositions in which their felt sense of an ultimate environment is inclusive of all being. They have become incarnators and actualizers of the spirit of an inclusive and fulfilled human community. They are contagious in the sense that they create zones of liberation from the social, political, economic and ideological shackles we place and endure on human futurity. Living with felt participation in a power that unifies and transforms the world, Universalizers are often experienced as subversive of the structures (including religious structures) by which we sustain our individual and corporate survival, security, and significance.[2]

Whether or not one agrees that human beings can be placed in specific categories of faith, it was clear to me that, even among this group of remarkable women, Anna had a special gift of faith and maturity. In her life, apparent opposites combine with grace: Reflection and action, thought and feeling, independence of spirit and appreciation of community norms, self-confidence and humility, hospitality and social courage, resistance to being outwardly pious and deep religiosity. I frequently found myself, in her company and since that time, thinking, "This is precisely what I wish to be like as an older adult."

As noted in the discussion of the focus groups, Anna was held in *Hochachtung* (high esteem) by the other women who attended the focus group. She said little, but they referred to her brief comments several times during the session, saying "As Frau M. said . . ." After the group meeting, I was unsure of the names of most of the women I had met. Selma, the pastor's wife, told me a little about Anna's life but nothing about her physical appearance. Later, I was able to guess who Anna was when I saw her at worship, simply from the way she carried herself. Selma said that Anna was the *"Grosse Dame"* (great lady) of the parish. She is not at all arrogant, but her dignity, style, and self-confidence set her apart immediately.

Anna is now 75 years old. At our closing interview, Karl and Selma told me they recommended her as a spiritual nominee because of her faith, her humility (Selma: "She doesn't know what she has."), her long years of church service, and her life of social action on behalf of the poor and weak. She is also concerned about ecology and active in the anti-war movement, and she was a foster mother to an Iranian refugee boy in her own home. The first woman ever to be elected as the leader of Wilster (called "the First Lady of Wilster" thereafter), Anna also worked for twelve years as church secretary and was on the church's *Vorstand* (governing council) for eighteen years, where, Karl reported, she was "very vocal." When I first met her, I mistook her dignity for aloofness or dislike of Americans and was afraid she might not agree to be interviewed. (She did not seek me out for conversation as did many of the other women, at worship and coffee hours). To my delight, she consented immediately.

Before arriving at Anna's house for our first conversation, I read an interview with her and several other townspeople in the book *700 Jahre Stadt Wilster* (*700 Years of the City of Wilster*)[3]. When I arrived for the first interview, I found that she had prepared coffee and cookies for us to share, as did all the German women, and she lit candles before we began.

I was nervous when we began, more than a bit intimidated by this "great lady," but her graciousness and warmth soon put me at ease. As soon as we began talking, it was clear that the war would be a dominant topic. Anna was born the daughter of a craftsman and married into a wealthy family. As a teen, she became enthusiastic about Adolf Hitler and, against her father's and later her father-in-law's warnings, joined the Hitler youth movement.

> In retrospect, I find it incredible. But I was so dumb. Then I was still so dumb. I did not see the way things are connected.

Those were times of economic hardship in Wilster; Anna felt that Hitler would improve things and make life more exciting and that the older generation was just being difficult and stubborn. Although her participation was limited to this political stance and allegiance and she did not take part directly in Hitler's atrocities, she does not attempt in any way to minimize her mistakes during those years.

Anna's faith has developed as a result of her early history. When her husband returned from the war and their children grew up and asked questions, she found that she had to come to grips with her membership in the Nazi Party. She has spent the rest of her life not so much focused on guilt as on making a positive difference. Although the regrets are clearly there and always will be, she has a faith based on *Nachdenken* (pensively thinking back), making sense of her own story and then moving on to trying to prevent a similar horror from recurring. Anna told her story as a contrast between the hubris of her youth and her current life in the faith community. Faith she called her *Geländer* (handrail). She objects to being called pious:

> I'm not pious. Piety is such a little, . . . do you understand what I mean, so very "lording it over."

And she mentioned that she does not attend church every single week. Although she prays and reads a little book of devotions every day, she told me she is no Biblical scholar. Instead, she has engaged in lifelong *Nachdenken*, in political action, and in a general learning process in which she attempts to integrate her current life in community with her historical past.

I like, I like to read, I read also—I have an adequate pension—but I always read only good newspapers, that is my hobby, that's how I get excited and then calm myself down, about politics, about everything.

The quiet, dignified voice I heard from Anna was, at times, intense and dramatic, as she related how she had to risk offending others in Wilster because she believes that the church and its people are not always sufficiently involved in justice issues, especially in ecology, peace, and anti-poverty work. From the Greenpeace sticker on her front door to the piles of books and newspapers in her small house, it was clear that Anna keeps herself well-informed and busily involved in justice issues. Now a Social Democrat, her local political participation has led her to feel that she must work for justice not only in Wilster, which she calls her *kleine Welt* (little world), but throughout Europe and the globe. "I'm a bit...nervy, yes," she says of herself. A particular point of passion is her insistence that Germans take responsibility for World War II and the Holocaust; this is not a stance that tends to make one very popular in a town where, as Karl told me, the personal biographies given to him before funerals tend to have a typical gap: the twelve Nazi years. Nevertheless, Anna has taken a strong stand in Wilster. When the editors of the local jubilee book[4] wanted to ignore the Nazi era, she was outraged.

They had worked on only the historic book two years, you see. And they had nothing [about] those twelve years, nothing, nothing on paper.

From her position in the church office, Anna told the young woman writing the book (who was seeking some documents from her),

She could just keep her book! She did not need to have it published, no?

The young woman finally agreed to include the Nazi era if Anna would give her a list of older people who might talk about Wilster during those years. Anna prepared a list; most people refused to help. Finally, a small group did meet for extensive interviews, including Anna. She paid a personal price for her stance, because she found the interview process *"wahnsinnig anstrengend"* (madly exhausting). But, she insisted repeatedly,

One must do that. In order for it not to happen again, one must speak.

And so Anna continues to risk speaking out about the war and the Holocaust, even risking a breach of another one of her values, *Gastfreundschaft* (hospitality). She told me of some tensions she felt when other women came to call on her socially and refused to talk about the Nazi period.

> A: Naturally I don't wish to abuse hospitality. But I'm not of a mind that one can lay this aside. I'm not of the mind, that one can act as though it were all only an accident, or something. I'm of the mind that one must keep these things in view, and must speak about it, so that it cannot be repeated, right? But, there are many of my good acquaintances, whom I value, and they don't like this much, this doesn't please them at all.
> J: Are they angry with you about it?
> A: No, they know this about me already. They excuse me.

Anna's spirituality-in-action, as it intersects with history and with her own life story, is an excellent example of what Payne described as spiritual maturity. Self-identity and life purpose are not assumed to be present at birth but rather are seen as evolving out of relationships with others and society in a specific period of history with its unique sets of events, values, and norms. It is out of such interaction that self-identity, values, and meaning emerge. Spiritual maturity, then, as it is used in sociological context, would relate to the development of self-identity and purpose in later life as a consequence of interpreting the meanings of past and present relationships.[5] Anna is, indeed, an evolving human being whose interactions with history have taught her the importance of Christian faith and community. Her ambiguous personal history has convinced her that a life of honest reflection and political action is preferable to a life of denial and passivity.

INGE: THE JOY OF LIVING

> When I was 70 years old, I invited sixty-five people here into the parish house, with food and drinks, with music and dancing. It was very, very wonderful. I can dance the whole night, I never get tired, I don't need to eat, I don't need to drink.

Even before hearing her incredible story, filled with so much suffering , one feels amazed by the joy and enthusiasm that characterize Inge's life. At age 74, Inge has been the *Küsterin* (sexton) of St. Bartolomäus for the past five years. She also works part-time as a fashion model. She has such a busy schedule that I had to make special arrangements to interview her before she left on her downhill skiing vacation (cross-country skiing, she told me, is too "boring"). But Inge was nominated not because of her energy for recreational activities but because most of her energy is used for purposes of building up the Christian community and sharing her special joy with others.

Inge was the first woman I met in Wilster outside of the pastor's wife, and that was not a coincidence, because she is always the first to arrive at church functions and the last to leave. Not only does she enjoy the fellowship, but also she stays busy setting things up, moving chairs, cooking, and lighting the ever-present candles. She greets people on Sunday mornings, collects the offering, arranges flowers, sets up for coffee hours, puts out the hymn books, brings older members to the Senior club when they need a ride, and says frequently,

This is my family. This I do gladly.

A few of these tasks fall into her job description, but most are done above and beyond the call of duty, simply because she enjoys doing them.

Inge was nominated quite naturally by Karl and Selma, not only because she is close to them personally but also because they consider her remarkable. She has had dramatic suffering in her life but has not become bitter. Also, although she has always had faith, only recently has she become highly involved in the Christian community. Now, her entire life centers on the church, even to the point of staying in Wilster over Christmas rather than visiting her daughter, so that she could be present for special services. Light as a butterfly and just as colorful, Inge's typical dress is purple slacks, a pink top, a bright scarf, and jogging shoes. She smiles frequently. Inge made a special effort to stop by the day she left for her ski trip to bring me flowers and say good-bye. She is one of those people about whom others say, "Doesn't she just brighten your day?"

But many of Inge's own days have been far from bright. When I went to her home to interview her, I already knew from the focus group that she lost a son in the war, but I did not know the details. During the three times I met with her, she became so teary in telling me the struggles she has had that I kept the interviews shorter than usual, just over an hour. Here is Inge's simple narrative of her greatest sorrow, the death of her baby, quoted in full because it is so central to her faith story:

I: We had never had sorrows . . . always much sunshine. . . Then [we] were at war, 1942. Then began the sorrows. My husband was, during all the years, [a soldier] in Russia and in France and Russia, until the end. Then I bore a child, in 1943, and then left as a refugee in flight. That was a very hard time. From Hinterpommern. . . . I was born in Stettin and was evacuated to Hinterpommern with my child because I couldn't hold out any more, with the daily bombing. I was mentally fully ready. I was there from '44 to '45. And the Russians were only four kilometers from the place. It was night, and I was fleeing in a loaded wagon, open, without a cover, totally filled with many people, all together. We had head lice; it was a very bad time.

J: How old was the child then?

I: Two years old. That child had a lot to go through. He was never completely dry, and one couldn't clean him up, and he was sick, and in April he died. (cries, pause)

J: I'm so terribly sorry.

I: Yes. (pause) And then came something that one can't believe, can't grasp. My child had not been baptized yet because my husband was in the war, and then I went to the pastor there, where I was—I didn't know anyone—and asked him to bury my child. And he refused, because the child wasn't baptized.

It may seem difficult to juxtapose this story with my picture of the present Inge, a person who dances and parties with her friends and so loves her church that she behaves with consistent joy and enthusiasm. At the very least, it would seem understandable if, after that pastor's behavior, she had never gone near a Lutheran church again. That was, in fact, her husband's response. But Inge said she refused to judge the entire church by the actions of one person.

Unfortunately, Inge's many difficulties did not end with that episode. Her husband became an alcoholic who left her to manage their children alone, take over their jewelry store, worry about finances, and, in short, assume all family and work responsibilities. She told of nursing her child, then rushing down to wait on customers, then rushing back to check on the baby. After her husband's death, her son became a drifter who constantly took her money and now refuses to see her. Since her adult years were so difficult, Inge still thinks most fondly of her childhood years. Although occurring some time ago, the deaths of her grandparents and parents are still difficult today for her to relate without tears. This woman has known enough *Sorgen* (sorrows) to lead her to understandable bitterness, the very opposite of what she has become.

But I have, in spite of it all, remained positive towards life.

Her positive attitude toward life, she told me, comes from her trust in God, the special relationship she has with the pastor and his wife, and the love she gives and receives in her church family.

I simply have trust in God, that He shall make everything right.

Simple trust is her antidote for the complexities of many deep pains.

ELISABETH: FAITH AND PERSONAL PEACE

My hope is the Lord Jesus Christ
when all else threatens to waver,
when my power is at an end
then I will still thank Him.
Old age approaches, my body decays
I can suffer so severely
but still I know what I must hold onto forever
the hope in my heart![6]

Elisabeth, at 65, was the youngest spiritual nominee in this study. She sat beside me at the focus group and spoke at length, in a carefully worded, sensitive response to Frau C.'s doubts about suffering and the God of love. Because she was able to testify to her own faith without appearing arrogant or judgmental, I was impressed immediately with her quiet confidence and by what she shared.

After the focus group, Karl suggested that I speak first with Elisabeth, since we were in immediate agreement about her as an appropriate woman for my interviews. Elisabeth, he told me, has a kind of evangelical piety. Since her childhood she has participated very regularly in many aspects of church life. She articulates her faith well and is open to new ideas. She is progressive politically and takes the initiative in meeting other people's needs. Her poetry also is an indication that she is a deeply spiritual person. In the past, she not only served as a lector in church but had total responsibility for the service on at least one occasion when the pastor was out of town.

Elisabeth grew up in Wilster, the daughter in a working-class family with definite gender ideas when it came to education. She explained to me why she had never been formally educated or learned to speak English, a fact that seemed to embarrass her.

Yes, I entered school in 1933, just as Hitler came to power. My father was a worker. In the shipping works, Blom and Voss, in Hamburg.

And we didn't have much money, no one could be sent to school. My oldest brother received a free place. And it seemed it was practically given to him. A stipend. He fell in Russia. He had been sent to Russia at 18. And so we in the technical school, we weren't instructed in English. For the common people, that was not permitted.

Elisabeth was an ideal person for my first German interview; she was gentle, kind, and patient with my poor pronunciation, putting me completely at ease. I found myself able to follow her German without difficulty. Most important, she was precisely the spiritually resilient woman I wanted to meet. When I discovered that she had written much poetry about her faith and was happy to share it with me, that became an extra bonus to my choosing her.

Elisabeth is the only woman in this study whose husband is still living. Her spouse, a former school master, is partially disabled and remained in his bedroom until after the last visit, when he came out briefly as I was leaving and met me. In dramatic contrast to Elisabeth, he immediately corrected my pronunciation. I felt as if I had been scolded in school, and Elisabeth looked embarrassed.

Throughout the interviews, Elisabeth spoke very softly, almost in a secretive tone, as though she did not want to be overhead. At one point, she told me a special secret and specifically requested that I not include it in any report. My impression was that, although she may not fear him, she is somewhat intimidated by her husband and is accustomed to keeping some of her life separate from him. As I discovered during the interviews, he no longer attends church. Elisabeth feels she may be responsible for that, because at one time she was so busy and overinvolved with church activities that he became disgusted with the whole topic. She does not, however, hesitate to invite friends from the church community into her home regularly, and he apparently does not object.

Elisabeth's faith, reflected in her writings, is rooted in her love of nature and her strong appreciation for Christian community, the aspect of her faith life that she identified as most important. Of all the women I met, she was most enthusiastic about nature and most specific about how her faith is often a thankful response to the beauties of the created world. Even though it was winter, it was obvious that the garden around her small house was cared for lovingly. Bird feeders hung by the windows, and at one point we were interrupted by the arrival of a beautiful small bird that resembled a hummingbird. She belongs to clubs with other gardeners and plant lovers and collect stones on her many *Urlaub* (vacations), most of which appear to be spent walking outdoors. Her precious stones are kept in a display case, and she brought them out to show me. One of the poems she gave me was typed on the back of a picture of her garden in bloom, and on my last days in Wilster, she arrived at the parsonage with flowers and another short poem as a farewell. Elisabeth is a warm, giving woman who, more than anything else, radiates a quiet spiritual peace, a peace that apparently grows from her strong relationship to both the natural world and to her friends in the Christian family.

Elisabeth has suffered physical problems, as her poem implies; she has had hip surgery. At 65, she anticipates more problems to come and watches as her older husband's health declines. Here, too, she uses her faith, often expressed in poetry, to solidify and strengthen the confidence, the *Hoffnung* (hope) she already feels. She told me that when she writes a poem, the faith that she expresses becomes more certain for her in the writing. Sometimes it is not even until she writes down her thoughts and feelings that she can really know what they are. Writing is the medium, then, for Elisabeth's spiritual growth. She does not, however, use this gift only for personal purposes, but shares it with the whole community.

NOTES

1. Karen Carter, a German friend who transcribed most of the German tapes, was very impressed with Emma and reported that her own spiritual life was affected by listening to Emma on tape.
2. Fowler, 1981, pp. 200-201.
3. Kurtz, 1982.
4. Kurtz, 1982.
5. Payne, 1990, p. 29.
6. Poem, *Hoffnung* (Hope), written by Elisabeth in 1994.

CHAPTER 7

Resiliency and Community

Jan: What things are most important to you because you are Christian?
Elisabeth: Community with others.

You have thus far been introduced to eight women who have obvious strengths and abilities, not only to transcend losses but also often to triumph over them. But in the previous chapters, we have only summarized their lives, faith, and coping styles. How did they manage? What themes of spiritual resiliency emerge from the interviews of women in both countries?

Reading, rereading, and coding our data confirmed the importance of a category of spirituality that was voiced repeatedly during the interviews: Christian community. Not only did the women speak of community as important directly, but this category was also *implicitly* present in the interviews in both countries, third in importance after faith and affect. Elisabeth called *Gemeinschaft* (community) the most important aspect of her life as a Christian; for Anna, it was the results of maturity, the opposite of the isolated idealism and foolishness of her youth. Rebecca said that community is the place where the truth is not only preached but also preserved, and Lovey spoke of a firmly based community where people are joined in love. For all eight spiritual nominees, the faith community was integral to their spirituality and a vital component of their general resiliency. They considered it to be an essential aspect of their spiritual lives, not an alternative choice for religious practice.

What is community? Because community is seldom emphasized as an important aspect of spirituality in the literature, its strong presence here is of particular interest. However, it is a word with different meanings in different contexts. M. Scott Peck wrote,

> Community is something more than the sum of its parts, its individual members. What is this "something more?" Even to begin to answer that, we enter a realm that is not so much abstract as almost mystical. It is a realm where words are never fully suitable and language itself falls short.[1]

The term *community* as used here acknowledges that mystery and has several layers of meaning. Concretely speaking, *community* refers to members of the women's home congregations (St. Bartolomäus, Wilster, and Glade Creek Lutheran, Blue Ridge). But in traditional Lutheran understanding, and as used by these women, the term is not tied exclusively to local groups. Rather, it includes all Christians, across denominations and across the globe, living and dead. Christian community, therefore, is both symbolic and actual, an everyday reality but also an intangible, mysterious concept.

The interviews are filled with so many references to community and to its importance in these women's lives that a separate book could be written on resiliency and spiritual community. Examples given here are representative but by no means exhaustive.

COMMUNITY AND THE GIFT OF OTHER PEOPLE

Community is, on its most basic level, the daily environment in which these women make friends. "I'm never bored," reported Inge, whose entire life centers on her church and its members. One of the most obvious contributions made by community to the life quality of these women is the social structure it gives their lives. For Inge, who loves fun and being with people, the community is an endless source of happiness and support.

> I am always happy if I can be in church. And, too, I have many friends and many invitations and I also invite many people to [visit] me.

But brothers and sisters (as Elisabeth and Lovey call them) in the faith community provide far more for these women than companionship and friendship. They are also *resources* for spiritual and practical assistance, teachers, role models, surrogate family members, connections to those who have died, and inspirations for the women's future faith development. Collectively, these special people in the Christian family become greater than the sum of the relational parts; they take on a larger, symbolic significance. They are not merely individual persons with whom one has relationships; they are, in the language of Christianity, *die Gemeinshaft der Heiligen* (the Community of Saints).

Emma and Elisabeth both told stories of asking for and receiving assistance with matters of faith from other members of their community. Emma asked one special person in her church to speak with her children and grandchildren about faith issues, hoping that he might be able to do what she has not managed: bring them back into church participation. Elisabeth described how she went to visit a younger woman for help during a period of doubt and depression.

For Miriam, Martha, and Rebecca, who had no children of their own, the children who are part of their religious community are a special joy. Said Miriam,

> You have to know the families. Of course I knew all the kids from teaching Sunday School, so I got to know their parents a lot better. I just enjoy it, I enjoy the circles. I hardly ever miss.

Pastors, both present and past, have become important people in the community for these women, to varying degrees. However, even though the pastors may be important both symbolically and realistically for the leadership and inspiration they provide, these women are quite capable of carrying on without them. In fact, the women reported that many of their most important spiritual experiences occurred at times when the pastor was not present. Said Emma, for whom Bible reading and study is a very important part of her spiritual growth,

> Pastor Steenbuck preaches wonderfully indeed, and one always takes something home with oneself.

But she went on to tell me that in her Bible study, where the pastor seldom visits, the free exchange of ideas has been especially helpful to her,

> If you read over the text with others, and struggle somehow, through that, one can somehow ask someone [about something] or say to someone, "I see it that way."

Christian community does not end at the grave for these women.

Lovey pictures heaven as one big family reunion. She is primarily connected to Christians, living and dead, through love, not blood.

> J: What way do you feel connected to them [those who have died]?
> L: Well, I don't know, just the love you have for them I guess. Because you have love for your parents, you know how you have love them, well, they have love the same way. Your grandparents and all, they mean so much to you. They do to me. . .
> J: How about people that you're not related to, that you know in the church?
> L: They're the same way. People that I remember, now B. D. just passed away . . . well, I knew them too and they seemed close to me. Just like I told a girl yesterday on the bus, I said, "You all just feel like my sisters. I'm still close to every one of you and love all of you."

For the women in Virginia, being Lutheran means being in a minority, so Christian community includes those outside their denomination. Martha, for example, spoke of her Brethren neighbors,

> I've had neighbors, the R.s , now they belong to the Brethren church. There were two old maids, and an old bachelor. For us children that was like going to grandma's house, to go visit those folks.

One of her non-Lutheran neighbors became like an extra parent.

> J (referring to Martha's special aunt): It's like you had three parents, isn't it?
> M: It really was, and really we had a fourth one. There was an old Black woman in the neighborhood. She came to help mother when I was a baby. S. would have gone through fire for any of us. She was a good old woman. She had a stroke in church and they came for my mother when it happened, because we had just gotten in from church. S. was a good old woman.

Lovey's memory was focused on denominational cooperation to an almost humorous extent. She talked about the people she currently gets together with in a senior's club and about her interdenominational church as a child.

> L: We have some wonderful times. We have people from the Brethren church, from the Baptist church, from the Lutheran church. When I was young, we were in a Union[2] church and the Lutherans had[3]

the first Sunday, Baptists had the second Sunday, the Brethren had the third Sunday, and the Methodists had the fourth Sunday. I think I'm wrong there, I think the Methodists had the first Sunday.

J: You had lots of denominations there.

L: Yeah, and then on the fifth Sunday, everybody could have that day.

The special people in these women's faith communities also extend beyond the immediate locality to include the writers, teachers, and pastors they have read and heard about. Sometimes these other persons serve as standards of and inspiration for faith and growth. Emma, for example, likes to read Christian biographies; she has read those of Paul Gerhard, Martin Luther, and a Pastor Busch, a young pastor-missionary. She compares herself and her faith unfavorably to their own and realizes she still has a long way to go on her *Weg* (way).

Dietrich Bonhoeffer has a very special place among the German women as an inspiration. Remarkably, all four of the women brought out and showed me (Ramsey) the same prayer written in prison by that German pastor, composed while he awaited execution by the Nazis; he had participated in an unsuccessful plot to take Hitler's life. My journal reflects that this prayer by Bonhoeffer, who has been a hero of mine since adolescence, is now a treasured part of my own spiritual life (see Figure 7.1):

Wonderfully secure through a benevolent power,
we await with confidence whatever may come.
God is with us in the evening and in the morning,
and entirely certain on each new day.

For me, in addition to its comforting religious meaning, it is also a reminder of the warm acceptance into Christian community I experienced in Wilster, of Anna and her struggles in particular, and also of the strength and courage I found in all the women I met and came to know in both countries. The long, emotional but comfortable pause that followed Anna's reading of this prayer aloud, just after she had shared her painful war memories, was by far the most unforgettable moment I knew in Germany.

COMMUNITY AND LOVE

Emma explained to me that community is based on the second part of Jesus's new commandment, "You shall love your neighbor as yourself." Echoing Lovey, she said that for her, the very basis of

Von guten Mächten
wunderbar geborgen,
erwarten wir getrost,
was kommen mag.
Gott ist bei uns
am Abend
und am Morgen
und ganz geiss
an jedem neuen Tag.

Figure 7.1. Prayer "Von guten Mächten" by Dietrich Bonhoeffer, 1945.
© Chr. Kaiser/Gütersloher Verlagshaus, Gütersloh. Reproduced by permission.

community is love itself.

> That is really, actually, the bounds of love, the love of Jesus for us and we for one another.

The voices of these women showed that, for them, this love is not only emotion, it is love in action. Love in their communities is by and *for* them; they are able both to give and take love from others. Miriam works to make quilts for Lutheran World Relief; she is proud that her little group made eight quilts last year.

> I've got one in here I just hemmed last week. I brought one of them home to hem. I should have sent it down there but I didn't. We save them up and give them to people who are in need.

She also visits church members who are in a nearby nursing home.

For Lovey, love both for individuals and for the community as a whole may mean just the opposite of being active at times. She has learned to step aside at times and let younger members of the community have a chance.

> L: Yes and I think that's a good thing 'cause the young ones have to carry on later. They're always going away.
> J: When you say you dropped out of some of the groups, do you still feel like you're a part of things at the church?
> L: Oh, yes, I still feel close. Of course if they need me I'm there.
> J: So you are kind of waiting to be asked?
> L: Uh, huh. Well, not exactly that, but you know, it does, there's a lot of people there and there's a lot that can take part, and as long as somebody else will take the part they won't do it. That's the way the young ones feel. They don't want to root the old ones out, and if you kind of step aside they can go in there and be satisfied.

Although Rebecca is now homebound and seldom moves from her special chair except for Sunday mornings, she also finds a way to put her love into action: She is bound to the faith community by the prayers she makes for them.

> Well, lately I've had a lot of people in trouble in our congregation. Some died and some have been real sick. So you have to pray for everybody, every day. You don't just pray one time and quit. You pray for your family. You pray for the overall church. You pray for the

seminaries that they'll turn out men and women that will spread the gospel light.

Several times during our interviews, she mentioned members who were ill or who had recently experienced deaths in their families, and each time she very naturally followed by saying that she was busy praying for them.

> Two of our church members lost their wives. Mr. W. and Mr. P. I have to pray for them, that the Lord will sustain them and help them.

Rebecca believes that God's Spirit assists her in her prayer life and heals others in the community.

> I hope the Holy Spirit will help me to say and do the right things all the time. You can't do it without the Holy Spirit. . . I pray for the ones that are real ill and need special prayers. I pray that the Holy Spirit will take over and help.

Love that is active in community moves outward but returns, and these women do not have high levels of ego or pride that might prevent them from being on the receiving end of the community's love. Most remarkable was Emma, who told me of two acts of love toward her by members of her church. One was a gift of money, enabling her to pay tuition for a church retreat she wanted to attend. The other she asked me to keep secret; it consisted of a direct gift to meet a life necessity. Emma's theology allowed her to accept the gifts graciously; she rejoiced at them and interpreted them as coming from God through the community. Speaking of the money she received to attend the retreat she said,

> And then she [the friend] sent me that! And that was indeed a gift from God.

But Emma is not always on the receiving end; she is constantly visiting others, especially shut-ins. With them she shares her time, her company, and her faith. One very special person for her is Frau A., who first invited Emma to attend the Bible study group. Emma reported that Frau A. taught her about prayer, namely that "it really creates community." Now Frau A. is sick and housebound, so Emma visits her weekly. Yet Frau A. continues to teach Emma and encourage her spiritual resiliency though example. Their relationship is mutually supportive and growth facilitating. Emma explained that she had been worried that Frau

A. might die alone, but Frau A. has assured her, "I'm not alone. Jesus is there." Now, because of what she has learned from this role model, Emma herself can cope with the most serious challenge of her own recent life: feeling alone "since my husband is no longer here."

Community love in action can be mundane and routine, but none the less, it is appreciated. There are times when having someone from the community just screw in a light bulb may be a definite advantage to an old woman, and these women are glad for that kind of direct help. Inge told me about a recent phone conversation in which her daughter teased her about always being able to find *"einen Dummen"* (a dummy) from her community to fix anything that may be broken. But, says Inge, sometimes it takes more than simple strength to do the job, so she does not even try to solve all problems herself:

Rather only, only out of contact with others around here [do I get things fixed]. And they don't say no.

COMMUNITY, AFFIRMATION, AND SELF-IDENTITY

Maintaining a positive self-image is often a challenge for elderly persons, but for these spiritual nominees, it is greatly facilitated by their life in community. They frequently experience warm acceptance and praise by friends in the church family, positive feedback that can then be internalized as part of their self-identity. The American focus group demonstrated this capacity for community affirmation. In the interviews in both countries, this theme also emerged. For example, Inge related how one member of the Church family expressed her appreciation for Inge's many contributions to the community at Christmas time,

At Christmas I received a package and a dear letter from a Church member, and she thanked me for my gracious and friendly style towards everyone in the church.

For Elisabeth, community is the place where she is able to combine her love of writing poetry with her faith and also the place where her gifts as a poet are recognized. At times, she spoke very directly of her self-identity, telling for example, how a retreat experience assisted her in forming her idea of who she is.

For example, we have, during a quiet day, a time of pausing, taken

[up] the topic , "Who am I?" And we have begun, all participants—it was old people and some in middle age—and then we all took paper in hand and, on the floor, got prepared, and we marked an outline [of their hands] and merely wrote our name, and that was also like an entry. And then we said, "What have we done today? What has my hand accomplished?"

The women's experience in community is one of safety and acceptance. Emma said she feels confident sharing some of her intimate experiences with sisters and brothers in the faith, who understand her better than her own family and who listen to her, keep her secrets, and do not look down on her.

Since I know that it [her thought] is well heard, that they won't repeat it, that they won't turn up their nose mockingly, and say, "Oh, what kind of a person is that" or something like that, you see.

COMMUNITY AND LIFESTYLE

The spiritual nominees believe that the spiritually mature life includes a place for social justice and peace. Several of the women in these interviews mentioned the importance to them of living a simple, nonmaterialistic life. None of them appeared to be wealthy, and none expressed a desire for more material advantages than they had. In their religious communities they are not required to make great financial contributions or to dress in a certain style (attire for worship in both communities ranged from very casual [blue jeans] to more formal [suits and jackets]). This is particularly important for Emma, who was left in poverty when her husband died.

Inge described the difference between having things and being happy. If one is a member of the community and lives with special people, then one is content.

I can envision leading the simple life. Together with good people, I can well envision that.

She expressed disgust with the materialism she sees around her in German society,

It's so terrible, that in today's times, one always wants to have more than the next [one]. I have a little car, [but] they must have a large one, still larger, it's frightful, frightful. People fret themselves over it;

they have no peace. They must forever have more, always more. And that I find to be a great disadvantage in today's time.

Faith for these women very definitely includes working for justice and peace. Emma does not feel that she has done enough for world justice: "However, I really haven't done much in that direction." But she feels that she works hard for justice in her local community, and says she believes justice must begin there. Across the ocean, Martha would agree that justice begins at home. With her typical, blunt style, she told me how she has taken the role of peacemaker in a dispute between two neighbors,

> Well, I think you try to feel right with everybody you have contact with. I think it [faith] affects your communications with other people. I had two neighbors up here that were at each others' throats all the time. I'm friendly with both of them, and I told them both that what they were arguing over wasn't worth neither one of them going to hell. They wouldn't believe me . . . I can't do a thing with either one of them, and they are fussing over a little strip of land about the width of this living room floor. I really do, I think that the way we live should be an example for other people.

Anna's involvement in justice issues was the most extensive and reflective. Her community is the church and also the world, and the risks she takes to work for justice are both personal and political:

> Previously . . . I've been a bit politically active. Then I also entered into community politics.

Her primary convictions—that the helpless must be helped, the mistakes of the past must not be repeated, and the coming generations must have peace and a healthy environment—are at the base of her spiritual vision. A word she uses often, *Zusammenhängen* (connectedness), reflects this dream. Her vision is one of human unity, a vision that requires the constant focus of a spiritually mature person. Anna understands not only love but also unconditional love, agape; she now recognizes that freedom (her dangerous choice as a young woman) must be tempered with will, duty, and concern for others.[4]

COMMUNITY AND RELIGIOUS SYMBOLS

The women in this study participated in a dimension less obvious than the good company, support of self-esteem, concern for social justice, and humble life style mentioned earlier. Juxtaposed to their positive experiences in relationships with other persons were the strength and the power they discovered through the symbolism of the religious community. The two Lutheran sacraments, Baptism and Holy Communion, are important parts of that symbolic life, and, in addition, two unexpected symbols were found: the lighting of candles (for the German women) and the church building itself (for both the German and the American women).

On every home visit I (Ramsey) made for an interview in Germany, the first thing the women did after my arrival was to light candles. In the parsonage where I lived, candles were also lit for coffee time, and they burned on every table at the coffee hour that followed *Gottesdienst* (worship). Even *Vorstand* (Church council meetings) were conducted by candlelight. My view of this act changed from seeing it as merely a simple cultural tradition (popular throughout Germany) to realizing that, for the church family in Wilster, it was also part of a larger meaning system. This realization came after hearing several of the women talk about *light* in their spiritual lives. The Biblical book of John calls God the "Light of the world," and for the spiritual nominees, the simple act of lighting a candle apparently served as a way to acknowledge God's presence in their homes, group meetings, and lives. Lighting the candles on the table before us during my second visit with her, Elisabeth told me why the lighting of candles had become so important for her. During a time of spiritual struggle, she visited a young woman from her community. Elisabeth was crying when she arrived at the woman's house, and the woman acted symbolically, without speaking a word.

> She took a candle and lit it and simply put it down before me. Between us. Then suddenly I stopped my wailing. Then I remarked, "What do I have to talk about here? That [talking] is not what will bring me around." That was so impressive, I said to her later. It is very important for us, the Light, by which we know, you see? By the way, it happens on this day, today, also. Well, that's what I experienced here in Wilster. That was for me primary [when] she placed the light before me.

Inge told me that when she is surrounded by the community and gazing on the lighted altar candles, or when she finds herself working alone in the church building Sunday evenings and thinks back on the community experiences of the morning, she feels peace and a lack of anxiety. She described those feelings to me during our second interview.

I: The most beautiful and best I feel is if I am in the church and many people are around me and the candles on the altar are glowing and—I could gaze forever on that. There is so much peace, and even when there aren't any people at all in the church. When it's Sunday, in the evening, and I'm in the church, then I lock up. Since some things have already happened with us, in the church—but not me, me in particular—here in the church I have no anxieties. . . In fact when I'm in the church, then I can really breathe deeply, and be at peace.

J: A special place.

I: Yes, indeed, a special place for me.

For Rebecca and for Miriam, the church building itself also has symbolic significance; so much of their time has been spent there, and so much family work had been invested there through the years. Rebecca narrated in detail the beginnings of the current church, where she and her husband were charter members. It represents for her permanence and continuity with her past religious life, and she talks about the exact dates of its completion just as others might speak of the birth of a child.

So it's been there ever since 1941, is when it was built. The first Sunday in January of '41 is when we had our first service over here.

Miriam thinks, too, of her deceased husband when she thinks of the church building.

Of course Johnny was a real good worker in the church. We worked and got home at 3:30. He worked digging foundations. My husband did what he could.

COMMUNITY AND OUTREACH

The spiritually resilient women in this study did not stop simply with feeling good about their community experiences; they shared their experiences with others. Anna referred to community as the place where "One somehow gives back." In our third interview, Inge spoke of how she shares the joy she finds living, and singing, in her volunteer work with "the older people" (she accurately places herself, a 74-year-old skier, model, and dancer, among the "young old"). We were talking about her favorite hymns.

I: "Let Us Sing with One Another" and "Praise the Lord" are also

wonderful.
J: "With one another." You have said that other people are important
   to you.
I: Yes, and I've already sung this hymn with the older people, if
   someone doesn't know it, or as a closing, and I find it so beautiful.
   "Let Us Sing with One Another."

COMMUNITY: A PLACE FOR SHARING DOUBTS, JOYS, AND SORROWS

Perhaps the greatest gift these women have experienced in community is the joy mentioned earlier. Simply being together pleases them. As Emma explained to me, the conversation might well be over little things and still bring joy. However, community also serves as a safe place for them to go when things are difficult, even when the issue is one of faith. In Germany, I not only heard about this process from the women in the interviews, I saw it occurring during the time of my visit. Frau C., who had spoken out with strong feelings about her theological doubts at the focus group, was then invited by her friends to discuss her feelings in smaller community groups. They were worried about her and wanted to be supportive to her during her "dark night" of doubt. Elisabeth told me that when a group got together to play cards, someone again brought up the topic, and they talked among themselves, trying to give Frau C. an opportunity to air her feelings. But Elisabeth feared that she was stuck for a time and would have difficulty moving on because, she said, Frau C. was ignoring a way of knowing and believing that Elisabeth considers important—using the heart along with the head.[5]

> And there we again talked about this topic, and she was very overwrought, and then she said, "I simply can't grasp it in my head" and "I simply can't grasp it." She believes in God, but she does it all with her head.

But Elisabeth knows, too, of the opposite community emotion, joy. She told me of the joy she feels when she, by chance, meets someone whom she knows from a spiritual retreat. Miriam's spirit, too, is enthusiastic and her manner joyful; she no doubt adds much joy to the many community groups of which she is a part. Speaking of a project at church she said,

> That's another hard job, but we have a lot of fun while we're doing it, 'cause we have more help with that than we do anything else. We'd

have sometimes twelve ladies at a time working. We are always gabbing and laughing and talking and stuff. . . I enjoy the fellowship, being with everybody. I'm a person that loves people. . . I've always loved to be out and be with a bunch that you can have fun with and still have time to get your work done.

The special anniversaries and occasions in these women's lives also become experiences in which the entire church family participates, and all of these elements—friendship, building of self-identity, practical help, symbolism, simple lifestyle, and sharing with others—all come together for these marker events. Inge is already planning such a time, her 75th birthday party, to be held next summer in the church parish hall, complete with the dancing she loves. (In Germany one typically gives oneself a birthday party with friends.) Whether in joy or sorrow, the community is the place where one is comfortable and among friends. In the words of Elisabeth, that is where the women feel *zu Hause* (at home).

COMMUNITY: THE RICHNESS OF ITS CONTRIBUTIONS

Emma was the most articulate of all these women in describing explicitly what community means to her. In my three interviews with her, she gave such a thorough picture of what community has meant in her life that it serves well as a summary of this aspect of spirituality for all these resilient women. She talked of how individual prayer is important, not only for the strength it gives each person but also for the community it builds. She talked of the believers' common faith in Jesus, and she described how, through that faith, another member of the church has taught her the courage not only to die but also to live. She mentioned some of the community activities that give her most joy and the equality created by Christian fellowship.

If also we can, when we visit, pray together, which I find very, very important. And we sing together, such wonderful songs, that makes one so very happy, and we sometimes study a text together, and all is somehow agreed upon—yes, out of the common belief. And that is true community. And then also, we believe that no one is better than the other, is more Christ-like, or believes better. We are all on the way to Him.

NOTES

1. Peck, 1987, p. 60.
2. "Union" refers to a practice to combine two or more denominations in one church building, with shared use of the facilities.
3. "Had" means that they were able to use the building for their worship service that day.
4. Hillery, 1992.
5. See section on Lutheran theology and spirituality in Chapter 2.

CHAPTER 8

Resiliency and Emotion

As we listened to the women in this study, and then listened again to their stories on tape, we heard evidence of many strong emotions. There were tears, sighs, whispers, and long pauses. Most of the women talked easily about their feelings and their affective experiences, relating them comfortably to their life stories and their spiritual lives.

AFFECT AND COMMUNITY

The relationship between affect and belonging to their religious group is strong for these women. Emotions are not seen simply as private matters but are anchored in the sacred symbols, history, and daily life of the faith community.

For Elisabeth, learning about her faith in a community setting is an emotional experience. She frequently gives voice to her feelings through poetry, thereby doing much of her emotional work and at the same time creating a means through which she can pass on her insights to others. Elisabeth experiences just walking into a room of fellow members in the Christian community as a kind of homecoming:

However, when one comes in there, then it is as if one is at home, and that is the beauty [of it].

Feelings and faith go together for Martha, too, who sees Christian community as extending beyond the grave. At one point in the second interview with her, she cried as she shared her beliefs about the community of saints.

> J: What about some of the Christians that have gone on before you, who have died?
> M: Yeah. I can't explain it, I know I'll see them. I guess that's one thing that makes it as easy to give them up as it was . . .
> J: To have that expectation?
> M: Uh huh. (pause, tears)
> J: It's a hard thing to talk about, isn't it?
> M: If we didn't have those feelings . . . that's where our faith comes in.

Love is the foundation of Christian community for Lovey. God is Love, and that love creates community. She moves comfortably and naturally back and forth, from reflecting on God's love to thinking of the love she feels for others. Nowhere did Lovey become more animated than when she spoke of the emotion for which she is named.

> The greatest thing is the Lord. And you know love is one of the greatest things on earth. Love for one another. If everybody loved everybody like I love them . . . there's always good. I don't care how bad a person is, there's always good there if you want to find it.

Later she said,

> I love people, I love everybody, I sure do. One of the greatest things. Love is one of the greatest things on earth. I'll say that all my life.

Lovey moves on to put her feelings into action, and she admitted to hoping she will be loved herself. For example, I asked her to tell me more about the large group always present at her holiday dinner table:

> L: Yes, I don't know how many. We've got a real good friend and he always comes 'cause his wife works on an airplane as a stewardess and she is seldom home for Christmas. . . We know she isn't going to be there to fix him breakfast.
> J: Open door, huh?
> L: Yeah. What I want is love.

AFFECT AND RELATIONSHIPS

Not surprisingly, emotions ran high when these women talked

about the people in their lives with whom they now are or have been most closely bound, their children, husbands, parents, pastors, and special friends. Family relations are sources of both joy and pain, and when relationships are troubled, the women suffer. Inge, for example, is deeply pained over a breach with her adult son, who will not work and repeatedly asks her for money and who demanded, after she had no more to give, that she borrow money from a bank to pay his bills. When she finally said no, he disappeared from her life, and she now hears of him only through mutual friends living in his city.

> J: You know that he is healthy.
> I: Yes, yes. And that, I now say, satisfies me. I can't do anything. But it troubles me (tears). That is my sorrow.

These women suffer emotionally when they see their loved ones making mistakes and causing themselves and their families pain. One of the poignant examples of this was during the interview with Emma, who spoke of her son in quiet, deep tones,

> I have a great, great sorrow: My second son is an alcoholic.

The women also experience many deep feelings of worry when their children, spouse, or others whom they love do not stay involved in the life of faith and community. This was especially troubling to the American women, for whom regular church attendance is understood as a necessary part of being Christian. And in Germany, too, Emma grieved that her grandchildren are not being raised in the Christian faith:

> My grandchildren have not all been baptized, and that makes me very sad.

For Lovey and Inge, breaches in human relationships seem to be among the most painful aspects of their lives, for these women live to love and to be loved. Rejections are very painful to them. Lovey told a story of her difficult stepmother, an event just as real to her now as it was many years ago. She and her young husband had to live temporarily with her father and his new bride.

> We showed our love towards him [her father], and our stepmother was jealous of us and made it bad. . . Then one morning after we stayed—I guess I stayed there for six months or something after we were

married—one morning she came down to the kitchen and we had all eaten and others had gone to work. Papa didn't go to work that day and he came over and sat in a chair, and he pulled her down in his lap and they sat there talking. I was fixing their breakfast, hot for them. She said to me, "I'll be so glad when you leave that I won't know what to do. I think it's time for me to take over." (pause, tears) As soon as we found a house, we moved out.

Joy is the other possibility in family relationships, and nowhere was it more poignantly expressed during these conversations than when Anna described the most memorable moment of her life, the birth of her first child. She spoke in response to the question, "When has God seemed especially close to you?" Because of the horrors of the war, the arrival of this baby became a sign of hope for Anna, a sign that God was close by.

And that first child I still remember. Ah, ah. And, do you realize, that was war? He was born in 1940. I lived above, in this house. I delivered the child, the oldest child, in the hospital. That was, now, 54 years ago; he is 54. And then the first night when I was alone with the child . . . and I had such a little basket, I laid him in it . . . and it was such a sweet child, you see. And then I felt his tiny little breath and then—you must imagine, it was war! My husband was always away. And you lived for the mail, that a letter would come. And this child! And if I had to answer the question, "What is happiness?" ah, that was indeed a happy moment, ah, and then God was totally close by. Then was one secure, and, one, one prayed, and one thanked, and one thought, oh, oh, that sweet child, born so healthy, and in spite of the constant uncertainty with the war, this was a sign that all was well and good and that God is love, and that one had [Him] near by, you see? That I have never forgotten.

AFFECT AND SELF

Emotions were high when the women spoke about aspects of their lives that related strongly to their self-identity. For example, Elisabeth spoke of her pride in being called a *Hausfrau* (housewife),

That's indeed what I wanted to be! That's what I still want to be!

In contrast, Inge's identity had been tied directly to her career outside the home. She recalled the time of her forced retirement at 65 with strong feelings.

That cost many tears, I was so unhappy and sad. I had liked being there so much. Then I thought, this won't do. Without work you can't exist at all.

AFFECT AND DIFFICULT TIMES

These women did not see the world with rose-colored glasses nor did they gloss over the troubles they knew. They did not understand Christianity to mean that one is required to deny pain and doubt. Elisabeth, for example, spoke directly and bravely of the high and low periods she has known:

Yes, as I already said, there are highs and lows, repeated over and over. And that's frequent. That's the way it goes with me.

One of the most painful moments in the American interviews came when Miriam told the story of the sudden deaths of her father and brother and her mother's subsequent depression. Losing both husband and son was more than Miriam's mother could bear.

She was 44, and my brother had just died, and my father had just died. . . . She had a nervous breakdown. She lost her son in May and her husband in September. It was more than she could take.

After long months in which her young mother could not attend even to her most basic human needs because of the depths of her depression, Miriam finally was able to see some small improvements.

We had it hard and finally I got her up into a chair and I brought one of her rockers down here, sitting by the window. When he [Miriam's husband] came home we'd get her up in a chair and she'd sit there at the window. After she got so she could handle herself, she started to get into better spirits. But, she cried a lot. . . She was so despondent too. She couldn't use her hands, and we got these big balls and we rubbed her hands with cocoa butter. And finally she got so she could use them a little bit, but that's as far as she got them even later in life. We got her some big needles, she loved to crochet. 'Course I had to do a lot of things for her, but she was able to sit on the stairs and wait on the steps.

For the German women, the present was also sometimes painful because of its echoes of the past. They spoke with deep emotions about current ethnic conflicts and European violence. Their war memories fill them with longings for peace and with hatred of war. These emotions were strongest in Anna, whose community is the whole world and who feels distress on a daily basis that people have not yet put an end to war. She has traveled in Yugoslavia and is especially heartbroken to see the destruction occurring there.

> This, this unrest that, also there in Yugoslavia, that is all so inconceivable. Such a beautiful country, don't you know, so often visited, all so like a picture book: little houses, mountains, the sun, water—oh, God, no, no, no. That is so very, very sad, that human beings will not become any smarter.

Emma also expressed strong negative feelings on this topic, saying that she could hardly bare to watch the scenes of Yugoslavia on television, "How terrible it is."

The women were courageous in being willing to talk about times when God seemed distant, even if others might misunderstand. Here, too, the affective element to spirituality was central to their experience. Said Lovey,

> Yes, at times I say to myself, "Lord, where are you? I can't *feel* you."

For Lovey, her doubts are experienced directly as affect, as a *lack* of feeling the divine presence. Emma remembers with sorrow that her husband taunted her about her times of doubt and fear.

> He would often say, if you believe in God, you would not be despairing. But this I don't know.

Miriam said she sometimes feels "depressed" when God seems far away.

> Sometimes I think that I lose sight. I get depressed and those things kind of come between us. But, I think He's always near, never that far away.

Miriam's last words capture an important theme in these interviews: Pain and down times are not the end of the story for these resilient women. They do not get stuck in their emotionality but soon again experience God as present with them, precisely *because of* and *during* their difficulties. Lovey expressed this:

L: It's just a wonderful feeling. You just feel sweet, you feel like you're loved all over. It's something that you can't express, you can't tell nobody.

J: What are some of the times when that's happened?

L: Well, just a lot of times. Lot of times when you are down and out. Then He can come in and make you feel wonderful.

A specific stress in her life occurred when her son left for Europe in World War II. (Lovey was the only American woman to refer directly to the war.) Lovey had vivid experiences of God's presence during that period.

But you know when he went into the service, after the Lord had talked to me on the porch, I felt like He was close.

This closeness to God led directly to her feeling able to cope with her anxieties for her son's safety and to feel confident that he was still alive.

L: Every night I could feel him in his bed. He was there.

J: Your son, you mean?

L: Yes.

J: So it sounds like feeling close to God made you feel close to him, too.

L: It did. If you're close to Him, He pulls you in.

Miriam, with no living family member as possible caretaker if her health continues to decline, sometimes feels anxious. She recognizes, too, that she is a woman who has always cried easily, and she believes that her ability to cry is part of her inherited nature.

Yeah, I cry at the drop of a hat. I got that from my mother, I reckon. She got it from her mother. (laughs)

But Miriam's resiliency arises from a courageous combination of spiritual faith and the ability to *allow* herself to cry, to feel emotional pain, and then to move on.

I have these spells when I'm here by myself, I cry and go on. It makes you feel better.

Ultimately, Miriam's trust in God prevails.

When you are by yourself you have a lot of time to think and if you dwelt on it, I don't believe you could take it. I believe you would go out of your mind if you dwelt on it a lot. I like to think over my good memories and my bad ones too. I do a lot of that laying in bed at night. But I think, well, I'm here for a purpose and it will work out for me. I know it will. I feel like it will. I'm going to try to keep my faith that it will. I feel like it will work out for me. There will be a way.

AFFECT AND FAITH EXPERIENCES

The women varied widely in their abilities to reflect on their faith in theological language, but they all recognized and accepted that faith includes feelings. Inge was most explicit in *defining* faith as feelings. When asked if her faith was more like a feeling or a thought, she responded, "These really are not thoughts; these are feelings." Many of the women described faith as a feeling, a safe or good feeling, and none seemed uncomfortable with this aspect of their spiritual lives.

The diverse ways in which the women reported the affective aspect of their spiritual lives were directly related to the unique themes of spirituality that emerged from each set of individual interviews. For example, it was when Martha spoke of her work that she was most moved and had to pause to compose herself.

M: I know I have a church bulletin somewhere that I saved. It shows an old scrub woman, cleaning between the pews at church, and it has the verse on there "Whatever you do, do it all for the glory of God." I thought, well if scrubbing the floor, . . . you don't think about praising God when you're down scrubbing the floor, do you? But I saved it. (pause, tears).

J: Looks like that really moves you, to talk about that. How did you think about that yourself?

M: After that I felt like everything I did, I should do it to the best of my abilities. If God had given me the ability to do these things, then I should do it the best I could. . . I truly feel that anything we do we should do it as a praise to God. 'Cause He has given us the strength to do these things.

Miriam, who loves music and who sang for many years in her church choir, spoke of her delight in hymns.

I like the spicy ones! Those joyful ones that we used for processionals all the time, "Bring Out the Banner," and that kind of stuff, you know.

Lovey claimed that she found it difficult to express her feelings of being close to God, but in the interviews she did so in colorful yet simple metaphors that captured her childlike, trusting faith. In explaining her relationship with God, she said,

> It's just one of those things you cannot express, really. You feel like. . . I can imagine how an angel feels, I feel that way. Just with the imagination, you know how you'd feel if you were an angel. That's the way it feels.

She speaks similarly about prayer,

> Great things the Lord enlightens you to. I think that's where you learn, if the Lord's with you and enlightens you to things. Have you ever felt like he is just talking to you? Now that's great when you feel like that.

Lovey's ability to use her imagination is intertwined with her emotional and spiritual life. About her favorite Bible story, Joseph in Egypt, she said,

> That story just touches me when I think about that old man, and his boy had been gone for all those years. He met him, come back and found him and joined him and they cried. It just makes me almost cry myself. Just put yourself in their place!

Speaking about her confirmation day, she said,

> When I walked down that aisle to make confession I felt like I just had wings, floating up there.

Emma finds it easy to discuss her faith with others, and she reports that it makes her happy to do so. Her fondest wish for the coming generation, and particularly for her children and grandchildren, is that they will discover what she has found in her faith.

> I wish my children, or the young people, that they may be open, that they may hear, that they may recognize that God indeed wants us again, helps us and calls us back. Therefore I always think that it would be so wonderful, the most beautiful present, for them, if I would see, . . . oh, I'd be happy. If I would see my children following Jesus, being in the succession!

Rebecca described a sacrament, Holy Baptism, in affective terms. She continues to have a sense of herself as baptized, and this leads to a feeling of security in daily life situations where physical limitations are a constant reality.

R: The Bible speaks of it. "He that believeth and is baptized shall be saved." That's what it says. So it's a good feeling. I've never been without that feeling. I think I'm talking too much.

J: No, no, that's the whole idea. It's interesting to hear you say that it gives you a good feeling.

R: Yes, you feel good inside you know. You feel safe.

J: A safe feeling.

R: Yes.

CHAPTER 9

Resiliency and Personal Relationships

THE IMPORTANCE OF PERSONAL RELATIONSHIPS

As you have seen in the chapter on resiliency and community, the interviews with these spiritual nominees were frequently interwoven with stories of relationships. As they talked about their faith, children, husbands, parents, grandparents, nieces, pastors, and friends all appeared, disappeared, and then reappeared on the stage of the women's lives. The women care deeply about other people, they learn from them, they appreciate other members of the community who are role models for their development, they nurture and care for others when needed, and they hope that their children and grandchildren will find the joy and strength they have found in the church. They suffer when there is conflict in their families (for example, Emma and her daughter or Inge and her son) and they rejoice when things go well for the special people in their lives (Anna and her professional children or Lovey and her affectionate daughter). Children are especially important to them, and those who have been married speak often of their husbands. Clearly, they value highly their relationships with others.

If relationships and faith are both important to these women, what do they do when they must choose one or the other? Emma is an example of how the mature person might balance her desire for good family relationships with enthusiasm for sharing her faith. Her daughter and son-in-law do not attend church, so Emma worries about her grandchildren and their future. However, she also wants to get on well with her children since she lives in their home.

Then naturally, they get into conflict, the children, isn't it so?

Because she is a mature person, Emma has devised ways to evangelize through modeling behavior rather than through preaching or arguments:

> And with my grandchildren, I must be educationally restrained, careful, because my daughter is totally against it [religion], and so evangelically restrained somehow, so that they [the grandchildren] notice, "Grandma thinks that," "Grandma loves the Bible."

The picture that emerges from the interviews certainly does not support the idea that "women tend to remain in Faith Stage 3 which is characterized by socialization and dependency"[1] To label their intricate, caring, and cognitively complex relationships with others merely as "socialization" is a gross simplification, and there is no evidence that these women are "dependent." Rather, as shown in the chapter on resiliency and community, the personal relations they had with others in their faith group were multifaceted and interdependent. Within their families, too, they played differing roles and met divergent needs with tact and flexibility.

The spiritual nominees nurtured and cared for their children, whether biological children or those they taught in Sunday School classes (for example, Martha). Anna now looks back on those days fondly; in one interview with me she talked at length about a conversation she had with her adult children, reminiscing about how, as young children, they would always ask "Where is Mommy?" whenever she went out for a while. These women were generative in an Eriksonian sense[2] that transcends the mere ability to care directly for children. Even immature women can, at least temporarily, nurture their own young. Generativity is "not just a stage for making little things grow."[3] These women also spoke often and passionately about their hopes and dreams for the coming generation, not just for their own descendants. Inge wished them *Frieden* (peace) that comes from "more believing in God." Anna hoped for peace, tolerance, and a clean environment. In Germany the women expressed concern for each *Mensch*, the general term meaning a human being.

Even though they enjoy other people, and feel it is necessary to be part of a faith community, these women are not clingy or dependent by any means. Their relationships are better described as interdependent because they give and take in an atmosphere of mutual support and acceptance. They realize that mutuality, a balance between giving and taking, is vital to human friendships. Said Inge,

> One must do something for the friendship. One must not expect the
> other to do everything. One must give herself, I think.

Also important is their ability to receive. *Receiving*, for some older
persons who have been very active all their lives, can be more difficult
than giving. In contrast, Rebecca is able to receive help graciously, when
others make tapes for her, help her with her daily care, and transport her
to worship. Similarly, Emma graciously accepts money and other forms of
help from her friends in the community.

All of those who lived alone did so successfully, again
demonstrating their lack of dependency. They were able to differentiate
between being alone and being lonely, a cognitive distinction that shows
both emotional and spiritual wisdom. Rebecca stated explicitly, "I'm
alone but I'm not lonely." Several of the women expressed similar views.
Although Miriam had found living alone difficult at first, she now sees it
as an opportunity.

> When you are by yourself, you have time to think and read and
> meditate more, and I think you grow closer [to God], I really do.

Because they are based on faith and mutual life together, the
women's relationships outside of families tend to cut across the lines of
rigid age divisions. Said Inge, "I like to get together with young people,
and I have almost all friends who are younger than I." Miriam talked
fondly of some neighbor "boys" (actually, young adults) to whom her
husband had given Bibles. Even though she said she sometimes feels
uncomfortable with young people, Martha, too, spoke of warm
relationships with younger neighbors and with her niece.

FAITH AS A RELATIONSHIP

A still more complex piece of this relationship puzzle is the
question of how the women conceptualize their faith lives. One of our
research questions had addressed the issue of whether the women would
speak of their faith primarily as a *personal relationship* with God (God as
a life companion) or as a *concept* (an abstract belief system). The latter
has typically been considered be more common to men's spirituality than
women's. Stokes wrote, "Significantly more women than men define
'faith' as 'a relationship with God' while more men than women define it

as 'a set of beliefs.' "[4]

All of the women who were interviewed did use relational language to describe their faith lives, and in some cases, this imagery and language dominated. But their rich spirituality was far more profound and multifaceted than is implied by Stokes. The women integrated both relational aspects of faith *and* abstract thought, "a set of beliefs,"[5] in other words, theology. For Inge, Miriam, and Lovey, relational language was prevalent but not exclusive. For Elisabeth, Emma, Martha, and Rebecca, there were many occurrences of both stated beliefs and principles. For Anna, this combination is extremely well integrated.

Lovey said that her relationship with the Lord was the most important thing in her life. But she also revealed her theology of faith as trust when she spoke:

> That's exactly what I would tell them [the children of the future], that's the greatest thing you could do. Be with Him and trust Him, and do what He enlightens you to do.

Rebecca said she has never really experienced God's absence,

> No, I know He's right here. I know He's always there. It has always seemed like that to me. Even when my husband had a stroke and was laid up for forty-eight years.

A feeling of God's nearness gave Martha courage to work on the farm, even in the middle of night.

> Oh, I feel that [God's presence] every day I'm home. If I didn't I don't believe that I'd even feel safe enough to lay down and sleep at night. . . To go to bed tonight, if I think there's a cow that might be having trouble in the barn, I'll go down there by myself and sit down by them.

Miriam was the most enthusiastic about faith as a personal relationship.

> I don't know, I guess the most important thing for any Christian is to believe in the Lord Jesus. And to know He's with you . . . I feel like the Lord is with me all the time, I don't have the feeling that He's too far from me.

She consistently spoke of feeling God's presence,

> I've always had that close feeling, so I don't know what it feels like. . .

> I've always felt like I've been close . . . 'Cause all you've really got to
> do is ask Him and He is there.

Through her suffering, her relationship with God has only strengthened
her. But she reflected on the meaning of her suffering as well.

> I don't know, maybe I've grown stronger in faith with all those
> troubles, 'cause you can look back and see and realize how much He's
> done for you.

Here it is not just the feeling, but the thinking back, that matters to her.

In Germany, Inge spoke often of God in relational terms. She
described her trusting relationship with God as childlike (not childish).

> I don't question why and how, I simply believe. Sometimes I think,
> I'm like a child, huh?

Emma, the "theologian" among the women, also balanced relationship and
concept. She called faith "a very close relationship with Him."[6] She
imaged herself in God's loving arms and she has, from childhood on,
always believed and trusted that God would keep her safe,

> As one always says, "I can't fall down deeper than God's hand." And
> I've always held with that.

Elisabeth, like Martha, believes God is her personal helpmate in hard
times.

> One is, to be sure, dependent on that [God's help], but by grace one is
> dependent and only need, fundamentally, so say, "Yes, I believe that
> you help me."

Anna gave many examples of her ability to integrate abstract
thoughts and a relational approach to faith. In discussing most topics, she
combined, with perfect ease and naturalness, her strong love and concern
for people with her passionate beliefs. She has reached this point through
a lifetime of both cognitive and emotional work. She spoke often of her
lifetime of *Nachdenken* (pensively thinking back). As mentioned
previously, during the interview, she read the Bonhoeffer prayer, pointing
to God's dependable presence in daily life. This occurred immediately
after the most intense part of our conversation when she had been
speaking of the concentration camps during the Nazi times. Many of her

sorrows over those years are relational in nature; she thinks of how she argued with her father-in-law, who hated Hitler, and was economically ruined by the war nevertheless. She thinks of having to explain her actions to her own children when they were old enough to understand. But she did not speak of hours spent on her knees, deep in confession. Those times may well have occurred, but they are past. She does not linger on her guilt but lives today, by her principles. By far the majority of our time together was spent on present-day issues of war, peace, ecology, ethnic tensions, and homelessness. The metaphor she has for faith is also a combination of relationship and abstraction: *Geländer* (handrail). God is a daily presence, a guide along the way.

Because she has this "handrail," Anna can take risks, and because she has definite beliefs, she can speak out with confidence. As described earlier, in the jubilee book, *700 Jahre Stadt Wilster*,[7] she was one of only a small group of her cohorts willing to be interviewed about the Nazi years. In that conversation, too, she demonstrated how deeply she has thought about those years and formed beliefs about God, the world, and human nature. At one point she said,

> It goes to show what entirely normal human beings will do if they are given power in their own hands.

She remained true to her principle to speak out about this unpleasant reality. At one point, the topic of the Wilster church's do-nothing stance during the war came up during the editor's interviews. She told the editor,

> Yes, it's true what you said. But remember, we all are the church. We all kept still.

The editor asked the group if they knew what was being done to the Jews. Several men on the panel said, in effect, "No, we did not know; we had not read *Mein Kampf*." But Anna courageously disagreed; she told what she saw in a Berlin woods one day during the war years,

> I first had a suspicion during a visit in Berlin. There I saw daily workers in the woods, hundreds in striped suits.

The last comment by Anna during that interview reveals her ability to take risks because of her orientation toward the future. She consistently attempts to combine principle with a concern for human relationships.

I say over and over to the young people: Don't be so sure, that something like this can't happen again. You must ponder it.

NOTES

1. Stokes, 1990, p. 175.
2. See Gilligan, 1982.
3. Vaillant, quoted in Gilligan, 1982.
4. Stokes, 1990, p. 175.
5. Stokes, 1990, p. 175.
6. Although Emma used sexist language for God here, at another point in the interview she spoke at length of how difficult it could be to use male language for God, including the term *Father*, if one has not had a close and good relationship with one's own father. Her granddaughter, she said, was a case in point. She herself had a good relationship with her father and prefers to use that term.
7. Kurtz, 1982.

PART III

Conclusions

CHAPTER 10

Implications for Thinking, Being, and Telling

You have met eight resilient old women, heard their stories, and reflected on the diverse ways in which community, emotions, and personal relationships have enriched their spiritual lives. You have listened to women who listened for God. But an engaging question remains: How might it profit you to have come to know them? How might becoming acquainted with Lovey, Miriam, Rebecca and Martha have everyday, perceptible applications for you as you age? Or if you are a therapist or social worker, of what use are models of spiritually resiliency, such as those of Anna, Inge, Emma, and Elisabeth, as you counsel older persons? How do the stories told here intersect with the cognitive, existential, or narrative approaches so useful in therapy with seniors?

If you are yourself a person who is facing aging-related losses, we hope that you have already been encouraged by reading of Lovey's ability to focus on the beauty of God's world on a winter day, by Anna's experience of God's forgiveness, by Miriam's sense of God's presence as she opens her front door. We hope that learning how Inge was able to dance and laugh and be joyful after such experiences as losing a baby in war and living with an alcoholic husband will challenge you to search out the spiritual joy in your everyday life. As you go about your daily tasks, perhaps the image of Martha, caring for her farm animals, will remind you that all you do is for the glory of God. Elisabeth found a sense of herself in the writing of her poetry, and we hope that you will feel empowered to honor whatever gifts of self-expression you have. If you are able to visit the sick and homebound in your community, you will, perhaps, come to see that work as giving back to your spiritual community, as having a second chance to comfort others with the Good News of God's love, as did Emma. Or, if you are coping with physical losses, perhaps when you came to know Rebecca, you realized that your losses do not have to mean an end to a powerful service of prayer, for, as she has, you can remain richly connected to the lives of others through this ministry.

IMPLICATIONS FOR WORKING WITH AGING PERSONS

It could be argued that hearing stories of resilient women would only discourage old people who are *not* coping successfully with difficulties in their lives. Would not listening to stories of strength make those who are currently having difficulties with a loss or transition feel even more inadequate? If you are an old woman who, because of fear, never goes out of her house, does it help to know about Inge and her skiing? If you are guilt ridden in your seventies, stuck on mistakes you made in your twenties, do you want to hear about Anna, who has managed to leave her guilt behind? If you are a widow of five years who cannot seem to stop grieving for her husband, what benefit is there to you in reading about Miriam and her ability to say goodbye to so many loved ones?

Certainly, sharing stories of resilient persons must be done with the same care, good timing, and tact required by any therapeutic intervention. It is important, too, that the women in this book not be held up as perfect saints. Doing that would fly in the face of both the reality of their mistakes and the Lutheran theology in which they believe.[1] The women in this book do not claim spiritual perfection; in fact they do not have a sense of being special or unusual in any way. To paraphrase Selma Steenbuck's words about Anna, they "do not know what they have." Rather, they humbly take their places among the members of a spiritual community.

The authors of this book believe that people similar to the eight women described here could be found in most places of worship across the world. There are untold stories similar to these everywhere; there are many spiritually resilient persons who could serve as models for others. These women are not unique, nor should they be described as such. They are part of the human family. At times they have felt nearly overwhelmed by their circumstances and exigencies. Transitions and losses have been difficult, but they have not found supernatural ways to escape the pain and ambiguities of life. They are robust examples of spiritual resiliency because they not only coped with losses, but transcended them. Not through extraordinary virtue or even spiritual sanctification, but through the strengths they found in spiritual community, in emotionally rich faith experiences, and in loving relationships, were they able to move on and out of difficulties and go to work for the larger fellowship. Community as the source of their strength was held up repeatedly and honored as the primary reason they could go on. They integrated their emotional and religious lives and they focused on strength-giving relationships with others. Those are the springs of the spiritual water they drank; to pour out carefully such waters for others who are thirsty is an act of compassionate ministry.

People who hurt are, indeed, thirsty for encouraging stories of "survivors." For example, although currently controversial for some of its practices, one of the most successful community-like organizations in this country is Alcoholics Anonymous. When people who are struggling to turn their lives around return from their first AA meeting, they frequently say something like, "It was so good to hear about someone else who had it worse than me and who has been sober for ten years." The vulnerability risked by those in recovery who share their journeys can be more than an inspiration for those who are slowly moving out of denial. It is also an embodiment of what survivorship looks like.

Often it is the loss of hope, the impossibility of moving past despair and seeing alternative outcomes, that overwhelms those who are aging. Stories of resiliency in old age can, like the stories of any group of survivors, be hope giving and life restoring. If the narratives of strong women, like those you read here, are told with a light, nonmoralistic, and empathetic touch, they can impart inspiration and fresh optimism to those who previously foresaw only catastrophe. We hope that many such stories will be told, as we all work together to re-create our idea of what it means to grow old.

FINDINGS IN RELATION TO CLINICAL PERSPECTIVES

We detected much congruence between our research findings and the three therapeutic orientations described in Chapter 2. Nevertheless, we believe that the picture of spiritual resiliency found in these old women offers important correctives to the individualistic and overly rationalistic themes sometimes emphasized by therapists using cognitive-behavioral, existential, and narrative therapies.

Cognitive Therapy

Like those who have successfully concluded cognitive-behavioral therapy, the women we met are experts both at reframing and at follow-through actions. They do not engage in self-talk that inspires irrational fears and contributes to the vicious cycle of anxiety. They combine calm, rational thinking with faith as a *felt* experience, including the experience of God's presence. Skilled at decisive thinking, they have learned to state a situation for what it is—a problem to be solved, not a disaster. They argue with themselves and with their own fears and go on, eventually, to replace anxiety with hope and confidence. They engage in lives of active serving and find ways to contribute to the community at whatever activity level they can manage.

Miriam, for example, has learned to reframe the frightening experience of going away from home alone. She asks the Lord "to take care of me and bring me home safe." Although it is hard for her not to have her loved ones there with her, she manages her anxieties through her interpretation that God is present as she opens the door and leaves her home. Similarly, Martha reported how her feelings about being alone differ from those of her sister, a "worrier."

> I know He's there. I believe if the devil walked through that door, I don't believe he'd scare me. I never have felt that way.

For both of these women, who no longer have family members living in their homes, spiritual resiliency allows them to reframe a potential frightening situation as one that, though not ideal, is tolerable. They can do this because the experience of God's presence leads them to feel they are not alone.

Although sometimes conceding the need to combine faith and cognitive therapies, counselors frequently do not understand how powerful this combination can be in working with older clients. Whether or not the counselor shares the client's belief system, it is important to recognize spiritual strength when one sees it and to be willing to help the client explore ways in which his or her faith in God's presence might lessen anxieties. The Christian faith is rich in beliefs that can aid in reframing catastrophic thoughts. "It's terrible that I am alone now" might be transformed via hopeful substitutions congruent with spirituality into "But I'm not really alone because God is with me." Rebecca explained why this sense of Presence has kept her from despair:

> I know He's right here. I know He's always there. It has always seemed like that to me. Even when my husband had a stroke and was laid up for forty-eight years. I never questioned God and I didn't get bitter like some people.

Other worries expressed by these women are common in old age, including the fear of dying alone (Miriam), anxieties about the next generation (Emma), and the fear of increasing disability (Elisabeth). They each found different ways to deal with their uneasiness, but all revealed some element of reliance on God's presence in their lives. Counselors spend much time and energy working with clients on expanding their "support systems," but how often do they speak with comfort and naturalness about the spiritual support system on which so many old people rely?

Perhaps the most commonly mentioned concern of aging people is the fear of becoming dependent on others. But this anxiety, too, is reframed by spiritually resilient old women. Neither dependence nor independence but *interdependence* becomes the focus of their lives, interdependence based on a lifestyle that embraces spiritual community. They see themselves neither as objects of care nor as fiercely individualistic and self-reliant. They need each other and they need God; they give to each other and they work for God. At one end of the activity spectrum is Rebecca. She is blind, almost deaf, and can go nowhere without the help of others. Yet she views her need for help not as an alarming dependency but as a natural opportunity for the church family to participate in mutual support and reciprocity. When she spoke of this, it was without self-pity or fear. Similarly, Emma was able to accept financial gifts from others without injury to her sense of dignity. For her, these were signs of God at work; she spiritually reframes as "God's gift" what others would dread as economic dependency. Referring to money given to her so that she could attend a retreat, she said,

> And then she [the friend] sent me that! And that was indeed a gift from God."

On the other hand, Martha's life appears at first glance as amazingly independent. She cares for herself and her farm with tremendous energy and with little outside assistance. Yet she became almost angry when labeled self-sufficient; she insisted on acknowledging her reliance on God.

> I truly feel that anything we do we should do it as a praise to God. 'Cause He has given us the strength to do these things.

Many examples of spiritual reframing go beyond personal belief to incorporating a sense of spiritual community. When Elisabeth writes her poetry, not only is she able to move from despair into confidence in God, but she feels she is writing for the whole community. Emma's visitations to sick and homebound persons are not for her own sanctification so much as on behalf of the congregation's outreach. Her effort is anchored firmly in a sense of community. But assuaging fears is not the only conceivable result of learning spiritual reframing. Joy is also a reality. Emma, who has moved past what she believes to be a German propensity for overseriousness, professes that this joy is hard-won.

> But, no, that one goes there [to communion] with joy and takes part in the Lord's Supper, that He is there and says to us, "Yes, I have died for you, and I have given myself up for you," that is a joy.

The eight women we met have learned how to *think*.

Existential Therapy

The questions of meaning that are the foci of existential therapies were richly evident throughout the interviews, confirming the appropriateness of this therapeutic approach for working with old persons. Here, too, community, affect, and relationships with others were consistently interwoven in the picture of resiliency that emerged.

Inge found pleasure and significance in being able to do simple things, such as dancing, being with others, and gazing at the beauty of the church interior. Rebecca, who is no longer able to leave her chair, believes that God is in charge of her life and that her ministry of prayer is important to the whole community. She lives to pray and to fulfill whatever God has in mind for her; she is God's servant and finds meaning in what she believes to be a morally upright, theologically sound life. Reminiscent of Frankl's stories of persons who watched the stars in the concentration camps,[2] Lovey finds meaning in her appreciation of nature, in looking at the world God made. Along with her love for friends and family, she finds sufficiency in taking her part as a creature in the Creator's world. Martha's meaning revolves around work, and she defines herself as a worker in God's Kingdom.

The women did not hesitate to share emotional aspects of their search for meaning. As they sought to find themselves and the meaning of their lives, they cried, laughed, and sighed. From the tears of the interviews and German focus group to the laughter in the American group, there was no gap between their existential questions and powerful human feeling. Because they felt safe in their communities, they could share what M. Scott Peck referred to as the "lost art of crying."[3] Miriam, for example, cried as she spoke of her mother's illness and death, but she also articulated how caretaking had given meaning to her life.

> When my husband died in '79, my mother lived next door. So she was

getting old and I felt like she needed to be with me, and I was alone so I brought her down here to live with me. Then she died in '86. But the last three years she was almost bedfast. So I had it real hard again, but I came through it, and I feel like I've been enriched by it.

Her emotional and existential courage cannot be understood apart from the community in which she lived and from which she drew strength. As Peck wrote about his own emotional experiences,

It was no accident that I relearned "the lost art of crying" at the age of thirty-six while I was in a true community setting. Despite this relearning, my early training in rugged individualism was sufficiently effective that even today I can cry in public only when I am in a safe place. One of my joys, whenever I return to community, is that the "gift of tears" is extended to me. I am not alone. Once a group has achieved community, the single most common thing members express is: "I feel safe here."[4]

The search for meaning is often characterized as a solitary matter, yet these women's endeavors were definitely communal. One vivid example of how the community functions to support those who are questioning occurred after the focus group meeting in Germany, when the women found ways to reach out to Frau C. She was despairing because of feeling God's absence, so the other women in the community took it as their responsibility to invite her into spiritual dialogue. Elisabeth spoke of how her spiritual retreats with other Christians address questions of self-identity and life purpose; Miriam learned to accept suffering and loss through gratitude for her pastor and friends in the church, her new family.

Clearly, these women have learned how to *be*.

Narrative Therapy

The world of these spiritual nominees is anything but "destoried."[5] They are able to externalize their problems, rewrite their plot lines, and visualize their narratives within a larger, ongoing story. They create their stories with heart as well as mind. They have a sense of the many ways in which their individual stories intersect with the stories of others to whom they relate, including friends and family. Their stories are part of the larger story of God's People, and they are, therefore, able to move along the path of spiritual development—*der Weg*, as Emma called it, "the way." Rather than telling problem-saturated stories in which they appear as victims, they tell stories rich in choices, empowerment, and second chances.

There is no question that even as they spoke, the women were participating in reconstructing the reality of their experiences. The ways in which our research project encouraged a narrative process that was helpful and healing are not all known to us; there is no way to unweave the narratives that were told into the parts that became different in the telling and the parts that remained as they were told before. Their stories created them as much as they created their stories. Such restorying was not the goal of the project, but it occurred nevertheless, as in all narrations of one's life.

When one considers the external events of their lives, there would be ample reasons for these women to write stories with the theme, "poor me!" An example is Rebecca's situation: she is homebound, blind, almost deaf, and disabled. Yet her narrative is totally lacking in self-pity; she sees her physical ailments as just one part of who she is, not as the defining element of her selfhood. She has vision problems; she is not "the blind woman."

Emma's story line, shortly after the death of her husband, was faltering. Here the love and concern of her children were helpful and led to a new story line. "Get a life," they told her, and the life she got was one so new and hopeful that she was almost sheepish in telling how much happier she is now. Her days are filled with Bible groups, worship, calling on the homebound. Her *Weg*, her faith pilgrimage, is now the theme of her life, and the time after the loss of her spouse has became a new chapter titled, "A Second Chance."

The women's narratives were full of continuity as well as change. Lifelong Lutherans, their old stories already contained important themes that had no need to be abandoned. Only revisions were needed, in keeping with new situations, new insights, and increased maturity. This is consistent with emphases in narrative therapy. Wrote Parry and Doan, "If these themes are important in the old story, there is no need to assume that they must be totally abandoned or labeled as bad or ineffective in the new version. Rather, they need to be reinterpreted."[6] One other example is the almost childlike persona Inge has created for herself. Now, however, she is no longer the child of the family of origin where she was once adored; rather, she defines herself as a child of God, a member of His family of believers.

Perhaps the most dramatic rewrite told in this book is that of Anna. Her narrative now is anchored in community, but her early chapters had been filled with the theme "me." Her persona was, she said, overly individualistic and rebellious. Then she found a more active role in the Christian community, where a *Geländer* (handrail) was available to guide her. She did not rewrite her story to excuse herself or deny that she had made bad choices in becoming a member of the Nazi Youth Party. Instead, she encouraged her whole community to participate in a rewrite, and one result was discussion of the Nazi era in the city jubilee book.[7] Anna's spirituality allows her to externalize evil, such as the evil that came with Hitler, and go on to work against corruption in a variety of ways—as her town's mayor, as an activist in ecology and world peace movements, and as a courageous host to those who would prefer to forget. When she says, in effect, "never forget," she is also saying, "Evil will never write my story again."

Anna, like the other women we met, knows how to *tell* her own story.

SUFFERING AND QUESTIONS OF MEANING

This book was written because of an intersection of the practical and the personal. Inevitably a moment comes when a question such as the following occurs to all of us who work with or on behalf of elderly people: How might *I* handle serious losses when I am old? We know that the need for emotional connections and supportive relationships is particularly urgent after a serious personal crisis. Yet persons who have lost a loved one or endured a health crisis often report that, in spite of the many caring people who assist and surround them, they experience a painful feeling of being alone. Friends, family members, even pastors and other professionals often seem either to pull back emotionally or rush in insensitively, saying or doing precisely the least helpful, most inappropriate thing. Why is this? Do people stop caring during hard times? Certainly not, for the cards and casseroles do arrive, sent with obvious love and compassion. Yet the bereaved one typically feels isolated in his or her grief.

Most likely it is fear, not lack of caring, that is at the root of this breakdown in effectual support. This fear may lead friends, family, clergy, and even counselors to emotional withdrawal. We withdraw, excusing ourselves, citing feelings of awkwardness, such as, "I didn't know what to say to her." Or we make remarks that sound more glib than reassuring, "I know this is God's will and it is all for the best." To understand this common failure in human outreach during times of grief, one must acknowledge and recognize a pervasive human fear. It prevents us from being fully present with someone who has just had a significant loss; it arises after we realize that the crisis our friend, client, or parishioner is experiencing could someday be our own. Their pain could someday come to us. We, too, could be hurting and alone. Especially after the blindness of youth has past, when we stand on the frightening pinnacle of middle age, able for the first time to look behind us at our imperfect history and ahead into an uncertain and limited future, we realize that we, too, will face limitations, losses, suffering, our own decline, and death. Not everyone is ready for the view from this hill; it is a hard reality to face. It brings up questions we would rather not ask. "What would I do if this crisis were to happen to me? Am I strong enough? Could I survive that? How would I manage if I lost my health? My husband? A child?"

The authors of this book believe that it is crucial for those of us who wish to comfort older persons to be aware of this intrapsychic dynamic. On the rational level, we may want to be fully available to people who are hurting, to be helpful beyond the level of practical assistance, to enter as completely as possible into their pain as well as celebrate with them their joys. But if we are stuck in personal fears that lead us to doubt our own abilities to survive, we will stay powerless and helpless. No amount of education, supervision, or clinical experience can compensate for the lack of ability to be emotionally present with a grieving person.

Spiritual growth and development is, therefore, crucial for the counselor, the pastor, the friend. And it is decidedly possible. As the stories you read here demonstrate, it is possible to begin life as a willful, rebellious young woman, trusting only in her own opinions, and to grow into a wise and respected leader in later years. It is possible to change one's perspectives about suffering so that even monumental losses can be survived and transcended, even the ultimate loss of separation at death. As these eight women found out, even "ordinary saints"[8] can be healed from a paralyzing fear of suffering, enabling them to participate in the healing of others. Both life experiences and these spiritual nominees teach us that, clearly, some people survive terrible losses with remarkable resiliency while others crumble under apparently trivial circumstances. To find the answer to this mystery, we turn not to the data of social science alone but to questions of meaning and issues of the spirit.

To meet older women of great spiritual resiliency and recount their stories is a life-altering experience. Both authors are grateful not only for the welcomes leading to international friendships but also for the spiritual growth it has facilitated in our own lives. Like the women in this study, our faith experiences became an intertwining of the personal, the emotional, and a strong sense of world community. In her personal journal, written during the initial stages of this project, Ramsey noted,

I will always be grateful for this experience. It's difficult to express all the feelings going on inside me. Being in a foreign country, feeling welcomed as a fellow Christian and as a woman. I constantly feel gratitude for all those who have brought me to this point. And above all, to God, who has kept me safe.

Blieszner described her involvement in this project as a pull toward a spiritual element within her that had been latent and not fully realized yet was often a highly attractive and powerful force. Soon after joining in the writing of this book, she e-mailed Ramsey,

This is all fitting into some strange call to live my faith more consciously than ever. You'll see—I've decided the only way I can write the journal is to write letters to you. If you're getting me into this extended spiritual journey, which is what I've come to think of our project, then you'll just have to read my letters along with everything else!

NOTES

1. See, for example, Tillich, 1963, p. 230.
2. Frankl, 1969.
3. Peck, 1987, p. 67.
4. Peck, p. 67.
5. White & Epston, 1990.
6. Parry & Doan, 1994, p. 50.
7. Kurtz, 1982.
8. Benne, 1988.

CHAPTER 11

Implications for Gerontology

IMPLICATIONS FOR RESEARCH ON SUCCESSFUL AGING

From its beginning in 1955, the motto of the Gerontological Society of America has called for "adding life to years, not just more years to life."[1] As the narratives of the women in this book have shown, the spiritually resilient life is one that can certainly be lively and worthwhile. This research takes its place in the academy beside other studies emphasizing the human capacity for adaptive competence. Like theirs, its two primary emphases are positive: (a) the conviction that later years offer opportunities and challenges as well as problems and losses and (b) the belief that elders are best viewed as resources in families and communities rather than as problems to be solved.

Currently, an important area in the investigation of adaptive competence is research on successful aging, which explores the boundaries of human potential in the later years. Influenced by the scientific concepts of *interindividual variability* and *intraindividual plasticity*, this research is based on the principles of selection, compensation, and optimization. Baltes and Baltes wrote that, beginning with the Roman philosopher Cicero (106-43 B.C.), at least some people have refused to view old age as merely a time of decay and decline and have emphasized, instead, opportunities for "positive change and productive functioning" in the later years.[2] For these people, fears and anxieties about old age can make way for new feelings that are more harmonious and satisfactory to persons as they age.

Although such thinking could be called unrealistic, elitist, or utopian, an important purpose for this line of thought is that it can expand the horizons of human imagination and potential. This study of older women's spirituality is related to research on successful aging through its positive emphasis on aging and because of its contribution to the search for those elusive factors that contribute to an optimal experience of aging.[3]

Similar to the approach of other research on successful aging, our positive emphasis here is juxtaposed to a recognition of the sometimes harsh realities of aging. Losses, death, and the possibility of deep regret have not been ignored in this project because they are themes that cannot be ignored in the women's stories. Just as Baltes and Baltes argued that biological realities of aging must be borne in mind when testing the limits of psychological potential, so it is important to acknowledge the emotional realities of loss and sorrow when exploring the limits of spiritual potential. Understanding this "in spite of" quality of faith is an option if one wishes to be credible with the very person who, as Baltes and Baltes wrote, "might be the one who has most often lost friends, most often stood at open graves, and perhaps, most often endured illness."[4]

FURTHER SIGNIFICANCE OF THIS RESEARCH WITHIN GERONTOLOGY

We present this study as a model for future research. To the best of our knowledge, triangulated, qualitative methodology with a cross-cultural focus and denominational specificity combine here for the first time in an empirical study of older women's faith. Our approach responds to the call of Atchley and others for the "evolution of adaptive new structural forms" in the study and research of gerontology. We have been energized by the "anarchy in the marketplace of ideas" in these postmodern, multidisciplinary times[5] and wish to join in the fight against the tendency to "leave religion off the map"[6] in gerontology. With other scholars who risk working without a positivist paradigm in order to open up new understandings, we have searched out themes and categories for understanding women's spiritual experiences in the later part of life. We recognize that this research is exploratory and will require much future work to fill in deeper levels of understanding.

We believe that the empirical (experiential) nature of this work is part of its significance. It was said several decades ago that anthropological work on religion since World War II has made "no theoretical advances of major importance. It is living off the conceptual capital of its ancestors."[7] Although this critique may no longer be completely true, empirical studies in religion and the social sciences are still rarely conducted, and, in gerontology, those that exist have been slow to use qualitative tools. Only through research that takes some methodological risks does the potential exist to discover new categories of meaning; from innovative methodology, new concepts are more likely to emerge that can then be used as assets for the future.

SIGNIFICANCE OF THIS RESEARCH WITHIN FEMINISM

In light of the debate over the work of Carol Gilligan,[8] it has been interesting to see how the *relational* and traditional sides of these women's spirituality come together, as discussed earlier. But more important, to us, this book has included an advocacy proponent. Saiving said, "As an older woman, I sometimes wonder whether the women's movement is made up exclusively of women between the ages of 16 and 45, for so little is ever said about what it means to be human after the latter age."[9] We strongly believe that paying attention to the voices of *older* women is long overdue in the women's movement. The mistake of ignoring diversity, which was made early on with different ethnic groups, is now being committed with respect to older women. This study takes a place among work that aims to correct that sin of omission.

The study also has significance within feminism because it reveals stories not yet told and gives heed to voices not yet heard. It has been exciting to see the interest in our book by the older women who participated in the focus groups and interviews. They *want* their stories to be told; they *wish* to be helpful to future generations. In her "Letter to Readers" in the second edition of her book *In a Different Voice*, Gilligan wrote that she sees her work as "part of the process that it describes—the ongoing historical process of changing the voice of the world by bringing women's voices into the open, thus starting a new conversation."[10] This study participates in the same process. Opportunities to listen to the special concerns and unique voices of older women of spiritual depth can only enrich all of us.

SIGNIFICANCE FOR THE STUDY AND PRACTICE
OF SPIRITUALITY

At the conclusion of his book tracing the history of spirituality, Holt suggested what he saw as needed by Christian spirituality in contemporary times. He called for "a *listening spirituality*" (emphasis in original), stating "We must be willing to hear the voices from continents and ages other than our own."[11] The findings of this study are not just academic; they have a role to play in expanding the horizons of the practice of the Christian life. There is significance in demonstrating how a partnership between the social sciences and religious institutions can focus on listening. This activity is vital not only in today's academic research, where scholars are often urged to find their voice, but also in spirituality, where listening for God has been central throughout the ages. Lovers of books though we are, we also agree that "A kind of knowledge is available to us from books, but personal knowledge, the kind that really counts, can come only from experience."[12] By listening to older women who listen for God, we can learn patterns of resiliency so important in gerontology, and we can experience something of God's passionate love.

IMPLICATIONS FOR CHURCH PRACTICE AND POLICY

The various ways in which the voices of these women might be relevant to church practices could be the topic of another book. We present a few initial observations here. If spiritual resiliency is, for many older Lutheran women, tied closely to their experiences in community, then those who participate in what is called "ministry to the elderly" must bear this in mind. An occasional pastoral visit to a shut-in and the receipt of the parish newsletter (too often published in small print and, therefore, unreadable) may be the only signs to an older person in frail health that he or she is still part of a religious community. Visits by a variety of members; being recognized as a minister through one's prayers on behalf of the church family; continuing education opportunities, especially Bible study for spiritual formation; calls, cards, and letters that remind the older person of the whole family's love and concern—all are crucial. But even when older members can attend church services, they often experience a youth-centered environment and ageist denials that make it difficult for them to feel incorporated into the group. Simmons[13] proposed that worship rituals should name the life-stage issues so important to older members publicly; this study validates such a suggestion.

Another minor but significant finding was the frequency of "memory words" in the conversations of these resilient women. We suggest an obvious application: that the planners of religious education reexamine their methods. In years past, memorization of Bible verses, creeds, and prayers was a common part of Sunday School and confirmation classes. Modern approaches have de-emphasized memory work in favor of explanations and discussions of relevance to daily life.

However, what are younger cohort groups receiving now that can replace these words and verses? Consider Rebecca, with her physical limitations, and how crucial her memory is to her. It allows her to work (or, she would say, God works) a wonderful chemistry, a spiritual reframing, so that her suffering and difficulties become blessings. She does so chiefly as she meditates on memorized texts and applies them to her life. Christian education that ignores this need may appear modern, but it will be less helpful during the long years at the end of life that most of us will experience.

Ultimately, the spiritual resiliency of another human being remains beyond the ability of scholars to describe or define. Just as each symphony creates a particular and special sound, so the marvelous, complex interweaving of the themes of personality, history, culture, and faith in each life story is unique. Yet if members of the religious community honor their older friends as the spiritual resources that they are, careful listening will allow them to recognize patterns of resiliency and to discover springs of strength more than sufficient for a lifetime of faithful living.

NOTES

1. Quoted in Baltes & Baltes, 1990, p. 5.
2. Baltes & Baltes, 1990, p.16.
3. Baltes & Baltes, 1990, p. 4.
4. Baltes & Baltes, 1990, p. 5.
5. Atchley, 1993, p. 16.
6. Thomas & Eisenhandler, 1994.
7. Geertz, 1973, p. 87.
8. Gilligan, 1993.
9. Saiving, 1988, p. 117.
10. Gilligan, 1993, p. xxvii.
11. Holt, 1993, p. 127.
12. Holt, 1993, p. 129.
13. Simmons, 1990.

The Gracious Encounters Continue

Writing this book has not only *led* to a series of gracious encounters, it was *built* on them as well. As we planned this work and then listened to women who listen for God, we participated in experiences of personal dialogues on a variety of levels. Some of these meetings were between the two authors. Some were interviews between the women and us, and still other encounters occurred among the women themselves, drawing them closer to one another.

But throughout all of these, we experienced another dimension as well. We believe that our human comings-together took place under the care of a Holy Presence, that God, too, encountered us. To our eyes, this divine dimension gave depth and power to the human meetings, and we find evidence that we are still being strengthened in this way today.

There were many times when the long interviews were difficult for the participants, when old sorrows reappeared and brought tears. Yet overall, the women have reported that this experience has deepened and enriched their own faith. As we discovered months later during our trips back to Blue Ridge and to Wilster, the women had found some questions to be troublesome yet growth provoking. "They were not easy to answer, but they have made me think and draw closer to God," was a comment we often heard.

Although we, too, experienced times of discouragement, worry, and dryness while we conducted this research and wrote this book, we believe that God was present with us, perhaps more so during difficult times than during those that were easy. The lives of our spiritual nominees suggest that this was so for them as well. Just as they could see, looking back on their lives, that God was their strength and the source of their resiliency, so we see now that God was present with us, even when we did not realize it and were too caught up in the moment to sense it. A typical journal entry, written soon after I (Ramsey) arrived in Wilster and before the first interview in German, certainly reveals need for this help.

> But will the women trust me enough to open up to me? Why should they? I guess I'll have to leave that concern to tomorrow, and to God.

Looking back on our conversations with these strong women, we can now see how God met and supported them as they spoke and enabled us to listen. While we recognize that not all readers will have this point of view, we risk labeling this as "a gracious encounter" with the ultimate Source of resiliency.

Since the time of the first interviews, the Steenbucks have met Rosemary Blieszner and served again as gracious host and hostess to us both. They traveled to Virginia and became acquainted with our families and our communities. Karl and Selma's contributions were of major significance, and it is no exaggeration to say that the German part of the research could not have been conducted without their help. It has been great fun for both of us to become close friends with them, to be addressed now as *du*, the familiar form of "you."

We were delighted to discover that the spiritual nominees extended gentle gestures of friendship across the ocean, expanding their Christian community in the process. In response to a letter from the American focus group, the German women wrote to their sisters:

> Dear Women of Glade Creek Lutheran Church,
>   Splendid thanks for your greetings which we received at Christmastime. We have much joy concerning our conversations with Jan Ramsey. We send you many greetings from Germany.
>   [Signed by the members of the focus group.]

Another delightful layer of continuing encounters is the increase in friendship bonds experienced by the old women themselves as a result of their coming together for this project. In Germany, particularly, the group that met for the first time as a focus group when this research began has been meeting on a monthly basis ever since. Together with their pastor, they discuss how their spirituality can be increased and woven into matters of everyday life. They support each other during times of crises and doubt, and they sing, laugh, and share faith stories. Needless to say, we are very pleased that this has occurred!

In Blue Ridge, the women have not met again but have gotten to know each other better through reading about each other in the interview transcripts we shared with them. When Lovey died last year, Pastor Maier read sections of the transcript at her funeral so that her own words of faith and encouragement could help her family and friends deal with their grief.

We could never have anticipated that the focus group in Germany would continue or that the interviews would become the stuff of funeral sermons. But by far the most exciting spillover occurred far away and was not known to us for some time. On our last trip to Wilster, we learned that Anna had been having difficulties in her relationship with her daughter for some years, primarily as a result of misunderstandings that arose when her daughter entered psychoanalysis. When the English-language transcript was mailed to Anna, this daughter translated it into German for her. After her daughter did so, they had some new dialogues, and an improved relationship resulted. It is nice to think that seeing Anna and her many gifts through our eyes may have helped.

When we visited Germany in the summer of 1997, we met with the spiritual nominees for feedback on the research report and we also participated in one of the monthly discussion meetings. Each of the four spiritual nominees proudly introduced herself to me (Blieszner) using her pseudonym; each had a copy of the section that summarized aspects of her spirituality. Anna's youngest daughter and Emma's son had translated their sections into German (the son had said he would do it when he had a chance, but he actually completed the translation one day later!). Karl translated Inge's and Elisabeth's sections orally for them.

First, we had a chance to speak with the four spiritual nominees. Jan asked the women to tell us their perceptions of the accuracy of the summaries and how they felt when reading about themselves. All four agreed that most of the description was accurate except for some minor details. Anna stated that the description of her as a model of faith was too grand, too complimentary—she does not see herself that way. The other three women were also very modest and said the descriptions of them were too kind. Elisabeth mentioned that she had not shown the transcript to her husband at first, but then she did later. Anna showed hers only to the daughter who translated it. But that daughter made copies for her siblings to read, and then they had a family meeting to discuss it—they were so proud of their mother!

Anna said that participating in the study gave her the possibility of reflecting on and seeing the fruits of her life. Then, reading the transcript was like looking into her life as in a mirror. All the struggles she experienced now have a new meaning because other people will know about them. Furthermore, Anna appreciated the way the research experience helped the women of St. Bartolomäus Kirche form the ongoing discussion group and enabled them to have interesting and meaningful conversations. She said she was honored to have been involved in the project, and she presented Jan with a letter expressing her joy at meeting her and her affection for her.

Inge mentioned that participating in the interviews had been difficult because the questions were more abstract than the topics she usually discusses with others. Thus, she had to concentrate hard in order to stay focused on the interview. All the women agreed that no one asks these questions in daily life. They have continued to think about these matters since the interviews had taken place. Overall, Inge thought taking part in the interview was a very enjoyable experience.

Emma came to realize how important her faith is and believed that participating in the study strengthened her faith. She showed the transcript about her only to one of her sons because her children do not share her faith or understand the depth of it. She and Inge wore the Holy Spirit (dove) pins that Jan had given them two years ago. Elisabeth said hers had "flown away!"

The women wanted to know why anyone would be interested in them, so we explained how we have used the stories in speeches, counseling, teaching, and in this book. We emphasized how the stories inspire and help people.

Our next meeting was with the members of the original focus group and some additional women who have since joined the monthly discussions. When I (Blieszner) entered the parish hall where the meeting was to take place, I was overwhelmed at the beauty of the room and tables. Inge and Selma had worked hard to make it look special. They had placed the tables in a large square and covered them with crisp white damask cloths. The tables were set with white china, bright yellow napkins poking out of the cups like big flowers, yellow lighted candles, and bouquets of huge-headed yellow and purple pansies. There were candles and flowers on the altar at the side of the room, as well. One of the women played the piano as everyone gathered and greeted one another.

Karl claimed everyone's attention and explained that first they would sing Jan and me a welcoming song, then he would introduce us to them, the women would introduce themselves to us, and we would discuss the research project. The beautiful song, based on Psalm 104, gave praise for the beauty of summer. The women sang in harmony—what a special moment! Then Karl interpreted for them my explanation of my work and our plans to write a book based on this research. The women were very curious about their American research project sisters and indeed, about how older adults fare in America. In introducing themselves, some women mentioned how much they appreciated the opportunity to meet and talk together every month.

After an interlude with coffee, pastries, and much animated conversation and laughter, Karl once again called for attention and asked Jan to speak. She told the group about her research and the fact that the journey continues, as evidenced by their ongoing meetings and by her use of the stories in her therapy sessions and speaking engagements. She described the three themes that emerged from the data analysis—the importance of community, affect, and personal relationships—and made some comparisons across the German and American women. In closing the meeting, Karl invited everyone to pray the Lord's Prayer and he blessed us all. The women sang a song of praise, again breaking into harmony spontaneously at the third verse, which gave me goose bumps. They arranged the meeting date and discussion topic for the next meeting and went out to the garden to take photos.

Our relationship as joint authors has led to many extended conversations about other aspects of our respective personal and professional lives, yielding an enlarged sense of our own spiritual community. Jan often told me (Blieszner) about her efforts to help clients in therapy write different narratives of their difficult situations by using examples of coping and resiliency from the women in this book. She has also found sources of inspiration to share with clients from our conversations. For example, one day I recounted to her a powerful religious experience that I had had: During Lent, our pastor asked the congregation to write their concerns, frustrations, sins, and other woes on small strips of muslin. The idea was to offer them to God as a way of releasing them. Each week, the strips were tacked to a cross that was carried in and out at the beginning and end of Mass, and the woes were woven into prayer petitions sung during Mass. More and more strips were added to the cross as the weeks of Lent progressed. During the Good Friday service, Father Lemay took up the strips, which had been sewn into a long narrow length, and while a hymn was sung, he wound the wrapping around and around the crucifix, until the figure of Jesus was completely bound up in woes. The crucifix remained shrouded until the triumph of Easter Sunday. Jan has used this story with several clients, all of whom have wept in response to the paradoxical idea of so much sadness borne by Jesus but then transformed into joyful relief.

This book began with an invitation to listen, and it concludes with one as well. After reading the stories of these eight remarkable senior women, we invite you to make a practice of listening to old persons, both men and women, and to the life stories they have to tell. In congregations of many faiths around the world exist powerful, healing models of spiritual resiliency—old people of strength and courage. Their stories not only instruct, they inspire. As you can see, these venerable elderly not only teach about coping during losses; their stories build friendship and hope. We hope that you have learned with us something of how the discipline of careful attending can have its rich rewards, particularly when one listens to women who listen for God.

Research Journal

The following pages contain the research journal written by Ramsey during the course of planning the study, conducting the focus group meetings and in-depth interviews, analyzing the data, and interpreting the results. Researchers keep such a journal to record their observations during and reactions to the investigative process. Such notes become a source of data to be analyzed as well as a check on the veracity of the interpretations offered in the discussion of the findings. Recording responses in a journal enables researchers to separate their own feelings and reactions from those of the study participants. We present these notes to aid readers in understanding both the research process and the person who conducted the main interviews.

SEPTEMBER 20, 1994

This morning I've been reading John's version of Jesus's conversation with the Samaritan woman (John 4:7ff), and a strange verse stood out for me, verse 27: *Just then his disciples came. They were astonished that he was speaking with a woman, but no one said, "What do you want?" or "Why are you speaking with her?"*

Not one of his disciples gave Jesus a hard time about breaking both the gender (and the racial) rules. They probably thought plenty, but they didn't say a word. The Samaritan woman ran off to tell everyone what she had learned and that Jesus might be the Christ. She wasn't sure, but she was excited enough to go tell everyone, just in case . . .

So often I see, or think I see, the same kind of look that I image was on the disciples' faces that day. "What are you doing, wearing that clerical collar . . . standing up there by that altar . . . even parking in the clergy parking lot?" I get so tired of it, of seeing the unspoken questions on faces. But I overreact, I am easily hurt.

Why I am so touchy, so easily bruised? Why can't I just ignore it and go running off, like the Samaritan woman, to tell everyone how thrilled I am that my Lord stopped for a while and "talked" to me, explained things to me, that He took a hard look at my life and told me to worship you "in spirit and truth"? No less incredible that He would do that with me than with her: I'm not Jewish, or male, and my marital history, like that of this woman, is less than perfect. Yet He has come to me, He gives me "the time of day," and so much more.

Sometimes I feel just as free and excited and spontaneous as she was that day, and those are the times I'm listening to God. But inside me, too, are places were I hurt, where I'm afraid and insecure, where I'm afraid that maybe I just don't measure up.

Lord, be with me through this day. Let your peace stay with me, guide me, give me security and the assurance that you care for me, want me to be yours. Forgive the stupid, petty times. Continue to heal the scars I've gotten from rejections by others and from self-inflicted wounds. Draw me near to you through the keeping of this journal, through my writing, through this research. Still voices within and help me to listen to your voice.

DECEMBER 29, 1994

I've just finished my first interview with a spiritual nominee. It was a good experience; I feel privileged to have listened to Rebecca, the 93-year-old woman I met, and to have been let into her life.

I also feel somewhat sad. Maybe I'm wrong, but I'm afraid that lives like Rebecca's are a thing of the past. The simplicity of her lifestyle, the firm values she holds, the lack of materialism in her environment, the peacefulness: how different and remote it all seems from our family life. Driving home after the interview I wondered, "Can I, can anyone, have a faith as strong and sure as she has in a world that has changed so quickly and is so much more complex than the one in which she grew up?"

Her struggles were in no way less serious than my own: caring all those years for an invalid husband, not having any children in a world where bearing children was expected, the frail health she has now. Yet it seems, on the surface, that her life was so much more quiet and that the distractions from the spiritual life fewer. I came home to write this and found the stereo blaring out from my 22-year-old son's room, the usual raunchy song, and I thought about Rebecca and her worries about people living together before marriage today. Our world has changed. Does she even guess all that is going on, how extensive those changes are?

I kept thinking about the quiet of Rebecca's world. She's no doubt still sitting there, in her chair, listening to a tape. Later she'll eat a simple supper and go early to bed. Yet she's happy, content. My children complain constantly about "boredom." My life is packed with activity and people, every moment of every day. Will I someday sit and remember as she does, my childhood, my family, my church friends and experiences? Will I ever know the kind of peace that she seems to know. "My life is very pleasant," she said. "It's the contentment," I wanted to say. Others would sit there and feel bitter. "I'm alone, but not lonely," she added. What a gift. Oh, how I want to be more like her. I was so alone after my first marriage broke up; growing into being OK with being alone was a real struggle. This trip that begins in two days to Germany will include many alone times, especially when I'm not in Wilster. Will I be able to be alone but not lonely? Do I have a quiet center, like Rebecca?

DECEMBER 30, 1994

I'm packing for the trip to Germany and preparing myself for this adventure. I have such a sense of people going with me, even though I'm traveling alone: Joe, family, friends, the women at Glade Creek and friends at Christ Lutheran. Through all of them, I have a sense of God's presence as well.

I have many anxieties about being able to complete the project in a land with another language and a less-than-familiar culture. I'm anxious, too, about being a burden on the Steenbucks, even though they must be very kind people. It makes me feel so connected to the church, being welcomed like this across the ocean by a pastor and his family. I wonder what life is like for people who have no church roots, connections? That sense of community has always been there for me, and I know often I've taken it for granted. I don't now; an experience like this really helps me to understand how wonderful it is to be part of the Church.

Meanwhile, I pray that my family will be safe and happy while I'm gone. I hope Joe's health will be good and that the children will all thrive. There's always so much to worry about with five kids, all of whom are at different places at different times. I feel none of them has the spiritual center and lifestyle I would wish for them, but I know part of that is their life stage. How ironic that as I study older women, it is my adolescent children who are so much on my mind. Maybe that's a good reminder that the women I'll meet in Wilster, and the women at Glade Creek, were once teenagers, with some of their own emotional and identity struggles. But what a different world they knew. But there must be strengths I can learn from women who grew up so long ago, in such a different world, that would help me and later my children to live courageously in this world, now.

I spoke to a former client who is very bitter about a divorce after a long legal struggle and who always has troubles with holidays. She spoke of the brokenness all around and I agreed, but after last night I wanted to add—but it's the brokenness, and our need for wholeness, that Christmas is all about. I don't fight that idea so much anymore, that the world is broken and imperfect. I don't romanticize my life, my family, as I once did; too much has happened. And I know now that it is the brokenness that makes Christmas necessary—for my family, for me. That includes the brokenness in me, the mistrust and greed and fear. How can you be almost broken by life and yet be whole? How can you "grow back," as Esther said? Maybe that's another reason I want to learn about being resilient. This work is about me, too, much more than I first realized when I picked a topic for a dissertation. Divorced yet happily remarried; disillusioned with my romantic dreams for life, yet hopeful; fearful and filled with doubts, yet believing and listening; clearly, this topic picked me.

JANUARY 2, 1995

I am in Wilster at last. This has been a hectic day of travel from Frankfurt, with the stress level compounded by missing luggage. But the good news is that Wilster is a complete delight and my host family is friendly and gracious. They treat me with warmth and courtesy even though they know me only as "Bob's friend" and as the woman who wrote them letters in simplistic German. Their two sons are also friendly. Michael is quiet and studious, studying to be a lawyer. He gave me an excellent tour of the church but speaks only in German to me because, as Selma, his mother says, he is a bit *genau* (precise). Hearing my German errors should cure him of that! Raphael, "Raf," is his opposite—outgoing, artistic, a long-haired guitar player in a rock band. He will speak English with me and does so very well. I suspect that Michael will do so too as time goes on. I'm trying not to panic, even though the luggage has not arrived by bedtime. Inside the bags is everything I need to do my work here, including cassettes, recorder, translations, laptop computer. I'm telling myself that I certainly need trust, not so much God (my bad planing is not God's emergency) as German efficiency (the bags were lost in the United States, but the German airlines promise to deliver them to our door).

There was interesting conversation with my hosts today despite the language differences. We were trying to get to know one another, especially checking out values and viewpoints. Being Christians doesn't necessarily mean that any two people are in agreement on social and economic issues, obviously. As it turns out, Karl and Selma are liberal in their views, much as I am. I think that increased our comfort level with one another somewhat, but from my point of view, anyone who serves incredible pastries like those I ate here today would be quite acceptable!

I called home for the first time tonight since arriving in Germany. Joe and Brian's voices had an echo, reminding me that there's a great distance between us. Yet love really does keep people close, and I feel my family's presence just as I had hoped I would. Does that mean that when God seems distant it's because our love has grown dim? Surely God's for us never does, so when there's a feeling of isolation and loneliness, it must be because we have tired of loving God and gotten lazy about working on that relationship. So when God has seemed distant to me in my life, it's been because of a failure of love on my part. Those are difficult words for me to say, even to write down in this journal: "I have not always loved God." Yet why should they be more difficult to say than "I have fallen short and sinned." The second statement is abstract; the first is personal. Faith is about this personal relationship, and if I could keep it more on that level in my life, I would love God more and sin less, because it's a lot easier for me to go against an idea than a loved one. Yet it is God whom I hurt when I turn away, God whom I fail to love.

From time to time I feel pangs of loneliness at being in such a strange environment. I keep trying to reframe this as a growth experience. When I start to feel blue, I think about how I'm proving to myself that I, a woman alone, can really do this. And it helps even more to remember Rebecca, the spiritual nominee in Glade Creek, who sits there, alone in her home, blind, 93, and who said to me without a trace of self-pity, "I'm alone, but I'm not lonely." Already one of these woman is a model of strength for me, and the project has just begun. I am so excited to think what stories I'll find here. But will the women trust me enough to open up to me? Why should they? I guess I'll have to leave that concern to tomorrow, and to God.

JANUARY 3, 1995

Today was much better and less stressful. Not only did my luggage finally arrive late today, but I have mostly gotten over that slightly nauseous feeling of jet lag. For the most part, it was a quiet day at home, getting acclimated. I took two walks around the neighborhood and felt very much the stranger. But the beauty of the snow-covered town and the regular ringing of the church bells remind me that I am no stranger to God. The Bible says we are all strangers in this world in a sense, since its values are not our own, not Christian values, and never will be. But because God made the entire earth, for all his creatures, I'm really no more out of place here, in an ultimate sense, than I am in Virginia. Culturally, though, and humanly, its quite different. There are so many things to get used to: the way that Germans eat so quickly (I'm *always* the last one to finish), the proper way to shop (you bring your own sack and bag your own groceries), the way to behave with strangers and acquaintances (don't speak, just nod to strangers who are sharing a close space with you). Of course you say *Guten Tag* (Good day) to acquaintances and *Angenehm* (pleased to meet you) when you meet someone new. *Tschuss* (so long) is for when you're leaving. I am anxious, worrying that I will do something to displease my hosts. If I feel insecure, it's because I'm so dependent on them, I guess; it certainly isn't because they have been anything but fantastic to me. With Selma I feel particularly comfortable. We communicate very well despite my poor pronunciation and her lack of English. It's as though being women and mothers (and overworked!) gives us much in common. We laugh together at women's kinds of issues; like me, she is a feminist but also very committed to her family. Karl is a wonderful person, intense and committed. He loves the church and is very interested in many things; he's so bright and quick, I really enjoy our conversations. He's given me a Barth book to read while I'm here. I can understand his German better than anyone else's because he speaks so succinctly. Yet sometimes he makes me a little anxious because I feel as though he hasn't made up his mind about me yet. I get the feeling that my informality and spontaneity make him a bit uncomfortable.

For my devotions tonight I finally have my own English Bible. It was slightly bent en route but looks so familiar and comforting. When I took it out of the suitcase, it was like seeing an old friend. I found myself yesterday realizing that this old leather Bible would be the personal object that I'd miss most if the suitcase didn't arrive, even though the tape recorders are what I most needed.

God, I ask that you use this experience to work with me and to help me grow spiritually. May even the moments of homesickness and anxiety I feel be reminders that I need to be stronger in my sense of self as your child, and that none of us are ever completely at home in this world.

JANUARY 4, 1995

This morning I woke up sick with a cold and had to cancel my plans to go to Hamburg to explore the city on foot. I couldn't risk spending a day outdoors and being sick tomorrow for the focus group. My hosts were as kind and solicitous as always, and Selma brought me fruit and yogurt in my room in spite of my protests. I must admit that it felt good to be nurtured. I keep thinking the same thing over and over, how small the world is for Christians. If I can travel half way around the world and be accepted here, made to feel part of the family, then that's what we mean when we talk about the "body of Christ." Yet so seldom do we actually experience this unity in a practical way.

Tomorrow is the focus group and my first meeting with the older women of this parish. Will they accept me as the Steenbucks have? Will they talk to me about their lives and their faith? I keep thinking, why *should* they open up to me? Why should they tell me anything personal about themselves? Will the language and cultural barrier make this experience very different from my conversations with Rebecca? My experiences outside this household have certainly not all been so positive. The train conductor overcharged me by several Marks for a cup of coffee and told me the wrong track number (deliberately?). The postmaster yelled loudly at me when he thought I did not understand German. Why should the women be different? Yet my hopes are that they will be, that they too will approach me as a fellow Christian and be kind and cooperative.

At each step of this adventure, I have had to learn to trust again that all will be well. Each difficulty seems to shake my confidence unreasonably. First, at the Roanoke airport, I thought I might not get to fly at all because of the weather. When the plane was announced as a "go," I had such a strong sense that God was helping me. Yet at the very next problem, the loss of my luggage, I had trouble trusting again. Now that I have my luggage and that all is going well with my stay here, I *again* have trouble trusting God. I keep thinking everything is up to me and my skills, yet I also have a strong sense that I have God's support with this project, that I am being used here in spite of my poor faith and many insecurities. Prayer helps; I find that when I take my concerns to God honestly and confess my anxieties, they diminish on the spot—not disappear, but diminish.

God, I ask now that you be with me on this day, and tomorrow. May my meeting with the German women be not only helpful to me, but to them. May they feel affirmed and strengthened as they realize what You have meant in their lives. May they grow through their cooperation with this project, as they realize how important they are to others. May I use all my talents and gifts in this work. Thank you for all that has brought me to this point. May the church bells I am hearing at this moment be a symbol of your presence and love, and may they ring in my heart when I have gone back home.

JANUARY 5, 1995

This afternoon will not be soon forgotten. I just returned from the focus group here in Wilster. To say that it was a success does not begin to capture the experience for either me or for the participants. It is definitely one of those rare times of my life when I feel absolutely confident that God's purposes took over and things happened far greater than I could have ever imagined. When the first woman, Inge, began sharing with me, telling me that she identified with Mary the mother of Christ because she, too, has lost a son, I was surprised and touched. That was only the beginning of my surprises. The emotionality of these women is so deep. They have been through terrible experiences. Being with them reminded me of being with the Vietnam vets last summer in one way: I felt respect for the seriousness of what they have survived. When one woman spoke of not knowing for days whether she would live or die, she cried. I suddenly realized that this research experience is going to be a lot more emotionally powerful than I had expected. I immediately had a sense of gratitude that she had allowed us to participate in such a moment. And I was astonished that they would be sharing such deep and meaningful things with me. I sensed that God was working, and that in spite of all my limitations, it was God's intention that the voices of these women be heard. Suddenly knew that what I am participating in here is far more important than my degree; it is important because it is another piece of God's work. I feel recommitted to this project, excited about how I stumbled onto it and determined to do my very best with it.

I will never forget the faces of these women, their *Angst* when they told of painful times and their pleasure when they heard that their faith stories were going to be heard. When the pastor explained that I would be sending word back to them and checking out my findings with them before publication, they looked especially pleased. I think they, too, have had a feeling of being a part of something larger than any one of them alone. I think now that the best thing for me is to get out of the way and let God's work be done; this journal will help me to do that. Tomorrow, my first visit with a spiritual nominee. I'm frightened, but on the other hand, I can hardly wait.

JANUARY 6, 1995

This day has been beyond description. This morning I had my first interview with a German spiritual nominee, and I was so moved by the experience. This woman, Elisabeth, has such a quiet confidence and so much to say about her spirituality. I couldn't believe how trusting she was with me. It was as though she was quietly delighted that someone cared about her ideas and stories. And as if all of that were not enough, she is a poet, and she shared with me several of her poems. Many are directly related to her spiritual strength. Everything keeps being so much better than I had ever hoped for on this trip.

Later, at *Mittags* (lunch break), I took all four of the Steenbucks out to eat at a local restaurant, and that was fun. It was good to see them relaxed and enjoying themselves without Selma's having to cook. It troubles me sometimes to think that here I am doing a research project for feminist purposes, and now a woman has to work harder because of my presence in the household! Before we began eating, Karl offered grace, very quietly. It was as though he did not want to disturb anyone or remind them of his piety, yet he was not willing to eat without giving thanks. He always says the same short prayer, which is the exact German version of the prayer we always said at home in Pennsylvania, "Come, Lord Jesus, be our guest." My German roots show up from time to time.

But by far the most fantastic part of the day was the evening. We drove to Itzehoe, a nearby city, for *Gottesdienst* (worship services) because today is Epiphany. I was expecting a small group and a simple service. What occurred was an experience I'll not soon forget. The church was old and beautiful with a large crucifix hanging in front. The only light was the candlelight from candles at the end of each pew and from the large *Tannenbaum* (Christmas tree) in front. The atmosphere was so quiet and hushed; no one spoke above a whisper except for those who presided. The celebrant and preacher was the provost, who is a church official somewhere between a bishop and a dean in our system. He has a dramatic voice which he uses well for worship. I sat with Selma and a few of the older women I had met yesterday, including Inge, because Carl was assisting with the service. I followed along with the German hymns and could understand the sermon completely since the preacher spoke slowly and precisely. He spoke of the mystery of the "three holy kings," as the Wise Men are known in Germany. He said that they brought their gifts in humility and that the mystery of Epiphany is to offer to God our pride and selfishness and materialism, to put all that at His feet so that we can experience newness of life with God. He said that it is difficult for us to do this, to live a spiritual life, because of all that we have. We mistake our material possession for riches. There was Holy Communion, and in that atmosphere, so quiet and spiritual, with my new German friends, so far from home and yet so *zu Hause* (at home). I was deeply moved. For some reason I thought about my mother during the service. I suddenly thought how incredibly fortunate I am to be having this experience. And I thought of how she has never been able to come to Germany; once she came close, but had a heart attack just before she and my father were to leave. She has had so little in her life and so much sorrow. I have had so much, so many incredible experiences, so much joy. I wish I could tell her how much I love her and wish to thank her for all that she has done. I guess having an experience like this one, one you're grateful for, makes you realize more than ever how deeply in debt we all are to those who have given to us. I am here because of the love and support of so many other people.

I kept feeling tears start in my eyes during the service. The Germany words were so beautiful. The same meaning as in English, the Creed, the Our Father, but somehow hearing them in German was so precious to me. One dramatic difference I noted in this service was how quiet the congregation was, how worshipful and formal. At Glade Creek, there was so much talking and informality. It's not as though the people in Virginia were any less sincere or close to God, it's just a dramatically different culture. A female pastor assisted with Communion. That was good to see.

After worship we went by car to a parish house and had *Abendessen*, which consisted of much conversation, beer, sausages, and dark rye bread. I sat with the group from Wilster and talked with the women and with Selma, who graciously tried to draw me into the conversation. Imagine my surprise when the provost asked Karl to introduce me and then when Karl asked me to speak to the whole room filled with people! He told the group gathered there, from various churches in this *Kreis* (circle, a geographic area) about my work. I noticed two women who whispered and joked with each other when he said that I was writing a book about older women. I told the group how much I appreciated the warmth and friendliness and how strong a sense I had that I was part of the church community, having come so far across the ocean and yet feeling so at home. The faces in the room lit up when I said these things.

Afterwards the same two women (not from our group) who had joked with each other about being "older" approached me in the coat room. They looked sophisticated and intelligent. The one who spoke English told me, in English, that she thought it was different in Germany from the United States because in Germany there are many older women without partners "because of other war." She said being without a man makes a difference. I responded very seriously, even though at first she was smiling, and I told her that this problem exists in the U.S. also, having more older women than men. Although, I said, it may be a still worse problem in Germany. She appeared to be shocked to hear this and said she wondered why this should be so. In addition to the war, I said, women live longer. I guess we're stronger. She told this to her friend and then asked me how she could get a copy of "my book." Once again I was moved to see how eager these women are to be heard, how important it is to them that someone cares about their situation.

On the way home I told Karl and Selma what a fantastic day it had been for me, and they said they enjoyed it too. But they could not have known how meaningful it was for me. It was one of those days when you think, well, even if nothing else ever happens to me in my life, I will always be grateful for this experience. It's difficult to express all the feelings going on inside me. Being in a foreign country, feeling welcomed as a fellow Christian *and* as a woman, has been doubly powerful. Of course it's personally satisfying to know that people here have accepted me for myself. But I constantly feel gratitude for all those who have brought me to this point. And above all, to God. God has kept me safe, God's Spirit has helped with everything from assistance with concentrating on German, to knowing what to say when I have to speak to a group, to finding courage in awkward situations. It is so true, as the provost said, when one loves and worships by putting herself at God's feet, mysteries and miracles occur.

JANUARY 7, 1995

I am finished with my interviews with Elisabeth, and I feel terrific about how they went, not just from a research point of view, but especially since they seemed to be so important to her. Her life seems peaceful, that's the word that keeps coming to my mind. She is clearly at peace with her life, her story, her faith. I think that her love of the natural world has a lot to do with this peace. Her garden, her stones, her birds: She seems to have a deep sense that she, too, is part of God's world.

Joseph Sittler, one of my favorite Lutherans, wrote once that those of us who live in these times are "diminished" because our roots aren't so deep or so widely spread into the natural world of field and forest as were the roots of our ancestors. I had so much more time to be outdoors when I was younger. As a child I would especially find myself so happy outdoors, away from the tensions of our household. Everything delighted me, and I felt a bond with the streams and the damp leaves and the smells, especially on autumn days. Knowing that winter was coming made those times particularly precious. My first spiritual experiences, separate from my family, were in the woods at the summer camp I attended. Perhaps being away from home made those times more powerful (just as being away from home now is making this experience so much more intense). We would build a worship area in the woods as part of our church summer camp experiences, and I remember looking at the cross we constructed and being amazed that just putting two large sticks together, ordinary sticks, would suddenly produce such a powerful symbol. The sticks were no longer mere objects, but mysterious, somehow, reminding me that God was present through the story of Jesus Christ. I never fail to feel some of that mystery when look at a cross or crucifix. The beautiful crucifix that hangs in the front of St. Bartolomäus *Kirche* here in Wilster is a far cry from the simple crosses we made in summer camp, yet it evokes for me many of the same feelings. Lately my experiences with nature have been few because of the pace of my life, and this is a part of my spiritual life I feel cut off from. At least when I had a dog to walk, I would get outdoors regularly, but lately I have been inside, working and studying, all the time. A regular walk with no practical purpose in mind needs to be part of my life again. Here in Germany I'll be walking often since I have no car; hopefully I can continue to do so at home. Perhaps realizing its place in my spiritual life will help me to get outside more. I'll think about Frau Elisabeth and her peace and that model should help me to get going and out the door.

The other thing I've learned from this peaceful woman is the importance of creative writing in spiritual life for those of us who feel comfortable with this form of self-expression. All her poems are spiritual in some sense; her faith in God permeates all she thinks and writes. I was especially impressed with her insight that writing the poems helps her to believe more deeply; she says reading over what she has written makes it all more real for her. That is true of so much of faith; it has to be spoken and heard and lived to be made real. Yet Elisabeth also loves to learn and to think; in spite of her lack of formal education, she is intellectually alive and growing, never missing an opportunity to attend a seminar or retreat. But she is able to interweave, so naturally, the findings of her brain with her inner faith experiences. This is very impressive to me and a goal I have. In some ways it's what I've been doing in graduate school, but not always. The times when I keep a journal like this I've done far more of that synthesizing of head and heart, knowledge and faith, but it simply doesn't happen by itself, and I don't always give writing enough time in my life. I don't stop to express the connections between what I can learn about God's world with my head and what I believe in my heart. From conversations with Elisabeth, I have come up with two "New Year's resolutions:" Spend more time (1) in the natural world, walking and noticing the beauty of creation and taking my part in it, and (2) regularly writing, either in poetry or journal form, about my experiences and how they intersect with my spiritual faith.

JANUARY 9, 1995

Today I met with a group of older members of the congregation, at Karl's request. Only Inge was there from the focus group; the others were all different individuals. After coffee and coffeecake, served as always in elegant fashion, with candles at each carefully set table, Karl introduced me and asked me to tell the people something about my work. There was quite a strong reaction from one woman, who had been invited to the focus group but who had not come (we learned indirectly) because she said she didn't want to be "interrogated." Today, however, she agreed enthusiastically that older women are not heard in society, at home, or in the church, as they should be, and their stories not told. She was also very interested in the Social Security system in America and what I said about the problems of older women in America who are divorced in later life. She later told Karl that she would like to be interviewed now, "So that she could ask me more questions," and then later called the parsonage to repeat this request.

Not everyone there, however, was on that wave length. Immediately after she spoke, another woman argued with her, saying that older women have no place trying to get all the attention and should accept their lot in life quietly and let the young take over. Karl whispered to me, in English, "She's internalized the very attitudes you are speaking about!" These women were the only two to speak or to ask questions. Overall there was a tremendous contrast between this group of older persons and the selective group of women at the focus group. The women in the focus group were more articulate and more interested in religious matters, as well as far more self-confident about speaking out.

JANUARY 10, 1995

I have been thinking about how connected I feel with the women I am interviewing, and I believe the connection has two strands. One is our common faith and the community it provides. The other is our commonality as women. I had never dreamed that the latter would be so strong across cultures, but when I sit down for coffee with these women, we are two women talking about life and death and sorrow and joy and faith. It is as though I've been prepared by all the experiences of my life, the pleasures of being young, the joys of loving a man, the happiness and sorrows of motherhood, and the sorrows I've experienced, like losing an infant and divorce—all of these have prepared me for understanding what these women have been through. I'll probably never, thank God, know what it's like to ride in an open cart as a refugee from war, holding a 2-year-old, sick, dirty child, as Inge had to. But I know what it is to worry and cry about a child so that you think your heart will break. I heard some guilt, too, in Inge, for the years she was so busy in the watch shop. She had to work because of her husband's uselessness as an alcoholic, yet she misses the times with her son, and she makes (too strong, I think) a connection between her lack of time for him and his current problems. This is so familiar to me, the irrational yet never-ending guilt. I had to go to work after my divorce, while the children were still young; I had no choice, yet I often feel bad that the children's years went flying by. I'm always thinking that their current difficulties are somehow my fault, that if I had only spent more time with them, they would have turned out to have fewer problems today. Yet Inge doesn't allow her sorrow over her son to dominate her entire life. She can sit down and have a cry, yet she has a happy and healthy life filled with giving to others through the church. Her sense that she is loved by others in the church keeps her joyful, keeps her saying, "*Ich bin sehr glücklich*" (I am so fortunate). What an inspiration she is; her problems have been so much more dramatic and overwhelming; I've had so many opportunities she has not, for an education, for travel. But my faith and joy haven't begun to approach her own. I know I'll think back to her many times in the years to come when difficulties come my way, especially difficulties with the children.

JANUARY 11, 1995

No sooner do I write pious words about trust in God than I am put to the test. Last night I had a call from home and found out that [Katie] my [18-year-old] daughter, about whom I worry the most these days, now weighs only eighty-eight pounds. She is taller than I am, and this weight borders on the dangerous. I think she may be depressed, and I know she isn't eating properly. It's extremely tough to be this far away. All my motherly nurturing impulses are frustrated. And so often it seems with my daughter that I don't really have anything to give her that she wants or that she will accept; she is so busy finding her own way, making her path into adulthood. Sometimes, briefly, she seems to want some mothering, but most of the time it's distance she needs and wants. I'm thinking of Inge, of her story about the son who never calls or writes to her or even responds to her letters. Surely if she can bear that, I can bear my anxieties.

My husband says a doctor's visit is scheduled for this Friday. Even though he said he'd call me Monday, I know I'll call Friday night to see what the doctor said. Until then, I can practice being the strong woman I'd like to be and am not yet. There is no question in my mind that the most difficult part of being a woman is being a mother and worrying about one's children. Even marriage and love problems don't touch it.

But I do have a connection to my daughter, through God. Though she wants her space, I can pray for her, no limits on that. And God understands all that is on my heart—the guilt because I haven't been the perfect mother, the fears, the hopes and dreams for her future. I think, too, I will use what I've learned from Elisabeth and write a letter to Katie today. She wrote one to me before I left, trying to explain, saying that she loves me. It was a big help; she'll never know how much it meant. It let me know that the relationship is still there, still important to her. God, I'm glad you're there for mothers (especially mothers of adolescents); we certainly need you!

JANUARY 12, 1995

Tonight I accompanied Karl to his meeting with the *Vorstand* (church council). He asked me to come and help him lead the opening section of the meeting, which is always something devotional or spiritually educational. He decided we should discuss the fourth commandment, "Honor your father and your mother," and try to get those in attendance to talk about what this commandment means today, how it may be different in America and Germany, and how it's changed in the past and present. Karl says that in the past this commandment in Germany basically meant that one had to respect and obey, at any cost, not only one's parents but also civil authorities. Luther's catechism, he stated, has had an enormous impact on German life in this way, especially his interpretation of this commandment. It's resulted in a mixture of good and evil: Obviously the Nazi times are the most dramatic example of the latter, when authority figures were followed against moral principles. In reaction to that phenomenon, the Evangelical (Lutheran) Church in Germany has recently been emphasizing a change in understanding this commandment, saying "honor" should mean "care," care for our elderly parents when they are old. We should minister to them as individuals and as a church.

But Karl says that since my visit and our many conversations, he's no longer comfortable with this emphasis. He now realizes that this approach, too, is limited, because it tends to make the elderly into a problem, into objects of care, not respected resources of wisdom and experience. Naturally, I was delighted that he was thinking about these things and that he was saying that he might have benefited from my visit in some way. He and Selma have been so wonderful to me, have done so much.

He wanted to discuss all of this with the council and did a good job of introducing the topic to them, relating all of the above. I then talked for a few minutes about my work and how I felt that, in America, we need to learn to listen to our older persons and learn from their lives. I spoke in German and there were nods and smiles, everyone was most kind in spite of my pronunciation and God knows what other errors.

However, the discussion that followed was not what Karl and I anticipated. The room quickly divided between a few of the older men and the younger men; the women present (about five) said nothing (to my disappointment and frustration). The older men began talking about problems with unemployment, and the younger men said that the older people don't "understand modern technology" and therefore shouldn't be in authority. Some of the speakers at least called for a two-way conversation, but in general there was not the dialogue we'd hoped for. I'm afraid pastors like Karl and me are sometimes too idealistic.

But Karl regained control at the end. He reminded us all that this commandment is the only one that includes a curse and a promise. He said that shows how important it must be to God. And he said it is the hearts of the parents and children that need to change, not just the behavior. Karl is really a terrific pastor; he brings his theological knowledge and personal convictions into everyday situations so sensitively. I'm learning much from watching him. All in all, a good ending to a strange experience.

JANUARY 13, 1995

I am more than halfway through my time in Germany, and I remain profoundly thankful that everything is going so well. One thing I really did not anticipate was that I would grow so close to my host and hostess during my visit. Selma and Karl have become real friends during the last thirteen days, and it is a friendship which will last, I know. They are planning a visit to the U.S. during the coming year; I can't wait for Joe to meet them, and it will be so good to be able to do things for them when they visit.

The other aspect of this experience that continues to amaze me is the way that the women share private details of their lives with me. Yesterday I met with the third of my spiritual nominees, Emma, for the first time. This interview may have been the most significant so far, because she has an amazing ability to interweave stories about her life with the significance of her faith and faith experiences. Emma has been a widow for only four years; her former husband was an artist, and they lived an isolated life out of town with no real neighbors or friends. The people in their lives were customers of his, not real friends. During that time, Emma stopped going to church regularly even though she continued to practice her faith at home, especially in raising her five children. But when her husband died of cancer, she found she had to find a new path through life for herself. It was then that she became active again in the church and has become a new and different person in the process—doing so much for others, including the older-old whom she visits, sharing her story, attending a weekly Bible study, which she says is even more important to her than the pastor's preaching.

Emma's changes, after she found herself alone, really took me back to the time immediately after my divorce. Like Emma, I had let my (first) husband's profession dominate our lives; like her, I had gotten lazy about church, and although we attended, I was not really very involved. Then suddenly I found myself alone, finding my own path, and I grew to realize how important the faith community was to me. Not only did I become a different person, far more interested in others than ever before, but, ironically, like Emma I found new meaning for my life through visiting older persons. My divorce was my second chance, even though it certainly didn't seem it at the time. In Christian language, I'd say we both found ourselves by losing ourselves.

And in both cases, it was only after we lost the men in our lives that we were able to do that. Loss, with God's chemistry, can become gain. But I found myself realizing, as she spoke, that I am really afraid of the idea of losing Joe. That would be no second chance; that would be absolutely terrible. People talk about how different he and I are; they have no idea of what goes on between us, how close we are. He is my dear soul mate and here in Germany I miss him so much. I appreciate as never before how precious he is to me, how much it means to have him in my life. Would I be able to bear losing him, as Emma lost her husband, and as so many of these women have? There is no way to anticipate how I would navigate my way through that darkness, but I know that the community would be there for me, and God, somehow, would bring me through, even that. In spite of it all.

That brings me back to one of the aspects of my conversation with Emma that seemed most powerful. It was when I pulled out of her sentence the word, *trotzdem* (in spite of). She really took off with that word and explained in a moving way that her faith is "in spite of" all that has happened, and "in spite of" the continuing pain she often feels when she sees other young-old couples enjoying their retirement years together. But she doesn't become bitter or stuck on these feelings; she doesn't feel jealous in the sense of self-pity. She has found a new way to organize both her life and her thinking so that it is God centered. I can't really say that I am at that point, yet. I still am so caught up in my own accomplishments and worrying about my own life too much to be at the mature level of faith this woman knows. She always refers to what God does through her, not what she does. She has such a blend of enthusiasm and realism, about what life is actually like.

I respect Emma and hope that someday I can be given a faith more like hers. That kind of faith is a gift, but it seems to be a gift that I can help to get ready for by getting "self" out of the way. As I continue to be concerned about my daughter, I recognize how universal these experiences seem to be for mothers. Emma has an alcoholic son and other children who do not go to church, one who is in a new-age cult. She worries about them but, like Inge, does not despair or allow her worry to rob her of either her convictions or of the joy she knows in her relationship with God.

As I mature, will my worries, too, become less dominant?

Actually, I can already feel that happening to some extent. Katie was on my mind off and on all day yesterday, yet I had a somewhat less overwhelmed feeling about it, not caring less or loving less, but with a feeling that I could trust God more. I'm sure all will someday be well with her and that I need to focus my own energies not on worry, which accomplishes nothing. Instead, there is, right now, my work, which can be helpful to others, and relationships with these new people, the nominees, the Steenbucks. Like Elisabeth, I can write about my concerns and doubts and faith; like Inge, I can take comfort from the love of other Christians who care (at the present time, Selma and Karl), and like Emma, I can continue to walk the path that God has chosen for me, not just stumble around on one of my own making (particularly the non-path of fear and worry).

After the interview was over, I told Emma I had seen one of her husband's paintings in my book on Wilster. She said there were three altogether in the book, and she looked in the index and found the other two. This seemed very important to her; she is obviously proud of his work. The paintings are appealing, rather impressionistic and pleasant. She then asked me again to tell her something about my own life, and, since the interviews were over, I did share a little. When I mentioned my divorce and how that was my second chance, she became openly teary for the first time. How remarkable that she was so much more moved by my sorrows than by her own! When we said good-bye, I gave Emma the same small pin (a dove to represent the Holy Spirit) I've been giving to all the women after the last interview. She seemed especially pleased with it.

JANUARY 15, 1995

I saw Emma in church today. She read the lesson during the service; she's a regular lay reader. She also sat with a group of her friends from the Bible Study, who now seem like my friends, too. Elisabeth is also one of them. After the service, Emma greeted me warmly and pulled back her winter coat to show me what she was wearing on her collar: the small dove pin I had given her. I also saw Anna again, and I'm very eager to begin my interviews with her. I find both her and her story intriguing.

JANUARY 16, 1995

I have returned from my second interview with Anna, and my head is spinning. I never dreamed that this experience would be so fascinating and so emotionally moving. It's hard to describe all that I thought and felt today with this deeply spiritual woman who has seen so much and grown so much from her experiences. Thank goodness for this journal so that I don't have to try to be objective about her. She is very special for me.

Ever since I first met Anna I have been fascinated with her and her story—her style, her smile, her quiet way of talking, the things she has accomplished. But I was afraid of her, as well—somehow I felt awkward around her, the way I'd feel, I guess, meeting a great person from history, like Lincoln. But after today I feel much more at ease, because of her graciousness, warmth, and almost casual manner with me. I certainly don't feel any less in awe, however.

More than anything, I feel honored that we shared such intimate moments as we did in the conversation today. At one point, after talking about the war and reading Bonhoeffer's prayer out loud, she became very quiet and there was about a two- or three-minute pause, maybe longer. Those minutes were the most impressive of any time on this trip, a trip filled with impressive times. During that silence, I felt connected to her, even though I also felt she was far away, lost in her memories, thinking of times and people I will never know. She smiled a little sheepishly at me when the pause was over, and I told her I found her to be a very deep person, very sensitive. *"Weil ich nachdenke?"* (Because I think back?), she asked. Selma is right: Anna really has no idea of how special she is; that is, perhaps, the most amazing thing about her of all.

I feel like I've saved the best interview for last here in Wilster. That's not only true from the point of view of this work, but also for myself, personally. It will take some time for me to articulate all that meeting Anna has meant—I know, even now, somehow it has to do with things that go back to my childhood, to those nights sitting on the stairs in my parents' home, listening to dramatizations of the Nüremberg trials, reading the *Diary of Anne Frank*, and thinking, "I'm German, too. What does all this mean? How could all these things be, and what does it mean about me, about people, about God?"

In Anna, there is certainly no final resolution of these questions—they have no answers. As she says repeatedly, these things are truly incomprehensible, unimaginable. Yet to meet someone who was actually a member of the Nazi Party at one time and is now this wonderful person—what does all that mean about human resiliency, about God's Grace, and second chances? Certainly it means that we don't have to get stuck in guilt; we go on, we *nachdenk*, yes, but we go on. Anna works for peace and justice but with a sense of loving concern, not as though she's trying to redeem herself. She is responding to the love of God, not trying to earn her way somehow. And everything she thinks and does is out of love and compassion for those who have not had the opportunities she has had.

I can't believe how non-self-referential this woman is. I didn't hear one word about her own health concerns or anything that even comes close to self-pity from her. Always it is others she thinks about, often the whole human race. What a vision, what a way to live.

Selma is very understanding about my strong reactions to Anna; she is also fascinated by her. *"Die grande Dame,"* she always calls her. Yes, the great lady.

JANUARY 24, 1995

I'm home at last. There has never been a sight so welcome as the faces of my husband and son at the airport. How I love them and my other children. It is so good to be here.

This trip has really changed me. I feel more peaceful, more calm, somehow, more of my own person—yet at the same time I realize more than ever how much I love and need other people. I do feel some frustration, already, at not being able to share with Joe enough details of the experience to feel like he *completely* understands (he's trying!). I've taken lots of pictures, especially the last few days in Berlin, but it just isn't possible to explain everything to him. I guess that's OK, too, and maybe even necessary. The Steenbucks are, hopefully, coming to visit in October. But if only he could meet Anna, Emma, Inge, and Elisabeth. Maybe someday he will, when I return to Wilster with him. I'm grateful for this journal, and for the tapes (I guarded them with my life on the way home!). They are the real treasure of this trip, other than my memories. It's incredible to me, to think that I'll be able to reexperience those conversations now, as I play the tapes and read the transcriptions. And then, after I write the dissertation and the book, other people can meet these wonderful women too.

Thank you, God, for my safe trip home, for this experience, and especially for keeping my family safe while I was gone.

FEBRUARY. 21, 1995 3:15 A.M.

I got up out of bed to write this because I was afraid of losing my thoughts and feelings. I had a dream that helped me to understand what I am doing in this project and how much I want to be close to God.

Like most dreams, all dreams, it was a bazarre mixture of parts of my life, parts of me. Alan and Jo, my friends (a couple) were telling me to go to Lake Constance (in Switzerland, the city where Michael Steenbuck is studying law) in order to meet God. They told me that they had recently been there on a vacation and had seen the face of God in a large wave. They were very precise on how I could go to a certain part of the lake and find this wave and see the face of God for myself.

Well, the dream is really outrageous in many ways. Theologically, it's ridiculous, of course, primitive and so literalistic—it's worse than Cecil B. de Mille and *The Ten Commandments*. And my dear friends Alan and Jo are special and close to me, but not really pious people by any means, not people whom I would expect to be looking for God in the waves on a vacation.

None of that matters, though, because the phone rang on the children's line at 2:30 a.m., in the middle of this dream, and woke me up, allowing me to remember the dream, not just with my mind but with my heart, to think and to feel all that it brought to me. As I lay in bed thinking, I saw the wave again, and I had a remarkably strong sense of God's presence, never mind the stupid theology and images. And I began thinking about this project and the women, including Martha, whom I interviewed yesterday. They were so honest about God's presence in their lives, so unconcerned about how theologically correct that sense of presence is. Martha can't really, or won't, talk about her relationship with God when asked directly, much as Inge could not or would not. Yet she could tell me about sometimes getting up in the middle of the night to deliver a calf and feeling no fear as she goes down to her barn alone, because God is with her. Or she can talk about, and cry about, the Sunday School picture of the woman scrubbing the floor "for God." She can question the suffering she has seen and admit that God's ways are beyond her.

As I lay there in bed, I felt such a longing for a faith like that, certainly not for the first time in the last months. But this time I put different words to the experience, and I realized that I want so desperately to be close to God, to "see the face" of God in my life, to experience a *daily* faith relationship with God in a new and closer way. And I realized, too, that this longing is what this project is really about. It's not only about helping others learn resiliency, it's not only about writing a dissertation or a book, it's not only even about learning how to age myself and endure losses, even the worst possible one. More than anything, it's about wanting to be close to God. There's an actually physical feeling, inside my heart, the way you feel right after you fall in love and then have to say goodbye for the night.

Which is what I'd better do right now so that I can get up tomorrow and get back to work on this research.

References

Aiken, L. R. (1995). *Aging: An introduction to gerontology.* Thousand Oaks, CA: Sage.

Atchley, R. C. (1993). Critical perspectives on retirement. In T. R. Cole, W. A. Achenbaum, P. L. Jakobi, & R. Kastenbaum (Eds.), *Voices and visions of aging: Toward a critical gerontology* (pp. 3-20). New York: Springer.

Baltes, P. B., & Baltes, M. M. (1990). Psychological perspectives on successful aging. In P. B. Baltes & M. M. Baltes (Eds.), *Successful aging: Perspectives from the behavioral sciences* (pp. 1-34). New York: Cambridge University Press.

Baltes, P. B., & Staudinger, U. M. (1993). The search for a psychology of wisdom. *Current Directions in Psychological Science, 2,* 75-80.

Baltes, P. B., Staudinger, U. M., Maercker, A., & Smith, J. (1995). People nominated as being wise: A comparative study of wisdom-related knowledge. *Psychology and Aging, 10,* 155-166.

Barnes, M. C. (1991). *Yearning: Living between how it is and how it ought to be.* Downers Grove, IL: InterVarsity.

Bart, P. (1997). Portnoy's mother's complaint. In M. Pearsall (Ed.), *The other within us: Feminist explorations of women and aging* (pp. 25-36). Boulder, CO: Westview.

Bateson, G. (1972). *Steps to an ecology of mind.* New York: Ballantine.

Beintker, H. (1961). *Die Evangelische Lehre von der Heiligen Schrift und von der Tradition (Evangelical teachings of Holy Scripture according to the tradition).* Luneburg, Germany: Heliand-Verlag.

Belenky, M. F., Clinchy, B. M., Goldberger, N. R., & Tarule, J. M. (1986). *Women's ways of knowing: The development of self, voice, and mind.* New York: Basic Books.

Benne, R. (1988). *Ordinary saints: An introduction to the Christian life.* Philadelphia: Fortress.

Berger, P. (1967). *The sacred canopy: Elements of a sociological theory of religion.* New York: Doubleday.

Birren, J. E. (1990). Spiritual maturity in psychological development. *Journal of Religious Gerontology, 7,* 41-54.

Bonhoeffer, D. (1949). *The cost of discipleship.* New York: Macmillan.

Bouncing back from bad times. (1998, February). *Harvard Women's Health Watch,* pp. 2-3.

Braaten, C. E. (1983). *Principles of Lutheran theology.* Philadelphia: Fortress.

Breytspraak, L. M. (1984). *The development of self in later life.* Boston: Little, Brown.

Cockerham, W. C. (1991). *This aging society* (2nd ed.). Upper Saddle River, NJ: Prentice-Hall.

Copper, B. (1997). The view from over the hill. In M. Pearsall (Ed.), *The other within us: Feminist explorations of women and aging* (p. 121-134). Boulder, CO: Westview.

Daly, K. (1992). The fit between qualitative research and characteristics of families. In J. F. Gilgun, K. Daly, & G. Handel (Eds.), *Qualitative methods in family research* (pp. 3-11). Newbury Park, CA: Sage.

Erikson, E., Erikson, J., & Kivnick, H. (1986). *Vital involvement in old age: The experience of old age in our time.* London: Norton.

Estes, C. P. (1992). *Women who run with the wolves: Myths and stories of the wild woman archetype.* New York: Ballantine.

Evangelical Lutheran Church in America. (1978). *Lutheran book of worship.* Minneapolis, MN: Augsburg.

Fonow, M. M., & Cook, J. A. (1991). *Beyond methodology: Feminist scholarship as lived research.* Bloomington: Indiana University Press.

Fowler, J. W. (1981). *Stages of faith: The psychology of human development and the quest for meaning.* San Francisco: HarperCollins.

Fox, M. (1981). *Western spirituality: Historical roots, ecumenical routes.* Sante Fe, NM: Bear & Company.

Frankl, V. E. (1969). *The will to meaning: Foundations and applications of logotherapy.* New York: World.

Friedan, B. (1993). *The fountain of age.* New York: Simon & Schuster.

Geertz, C. (1973). *The interpretation of cultures.* New York: Basic Books.

George, L. (1990). Social structure, social processes, and social-psychological states. In R. H. Binstock & L. K. George (Eds.), *Handbook of aging and the social sciences* (3rd ed., pp. 186-204). New York: Academic Press.

Giesen, C. B., & Datan, N. (1980). The competent older woman. In N. Datan & N. Lohmann (Eds.), *Transitions of aging* (pp. 57-72). New York: Academic Press.

Gilligan, C. (1982). *In a different voice: Psychological theory and women's development.* Cambridge, MA: Harvard University Press.

Gilligan, C. (1993). *In a different voice: Psychological theory and women's development* (2nd ed.). Cambridge, MA: Harvard University Press.

Goldenberg, I., & Goldenberg, H. (1996). *Family therapy: An overview* (4th ed.). New York: Brooks/Cole.

Gubrium, J. F. (1993). Voice and context in a new gerontology. In T. R. Cole, W. A. Achenbaum, P. L Jakobi, & R. Kastenbaum (Eds.), *Voices and visions of aging: Toward a critical gerontology* (pp. 46-63). New York: Springer.

Hashimi, J. (1991). Counseling older adults. In P. K. H. Kim (Ed.), *Serving the elderly: Skills for practice* (pp. 33-49). New York: Aldine de Gruyter.

Heinecken, M. J. (1986). Exchanging metaphors between science and religion. *Journal of Religion and Aging, 2,* 17-27.

Hendricks, J., & Leedham, C. A. (1991). Theories of aging: Implications for human services. In P. K. H. Kim (Ed.), *Serving the elderly: Skills for practice* (pp. 1-28). New York: Aldine de Gruyter.

Hillery, G. A. (1992). *The monastery: A study in freedom, love, and community.* Westport, CT: Praeger.

Holt, B. P. (1993). *Thirsty for God: A brief history of Christian spirituality.* Minneapolis, MN: Augsburg.

Johnson, R. P. (1998, Winter). A unique credential. *National Board for Certified Counselors News Notes, 14*(3), 11.

Kaufman, L. L. (1989). *Old age is not for sissies.* White Plains, NY: Peter Pauper Press.

Kaufman, S. R. (1986). *The ageless self: Sources of meaning in late life.* Madison: University of Wisconsin Press.

Kim, P. K. H. (Ed.). (1991). *Serving the elderly: Skills for practice.* New York: Aldine de Gruyter.

Kimble, M. A. (1990). Aging and the search for meaning. *Journal of Religious Gerontology, 7,* 111-130.

Kimble, M. A. (1993). A personal journey of aging: The spiritual dimension. *Generations, 17,* 27-28.

Kinsella, K., & Taeuber, C. (1993). *An aging world II* (U.S. Bureau of the Census International Population Report No. P95/92-3). Washington, DC: Government Printing Office.

Kleinman, S., & Copp, M. (1993). *Emotions and fieldwork.* Newbury Park, CA: Sage.

Kohlberg, L. (1973). Stages and aging in moral development: Some speculations. *The Gerontologist, 13,* 497-502.

Krause, N., & Van Tran, T. (1989). Stress and religious involvement among older blacks. *Journal of Gerontology: Social Sciences, 44,* S4-12.

Krieger, S. (1991). *Social science and the self: Personal essays on an art form.* New Brunswick, NJ: Rutgers University Press.

Kurtz, J. (1982). *700 Jahre Stadt Wilster (700 years of the City of Wilster).* Hamburg, Germany: Verlagsbuchbinderei Ladstetter.

Langer, S. (1942). *Philosophy in a new key.* New York: Harcourt Brace & World.

LaRossa, R., & Reitzes, D. C. (1993). Symbolic interactionism and family studies. In P .G. Boss, W. J. Doherty, R. LaRossa, W. R. Schumm, & S. K. Steinmetz (Eds.), *Sourcebook of family theories and methods: A contextual approach* (pp. 135-163). New York: Plenum.

Laslett, P. (1991). *A fresh map of life: The emergence of the third age.* Cambridge, MA: Harvard University Press.

Le Guin, U. K. (1997). The space crone. In M. Pearsall (Ed.), *The other within us: Feminist explorations of women and aging* (pp. 249-252). Boulder, CO: Westview.

Levin, J. S. (1989). Religious factors in aging, adjustment, and health: A theoretical overview. In W. M. Clements (Ed.), *Religion, aging and health: A global perspective* (pp. 133-142). New York: Haworth.

Levin, J. S. (1994, March/April). Researching the "r-word." *The Aging Spirit, 15*(2), 11.

Lutheran Church. (1959). *Book of Concord: The confessions of the Evangelical Lutheran Church.* Philadelphia: Fortress. (Original work published in 1580).

Making a place for spirituality. (1998, February). *Harvard Health Letter, 23*(4), 1-3.

Marshall, C., & Rossman, G. B. (1989). *Designing qualitative research.* Newbury Park, CA: Sage.

Marty, M. E. (1983a). *A cry of absence: Reflections for the winter of the heart.* San Francisco: Harper & Row.

Marty, M. E. (1983b). Suffering: The theology of the cross. In M. E. Marty & K. L. Vaux (Eds.), *Health and medicine in the Lutheran tradition: Being well* (pp. 50-64). New York: Crossroad.

McCracken, G. (1988). *The long interview.* Newbury Park, CA: Sage.

Minkler, M., & Cole, T. R. (1991). Political and moral economy: Not strange bedfellows. In M. Minkler & C. L. Estes (Eds.), *Critical perspectives on aging: The political and moral economy of growing old* (pp. 37-50). Amityville, NY: Baywood.

Moberg, D. O. (Ed.). (1979). *Spiritual well being: Sociological perspectives.* Washington, DC: University Press.

Moody, H. (1994). Foreword: The owl of Minerva. In L. E. Thomas & S. A. Eisenhandler (Eds.), *Aging and the religious dimension* (pp. ix-xvii). Westport, CT: Auburn House.

Morse, J. M., & Johnson, J. L. (1991). *The illness experience: Dimensions of suffering.* Newbury Park, CA: Sage.

Myerhoff, B. (1978). *Number our days.* New York: Simon & Schuster.

Nelson, E. C. (1982). *The rise of world Lutheranism: An American perspective.* Philadelphia: Fortress.

Nouwen, H. (1974). *Aging: The fulfillment of life.* New York: Image.

Nouwen, H. (1976). *The Genesee diary: Report from a Trappist monastery.* New York: Doubleday.

Owen, B. (Ed.). (1993). *Daily readings from Luther's writings.* Minneapolis, MN: Augsburg.

Pargament, K. I. (1997). *The psychology of religion and coping: Theory, research, and practice.* New York: Guilford.

Parry, A., & Doan, R. E. (1994). *Story re-visions: Narrative therapy in the postmodern world.* New York: Guilford.

Payne, B. (1990). Spiritual maturity and meaning-filled relationships: A sociological perspective. *Journal of Religious Gerontology, 7,* 25-39.

Peck, M. S. (1987). *The different drum: Community-making and peace.* New York: Simon & Schuster.

Pearsall, M. (Ed.). (1997). *The other within us: Feminist explorations of women and aging.* Boulder, CO: Westview.

Randour, M. L. (1987). *Women's psyche, women's spirit: The reality of relationships.* New York: Columbia University Press.

Remen, R. N. (1996). *Kitchen table wisdom: Stories that heal.* New York: Riverhead.

Sager, A. H. (1990). *Gospel-centered spirituality: An introduction to our spiritual journey.* Minneapolis, MN: Augsburg.

Saiving, V. C. (1988). Our bodies/ourselves: Reflections on sickness, aging, and death. *Journal of Feminist Studies in Religion, 4,* 117-125.

Senn, F. C. (1986). Lutheran spirituality. In F. C. Senn (Ed.), *Protestant spiritual traditions* (pp. 9-54). New York: Paulist.

Simmons, H. C. (1990). Countering cultural metaphors of aging. *Journal of Religious Gerontology, 7,* 153-166.

Sinclair, K. (1986). Women and religion. In M. I. Duley & M. I. Edwards (Eds.), *The cross-cultural study of women: A comprehensive guide* (pp. 107-124). New York: The Feminist Press.

Sittler, J. (1987). The last lecture: A walk around truth, eternal life, faith. *Religion and Intellectual Life, 4,* 59-65.

Sokolovsky, J. (1985). Ethnicity, culture and aging: Do differences really make a difference? *Journal of Applied Gerontology, 4,* 6-17.

Sokolovsky, J. (Ed.). (1990). *The cultural context of aging: Worldwide perspectives.* New York: Bergin & Garvey.

Sontag, S. (1997). The double standard of aging. In M. Pearsall (Ed.), *The other within us: Feminist explorations of women and aging* (pp.19-24). Boulder, CO: Westview.

Stewart, D. W., & Shamdasani, P. N. (1990). *Focus groups: Theory and practice.* Newbury Park, CA: Sage.

Stokes, K. (1990). Faith development in the adult life cycle. *Journal of Religious Gerontology, 7,* 167-185.

Strauss, A., & Corbin, J. (1990). *Basics of qualitative research: Grounded theory procedures and techniques.* Newbury Park, CA: Sage.

Tarnas, R. (1991). *Passions of the western mind: Understanding the ideas that have shaped our world view.* New York: Ballantine.

Teri, L., Curtis, J., Gallagher-Thompson, D., & Thompson, L. (1994). Cognitive-behavior therapy with depressed older adults. In L. S. Schneider, C. F. Reynolds, II, B. D. Lebowitz, & A. J. Fridhoff (Eds.), *Diagnosis and treatment of depression in late life* (pp. 279-291). Washington, DC: American Psychiatric Press.

Thomas, L. E., & Eisenhandler, S. A. (Eds.). (1994). *Aging and the religious dimension.* Westport, CT: Auburn House.

Thorson, J. A., & Cook, T. C. (1980). *Spiritual well-being of the elderly.* Springfield, IL: Charles C. Thomas.

Thursy, D. (1991). Foreword. In P. K. H. Kim, (Ed.), *Serving the elderly: Skills for practice* (pp. xi-xv). New York: Aldine de Gruyter.

Tillich, P. (1963). *Systematic theology* (Vol. III). Chicago: University of Chicago Press.

Tobin, S. S. (1991). *Personhood in advanced old age: Implications for practice.* New York: Springer.

Tripp, D. H. (1986). Luther. In C. Jones, G. Wainwright, & E. Yarnold, S.J., (Eds.), *The study of spirituality* (pp. 343-346). New York: Oxford University Press.

Turner, V. (1978). Foreword. In B. Myerhoff, *Number our days* (pp. xiii-xvii). New York: Simon & Schuster.

Vaswig, W. L. (1994). You can keep your spiritual focus: Take a fresh look at what God is doing in your world. *The Lutheran, 7,* 16-17.

Wakefield, G. S. (1983). *The Westminster dictionary of Christian spirituality.* Philadelphia: Westminster.

White, M., & Epston, D. (1990). *Narrative means to therapeutic ends.* New York: Norton.

Wood, J. T. (1994). *Who cares? Women, care, and culture.* Carbondale, IL: Southern Illinois University Press.

Yates, G. G. (1983). Spirituality and the American feminist experience. *Journal of Women in Culture and Society, 9,* 59-79.

Index

About the Authors

Janet L. Ramsey is a pastoral counselor and licensed marriage and family therapist at the Pastoral Counseling Center of the Roanoke Valley in Roanoke, Virginia. She received the Ph.D. from Virginia Polytechnic Institute and State University in Family and Child Development with a major concentration in adult development and aging, the M.A.R. from Yale Divinity School, and the M.Div. from Lutheran Theological Seminary at Philadelphia. She was ordained by the Evangelical Lutheran Church in America in 1985 and has served as both a nursing home chaplain and a parish pastor. A Fellow in the American Association of Pastoral Counselors, her clinical work focuses on issues related to the aging process, caretaking, and chronic illness. She participates in a variety of community activities and serves on community organization boards. She has presented numerous workshops on spirituality, aging, caretaking, and coping with chronic illness.

Rosemary Blieszner is Professor of Gerontology and Family Studies in the Department of Human Development and Associate Director of the Center for Gerontology at Virginia Polytechnic Institute and State University, Blacksburg. She received the Ph.D. from Pennsylvania State University in Human Development—Family Studies with a major concentration in adult development and aging and a minor in sociology/social psychology. Her research, funded by the U.S. Administration on Aging, U.S. Department of Health and Human Services, AARP Andrus Foundation, Virginia Tech Women's Research Institute, and Virginia Tech Educational Foundation, focuses on family and friend relationships, life events, and psychological well-being in adulthood and old age. A fellow of the American Psychological Association, the Association for Gerontology in Higher Education, and the Gerontological Society of America, Blieszner is coeditor of *Older Adult Friendship: Structure and Process* (Sage, 1989), coauthor of *Adult Friendship* (Sage, 1992), and coeditor of *Handbook of Aging and the Family* (1995). She is also author of numerous articles published in gerontology, family studies, personal relationships, psychology, and sociology journals.